Change

Political
Change
in China

Comparisons with Taiwan

edited by
Bruce Gilley
Larry Diamond

LYNNE
RIENNER
PUBLISHERS

BOULDER
LONDON

Published in the United States of America in 2008 by
Lynne Rienner Publishers, Inc.
1800 30th Street, Boulder, Colorado 80301
www.rienner.com

and in the United Kingdom by
Lynne Rienner Publishers, Inc.
3 Henrietta Street, Covent Garden, London WC2E 8LU

Library of Congress Cataloging-in-Publication Data
Political change in China : comparisons with Taiwan / Bruce Gilley and Larry
Diamond, editors.
    p. cm.
  Includes bibliographical references and index.
  ISBN 978-1-58826-568-5 (hardcover : alk. paper) — ISBN 978-1-58826-593-7
(pbk. : alk. paper)
  1. China—Politics and government—2002– 2. Taiwan—Politics and
government—2000– 3. Comparative government. I. Gilley, Bruce, 1966–
II. Diamond, Larry Jay.
  JQ1510.P64 2008
  320.951—dc22

                                     2007051549

British Cataloguing in Publication Data
A Cataloguing in Publication record for this book
is available from the British Library.

Printed and bound in the United States of America

5 4 3 2 1

Contents

Acknowledgments

This book represents the first product of a new research program, Democracy in Taiwan, at Stanford University's Center on Democracy, Development, and the Rule of Law (CDDRL). We would like to thank CDDRL; its director, Michael McFaul; and its parent organization, the Freeman Spogli Institute for International Studies, for providing a stimulating and welcoming intellectual home for the Democracy in Taiwan program. We particularly extend our thanks to the Taiwan Foundation for Democracy and the Taipei Economic and Cultural Office in San Francisco for their support. We also owe a large debt to the gifted manager of the Democracy in Taiwan program, Eric Chen-hua Yu; to Larry Diamond's administrative assistant, Alice Carter, who has provided invaluable support; to Kathryn Stoner-Weiss, associate director for research; and Alice Kada, administrative manager of CDDRL.

The chapters were improved by the comments of a number of people. For their contributions in this regard, we thank (in addition to the authors in this book) Richard Baum, Melissa Brown, Mao-Kuei Chang, Tsungfu Chen, James Fishkin, K. C. Fung, Thomas Gold, Louisa Greve, Baogang He, Szu-chien Hsu, Samuel C.Y. Ku, Da-chi Liao, Junning Liu, Alice Lyman Miller, Ramon Myers, Andrew Nathan, Barry Naughton, Kevin O'Brien, Minxin Pei, Henry Rowen, Scott Rozelle, Tianjan Shi, Rana Siu, Hongying Wang, and Suisheng Zhao.

We also thank the anonymous reviewers who provided detailed and constructive feedback on the draft chapters; Marilyn Grobschmidt, our able editor at Lynne Rienner Publishers; and not least, Lynne Rienner herself, whose keen sense of what makes for a good scholarly book helped to make this a better one.

—Bruce Gilley
Larry Diamond

1

Comparing and Rethinking Political Change in China and Taiwan

Bruce Gilley

Political change in rapidly modernizing societies has been the bed-
rock concern of political science since World War II, when United
Nations–led decolonization ushered 59 new states into being in the space of
just 25 years. Two other states founded in this period have a special relevance
to the field: Communist China and non-Communist Taiwan. China's 1949
Communist revolution was the biggest experiment in social engineering in the
face of modernizing pressures that the world had ever seen, whereas Taiwan's
rump status as the island not conquered by Communist forces would forever
make it the symbol of the path not taken on the mainland, with all the implications this had for the study of China itself.

In the subsequent half century, history created an experimentally ideal
comparison between the two states. Taiwan witnessed a dramatic economic
transformation that was followed after 1986 by a phased and largely successful democratization. China experienced an equally dramatic economic transformation, but sustained growth did not begin until the early 1970s, following
a quarter century of disastrous Maoist campaigns. Moreover, although economic growth in Taiwan was accompanied by a predictable and steady deterioration of authoritarian control, punctuated by periodic acts of repression,
China's economic boom led instead to an apparent resurgence of authoritarian
control following the repression of prodemocracy forces in 1989. Taiwan
today is a liberal democracy that fulfills the presumptions of cultural universalists, whereas China is an illiberal autocracy that fulfills the presumptions of
cultural particularists. Comparing the two Chinese republics remains irre-
sistible, therefore, not just to scholars, politicians, and the general public but
also to activists and politicians on both sides of the Taiwan Strait.

This book is an attempt to rethink comparative political change in China
and Taiwan. At present, there are several highly valuable comparative studies
of particular aspects of politics in the two countries. These cover a range of

issues. Some deal with basic issues of political culture[1], national identity[2], and democratic norm diffusion[3] in the two societies. Others consider the politicization of the two societies as they developed, covering topics that include student protest,[4] civil society and elections,[5] urban politics,[6] and intellectuals in politics.[7] A final type of comparative works looks more closely at party adaptation[8] to this rising politicization. There are also, of course, dozens of volumes on the military, strategic, and diplomatic relations between the two states, which technically remain in a state of war. And a few make the link between domestic developments and their cross-Strait implications.[9] Yet there has been no sustained and systematic comparison of the causes and pathways of domestic political change in the two places, nor of the lessons this holds for theories of political change as a whole. This book intends to fill that void.

In particular, this book has three aims: to better understand the Taiwan and China cases individually, to contribute to debates on the theories of political and institutional change, and to use this knowledge to make predictions about China's evolutionary future. Each chapter was commissioned so that the volume as a whole would offer a comprehensive view of political change in the two places. Each chapter considers the theoretical literature relevant to its particular subject and asks how that theory travels when applied to the cases of China and Taiwan. The results lead to a reinterpretation of both places in many significant respects and to a reconsideration of several strands of political development theory.

Brief Histories

The People's Republic of China (PRC) was founded in 1949 following the defeat in civil war of the ruling Kuomintang (KMT), whose Republic of China had been created on the ruins of the Qing Dynasty in 1912. Measured by the Human Development Index (HDI) indicators of life expectancy, primary education enrollment, and income gains, the PRC did reasonably well: between 1950 and 1973, its historical HDI as calculated by Crafts improved by 50 percent, less than gains in Mexico, Brazil, and South Korea but well above gains in most other developing countries, such as India (32 percent) or Indonesia (24 percent).[10] Yet the costs of these gains were enormous. In the twenty years after 1956, the progressive ideals of the Chinese Communist Party (CCP) were subverted by Mao Zedong's paranoid rule, leading to the deaths of tens of millions (estimates range from 40 to 70 million) from famine and persecution. Maoism became synonymous with the worst horrors of the twentieth century. The renunciation of Maoism by his Long March ally Deng Xiaoping, who came to power in 1977, cleared the way for a period of economic expansion and political liberalization in the 1980s that many believed was taking China in the direction of democracy. But something strange happened on the way to the forum. The massacre of civilians in Beijing in June 1989 did not mark the last gasp of a regime collapsing amid the accumulating rubble of world Communism. Rather it marked the reassertion of state and party power. Nearly two decades since that event, with China's economy surging, its international role growing, and domestic political legitimacy intact, it is difficult to argue that the CCP regime is on its last legs. China's HDI score for 2004 surpassed that of the Philippines for the first time, marking the end of a half century closing of a material gap between what were Asia's poorest and richest nations after World War II.

The transfer of paramount power from Deng's post-1989 successor Jiang Zemin to the youngish Hu Jintao was achieved without major incident in 2002, and the party installed two cadres in their 50s, Xi Jinping and Li Keqiang, onto its Politburo Standing Committee in 2007, indicating that they will assume command for the decade beginning in 2012. Institutional innovations such as controlled local elections, greater legislative oversight by people's congresses, and a functioning legal system have been introduced since the 1980s without any notable erosion of party preeminence. China in the early twenty-first century is increasingly described as a form of authoritarianism with positive adjectives: soft, developmental, adaptive, institutionalizing, pluralistic, or resilient. Less flattering adjectives such as decaying, late, or sclerotic are used much less.

Taiwan's experience is often cited as the foil for the China case. The island of Taiwan lies off China's south coast and is geographically smaller than any of China's provinces or autonomous regions. Japan seized Taiwan after expelling the Qing dynasty from the Korean peninsula and seizing ports around Beijing in the first Sino-Japanese war of 1894–1895. Under Japanese sovereignty and then direct colonial rule from 1910 on, Taiwan's economic and administrative infrastructure improved markedly. Taiwan was turned over to the KMT in 1945 as part of the postwar agreement among the Allied Powers. Within a few short years, that minor possession took on life-and-death significance for the KMT. As Communist armies swept across China during the 1946–1950 civil war, KMT forces retreated to the island, which soon constituted the entire de facto territory of the Republic of China.

Under KMT leader Chiang Kai-shek, Taiwan was run as an authoritarian state. But private ownership and semicompetitive local elections made Taiwan a far more liberalized regime than the CCP regime on the mainland from the very start. Moreover, as KMT plans to retake China withered in the 1960s, it began to widen the scope and competitiveness of elections. In 1969, three years *before* the Sino-US rapprochement that followed Taiwan's expulsion from the United Nations, the first in a series of national-level elections was held for a portion of the seats in the three branches of parliament (the Legislative Yuan that passes bills, the National Assembly that chooses the president, and the Control Yuan that monitors government corruption). The

Taipei City Council also elected new members for the first time in that year. This built upon a continuous expansion of local elections for mayors and city councillors that had been initiated in 1946, contests in which non-KMT candidates had consistently won between 20 and 30 percent of the votes.[11] Legitimate opposition to KMT rule, in other words, was seeded very early on Taiwan.

Credit for the final stage of liberalization is generally accorded to Chiang's son and successor Chiang Ching-kuo, who became deputy premier in 1969, rising to president by 1978. For a host of reasons—domestic and international pressures, and genuine personal beliefs—Chiang accelerated the liberalization begun in 1969 while keeping a careful grip on the pace of change. By 1986, roughly a fifth of seats in the Legislative Yuan and National Assembly were held by non-KMT figures. In that year, Chiang convinced the KMT leadership to complete the major political reforms by lifting martial law, legalizing opposition parties, and expanding direct elections.

From 1986 onward, Taiwan embarked on the final stages of a decisive if gradual democratic transition, culminating in the first free and fair election of the entire Legislative Yuan in 1992 and of the president in 1996. Some date the end of Taiwan's democratic transition to 2000, when the opposition Democratic Progressive Party won the presidency, breaking the symbolic link between the governance of Taiwan and the unification of China that the KMT had long represented. Taiwan's democratic transition sits squarely within the Third Wave transitions that began in the early 1970s in southern Europe and spread to Latin America, Asia, and Eastern Europe through the mid-1990s.

Can China and Taiwan Be Compared?

The conceit of the comparative method is that it is the *only* method by which to arrive at an understanding of any one place. By that precept, an understanding of either China or Taiwan must be couched in comparative research. Because of its apparently universalistic trajectory, studies of Taiwan have tended to be better at making such comparisons than those of China, with its pretensions to political if not cultural uniqueness. So can Taiwan and China be usefully compared?

For some, the structural differences between the two places make comparisons inapt. Taiwan had particular security concerns with respect to the mainland that accelerated its democratization in order to maintain US support, for example. In this sense, its democratization was externally driven. A host of domestic conditions also differ, it is argued: the particularity of Taiwan's ethnic politics, its colonial experience, China's size, China's more orthodox Leninist regime, and China's latecomer status. In addition, the KMT never explicitly rejected democracy as a long-term goal, whereas the CCP rejects democracy, as commonly understood, as a future political model for China.

There are two possible responses to these claims. One is to argue that they are not, in fact, differences, that on all these points the countries actually look quite similar. China has its own ethnic tensions, faces international pressures to democratize, has moved in the direction of a universal understanding of democracy, and since 1989 has shifted to a developmental model that looks increasingly like right-wing authoritarianism. Although its commitment to "socialism" remains, the regime's emphasis on cultural nationalism, tutelary democracy, and capitalist accumulation echoes the KMT more than the Comintern. Reading accounts of the decades leading up to Taiwan's democratization is to be reminded of the strong parallels between the experiences of the postrevolutionary KMT and the postrevolutionary CCP.

Yet this argument misses the larger point that merely by making such claims we are engaging in comparison. Thus the more apt response is to say that these differences do not foreclose comparison but are rather comparison itself. Arguments about noncomparability are question-begging because they raise substantive issues that properly belong to the comparison itself. The assertion of noncomparability is a substantive claim whose analytic basis should serve to enlighten conditions in both countries.

For political scientists, comparability at a certain level is assumed across most states. Establishing comparability in any particular instance depends on the nature of the question being asked. In this book, we are asking about the comparability of political change in Taiwan and China, a broad and universal phenomenon that imposes no a priori conditions to establish comparability other than the existence of a functioning state. The basic facts of a state—a well-defined territorial boundary within which a self-identified political community exists—are all that is needed to establish comparability. These certainly exist in China and Taiwan. Beyond that, their similar cultural backgrounds, common histories in the modernizing influences born of the collapse of Qing dynasty rule, and shared regional setting make comparison particularly apt.

Comparability, however, does not mean similarity. To say that two places can be compared does not mean that the results of that comparison will be a finding that their actual experiences are the same: the finding may be instead that they are very different. One is bound to find in any comparison that the descriptive facts differ widely. Thus to take the chapters of this book, in some areas—value change, social modernization, and regime adaptations—the parallels between the China and Taiwan cases are striking. In other areas—intellectual pluralism, international pressures, and multiparty pluralism—the parallels are more strained. In all cases, the findings are only valid insofar as the premise of comparability is accepted in the first place. The China-Taiwan comparison is thus both apt and fruitful.

Periodization

A second methodological consideration concerns periodization: how to ensure we are comparing like periods. One approach, drawing on modernization theory, is to take levels of economic development as the basis of comparison. On this view, China and Taiwan can be most closely compared by imposing a 26-year lag on China (see Figure 1.1). Taiwan's 35-year period from 1951 leading up to its 1986 democratic breakthrough can be closely fitted to the period in China beginning in 1977 and ending in 2012 (which interestingly enough is when a new leadership will take command in China). (A recent World Bank recalculation has lopped about five years of growth off of China's gross domestic product (GDP) per capita, implying a revised 31-year lag from Taiwan.)

Modernization theory's simple proposition is more descriptive than causal: societies experiencing sustained economic growth will be characterized by parallel social and political transformations that lead in the same direction: a democratic, constitutional, and nonideological state characterized addi-

Figure 1.1   Income Levels in Taiwan (1951–1986) and China (1977–2004)

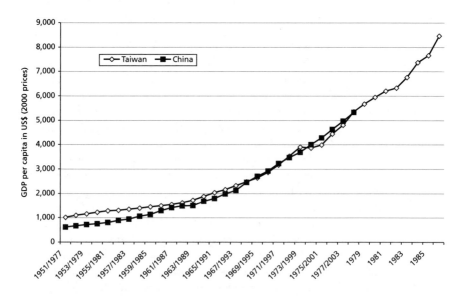

Source: Alan Heston, Robert Summers, and Bettina Aten, "Penn World Table Version 6.2," Center for International Comparisons of Production, Income, and Prices at the University of Pennsylvania, September 2006. Available at http://pwt.econ.upenn.edu/php_site/pwt_index.php.

Note: Real gross domestic product (GDP) per capita, US$ purchasing power parity (PPP) in 2000 prices computed using the Laspreyres Index.

tionally by mass participation and an institutionalized state. There is a spirited debate among econometrians about whether a discrete, constant, and irrefutably independent causal influence on politics can be attributed to economic growth.[12] However, modernization theory has an enduring utility for a qualitative understanding of political change in places as diverse as Communist Bulgaria[13] and industrializing South Korea,[14] not to mention Taiwan itself.

One implication of the modernization-based periodization is that *China has not yet reached the income level at which a democratic transition would be expected.* If so, then the many explanations offered in recent years of why China has not transitioned to democracy are premature. As Wang has argued, China has not reached the inflection point where demands for strong rule are replaced by demands for fair rule.[15] It is therefore neither an outlier from modernization trends nor even a laggard. Inglehart and Welzel predicted in 2005, using cross-national data on value change, that "if socioeconomic development continues at the current pace (as it shows every sign of doing) . . . China will make a transition to a liberal democracy within the next two decades."[16] Plainly put, we cannot determine whether the CCP has outlasted modernization pressures until China reaches an income level at which those pressures would be expected to be most acute. As Zheng puts it: "By the East Asian clock . . . democratization is not delayed or 'late' in China. It has taken Taiwan and South Korea more than 30 years to accomplish the political transition from a developmental authoritarian state to an emerging democracy. . . . China needs at least another 20 years before enough empirical data can be gathered to confirm or disconfirm the validity of the modernization-developmentalism-democratization thesis."[17]

Authors in this book also point out several unique conditions—international pressures, a perspicacious leader, and legacies of elections begun on the mainland—that may have made Taiwan *particularly early* in its democratic transition. If so, we might consider the second decade of the twenty-first century as the "earliest" date for democratization in China. Moreover, if there are conditions in China that are likely to make it *particularly late,* a laggard in other words, then the predicted date of transition might be further off still. Strict parallels with Taiwan's pre-1986 political experiences are contestable for contemporary China. Therein lies the analytic richness of the Taiwan-China comparison and the reasons for the intensity of contemporary debates on China's political future.

The more that particularistic conditions need to be invoked to explain China's divergence from the modernization paradigm, the more we should look for other ways to periodize the China-Taiwan comparison. A second approach to periodization is to find the periods in which state-society relations look the most similar, where the stirrings of civil society activism and a state reluctant to repress it look most similar, irrespective of income levels. One answer is to look for the point at which state-society relations were decisively fractured in the face of increasingly strong social forces such that limited accommodation, rather than total repression, became the new norm of authoritarian rule. At what point did ruling parties become governing parties in both states? Both countries have had well-known "massacres"—events that signaled a new accommodation or social contract as a result of the trauma they caused. In Taiwan, initially, KMT rule was seen as a liberation from Japanese colonialism. But rising tensions between a strongly authoritarian KMT with its mainland immigrants and the native Taiwanese population culminated in four days of unrest beginning on February 28, 1947, that left at least 10,000 dead. "2/28" forever changed KMT rule on Taiwan. It was the end of the honeymoon and the onset of an increasingly contentious state-society relationship in Taiwan.

The June 3–4, 1989, Tiananmen Massacre (known as "6/4" in China) is the closest parallel in China. The numbers dead are far smaller—perhaps 2,000. But the popular effect was just as great, since the movement had spread to some three-quarters of China's cities, and the official verdict on "6/4" would remain a highly volatile political subject thereafter. Both points mark the shift from totalitarian to authoritarian regimes, whence private business and incipient social movements first took root and then expanded in a linear fashion. By that measure, the period of liberalizing authoritarianism in Taiwan that began in the 1960s and 1970s in the lead-up to the 1986 breakthrough would not be expected to have a parallel until the 2000s and 2010s in China. Again, this suggests that given a proper periodization, it is too early to say whether China is following in the footsteps of Taiwan.

Civil Society and the State

Chapters 2 through 5 in this book deal with the question of socioeconomic development and change in Taiwan and China.

Chapters 2 and 3 deal with two of the most important hypothesized mechanisms of modernization theory: value change and intellectual pluralism. Yunhan Chu is optimistic about liberalization in China, noting the steep changes in values evident on the mainland from the early 1990s to the early 2000s. There is little doubt, he finds, that socioeconomic development profoundly changes values, as evidenced in Taiwan, Hong Kong, and China, and that this is accelerated under democratic conditions. Value change is in a sense a refutation of culturalist theory insofar as cultural theory posits a relatively stable and distinctive set of social values that pervade a given society irrespective of its developmental level or institutional conditions. But Confucian views about pluralism and authority continue to exert a strong-level effect in all three places, Chu finds. There are limits to liberalism in Chinese societies. Chu believes, however, that socioeconomic development and institutional effects are sufficient to create values in support of democracy. Chu finds educational levels in Taiwan and China were strong predictors of democratic orientations. Merle Goldman and Ashley Esarey are less sure about the transposition of the Taiwan experience to China. In both places, it was "establishment intellectuals" who were the most important sources of dissent. The nonparty movements grew out of these party movements. They also note how major crackdowns on dissidents in both places usually prefigured a period of regime adaptation. However, China's dissident intellectuals did not have the same media space and social support, and they were more likely to be either repressed or co-opted by the state than those in Taiwan. As with Chu's findings about culture, Goldman and Esarey find that Confucian literati traditions continue to bind in China as long as countervailing modernization or institutional trends do not unbind them.

Two further chapters—by Richard Madsen and Dorothy J. Solinger—deal with the question of organized social forces. Patterns of civil society and civil resistance form an intermediate link between socioeconomic development and political response. Both chapters question conventional approaches to civil society and resistance. For one, the notion of civil society as standing in an adversarial relationship to the state may be largely inaccurate. Civil society may flourish under authoritarianism through close cooperative ties to the state without losing its status as relatively autonomous of that same state. Second, both authors argue that civil society can often be highly illiberal in its orientations and behavior, particularly evident in contemporary China. This means that even though it may promote political liberalization, it will not necessarily promote liberal politics. And finally, growing civil society need not lead to democracy. Authoritarian regimes may often be strengthened by civil society or made more repressive. Civil society may be more a result of democratization than its cause. Although similar criticisms are now well established, even conventional, in the academic literature,[18] their applicability to civil society in China and Taiwan suggests that notions of civil society developed in Western countries may be the outliers. Indeed, given that Taiwan itself has often been portrayed as a classic case of Western-style civil society, these chapters imply that perhaps the role of civil society in the West itself has been misunderstood, a hypothesis that has generated much new debate in the field.

As Madsen notes, classical Western theories of civil society were ambivalent about whether or not it was a force for good. Both left-wing and right-wing critics of liberalism in the contemporary West, then, may be mistaken in arguing that liberalism is unique to the West. But the reason is not that liberalism is universally shared. Rather, it is that liberalism is universally miraculous, as unusual in the West as anywhere else. This is a reminder that the essentialization of the West is so often a mental stumbling block to understanding non-Western societies because it leads to a search for difference in the non-Western world that is contrasted to a nonexistent and essentialized West.

Madsen notes that the states in Taiwan and China tended to adopt mixtures of Marxist, corporatist, and republican views of civil society—where its positive virtues depend on certain institutional or cultural contexts—rather than a liberal view—where its positive virtues are invariant to such contexts. Perhaps all authoritarian regimes do so similarly since they find a convenient correspondence between these illiberal approaches and their own survival. Taiwan's civil society eventually broke free of such constraints and since 1986 has tended to look more like the liberal view, on the whole a positive force for democratic consolidation. One question raised, then, is whether the increasingly popular academic view of "illiberal" civil society is merely a function of institutional context: authoritarian regimes make civil society illiberal in the first place.

Solinger also takes the Taiwan case as a stylized example of civil society, in this case private business, acting as an oppositional and largely liberalizing force. She finds that a similar story is not unfolding in China, where private business is co-opted by and supportive of the authoritarian regime, partly as a result of regime efforts and partly because of more fractured social networks among business groups on the mainland. As she notes, however, one must distinguish between two parts of the Taiwanese business community—the largely autonomous native community and the more state-dependent mainland community. The latter, which dominated the economy until the 1980s, was as co-opted and regime-supporting as that of today's China. Yang's data suggest that the broader middle class in late-authoritarian Taiwan was also fully co-opted by the regime.[19]

Solinger's chapter raises two questions, then. What is a "typical" or "normal" relationship between business and democratization? And what did that relationship look like in Taiwan? Although private business groups usually move to the side of reform once democratic transitions begin, their role in the prior liberalization process seems to vary widely. Indeed, several studies suggest that a co-opted business community is more the rule than the exception in the liberalization phase. In both Latin America and Europe, business classes were often regime supporters until very late in the game.[20] Indeed, the only region where business stood unambiguously in opposition to authoritarian regimes from the beginning was Africa.[21] The role of business as a liberalizing force in Latin America and Europe was more as an agent of within-regime rather than outside-of-regime transformation, arguing for greater transparency and inclusiveness in the policymaking process.[22] In China, a similar within-regime dynamic seems to be at work.[23] If so, then China is more typical of the typical Western model, and Taiwan is, if anything (even if we accept the standard account of its business and middle classes as regime opponents), an example of the relatively unusual African model. The debate on China and

Taiwan thus forces us to reconsider the conventional wisdom of a core issue in comparative politics itself.

Regime Responses

The chapters in Part 2 deal with the ways that regimes in China and Taiwan actively and consciously responded to the domestic and international pressures that they confronted. This section pays particular attention to the ways in which similar innovations have had dramatically different consequences for regime persistence in the two places.

Robert P. Weller's chapter makes two essential points linking Parts 1 and 2 of this book. First, civil society's importance to political change may lie in its emphasis on "difference" rather than its emphasis on "resistance." Merely by separating itself from the state, civil society's diverse forms of cultural activity can create the space that undermines regimes on the quiet, even if there are often uncivil aspects to that activity. Second, authoritarian regimes such as KMT-ruled Taiwan and CCP-ruled China can and did develop feedback mechanisms to prevent the emergence of political movements among this proliferating civil society. Those mechanisms may be nonelectoral and yet just as effective as elections in keeping apolitical groupings apolitical. Given a set of contingent circumstances that limit broader pressures on China, the CCP may live much longer off such "responsive authoritarianism" than did the KMT. Indeed, a new emphasis on reviving feedback mechanisms within the ruling CCP ("inner-party democracy" or *dangnei minzhu*) articulated by CCP general secretary Hu Jintao at the party's seventeenth congress of 2007 may herald an even more responsive party-state.

In the 1960s and 1970s, scholars adopted a bureaucratic-authoritarianism model in order to explain the reversal of democracy or the persistence of authoritarianism in Latin American states.[24] States that captured the gains of economic development could use those resources to strengthen their administrative and repressive capacities, averting the specter of democracy by a mixture of technocratic legitimation and brute coercion. Might a similar approach explain the longevity of KMT rule on Taiwan and the persistence of CCP rule in China? Might it be possible, in other words, for states to navigate the treacherous waters of the "transition zone" in which pressures for democratization rise through the implementation of governance reforms alone?

Chapter 7 by Randall Peerenboom and Weitseng Chen focuses on the ways in which regimes in China and Taiwan strengthened administrative and legal mechanisms in the face of rising governance challenges—ways that seem to mirror the bureaucratic-authoritarian model. For them, China and Taiwan's legal system developments were part of a broader sequencing of governance reforms prior to democratization. Institutional reforms aimed at establishing a thin or procedural rule of law, enhanced spheres of freedom, and nascent constitutionalism combined with tight restrictions on civil and political liberties when the exercise of such rights was perceived to threaten the state are common features of both countries at similar development levels. Peerenboom and Chen conclude that democratization in China is not late by Asian standards and may threaten some of the gains in the rule of law if introduced too early. Nonetheless, they suggest that some form of electoral democracy, although not inevitable, is likely in China's future because pressures for political participation are rising there, as they did in Taiwan.

Thus both feedback mechanisms and rights-protections mechanisms provided an extended lease-on-life for authoritarian regimes in Taiwan and China. In Chapter 8, Tun-jen Cheng and Gang Lin consider yet another type of regime response to modernization pressures: the institutionalization of local elections. Their chapter reminds us of how similar institutions may behave very differently depending upon the context. Bound by the promises of its inclusive ideology and democratic goals, the KMT in Taiwan allowed itself to be challenged and eventually transformed by the spread of local elections. The Taiwan experience was typical of broader comparative evidence: elections in authoritarian regimes create "unintended" openings that generate momentum for democratization.

The CCP, by contrast, has so far managed to contain, even subvert, local elections to its advantage. A key to this is that the CCP has maintained a distinction between local elections and future national political organization. Seeking a "third way" has ensured that local elections in China are *not* seen as a prelude to national-level democracy but merely as an adjunct to new forms of accountability.

As Cheng and Lin note, however, elections have a momentum that is very difficult to slow for a protracted period. Lindberg, for example, has argued that semicompetitive local elections provided the route to democratization throughout Africa.[25] The big question is how long the CCP can continue to limit the trickle-up effects of elections. Cheng and Lin believe that ultimately the democratic discourse is ineluctable, no matter how many adjectives precede the word. Even if the CCP can maintain a nonelectoral ideal type in the minds of China's citizens, the practical needs of governance, such as controlling corruption (also an argument made by Peerenboom and Chen) could force the party to embrace national elections despite its best intentions.

A key difference that Cheng and Lin cite to explain the different implications of local elections in Taiwan and China is the international pressures on the two states. The KMT was more vulnerable to domestic trickle-up pressures because it was simultaneously trying to respond to trickle-in pressures from abroad. China, they note, has used nationalism and a new discourse of global political diversity to limit such external pressures. This is the question taken up by Jacques deLisle in his exploration in Chapter 9 of how the two regimes responded to differing international contexts.

DeLisle notes the window in which international pressures worked in favor of democratization in Taiwan in the 1970s and 1980s. He finds those influences to be particularly important to Taiwan's democratization. Periodization in a global polity model is particularly difficult because global effects are, almost by definition, constantly evolving. There can be no strict parallels to the global effects felt by Taiwan in the lead-up to its democratic breakthrough of 1986. The question of noncomparability is a big one in this area. On the other hand, at a certain level of abstraction, one can delineate the main features of global effects on Taiwan in the 1970s and 1980s: diplomatic pressures from the United States; an increasingly cosmopolitan middle class that felt embarrassed by its autocratic political system; and border effects from major liberalization in other Asian states, including the Philippines and South Korea.

It is easy enough to find parallel global effects being exerted on China in the 1990s and 2000s. Weller, for instance, wonders whether the prodemocracy environment that Taiwan found itself in during the 1980s is absent for today's China. Yet deLisle notes several ways in which it might be stronger. Moreover, several important democratizations took place in the 1990s (in Indonesia and Thailand, for example) and in the 2000s (in Ukraine and Georgia, for example). Thus, as deLisle shows, it is not so much the presence or absence of global pressures to democratize that matters so much as how those pressures interact with particular domestic conditions. What seems more important is why similar objective conditions have different actual impacts: Why do Chinese leaders and people not read these events as evidence of the need for democratic change? Or why did global democratic contagion engulf Taiwan in the 1980s but not China in the 1990s and 2000s?

DeLisle offers one answer: the KMT was unable to muster the kind of pushback against international pressures to democratize that the CCP could decades later. For most Taiwanese, democratization was a means of liberation from the state imposed upon them at the Cairo Conference of Allied leaders in 1943. For the people of China, by contrast, democratization was often portrayed as a threat to the freedoms they won after the death of Mao. And given China's enormous size and thus the comparative insularity of large parts of its population from global forces, the ability to muster pushback was all the greater.

The claim that global pressures were important to Taiwan's democratization is most often presented as an assertion. Yet global forces may have simply accelerated domestic trends well under way in Taiwan and done so without any notable pushback from the regime itself. In China, global forces are acting on a less momentous domestic trend, and they are moreover being resisted by the CCP tooth and nail. This dual contextualization is critical to explaining the impact of global pressures on political change in Taiwan and China.

What does the comparative study of these regime adaptations portend for China's political future? The writers here share a general view that the Taiwan comparison brings out the differences in China and by implication the different political future it faces. Although they all see the seeds of democracy lying in wait, most believe that in the immediate future, the CCP will successfully manage the political consequences of socioeconomic change.

Yet history is fond of playing tricks on predictions, and in any case it seems likely that at some point a CCP-ruled China will face a democratic transition. In Chapter 10, following a general theory of transitions and the experiences of Taiwan from 1986 to 1996 and China in 1989, I trace the likely implications for a future democratic transition in China. Would it succeed as in Taiwan or fail again as in 1989? I argue that it would likely succeed, given the dramatic changes in institutional and developmental conditions in China since 1989. How can we assess the likely nature of that transition as well as its consequences, if successful, for the democracy that follows? The answer here is more pessimistic: unless social forces gain much strength between now and the day of the next attempted transition, China risks falling into the category of feckless democracies, a "People's Republic of Chinastan," as I call it, where democratic freedoms advance barely at all, and the CCP remains dominant, if not hegemonic.

In Chapter 11, Larry Diamond stresses how the structural differences between the two states will likely bring about dramatically different denouements for authoritarian rule. China's large size, its different institutions, and its worsening inequalities and corruption, he believes, will make it harder for the CCP to engineer the sort of soft landing to democracy achieved in Taiwan. Given that pressures for democratization are unlikely to abate, this implies a tumultuous future for the world's biggest nation.

Intersubjective Comparisons, Intertwined Fates

These and other important *objective* comparisons between Taiwan and China should not overshadow the equal importance of the *subjective* comparisons made in China about the Taiwan experience. All human experience holds lessons for all humans, especially when humans choose to make it so. Some experiences may be more directly relevant to a given people at a given time and place. However, some experiences may become relevant through subjective perception, selection, interpretation, and application. There are few *objective* reasons, after all, why tiny Singapore—an ex-British microstate of four million people in Southeast Asia with a per capita GDP in price-equivalent (purchasing power parity, or PPP) terms of $45,000—should be considered to have lessons for China's political future. Yet this distant statelet is widely cited in domestic Chinese discourse (and by Peerenboom and Chen) as being relevant to China. That discourse in turn has effects on actions. Subjective lessons are as important as objective lessons. In light of the importance of subjective perceptions to democratizations worldwide, much greater attention should be paid to the ways in which the Taiwan experience is exerting an influence on *subjective* perceptions in China. Like Singapore, Taiwan may be relevant to China because people in China decide to make it so, as either a negative or a positive example of their own menu of choices.

A brief glimpse at policy journals in China will reveal the interest with which China's elites study the Taiwan experience. For many writers in China, the Taiwan experience serves as a negative example.[26] Democratization may result in the ruling party's losing power, a rise in social discord, worsened ethnic divisions, and slower economic development, they believe.[27] Taiwan's resurgent ethnic politics is interpreted by China in light of its own unresolved national identity.[28]

For others, especially since the KMT's 2005 reconciliation with the CCP, the Taiwan experience is serving as a positive example.[29] Not only did democracy rein in endemic corruption, on these accounts, but it also gave Taiwan an international dignity that China itself lacks. Guo notes that six of his interviewees from officialdom in China voluntarily offered the opinion that Taiwan's transition is "a powerful indication that Chinese culture can transit to democracy."[30] Beijing University professor He Weifang was quoted in a Taiwan newspaper in 2006 praising the virtues of Taiwan democracy. "It has shown the Chinese people that they are not born with a saddle attached to them so that they can be ridden, driven, and whipped. . . . Taiwan's today is the mainland's tomorrow," he says.[31] Most notably, Chinese Academy of Social Sciences professor Zhang Boshu published a lengthy essay in 2007 arguing that Taiwan's democratization provided "valuable lessons" for China's own future transition across a range of areas, from social movements to political leadership.[32]

Moreover, Taiwan itself is generally cited as a successful example of the East Asian developmental model, not just by Peerenboom and Chen but also by domestic analysts in China, wherein political civil liberties are slowly expanded while the state remains an active agent in economic development.[33] Properly periodized, the CCP could subjectively imagine itself as a KMT of the 1960s and 1970s. Chao and Lee argue that "Taiwan has much to offer [to China] as to what a party-state structure should do to accommodate demands for more liberalization and participation."[34]

It is difficult to ascertain where the balance of opinion lies among politically salient groups in China, not least because identifying who the politically salient groups are is notoriously difficult in authoritarian regimes. At the very least, the ability of scholars and analysts in China to publish works suggesting the *positive* aspects of the Taiwan democratic experience shows that a counterhegemony is at work. As deLisle notes, it is all too easy to point to the "official" and "approved" opinion in China and to ignore the potentially much more pervasive "unofficial" and "popular" opinions of Taiwan in China, views that censors cannot control and that continuously challenge official opprobrium of Taiwanese democracy. According to a Radio Free Asia report, one reason for the closure of the popular weekly *Bingdian* (*Freezing Point*) in 2006 was that it had published admiring reports on democratization in Taiwan that violated the party's proscription against anything but negative reports.[35] Indeed, the counterhegemonic view is often, perhaps most often, born of the hidden transcripts found in or decoded from the official view itself, just as salacious reporting on social and economic problems in West Germany by East German television stations during the Cold War tended instead to reinforce the virtues of the West German system in the minds of East German citizens. The balance of that debate, and how it is used in internal CCP debates, cannot be overestimated. The learning that takes place at the subjective level—informed perhaps by objective comparisons such as those contained in this book—may alter the course of political change in both places, transforming the objective comparisons themselves. Regime adaptations in China, for instance, have often been consciously grounded in perceived comparisons with Taiwan. Whatever the objective reality of electoral democracy in Taiwan, the *perception* among key political actors in China that it has *not* led to a more representative or well-considered system of rule has spurred the search for alternatives on the mainland. If so, what are the policy implications for Taiwan? Should it be more proactive in promoting the positive side of its democratic experience in order to counter negative views on the mainland?

Finally, Taiwan's experience is important to understanding China because the two are also *structurally* related. What makes this comparison particularly intriguing is that the two countries are causal factors in political developments in each other, not just through ideas but through a host of intertwined historical, economic, social, and political structures. At the most basic level, the origins of Taiwan's successful democratization were in China itself, where the KMT experimented with local democracy in the 1930s and held a national election in 1946. Taiwan's own democratization, based on a 1947 constitution written in China, was also in turn heavily driven by its anti-Communist stance and rhetorical adherence to the Three Principles of the People and then later accelerated by the US recognition of China. More recently, China's rise and its role in the livelihoods of increasing numbers of Taiwan citizens have generated greater support for the relatively pro-China political parties in Taiwan. China's diplomatic isolation of Taiwan, meanwhile, has retarded the growth of civil society in Taiwan by delinking it from its transnational counterparts.[36]

Taiwan has also structurally affected China in manifold ways. China's implementation of elections for village governments, passed into law in 1987, was based in part upon borrowing Taiwan's practice with its own village elections since the 1950s. Village elections in Fujian Province, meanwhile, have begun to mimic the electioneering styles of Taiwan. Taiwan's vast investments in China ($100 billion worth), exports to China (its number one market), and social migration to China (one million citizens) are also bringing with them both the norms of a liberal society and the society-empowering forces of economic modernization. Economic and social interdependence is, after all, a two-way street. Taiwan may be exporting its democracy to China along with its people and capital, even as it feels constrained in its own domestic political development by those same factors. For some analysts, Taiwan's push for greater autonomy or even independence subverts the democratic project in China itself by strengthening chauvinistic nationalism in China. If so, should Taiwan rein in its domestic political change? In other ways, Taiwan's strengthening of democratic commitments in Asia has altered the regional landscape of which China itself wants to be a part.

The comparison of Taiwan and China then must always keep in mind not just objective analytic comparisons (the topic of this book) and subjective analytic comparisons, but also how both of these are shaped by the actual interdependencies across the Taiwan Strait. Reality, in this case, has a way of intruding upon scholarly analysis.

Lessons Learned

In answer to the first of the three aims of this book, this chapter forces us to rethink the Taiwan and China experiences in a fundamental way. Simply put, once one examines the Taiwan case in any detail, the simplifying assumptions of modernization theory begin to have less and less analytic power. Value change, socioeconomic development, and rising social forces were preconditions for democratization, to be sure. However, these only provided background conditions. The critical reasons why democratization, as opposed to some continually adapting form of authoritarianism, emerged in Taiwan lie elsewhere. One reason is the international environment and its subjective interpretation by Taiwanese leaders. Another has to do with the ideals and expectations set in motion by the Three Principles of the People and Taiwan's attempts to distinguish itself from China. Another concerns the shift of civil society from co-opted to oppositional, partly as a result of adaptations by the state itself.

If this "most typical" case of modernization cannot be explained except with reference to state actions, then the opposite might be true of China. Often set out as a foil to modernization theories, China may fit the broad contours of such a theory more than is widely assumed. The same value changes, socioeconomic development, and rising social forces are evident in China, and properly periodized it would not be expected to experience major political transformation until the 2020s. More to the point, the ability of the CCP regime to resist the pressures for political opening that the KMT eventually succumbed to is not itself evidence that those pressures—the "modernization pressures" as we might call them—are not at work in China. China's ability to subjectively interpret the global environment as arguing in favor of continued authoritarian rule, and its ability to ensure that regime adaptations and a rising civil society do not unseat the party itself, are evidence of an ability to resist these pressures, not evidence that such pressures do not exist. Again, state actions are paramount in any explanation of regime outcomes.

This inversion of conventional wisdom about Taiwan and China bespeaks the importance of case histories in understanding political change in any place. The argument for case histories is not just that they lard simplified understandings with complex details but that they may change the simplified understandings themselves. The details provided on the China and Taiwan cases certainly afford the possibilities of such a rethink, as outlined above. Yet the cases also simultaneously attest to the relevance of one of the most enduring macrostructural theories of political change, once properly interpreted. It may be more accurate to describe modernization theory as a paradigm rather than a theory—a general model rather than a specific hypothesis about political change. These case studies illustrate the continued value of such paradigms for contextualizing and comparing case studies.

The analytical richness of the Taiwan-China comparison and the consciously theoretical way in which the comparison is tackled by the authors of these chapters yield several substantive lessons for political science as well. For one, as mentioned, modernization theory should be properly understood as a source of pressures for political changes but not as a cause of them. Developmental conditions are too far removed from the causes of political change. Moreover, they may operate in opposing directions. Delays and countervailing pressures brought about by authoritarian regimes are always possible. Regimes that continue to adapt to changing demands and that bottle up path-dependent expectations of democratization may endure the pains of rapid development without a grimace. To use Goodwin's terms, states that become more inclusive (as opposed to exclusive), more bureaucratic-rational (versus patrimonial), and more capacity rich (versus capacity starved) stand a good chance of averting revolutionary change.[37] The KMT could not sustain itself without a democratic transformation because its exclusiveness threatened a legitimacy crisis. China appears to have averted a similar fate by remaining sufficiently inclusive, empowered, and rational. But these variables are subjective, not objective. Necessary state action to avert democratic change in China is being constantly redefined in the face of changing social values and expectations.

Second, strong civil societies tend to go hand in hand with strong states.[38] The two may become oppositional, and it may remain analytically useful to compare their relative power—as I do in Chapter 10 to understand the implications for democratic consolidation. But in terms of absolute power, the two tend to move in tandem. One cannot understand the rise of civil society in Taiwan or China except in the context of the rise of an institutionalized state in both places.

Closely related to this is that civil society changes regimes, usually from the inside, but the direction of those changes is uncertain. The role of civil society in promoting democratization may not be one of promoting liberal ideals but merely one of fomenting internal regime pluralism. A truly "civil" society is a result of democratization itself. The KMT's increased fissiparousness on how to deal with the nonparty candidates and media led eventually to a preemptive move to keep ahead of those forces through phased liberalization. The penetration of the CCP by groups as diverse (and illiberal) as the Falungong religious sect and private business may likewise be creating the internal regime pluralism that makes regime unity harder and harder to maintain. Democracy, in this sense, could arise as a "fortuitous byproduct" of regime decay.[39]

Finally, subjectivity matters, and it matters far more than political scientists have generally been willing to admit. Underlying the assumptions about "social pressures" and "regime adaptations," for example, is the central question of subjective legitimacy. Legitimacy is not a fixed function of certain objective attributes of regimes but a variable function of them with wide latitude for subjective interpretation. Subjectivity also matters in how regimes themselves perceive and act upon the domestic and international environment they face. It might seem "inevitable" today that Taiwan's leaders saw the Nixon visit to China in 1972 as a sign that they needed to embrace democratic change, but this was by no means obvious at the time. This was after all the high point of the Cold War, and the United States continued to support authoritarian regimes around the world (witness Augusto Pinochet's coup in Chile the same year) as part of its containment of Communism. Nixon gave Chiang mixed signals about his intentions from 1967 onward, but his vice president, Spiro Agnew, told the press in 1970 that rumors of decreased support for Chiang's regime were "bothering the hell out of me." As Tucker notes: "If officials in Taipei had reservations about the Agnew channel, none was made apparent."[40] Agnew and other US officials gave every indication that US support of Taiwan was nonnegotiable. To retrospectively see objective "facts" in the leadership's subjective interpretation of the world climate is to ignore this alternative possibility.

Indeed, that lesson is made clear from China. The contemporary global environment surely brings as much objective democratizing pressure to bear on China as did the Sino-US détente on Taiwan. It has nonetheless been interpreted, and propagated domestically, by the CCP as an environment in which democratization is inadvisable. Again, there is nothing objectively true in this view, which depends instead on the subjective perceptions of leaders and their ability to convince society they are right.

Last, subjectivity also arises in the Chinese understanding of Taiwan. As comparativists, we have argued that the China-Taiwan comparison is both valid and fruitful. Yet subjectively, that view may not be widely held on the mainland. Chinese see in Taiwan an ethnically divided society and in Singapore a homogenous Chinese one, even though non-Chinese account for 25 percent of Singapore's population but only 2 percent of Taiwan's. This subjective seeking of parallels with a state whose stability and wealth are seen as more attractive to some reflects the persistence of intersubjective views and their importance to concrete action.

China's Future

Given its population, a democratization of China would represent more than the proportion of world population that was included in any of the previous three waves of global democratization. The effects of such a transformation would extend far beyond China's borders, probably fatally undermining Communist regimes in North Korea, Myanmar, and Vietnam and fundamentally changing the security situation in East Asia. China's political future is thus arguably the single most important question in contemporary political science. What do the studies here tell us about this most important of questions?

For a start, it is far too early to be pessimistic about democratic prospects in China. Although there is evidence that China's administrative reforms have lessened the influence of democratic demands, a proper periodization of the China case from any of several perspectives leads to the conclusion that the country is not yet at the point at which democratization should occur.

Another reason for caution in being pessimistic is that a reconsideration of the Taiwan case itself—considered a classic case of both modernization as well as state-society approaches to democratization—shows more parallels than was previously known. From the perspective of the mid-1970s, for example, many observers believed that the Taiwanese state had effectively co-opted business, repressed dissent, and institutionalized good governance and non-electoral feedback mechanisms. The country's long economic boom was seen, as with Latin America at the time, to have strengthened the state's ability to justify its rule to Taiwanese.[41] It is only retrospectively that we see how all these factors were either weaker than supposed or else were working in precisely the opposite direction.

Still, as Diamond has noted, the problem with comparisons across time is that global conditions change.[42] And one of the most important conditions that may change on the question of democratization may be the subjective lessons that have been learned about previous democratizations by the Chinese themselves. China's regime and to some extent its people are determined to avoid being "de-centered" by the global force of democratic norms.[43] In response, many fine minds, both Chinese and Western and working both in China and abroad, have been trying hard since Tiananmen to develop alternative conceptions of final resting places for modernity that look very different from contemporary liberal democracy. Various conceptions of a vaguely left-wing orientation such as "*xiaokang* socialism" and "decent democratic centralism" and others of a vaguely right-wing orientation such as "Confucian democracy," "traditional Chinese authoritarianism," and "consultative rule of law" have been proposed as alternatives to liberal democracy for China.[44] To some extent then, the field is wide open and everything is to play for.

Of course, caution is the byword when seeking new modernities in the experiences of authoritarian regimes. Some scholars found Yugoslavia to be on the forefront of political innovation in the 1960s and 1970s, only to be blindsided by that country's spectacular collapse, with the loss of half a million lives, in the 1990s. Latin American bureaucratic-authoritarianism and African socialism likewise had their brief moments in the social sciences sunshine before economic and political breakdown revealed them to be unsustainable bases of political order even for the places where they began.

Asian authoritarianism—delaying democratization until at least middle income levels have been reached—has been historically vindicated by the successful experiences of Taiwan and South Korea, but less so by those of Thailand and Indonesia. The record of countries that democratized at relatively low income levels is also mixed: India and Mongolia have sustained democracy and growth despite democratizing at low income levels, whereas Pakistan, Sri Lanka, Bangladesh, and the Philippines have done less well after transitions at low income levels. In the contemporary period, continued authoritarianism has served Singapore and Malaysia well economically and may be starting to pay dividends in Vietnam. It has been an obstacle to growth in Burma and Laos and an unmitigated disaster for North Korea. China thus steps into the spotlight as a critical test case of whether delayed or wholly averted democratization serves the long-term interests of societies better than early democratization.[45]

Authors in this book are torn about the implications of China's delayed or wholly averted democratization. Premature democratization may lead to stronger ethnic alliances, rising protest, or an uncivil society, all of which may increase the clamor for a return to authoritarian rule in order to reestablish growth and good governance. A hybrid regime or an outright democratic failure may result. A failure to democratize, or a long delay in doing so, on the other hand, may lead to rising inequalities, festering minority grievances, and weaker democratic norms. Again a hybrid regime or democratic failure may result, not because the state is too weak but because it is too strong.[46]

Viewing China through the lens of Taiwan is a great vindication of the comparative method. For not only does this provide a useful prism for thinking about China, but we are also forced to rethink nostrums about the Taiwan experience itself. Comparison, after all, goes both ways, and in this case it sends us back into history to conduct new research on what is often thought to be a closed case. There is already evidence of similar learning going on in China. The implications of that learning will shape China's future.

Notes

1. Ch'iu 1995; Weller 1999.
2. Lai 2008.
3. Lynch 2006.
4. Wright 2001.
5. Bellows 2000.
6. Tang and Parish 2000.
7. Ch'iu 1995.
8. Dickson 1997.
9. Herschensohn 2002.
10. Figures are the percentage gain in the log value of the HDI as calculated by Crafts. Logs are used because of the nonlinearity of the HDI function over time. Crafts 1997.
11. Huang 1996, 109, Table 5.1.
12. Those arguing against a causal link include Londregan and Poole 1996; Mainwaring and Perez-Linan 2003; Przeworski and Limongi 1997. Those arguing in favor of a causal link include Boix and Stokes 2003; Epstein et al. 2006; Kennedy 2004. Kennedy's conditional probability analysis—regime transitions are more likely to be democratic where there are higher levels of development—is perhaps the most intuitive and empirically robust statement of the relationship. Several authors, such as Diamond (Diamond 1992, 108–109), have argued that the relationship is nonlinear at points (development at a certain level will strengthen authoritarian regimes) and may change over time in light of global political conditions.
13. Vassilev 1999.
14. Han 2001.
15. Wang 2005.
16. Inglehart and Welzel 2005, 190. Inglehart's powers of prediction using World Values Survey data should not be underestimated. In a book published two months before the defeat of the Institutional Revolutionary Party in Mexico in July 2000, he wrote: "Mexico seems ripe for the transition to democracy." Inglehart 2000, 95.
17. Zheng 2003, 62.
18. Edwards, Foley, and Diani 2001; on China see, for example, Beja 2006.
19. Yang 2007.
20. Booth 1998, 146–147; Campero 1995; Huber and Stephens 1999; O'Donnell 1973; Rueschemeyer, Stephens, and Stephens 1992, 6.
21. Bratton and Van de Walle 1997, 88–89.
22. Silva 2002, 89–90.
23. Li, Meng, and Zhang 2006.
24. Collier and Cardoso 1979; O'Donnell 1973.
25. Lindberg 2006.
26. Ma 2005.
27. "The Taiwan model is unlikely to spread to China . . . [because] the performance of the Taiwanese democracy has not been attractive." Pan 2003, 40.

28. Dittmer 2006.

29. Wang 2006; Zhang 2007.

30. Guo 2003, 231.

31. Zhu 2006, 4.

32. Zhang 2007.

33. Lin 2005.

34. Chao and Lee 2006, 227.

35. Radio Free Asia, Investigation Report, January 10, 2007: "According to our research, *Freezing Point* magazine, which has been very well-received by readers, has published articles deviating from official propaganda requirements on the subjects of the Opium War, the War against Japan, *the democratization of Taiwan*, praising Hu Yaobang, and criticizing academic corruption." (italics added)

36. Chen 2006.

37. Goodwin 2001.

38. Shue 1994.

39. Waterbury 1999.

40. Tucker 2005, 120.

41. "These private justifications have been acknowledged and even to a growing degree accepted by the Taiwanese." Johnson 1987, 144.

42. Diamond 1992, 108–109.

43. Lynch 2006.

44. Angle 2005; Bell 2006; Ng-Quinn 2006; Pan 2003.

45. Feng 2003; Gerring et al. 2005; Halperin, Siegle, and Weinstein 2005.

46. Way 2006.

PART 1

Civil Society and the State

2

The Evolution of Political Values

Yun-han Chu

S ocial and political values are a key source of political change. In the case of China, the evolution of political values may hold the key to whether a democratic transition will occur in that country, an event that would be of momentous significance for Asia as a whole.[1] This chapter analyzes and explores the extent to which the political values of the Chinese citizens have undergone profound transformation, in particular in the direction of increasing democratic orientations, as a consequence of the far-reaching and rapid economic, social, and institutional changes occurring in China. It tries to accomplish a dynamic understanding of the sources of value changes by employing a longitudinal comparative survey conducted respectively in China, Taiwan, and Hong Kong at two time points, 1993–1994 and 2001–2002.[2] This unprecedented longitudinal trilateral data set allows us to pursue a systematic understanding of the lingering impact of these countries' common cultural heritage, the socializing effects of their divergent political institutions, and the transformative power of their sequential rapid socioeconomic modernization on political culture.

Hong Kong and Taiwan are arguably the two most relevant cases of reference for exploring the trajectory of China's political values. In many ways, the CCP regime today resembles the KMT regime of yesterday. It reigns over its society as a progrowth, market-conforming authoritarian regime and remains fused with the state in a typical Leninist fashion. The Communist leaders today are wrestling with the same kind of challenge that the KMT leadership faced two decades ago: how to retain their hegemonic presence in the society with dwindling capacity for ideological persuasion and social control, how to accommodate the rising popular demand for political representation and participation, how to co-opt the newly emerged social forces that came with a rapidly growing private sector, and how to cope with the political consequences of economic opening-up.

From the viewpoint of research design, the three societies offer a vantage point of entry for a systematic understanding of sources of culture shift, as the three exhibit great diversity among themselves in terms of both the level of socioeconomic development and political democratization while being bound together by a common cultural heritage. The three societies have traveled down different trajectories of regime transition. Taiwan has completed its democratic transition since 1996. Hong Kong has experienced some limited democratic experiments, starting with the introduction of popular elections in selecting a portion of the legislature in 1991. However, the momentum of democratization is now largely truncated as popular demands for the direct election of the chief executive are being rejected by Beijing. A parallel comparison of the three cases should help us decipher the relative importance of socioeconomic structural and institutional factors in driving change in political culture. In addition, our sampling design for China enables us to divide the nationwide survey into two subsamples: one for urban residents (with urban household registration) and another for rural residents. The advantage of doing this lies in being able to more clearly decipher the influence of modernization while holding political system and cultural legacy constant.

The chapter will proceed in four steps. First, we briefly review the ongoing theoretical debate over the mechanism and sources of value changes. Second, we introduce our conceptualization of democratic value orientations and their measurements. Third, we report the empirical findings of our statistical analysis of the trilateral survey. Last, we explore the implications of our empirical findings for China's democratic future.

Theories of Culture Shift

There are currently three main explanations of value change: modernization (or postmodernization) theory, institutionalism, and culturalist theory.

The central claim of modernization theory is that economic, cultural, and political changes go together in coherent patterns that change in predictable ways.[3] Modernization theory was understood by some as a variant of structural explanations.[4] Many modernization theorists emphasize social mobility and location in modern parts of the social structure as the leading cause of cultural change.[5] Although there has been continuing debate over the causal linkages, many empirical findings do support the claim that socioeconomic development generates more modern attitudes and values—greater tolerance and valuing of freedom, higher levels of political efficacy, and greater capacity to participate in politics and civic life.[6]

The postmodernization theory developed by Ronald Inglehart and his colleagues agrees with the modernization theorists on their central claim but differs on four essential points: change is not linear; economic determinism is oversimplified; the rise of the West is not the only version of modernization; and democracy is not inherent in the modernization phase, but only as societies move *beyond* this phase.[7] Inglehart and his colleagues have accumulated three decades of time-series data to demonstrate an intergenerational shift toward postmodern values, linked with rising levels of economic development.[8]

The three culturally Chinese societies provide the most challenging as well as the most fertile testing ground for the modernization/postmodernization perspective because the rapid socioeconomic transformation that the three societies have experienced over the past 25 to 40 years was unprecedented in human history. Even though all three societies have undergone rapid socioeconomic transformation, in terms of level of socioeconomic modernization they are still miles apart, with Hong Kong leading the pack and China trailing much behind. If modernization theory is correct, citizens of Hong Kong should register the highest level of support for democratic concepts and values, other things being equal. It should be immediately followed by that of Taiwan's citizens, then by the urban residents in China, with residents in rural China trailing behind.

Institutionalist approaches to value change posit that people develop certain orientations toward democracy as well as nondemocratic regimes as a consequence of the organizing principles of formal and informal institutions: specifically, the incentives, disincentives, and habits created by the rules embedded in differing forms of political institutions.[9] Participation in formal procedures such as voting, working for parties or candidates, attending election rallies, attending community meetings, joining with others to raise issues, or contacting elected leaders can have an educative effect that increases interest and efficacy as well as builds support for democracy.[10] Also, membership in civic organizations may build up social capital and cooperative practices and organizational and communicative skills that individuals apply in other and larger political arenas.[11] The historical institutionalist perspective, in particular, emphasizes the socializing effects of institutions in shaping citizens' preferences or even identity over time.[12] Practicing democracy over time would help citizens develop a new and longer-term perspective on judging democracy, based on an appreciation of the intrinsic nature of democracy rather than its consequences.

In short, according to institutional theory, institutions guide political behavior in such a way that after a certain period of time they also help determine changes in attitude and values. If institutionalism is correct, the socializing effect of democratic institutions should leave its clearest footprint on the soil of Taiwan, where the process of democratization has run its full course. In Taiwan, democratic culture would be expected to strengthen along with increasing experience in democratic participation, whereas in Hong Kong it would be expected to stagnate as the democratization process was largely stalled. In China, the practice of grassroots democracy would also induce value change over time, albeit its effect would be limited.

Finally, culturalist theory argues from a postulate of "cumulative" social-ization that privileges early learning. Prior learning is a basis for later learn-ing, and therefore early learning not only conditions later learning but the beliefs learned early also are much more resistant to change. Exceptionally great forces are needed to induce great changes in these basic orientations. Harry Eckstein, for example, describes the most likely cultural changes as pat-tern-maintaining change.[13]

According to this perspective, East Asian political culture and liberal democracy are not compatible, since each is specific to its own respective cul-ture. Lucian Pye has argued that in East Asian cultures traditional authoritari-an and paternalistic relations between superiors and inferiors will remain even after modernization.[14] The pattern of dependency established in the family will interact with an individual sense of insecurity brought about by rapid socioeconomic change to create new forms of power-dependency.[15] This psy-chocultural analysis is consistent with how Samuel Huntington draws a sharp distinction between Chinese and Western civilizations, the former valuing group interests over individual interests, political authority over individual freedom, and social responsibility over individual rights.[16] The cultural rela-tivists argue that Confucian tradition never developed a political philosophy supportive of liberal democracy as the West did. Advocacy of government by virtuous men, rather than law, is not conducive to individual rights, and mod-eling the state after the family leads to a paternalism that slides easily into authoritarianism. Essentially, Confucianism sees the ideal state as leading by moral suasion,[17] so as not to require coercion to fulfill its chief function of cul-tivating virtue and social harmony.[18]

The culturalists turned our attention to the incompatibility of liberal democ-racy with the region's Confucian political culture and traditions to explain why so many East Asian countries have failed to complete the democratic transfor-mation of their authoritarian or totalitarian Communist states.[19] Paradoxically, their view is echoed by defenders of Asian values who have claimed that Western-style liberal democracy is neither suitable for nor compatible with Confucian East Asia, where collective welfare, a sense of duty, and other prin-ciples of Confucian moral philosophy run deep in people's consciences.[20]

According to culturalist theory, value change in Confucian societies would have been rather slow and uneven, regardless of the transformative forces of modernization and globalization or the socializing effects of demo-cratic practice. For ordinary citizens, values that are more compatible with tra-ditional values, such as equality, might be relatively easy to acquire. Certain liberal values not so compatible with traditional values, such as individual freedom and rights, pluralism, and limited government, would have more difficulty in making their way into the prevailing value structure. Even if the political system of a given Asian country might become formally democratized, the new democracy would still carry many illiberal characteristics owing to the slow acquisition of liberal democratic values and beliefs among its elite and populace.[21] On the other hand, if the perspective of modernization is correct, then traditional Confucian values will decline in importance along with modernization, and liberal democratic values will be reinforced through improved educational standards and generational replacement.

Measuring Political and Social Values

There are a plethora of philosophical studies examining the linkage between Confucian values and the universality of human rights and basic democratic norms or their absence.[22] However, with a few exceptions,[23] empirical studies that systematically explore how traditional values actually affect the development of civic culture in Confucian East Asia are quite scarce. Most of the political science literature is based on anecdotal or impressionistic accounts of political attitudes and behavior among the masses and political leaders.[24] A systematic exploration requires both a conceptual scheme for measuring culture-specific traditional social values that people acquired during preadult life and a coherent conceptual framework for a cross-system and cross-time comparison of political culture.

Since the late 1970s, Hu Fu and his colleagues have pioneered the view that system culture—that is, value orientations toward the normative principles that govern the organization of political power and authority in a society—should be the pillar of the political culture approach and that the existing literature on political culture places too much emphasis on what Gabriel Almond termed process culture, such as efficacy, compromise, trust, and tolerance.[25] Hu's Taiwan-based team has developed an original battery measuring popular orientations toward a political regime on five dimensions: *political equality, popular accountability, political liberalism, political pluralism,* and *separation of power* (or *horizontal accountability*), also known as five democratic versus authoritarian value-orientations toward power.[26]

Hu Fu and his colleagues have tracked the evolution of political culture in Taiwan for more than two decades, covering the entire span of the island's regime transition, from the weakening of authoritarianism to the completion of the democratic transition.[27] They found that the acquisition of prodemocratic value orientations along the five dimensions has been uneven, suggesting the lingering influence of traditional values. Support for political equality was high from the beginning, and endorsement of popular accountability rose dramatically from 1984 to 1993 (as did belief in political pluralism, even though it remained rather low). Their data also show that by the late 1990s substantial segments of Taiwan's public still manifested the fear of disorder and preference for communal harmony over individual freedom that Lucian Pye takes to be generally characteristic of Asian attitudes toward power and authority. Yet, they also note the generally steady increase since democratization began in the mid-1980s in the proportions of the public expressing prodemocratic value orientations and rejecting the paternalistic, collectivist, illiberal norms associated with the Asian values perspective.

This approach was later on applied to the comparative study of political culture among three Chinese societies: Taiwan, Hong Kong, and China. The first-wave trilateral survey was conducted between summer 1993 and spring 1994.[28] The second-wave trilateral survey, which by then had become a part of a larger region-wide comparative survey known as East Asia Barometer, was conducted between summer 2001 and summer 2002.[29]

The democratic versus authoritarian value-orientation battery that has been consistently applied in all three localities consists of the following six items (one question for each of the five dimensions except for popular accountability, which has two):[30]

Political Equality

1. People with little or no education should have as much say in politics as highly educated people.[31]

Popular Accountability

2. Government leaders are like the head of a family; we should all follow their decisions.
3. If we have public leaders who are morally upright, we can let them decide everything.

Separation of Power

4. When judges decide important cases, they should accept the view of the executive branch.

Political Liberalism

5. The government should decide whether certain ideas are allowed to be discussed in the society.

Political Pluralism

6. Stability and harmony of the community will be disrupted if people organize lots of groups.

What are the specific components of Confucian values? Values widely cited as Confucian include the importance of family; a concern for ethics and virtue; the primacy of the group over the individual; and an emphasis on unity or harmony, hard work, thrift, and the importance of education.[32] Our analysis largely follows Tu Weiming's elaboration of Confucian personal ethnics.[33] According to Confucian personal ethics, it is imperative to obey family elders, and the ultimate objective of one's personal behavior is to honor one's ancestors. In order to bring honor to the family, it is also imperative to take on the responsibility of bearing children and continuing the family line. Finally, in one's social relations, it is imperative to respect the opinions of nonfamily elders and the educated, so that a harmonious and well-ordered society can be preserved.

We have developed a ten-item battery for the trilateral survey to measure Confucian personal ethics. These ten items can be subdivided into ethics for three social domains, namely family-related, interpersonal-related, and work-related ethics. We employed the following ten items consistently in the three localities and over time.

Traditional Family Values

Do you agree with the following statement?

1. Even if parents' demands are unreasonable, children still should do what they ask.
2. The main reason to work hard and get ahead is for the glory of the ancestors and the family.
3. When a mother-in-law and a daughter-in-law come into conflict, even if the mother-in-law is in the wrong, the husband should still persuade his wife to obey his mother.
4. If one wants to have only one child, it's better to have a son than a daughter.

Traditional Interpersonal Ethics

Do you agree with the following statement?

1. When one has a conflict with a neighbor, the best way to deal with it is to accommodate the other person.
2. If there is a quarrel with others, we should ask an elder to resolve the dispute.
3. Even if you have knowledge and ability, you need not make a big show of it.

Traditional Work-related Ethics

Do you agree with the following statement?

1. When hiring someone, even if a stranger is more qualified, the opportunity should still be given to relatives and friends.
2. It's embarrassing to accept payment for things you do for friends.
3. Wealth and poverty, success and failure are all determined by fate.

Results: The Big Picture

The distribution of popular political attitudes based on our six-item battery for measuring political values is displayed item-by-item in Figures 2.1 through 2.6. The most striking finding is the powerful impact of socioeconomic modernization on the growth of democratic value-orientation (indicat-

Figure 2.1   Support for Political Equality: "People with little or no education should have as much say in politics as highly educated people."

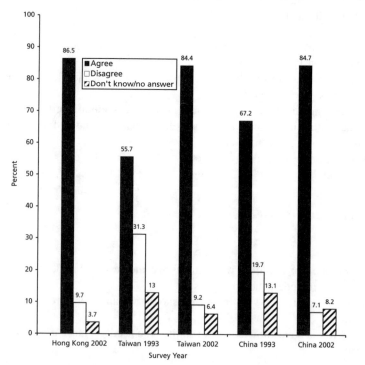

Figure 2.2   Support for Popular Accountability I: "Government leaders are like the head of a family; we should all follow their decisions."

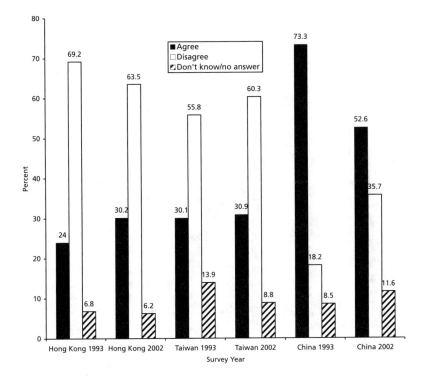

ed by the percentage of respondents who answered "agree" in Figure 2.1 and percentage of respondents who answered "disagree" in Figures 2.2 through 2.6). For most indicators, Hong Kong's overall level of democratic value-orientation is slightly higher than Taiwan's and significantly higher than that of China. This pecking order (descending with level of socioeconomic modernization) is most evident for indicators measuring the concept of popular accountability, political liberalism, and political pluralism despite the fact that Taiwan enjoys a more advanced status in terms of democratic development than Hong Kong. The only notable exception is the fact that the level of popular support for the principle of separation of power in Hong Kong is lower than that of Taiwan.

For both Taiwan and China, there is also a strikingly similar pattern of rising level of democratic value-orientation over time. For instance, on the question "Government leaders are like the head of a family, we should all follow their decisions," 55.8 percent of our Taiwanese respondents answered "dis-

Figure 2.3   Support for Popular Accountability II: "If we have public leaders who are morally upright, we can let them decide everything."

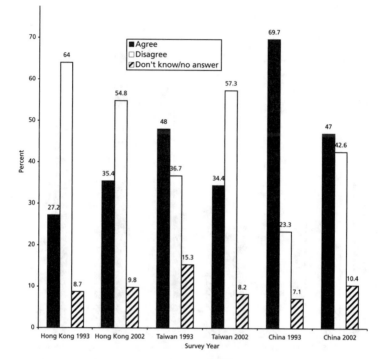

agree" or "strongly disagree" in 1993; that had increased to 60.3 percent in 2002. In China, only 18.2 percent of our respondents expressed disagreement to this statement in 1993, but 35.7 percent of them did in 2002. This pattern holds up for the second item measuring the concept of popular accountability (see Figure 2.3) and the item measuring political liberalism (see Figure 2.5). However, for the paired comparison between Taiwan and China, it is difficult to tell whether this longitudinal pattern should be attributed more to the influence of socioeconomic modernization or of political democratization because during this period both societies had made progress on both scores.

The paired comparisons between Taiwan and Hong Kong help us to clearly identify the socializing effects of participation in democratic process on the growth of democratic value-orientation. The political tempos in the two societies during the nine-year interval of the two surveys were quite different. Taiwan completed its democratic transition during the period, whereas Hong Kong's momentum for democratization suffered a setback. The divergent trajectories of regime evolution between the two societies manifest themselves in an opposite pattern of value changes. In Taiwan, popular belief in political equali-

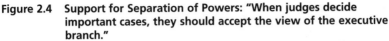

Figure 2.4   Support for Separation of Powers: "When judges decide
important cases, they should accept the view of the executive
branch."

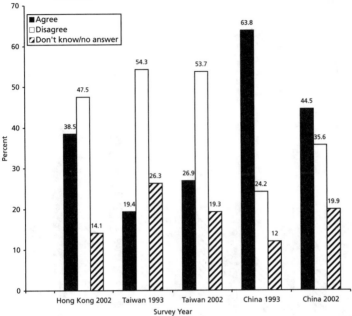

ty, popular accountability, and political liberalism gained strength during this period (see Figures 2.1, 2.2, 2.3, and 2.5). In Hong Kong, during the same period citizens' commitment to the principles of popular accountability and political pluralism lost ground, albeit at a modest pace. This suggests that political institutions can exert significant socializing influence independent of the forces of socioeconomic modernization, which are perhaps more powerful as indicated by Hong Kong's higher average level of democratic value-orientation.

Across the three culturally Chinese societies, we also detect some constraining as well as enabling effects of the traditional values. Most notably, the concept of political pluralism does not bode well with the populace in all three societies (see Figure 2.6). There were still large numbers of citizens in all three societies who worried about the implications of competition and contestation among diverse interest groups for social stability and harmony. Although Hong Kong houses the largest number of respondents who embrace of idea of political pluralism, in both surveys the level of support is still well below the 50 percent threshold. In both Taiwan and China, the number of respondents registering "disagreement" to this question never reached 35 percent. As a matter of

Figure 2.5   Support for Political Liberalism: "Government should decide whether certain ideas should be allowed to be discussed in society."

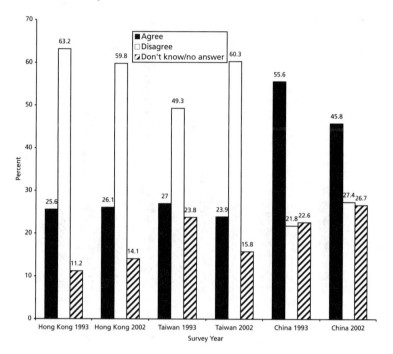

fact, in Taiwan, with the mushrooming of civic organizations and social movements during the 1990s, the level of support for political pluralism actually went down. It is interesting that in our surveys for China we witness a similar pattern of receding support for political pluralism just as many Chinese citizens had their first taste of associational life (see Figure 2.6). The distribution of attitude toward the principle of political equality is a mirror image of political pluralism. In all three societies, the concept of political equality reached an overwhelming consensus. In our 2001–2002 survey, there is virtually no difference among the three societies, with more than 80 percent of the respondents professing a democratic orientation. This suggests that the concept of equality is more compatible with traditional Chinese ethos so that it can be more readily assimilated into the core belief (see Figure 2.1). The concept of separation of power also ran into some resistance in all three localities. Despite a strong tradition of rule of law under the British rule, less than a majority of our Hong Kong respondents embraced the idea of judicial independence in our 2001 survey. It gained slightly stronger support in Taiwan, but there was virtually no change in the level of support between 1993 and 2002 (see Figure 2.4).

Figure 2.6   Support for Political Pluralism: "Stability and harmony of the community will be disrupted if people organize lots of groups."

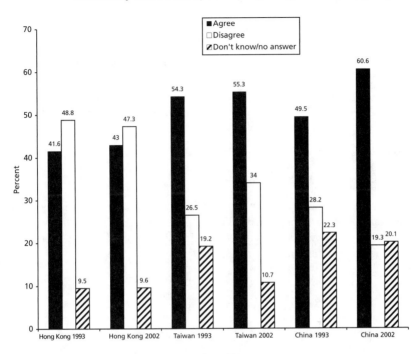

However, the influence of traditional values has by and large steadily receded over time as the process of modernization and democratization presses on. For instance, in our 1993 Taiwan survey, nearly half of our respondents embraced the idea that "if we have public leaders who are morally upright, we can let them decide everything." This traditional deference to virtuous leader has nevertheless waned over time. This concept commanded the allegiance of just a bit more than one-third of respondents in Taiwan around 2002. In China, it dropped from 69.7 to 47 percent between 1993 and 2002 (see Figure 2.3).

Table 2.1 offers a summary of the characteristics of the emerging political culture in Hong Kong, Taiwan, and China. Culturally speaking, Hong Kong provides the most fertile soil for a striving liberal democracy, but that overall advantage has been slightly eclipsed in the recent past. Taiwan came from behind but is catching up in a significant way. By 2002, on most of the indicators of democratic value-orientation, Taiwan was on parity with Hong Kong. The former also enjoys a more favorable trend line than the latter. By 2002, the majority of the citizens in China still embraced authoritarian orien-

Table 2.1   Support for Liberal Democratic Values

	Hong Kong		Taiwan		China	
	1993	2002	1993	2002	1993	2002
Political equality	N/A	very high	high	very high	high	very high
Popular accountability	very high	high	modest	high	very low	low
Horizontal accountability	N/A	modest	modest	modest	very low	low
Political liberalism	high	high	modest	high	very low	very low
Political pluralism	modest	modest	very low	very low	very low	very low

Notes: Support above 65%: very high; 64–55%: high; 54–45% modest; 44–35% low; below 34%: very low.

tation despite the fact that a significant number of citizens have been shedding their attachment to authoritarian values in the recent past. China still has a long way to go before a full-fledged democratic culture emerges, even though its trend line does offer a ray of hope.

Results: Microlevel

The patterns that we have observed at the macrolevel so far provide us with only some clues to the explanatory power of different causal mechanisms. To ascertain the implied causal relationships, we have to analyze our survey data in a more rigorous way. I will undertake this in three steps: First, I will look at the patterns of value changes at the subnational level, beginning with the urban-rural divide. Next, I will examine the impact of the level of education and age cohort respectively on the level of democratic value-orientation at the individual level. Third, I will run a regression analysis to examine the constraining effect of traditional Confucian values on the growth of democratic value-orientation in a multivariate framework.

In Table 2.2, the China sample is disaggregated into two subsamples, one representing the urban adult population and the other the rural adult population. For each of the six indicators, an F-test is conducted to ascertain if there is a statistically significant difference in the average level of support for democratic value between the urban and rural population. As this exercise is confined to a single country, the cultural attributes and regime characteristics at the system-level are in a crude sense held constant. The observed differences between the rural and urban population and over time can be more conclusively attributed to the influence of socioeconomic modernization. The patterns of value changes that emerge out of Table 2.2 are highly consistent with the patterns we identified earlier through trilateral comparison. Over the measures of

Table 2.2   Distribution of Democratic Value Orientations in China

Question		1993 Survey		2002 Survey	
		Rural	Urban	Rural	Urban
Political Equality					
1. People with little or no education	Mean	0.714	0.279	0.910	0.669
should have as much say in	Std.	0.776	0.989	0.970	0.643
politics as highly educated people.	F-test	83.247***		3.000*	
Popular Accountability					
2. Government leaders are like the	Mean	−0.779	−0.396	−0.448	−0.021
head of a family; we should all	Std.	0.741	0.990	0.968	1.058
follow their decisions.	F-test	71.454***		62.738***	
3. If we have public leaders who are	Mean	−0.684	−0.322	−0.327	0.140
morally upright, we can let them	Std.	0.828	1.028	1.000	1.038
decide everything.	F-test	55.391***		73.318***	
Separation of Power (Horizontal Accountability)					
4. When judges decide important	Mean	−0.631	−0.063	−0.473	0.141
cases, they should accept the view	Std.	0.851	1.071	0.971	1.067
of the executive branch.	F-test	118.753***		110.273***	
Political Liberalism					
5. The government should decide	Mean	−0.680	−0.198	−0.514	−0.097
whether certain ideas should be	Std.	0.807	1.038	0.893	1.031
allowed to be discussed in society.	F-test	84.372***		51.463***	
Political Pluralism					
6. Stability and harmony of the	Mean	−0.344	−0.282	−0.504	−0.594
community will be disrupted if	Std.	1.015	1.026	0.950	0.904
people organize lots of groups.	F-test	1.051		5.773**	

Notes: ***< .001; **< .01; *< .05.

popular accountability, separation of power, and political liberalism, residents in Chinese cities consistently exhibit a lower degree of authoritarian value-orientation than the people living in the countryside. Also, for both the urban and rural populations, the level of support for authoritarian values significantly declined between 1993 and 2002. These findings are consistent with Tang Wenfang's analysis that shows that China's authoritarian political system proved to be less effective than traditional culture, marketization, and industrialization in shaping public opinion and mass political behavior. Liberal ideas and bottom-up political participation can emerge even in the absence of direct elections.[34]

However, there are two notable exceptions. First, it is the rural people that more readily embrace the idea that "people with little or no education should have as much say in politics as highly educated people." This suggests that the people living in the Chinese countryside, who are typically less well educated than urban residents, are very conscious of their rights of political participation. This may have something to do with rural China's stronger socialist legacy as well as its longer experiences with grassroots democracy. This pattern is confirmed by both our 1993 and 2002 surveys. Our data also show that the concept of political equality continues to gain wider acceptance over time among both the rural and urban population. Next, there remains widespread aversion to political pluralism, and there is no difference between the people of the rural area and those living in the cities. Also, this popular aversion to pluralism has gone up rather than come down in the recent past. This resembles the pattern emerging out of the trilateral comparison.

Next (see Table 2.3), we disaggregate the 2002 China sample into three age cohorts, people who were born in or before 1949 (or above 55 years old by the time of the 2002 survey), between 1949 and 1968 (i.e., aged between 54 and 35), and after 1968 (i.e., 34 years old or younger).[35] For each of the six indicators an F-test is conducted to ascertain if there is a statistically significant difference in the average level of support for democratic value among the three age cohorts. The patterns of value changes that emerge out of this cross-generational analysis are again highly consistent with the patterns we identified earlier through trilateral comparison. The three age cohorts vary significantly over the various measures of popular accountability and political liberalism, and to some extent separation of power as well. More important, there is an easily identifiable linear pattern across these various measures: the younger the generation, the lower the support for authoritarian value-orientation.

Much like what we found earlier, this linear pattern does not hold up for the question on political equality, nor on that for political pluralism. However, the two deviate from the general pattern in the opposite way. People from all three age cohorts embrace the idea of political equality overwhelmingly, whereas they all harbor reservation toward political pluralism, albeit to a varying degree. Most important, it is among the youngest generation (aged between 20 and 34) that we found that the average scores on virtually all the measures (except for political pluralism) had moved into the positive territory, that is, more people were embracing democratic value-orientation than were attaching themselves to authoritarian values. By these measures, the contrast between this generation and the two older generations is truly stark. This suggests that in the midst of China's rapid socioeconomic transition, a culture shift has indeed taken place within two generations.

To dig more deeply into the causal mechanisms that could account for this significant transformation, we first examine the bivariate association between level of education and democratic value-orientation. We apply correlation analyses to all six indicators (plus their sum score) for both waves of

Table 2.3   **Generation and Democratic Value-Orientations: An Analysis of Variance of China, 2002**

Question		Born Before 1949	Born Between 1949 and 1968	Born After 1968
Political Equality				
1. People with little or no education	Mean	1.011	0.927	0.912
should have as much say in politics	Std.	0.607	0.673	0.660
as highly educated people.	F-test		5.223*	
Popular Accountability				
2. Government leaders are like the	Mean	−0.366	−0.231	0.017
head of a family; we should all	Std.	0.990	1.030	1.081
follow their decisions.	F-test		25.296**	
3. If we have public leaders who are	Mean	−0.234	−0.102	0.203
morally upright, we can let them	Std.	1.029	1.038	1.038
decide everything.	F-test		34.494***	
Separation of Power (Horizontal Accountability)				
4. When judges decide important	Mean	−0.151	−0.150	0.011
cases, they should accept the view	Std.	1.068	1.073	1.067
of the executive branch.	F-test		5.455 *	
Political Liberalism				
5. The government should decide	Mean	−0.489	−0.308	0.044
whether certain ideas should be	Std.	0.894	0.989	1.042
allowed to be discussed in society.	F-test		45.273***	
Political Pluralism				
6. Stability and harmony of the	Mean	−0.605	−0.494	−0.637
community will be disrupted if	Std.	0.917	0.949	0.873
people organize lots of groups.	F-test		6.274 *	

Notes: ***< .001; **< .01; *< .05.

the China survey. We then compare the statistical results with that of the two concurrent Taiwan surveys to ascertain whether there is one common mechanism of value changes between the two and over time despite the huge difference in their trajectories of regime evolution. The results (displayed in Table 2.4) are truly impressive. For most indicators (again with the exception of measures for political equality and political pluralism), we found very significant positive correlation between level of education and attachment to democratic value-orientation. Both the strength and direction of this association are very similar over time and between the two societies. This provides very convincing evidence for confirming the potent transformative power of an improved educational standard, arguably a good surrogate measure of the degree of exposure to forces of modernization at the individual level, in fos-

Table 2.4   Education and Democratic Value Orientations: Correlation Analysis of China and Taiwan

		China		Taiwan	
Question		1993	2002	1993	2002
Political Equality					
1. People with little or no education should have as much say in politics as highly educated people.	Correlation	–0.295	0.004	0.308	–0.016
	Sig.	0.000	0.833	0.000	0.573
	N	2849	2918	1204	1237
Popular Accountability					
2. Government leaders are like the head of a family; we should all follow their decisions.	Correlation	0.279	0.309	0.339	0.163
	Sig.	0.000	0.000	0.000	0.000
	N	2995	2807	1194	1213
3. If we have public leaders who are morally upright, we can let them decide everything.	Correlation	0.297	0.335	0.230	0.227
	Sig.	0.000	0.000	0.000	0.000
	N	3045	2851	1178	1225
Separation of Power (Horizontal Accountability)					
4. When judges decide important cases, they should accept the view of the executive branch.	Correlation	0.352	0.347	0.162	0.110
	Sig.	0.000	0.000	0.000	0.000
	N	2864	2551	1021	1121
Political Liberalism					
5. The government should decide whether certain ideas should be allowed to be discussed in society.	Correlation	0.319	0.331	0.344	0.215
	Sig.	0.000	0.000	0.000	0.000
	N	2518	2331	1058	1155
Political Pluralism					
6. Stability and harmony of the community will be disrupted if people organize lots of groups.	Correlation	0.043	–0.046	0.245	0.153
	Sig.	0.029	0.020	0.000	0.000
	N	2516	2541	1148	1198
Cumulative Index (Sum of Items 1–6)	Correlation	0.359	0.398	0.351	0.250
	Sig.	0.000	0.000	0.000	0.000
	N	2069	1878	855	1012

tering the growth of a democratic political culture. Its transformative power works in all Confucian cultural contexts and works under both authoritarian and democratic regime.

Last, we apply a regression analysis to our second-wave China survey. The dependent variable is the cumulative index of democratic value-orientation (i.e., the sum score of the six indicators). On the right-hand side of the equation, we include the following ten independent variables: (1) age; (2) gender (female as the default value); (3) education; (4) subjective social status;[36] (5) interpersonal trust;[37] (6) traditional family values; (7) traditional interpersonal ethics; (8) traditional work-related ethics; (9) perceived improvement in political rights since 1979;[38] (10) rural or urban household registration (rural as the default value).

The results of the regression analysis are reported in Table 2.5.[39] There are several important findings: First, the model provides a reasonably good fit to the data as indicated by an impressive adjusted R-square. Second, there is strong evidence that certain traditional values and democratic values are incongruous belief systems. All three composite measures of traditional personal ethics exhibit a significant negative impact on the level of democratic value-orientation. Their inhibiting effects are stronger than the positive impact of education, age, or urbanization. Third, among the six sociological variables, only education, urbanization, and gender (i.e., male) exert significant positive influences on level of democratic value-orientation. Age ceases to be a source of explanation once the effects of education, gender, and urbanization are taken into account. Among the three relevant sociological variables, education exerts by far the strongest positive influence on the strengthening of democratic orientation. Last, the people who perceived improvement in the areas of citizen rights and freedom since 1979 are more likely to embrace authoritarian value-orientation. We suspect that the causal relationship actually works in reverse. People with stronger attachment to democratic values tend to be more dissatisfied with the pace of changes in the areas of citizen rights and freedom during the reform era. This implies that a further strengthening of popular belief in democratic values will either weaken the legitimacy of the current

Table 2.5   Explaining Democratic Value-Orientations in China (2002 China Survey)

Explanatory Variables	Beta	Standard Error
Age	−0.03	(0.00)
Gender (female = 0) male 0.05		(0.09)*
Level of education	0.15	(0.01)***
Subjective social status	−0.01	(0.05)
Interpersonal trust	−0.00	(0.05)
Traditional family values	−0.14	(0.02)***
Traditional interpersonal ethics	−0.28	(0.02)***
Traditional work-related ethics	−0.13	(0.03)***
Perceived improvement in political rights since 1979	−0.10	(0.02)***
Household registration (rural = 0) urban	0.06	(0.10)**
R-square		0.314
Adj. R-square		0.308
N		1,115

Notes: ***< .001; **< .01; *< .05.

regime (as its admissible scope of political liberalization is not fast enough) or precipitate stronger popular demand for democratic reform.

Conclusion

The three perspectives—institutionalism, modernization theory, and culturalist theory—are all indispensable in formulating a full explanatory account of the steady growth of democratic orientation in the three Chinese societies.

Our empirical findings lend strong support to modernization theory. Rapid socioeconomic changes brought about by economic reform have had a significant positive influence on the growth of democratic orientation among citizens across Hong Kong, Taiwan, rural China, and urban China. I demonstrate the power of modernization theory at both the macro- and the microlevel. Its significant contextual effect on the acquisition of democratic orientation was demonstrated through a comparison of trilateral longitudinal survey data. At the individual level, our analysis confirms the potent transformative power of an improved educational standard—arguably a good surrogate measure of the degree of exposure to forces of modernization at the individual level—in fostering the growth of a democratic political culture. Its transformative power works in all Confucian cultural contexts and under both authoritarian and democratic regimes.

The paired comparison between Taiwan and Hong Kong helps us clearly identify the socializing effects of participating in the democratic process on the growth of democratic value-orientation. Our regression analysis also provides supporting evidence for the culturalist perspective. It shows that in Confucian societies traditional values do stand in the way of acquiring a democratic value-orientation. However, there is little ground to be pessimistic about the future of democracy in China because further socioeconomic modernization will weaken traditional values. It is most encouraging that we found that in the midst of China's rapid socioeconomic transition, a culture shift has indeed taken place within two generations. A democratic culture is emerging among China's youngest generation, the generation that has received the best education ever and grown up virtually exclusively in the reform era. In a nutshell, our analysis offers a ray of hope for the prospect of China's further political liberalization and eventual democratization as the momentum of socioeconomic modernization continues to be strong.

Notes

1. Chu 2006.
2. This trilateral comparative survey project was codirected by Hu Fu, Andrew Nathan, Hsin-chi Kuan, Tianjian Shi, and Chu Yun-han. It was financed by the National

Science Foundation of the United States, the National Science Council of the Republic of China, the University Research Grant Council of Hong Kong, the Henry Luce Foundation, and other funding agencies and implemented under the auspices of the Political Participation and Political Culture in China, Taiwan, and Hong Kong Project. After 2000, it became a subproject of a larger region-wide survey known as East Asia Barometer (and later on Asian Barometer after enlargement), which is supported by the Ministry of Education of Taiwan, the Academia Sinica, National Taiwan University, and other national funding agencies. For more details about the project, please visit www.asianbarometer.org.

3. Inglehart 1997, 7.

4. Bratton and Mattes 2001.

5. Inkeles and Smith 1974; Pye 1985.

6. Diamond 1999.

7. Inglehart 1997, 10–25.

8. Ibid.; Inglehart and Welzel 2005.

9. Bratton and Mattes 2001; Muller and Seligson 1994; Norris 1999; Steinmo, Thelen, and Longstreth 1992.

10. Finkel, Sabatini, and Bevis 2000.

11. Brady, Verba, and Schlozman 1995; Hall and Taylor 1996; Putnam 1993; Shin 1999.

12. Steinmo, Thelen, and Longstreth 1992.

13. Eckstein 1988, 793–795.

14. Pye 2001, 381.

15. Pye 1985, 325.

16. Huntington 1996, 108.

17. Mote 1989, 41.

18. Hsu 2005, 102.

19. Emmerson 1995; Hu 1997; Hua 2001; Huntington 1991; Zakaria 2003.

20. Barr 2000.

21. Zakaria 2003.

22. Bell 2000; Tamney and Chiang 2002; Tremewan 1993; Tu, Hejtmanek, and Wachman 1992.

23. Shi 2000, 2001; Park and Shin 2006; Chang, Chu, and Tsai 2005.

24. Huntington 1996; Pye 1985.

25. Almond 1990.

26. Hu 1998; Chu and Hu 1996.

27. Hu 1998; Chu and Hu 1996.

28. For the first-wave trilateral survey, in all three localities territory-wide stratified samples based on the probability proportional to size (PPS) criterion were drawn. Each sample represents all adult population above voting age in a given territory. Our Hong Kong survey yields 892 valid cases, the Taiwan survey 1,402 cases, and the mainland survey 3,296 cases. All three samples are sufficiently large, relative to their respective degree of demographic heterogeneity.

29. For the second-wave trilateral survey, the same stratified sampling strategy was applied. Our Hong Kong survey yields 811 valid cases, the Taiwan survey 1,415 cases, and the mainland survey 3,183 cases.

30. Items 1 and 4 were not asked in the 1993–1994 Hong Kong survey, however.

31. The wording of this item for the 1993–1994 survey is slightly different.

32. Bauer and Bell, eds. 1999.

33. Tu classifies Confucian values into two categories: political Confucianism and Confucian personal ethics; see Tu 1996.

34. Tang 2005.

35. The Chinese people born after 1968 were little affected by the Cultural Revolution, are the best-educated generation that China has ever known, and grew up almost exclusively under the reform since their adolescent years.

36. The wording of the question for measuring subjective social status is as follows: "People sometimes think of the social status of their families in terms of upper class, middle class, or lower class. Where would you place your family on the scale? Upper class, upper-middle class, middle class, lower-middle class, or lower class." It yields a five-point scale ranging from 5 to 1.

37. The question measuring interpersonal trust is worded as follows: "Generally speaking, would you say that 'Most people can be trusted' or 'You can't be too careful in dealing with them'?"

38. The index of "perceived improvement in political rights since 1979" is the sum score of the five questions asking the respondents to evaluate the changes between the present and the era before 1979 (the beginning of the reform) in the five areas: (1) freedom to express one's view; (2) government treats everyone equally; (3) people like me can have a say in government policy; (4) judges and courts are free from political interference; (5) join any organization you like. The five questions are preceded by the following lead statement: "We would like you now to compare the present system of government with the one our country had before the Reform. In each of the following areas, would you say that today things are much better than before, somewhat better, much the same, somewhat worse, or much worse?" Each question yields a five-point scale, ranging from –2 to +2.

39. We adopted listwise deletion of cases with missing values. As a result we had to throw out almost two-thirds of the cases. So this scaled-down sample is no longer a true representative sample of the population. People with better political knowledge and higher education are overrepresented in this scaled-down sample.

3

Intellectual Pluralism
and Dissent

Merle Goldman and Ashley Esarey

During the mid-twentieth century, the regimes in Taiwan and China were governed by nondemocratic leaders supported by hegemonic Leninist political parties. In the last two decades of the twentieth century and the early years of the twenty-first century, new forms of intellectual and political expression emerged in both places. Even though China is still governed by a Leninist party, its move to the market and opening to the outside world in the post–Mao Zedong era has been accompanied by the growth of rights consciousness, the development of ideological pluralism, and the periodic expression of dissent. Nevertheless, it remains a regime where dissent is a dangerous enterprise and political activism is repressed. At the same time, Taiwan has established and consolidated a democratic system of government, in part owing to the efforts of intellectuals who pressured the regime from inside and outside the political establishment, propelling and guiding the process of political liberalization. How did two regimes with such strikingly similar governments and political cultures take such radically different paths? What are the prospects for state-society relations in China to resemble those of Taiwan at some time in the future? Our chapter addresses these questions by comparing the role of intellectuals and the effect of dissent during an era of economic transformation.

In China in the 1980s, two groups of scholars, writers, and journalists led the way by expressing dissident views and engaging in public ideological debates contributing to intellectual pluralism.[1] One group—to use the term coined by Carol Hamrin and Timothy Cheek[2]—was the "establishment intellectuals," who staffed the party's research institutes, national media, official commissions, universities, and professional organizations. Establishment intellectuals were associated with the reformist party leaders, particularly Hu Yaobang, general secretary from 1980 to 1987, and his successor Zhao Ziyang from 1987 to 1989.[3] They sometimes expressed views that diverged from those of the leadership, but they generally expanded on the reformist views of their official patrons. In the 1990s, a small number of establishment intellectuals broke away or became disentangled from party patronage and began to express a broad range of ideological views that not only diverged from the party's Marxist-Leninist ideology but at times openly criticized party policies. They were dismissed with the purge of their patrons, Hu Yaobang in January 1987 and Zhao Ziyang on June 4, 1989. Both men had promoted reforms that the party elders, including Deng Xiaoping, believed went too far in undermining the party's rule and their power. Establishment intellectuals in China were most influential when their patrons were politically powerful and supportive of their causes.

The other group, which articulated and sought to assert their political rights, can be called the "disestablished intellectuals." They were expelled from the establishment for their nonsanctioned political views or activities, as Red Guards in the Cultural Revolution and the Democracy Wall movement of the late 1970s and as leaders of the 1989 demonstrations calling for political reforms. Along with a small number of establishment intellectuals, they not only challenged party policies but even called for a new political system.[4] At times, they joined with other classes, such as workers, farmers, and small entrepreneurs (*getihu*), in political movements. However, state control over the media and the regime's harsh crackdown on any independent political activity or organization made it difficult for disestablished intellectuals in China to win widespread support for political reform.

In Taiwan in the 1950s and 1960s, the most prominent establishment intellectuals were recent arrivals from mainland China who were members of the ruling KMT party, had ties to state leaders, and served as advocates of political liberalization or Western-style democracy. Their views were opposed by President Chiang Kai-shek. They entered the ranks of the disestablished, depending on Chiang's willingness to accommodate their challenges to his government. In the late 1970s, a new group of Taiwan-born intellectuals advocated liberalization by publishing in magazines and speaking at rallies in defiance of restrictions on large public gatherings. Eventually, many of these intellectuals were imprisoned. When they were released, they again sought to be politically active but were harassed by agents of the state or had their political rights revoked. Disestablished intellectuals gained influence after the cessation of martial law in 1987, which provided the mass media with more freedom to report on their prodemocracy views and afforded opportunities for intellectuals to speak to large gatherings of enthusiastic supporters. Beginning in the 1990s, the Lee Teng-hui administration pardoned many disestablished intellectuals who then began to participate in mainstream political debates over democratization.

A significant difference between China and Taiwan that shaped their developmental trajectories was that of regime type. The work of Juan J. Linz, who coined the term *authoritarian regime*, and his coauthor Alfred Stepan has encouraged social scientists to make a distinction between authoritarian regimes and other types of nondemocratic government.[5] In the Linz and Stepan typology, Taiwan under the KMT corresponded well to the authoritarian regime type, with its limited political pluralism, legally protected civil society, and less comprehensive political ideology. En route to democratic consolidation marked by the first direct, multiparty election for president in 1996, Taiwan's regime experienced "soft" authoritarian status from 1980 to 1988 and "hybrid" status from 1989 to 1995,[6] demonstrating the characteristics of what Larry Diamond and others have called "hegemonic electoral authoritarian" and "competitive authoritarian" regime types.[7]

Autonomous civil society has existed in Taiwan since Japanese rule in the 1920s, providing support for reform initiatives, such as the Movement for the Establishment of a Taiwanese Parliament, sponsorship of opposition journals, and funding scholarships for Taiwanese students to seek higher education overseas.[8] Under KMT rule the state apparatus dominated the state-society relationship. Yet civil society organizations, such as the pro–Taiwan independence Presbyterian Church, were allowed to survive, and private businesses had considerable autonomy and enjoyed legal protection.[9] Personal wealth in the hands of key reformers has financed support for democracy advocates in Taiwan since the 1920s. Though Leninist, the KMT was not Marxist and, therefore, did not claim a monopoly over "truth" or seek to impose nomenklatura appointments to all important positions within government and society. As Thomas B. Gold has pointed out, the KMT did not see itself as representing the interests of any particular social class; it promoted the goal of constitutional democracy, after various stages of tutelage.[10]

By comparison, the People's Republic under Mao Zedong (1949–1976) more closely resembled what Linz and Stepan have defined as a totalitarian regime, with an elaborate Marxist-Leninist ideology, a planned economy, and charismatic leadership seeking complete control over everyday life. In the People's Republic's first decade, the CCP won hegemony in the arena of civil society in the Gramscian sense;[11] all legal social and civil organizations were required to register with the state under the Organization Law mandating supervision by a party or governmental unit.[12] Preexisting civil society in China was completely destroyed or subjugated to state-appointed leadership. Even though pluralism emerged in China briefly during the Hundred Flowers Campaign from 1956 to June 1957, it was mandated by Mao in an effort to reinvigorate the party. In the post-Mao era, intellectual pluralism accompanied China's move to a market economy, opening to the outside world, and loosening of controls over nonpolitical spheres of life. Consequently, when a movement calling for political reforms, among other things, occurred in Tiananmen Square in 1989, it spread to virtually every large Chinese city. Yet, each wave of pluralism was muffled by party rectification campaigns and dissent silenced by widespread and often public forms of repression.[13] Thus, like the former Soviet Union before glasnost, China under Mao and in the post-Mao era is noteworthy for the absence of long-standing social and political organizations independent of the state, with the potential to serve as rallying points for political opposition and shelters for independent thought.

In the post-Mao era, China has come to resemble what Linz and Stepan have defined as a posttotalitarian regime. The Chinese regime's official ideology has been imposed with less intensity, and the regime has put less reliance on mass campaigns than under Mao. The post-Mao leadership of Deng Xiaoping, Jiang Zemin, and Hu Jintao has been less charismatic and more technocratic and pragmatic. In posttotalitarian China, citizens have more personal, intellectual, and artistic freedom. Yet, there are also significant differences from authoritarian Taiwan from 1945 to 1996. The CCP does not permit autonomous and legally protected organizations, such as political parties, religious organizations, or citizen's groups. Although nongovernmental organizations (NGOs) have been established in the post-Mao period, social and so-called nongovernmental organizations still must be registered with the state under an official sponsor. The ruling CCP fears freedom of association more than freedom of expression by individuals. Therefore, China's posttotalitarian regime not only suppresses independent political organizations, it also bars social, religious, and environmental organizations from involvement in independent political activities. The difference in regime types in Taiwan and China means that the former had powerful social organizations capable of pressuring the ruling party for democratic reform.[14]

In both Taiwan and China, dissidents and intellectuals have sought political reforms *within* existing political institutions. Whether reformers called for democracy, rule of law, freedom of speech and association, or religious freedom, they have done so in a manner that did not seek to topple the existing state structure. In addition, appeals for reform by intellectuals have benefited from popular support, in part due to attempts to portray political change as for "the good of the nation."[15]

At the same time, in both countries, political dissent has encountered varying degrees of repression, applied in a multiplicity of ways, ranging from imprisonment of dissidents to removal of individuals from government posts, restrictions on publication, interference with private business interests, and various forms of harassment. Often merely the threat of repression proved a considerable deterrent to the expression of most forms of political opposition. At the same time, the regimes sought co-optation of elites by providing incentives for compliance with policy or ideology. Nevertheless, even though in the later decades of the twentieth century Taiwan tolerated political dissent, China repressed it and usually ostracized or imprisoned the dissenters.

In terms of government structure, Taiwan and China once had similar

Leninist party-states run according to the principle of democratic centralism, which concentrated power in the top leader and gave the party control over the government and military. The regimes also enforced bans on political activity outside the party, established controls over the media and civil society, and advocated transformational goals through economic policy, mass mobilization, and use of propaganda.[16] Since the 1980s, the KMT and the CCP have both coped with the advent of rapid and increasingly global information flows, travel abroad, and use of cell phones and the Internet that have also spread knowledge and skills necessary for democratic governance.

Although Taiwan and China are post-Confucian societies, where the majority of the population is Han Chinese, the two populations differ in terms of their size and education level. Taiwan is much smaller and enjoys higher rates of education and literacy. In addition, Taiwan after the 1970s had a sizable middle class. By comparison, a middle class was just emerging in China in the early years of the twenty-first century and has yet to perceive its interests as independent of those of the regime, in part due to attempts by the CCP to co-opt entrepreneurs into the party and limit their influence in the political sphere.

The actions of political leaders during crucial historical periods profoundly shaped the emergence of pluralism and opportunities for dissent.[17] Unlike Taiwan's top leaders, who in the 1980s were willing to accommodate rather than repress political dissent and autonomous political groups, China's Communist leaders have repressed political dissent and cracked down harshly on any effort to establish an independent political group. In 1998, they suppressed the one effort to establish an alternative political party, the China Democracy Party, and imprisoned its leaders. Although they have allowed a degree of ideological pluralism ranging from Confucianism to the New Left, China's leaders have not permitted political pluralism.

By comparison, Taiwan's leaders, Chiang Ching-kuo from 1986 to 1987 and Lee Teng-hui in 1990, tolerated and even encouraged the emergence of democratic opposition. Chiang Ching-kuo's tolerance of the September 1986 founding of the Democratic Progressive Party (DPP) made possible the emergence of a multiparty political system. His decision to end martial law in July 1987 led to a formal lifting of the ban on political parties, and after January 1, 1988, opposition politicians were permitted to found new and independent media organizations.[18]

In April 1990, Lee Teng-hui heeded student demonstrators demanding a schedule for democratic liberalization and sweeping constitutional reforms, such as retirement of mainlander parliamentarians who had lifetime terms of office. Several of the students' demands were later incorporated into the agenda of the National Affairs Conference at which the KMT and the opposition DPP agreed that all seats in the National Assembly and Legislative Yuan should be opened to competitive elections and that the president, governor of

Taiwan Province, and mayors of the major cities of Taipei and Kaohsiung should be popularly elected. Lee also granted political amnesties to a number of opposition leaders, making them eligible to participate in elections held for local and national offices.[19] In 1996, Lee participated in and won Taiwan's first-ever direct election for president. By contrast, as of the first decade of the twenty-first century, in China there are elections only for village heads and village councils. With a few exceptions, elections have not yet reached the township level.

Intellectual Pluralism and Dissent in Taiwan

Following the KMT's defeat by the Communists in the Chinese civil war in 1949, Chiang Kai-shek's armies fled to Taiwan with the tattered remnants of the KMT Leninist party-state. Despite the fact that most islanders, especially the elite, spoke Japanese and identified themselves as Taiwanese, the KMT's official view was that all Taiwanese were liberated "Chinese," who were expected to lend unstinting support to Chiang's goal of "retaking the mainland." In the early 1950s, advocates for liberalization emerged from the ranks of mainland establishment intellectuals whose motivation for democratization differed considerably from that of the Taiwanese, who linked democratization to ethnic empowerment. Mainlanders such as Lei Chen, who founded the magazine *Free China* (*Ziyou Zhongguo*), were profoundly anti-Communist and sought to "take back the mainland" by creating an exemplary multiparty constitutional democracy in Taiwan—a system of government that would eventually be extended to all of China.

In the late 1940s, Lei Chen enjoyed a positive relationship with Chiang Kai-shek, and by virtue of his position as a national policy adviser, was solidly an establishment intellectual, albeit one in favor of reforming the KMT. The famous Chinese intellectual, Hu Shih, who was a contributor to *Free China,* also believed improving democracy and freedom of speech would prove useful for the purposes of retaking the mainland.[20] These two intellectuals differed over the role of Chiang Kai-shek's leadership. Hu Shih believed the goal of retaking the mainland and establishing a constitutional democracy required Chiang's leadership. Lei Chen and like-minded intellectuals in the KMT's "liberalization faction" (*ziyoupai*) believed in the merits of limiting Chiang's power. By the mid-1950s, Lei Chen's advocacy of democratizing the KMT leadership structure led to intense resistance from Chiang and conservatives in the party; as a result, Lei Chen was stripped of his party membership after three decades as a member. He then began to advocate the formation of an opposition party, the China Democratic Party (*Zhongguo minzhudang*) and to discuss collaboration with a small group of Taiwanese candidates who had formed a non-KMT alliance to contest local elections. Lei assumed that working through existing electoral institutions was the best way to influence politics, rather than by attempting radical reform at the national level. However, the Taiwan Garrison Command arrested Lei Chen on suspicion of spreading Communist propaganda and harboring a Communist, which led to the unraveling of Lei's coalition-building attempts and to the closure of *Free China.* Lei spent the next decade in prison.[21]

The Lei Chen Incident signaled to reformers inside and outside the political establishment that challenging Chiang Kai-shek's leadership was a risky endeavor. In the 1960s, independents defeated KMT candidates in mayoral elections in Tainan, Keelung, and Taipei; opposition politicians criticized the KMT from elected positions in the Provincial Assembly.[22] However, there were no efforts by incumbent politicians to organize an opposition political party, advocate democratization, or challenge Chiang's claims to be the legitimate government of Taiwan and mainland China.

In 1964, the first establishment intellectual to call for democratization and Taiwan independence was Taiwan University political scientist Peng Ming-min. The son of a wealthy doctor in southern Taiwan, Peng Ming-min was one of a few Taiwanese to study law and political science in Japan prior to 1945. In the late 1940s, his career as an establishment intellectual in postwar Taiwan was supported by KMT reformer Hu Shih, who lobbied for Peng to receive a state chair of the National Committee for Scientific Development, an honor shared by only 12 Taiwan scholars.[23] However, Peng grew profoundly disillusioned with Chiang Kai-shek's claims to represent all of China from his base in Taipei. With Hsieh Tung-min and Wei Ting-chao, Peng wrote a "Declaration for Taiwan Self-Salvation" (*Taiwan zijiu yundong xuanyan*) that urged overthrowing Chiang's government, drafting a new constitution guaranteeing basic human rights, establishing Taiwan as an independent democratic country, and joining the United Nations as a new member.[24] Before Peng, Hsieh, and Wei could distribute their declaration, secret police confiscated 10,000 copies of their manuscript and imprisoned the three men. Overnight Peng had become a disestablished intellectual. After his release in 1965, Peng was spirited out of Taiwan by supporters of the Taiwan Independence Movement; once overseas, he became an influential advocate of political reform within Taiwan.

Although the United States did not sever formal ties with Taiwan until early 1979, movement in this direction became clear after the visits of Kissinger and Nixon to Beijing in 1972 that resulted in the Shanghai Communiqué, which acknowledged that both sides of the Taiwan Strait believed that Taiwan was part of China. In the 1970s, changes in Taiwan's international status led to new pressures for democratization. With Chiang Kai-shek's decision to withdraw from the United Nations, Taiwan was barred from participating in key international organizations and lost many of its formal diplomatic allies.[25]

In the late 1970s, a number of native Taiwanese intellectuals, such as future two-term vice president Lu Hsiu-lien, a feminist and legal scholar, argued that democratization and de jure independence would differentiate Taiwan from China in the eyes of the international community and serve as a defense against Chinese claims that Taiwan was a renegade province for which the legitimate government was Beijing. Economic shocks caused by the 1973 oil embargo of the Organization of Petroleum Exporting Countries (OPEC) further decreased support for the KMT regime, at a time when Taiwan imported three-fourths of its oil from OPEC sources. The OPEC embargo highlighted the vulnerability of Taiwan's economy to changes in the global economy.[26] Moreover, all national representative bodies in Taiwan were dominated by representatives elected on the Chinese mainland in the 1940s, a fact that led to grumbling that permanent seats held by mainlanders were not representative of Taiwanese public opinion.

The KMT response to weakening regime legitimacy was to permit political participation by Taiwanese at the national level. Thus, in 1969, 1972, and 1975, supplementary elections were held for a small number of seats vacated by mainlanders in the National Assembly, the Legislative Yuan, and the Control Yuan. Although the majority of new positions were filled by KMT politicians, a small number of independents were elected, such as legislators Huang Hsin-chieh and Kang Ning-hsiang, who opposed KMT policies and favored liberalization of political discourse, media freedom, greater autonomy for social organizations, and multiparty democracy in Taiwan.

Prior to the 1978 elections for the Legislative Yuan and National Assembly, a group of opposition politicians founded the Dangwai (outside the party, or non-KMT) Organization to Promote Elections against KMT candidates. The 1978 election campaign, however, was cut short days before the election, when Chiang Ching-kuo declared a state of emergency, following the announcement by US president Jimmy Carter in December of US plans to abrogate diplomatic ties with Taiwan and establish formal relations with China. On January 18, 1979, President Chiang Ching-kuo announced that elections would be suspended for an indefinite period of time, forcing opposition politicians and reform-minded intellectuals to search for a new political strategy to challenge the KMT.

The Political Legacy of *Formosa Magazine*

In 1979, Dangwai activists established the *Formosa Magazine* (*Meilidao zazhi*), which included on its staff establishment and disestablished intellectuals, including incumbent politicians, political activists, and well-known writers who hoped the magazine could serve as a de facto political party by reaching out to supporters through 12 offices around Taiwan.[27] From the outset,

Formosa Magazine encountered intense opposition from KMT operatives who opposed Dangwai positions on democratization and Taiwanese sovereignty. Its offices around Taiwan were vandalized, and a riot broke out in Taipei during a public relations event to promote the magazine's first edition.[28] Media coverage of the riot proved effective "advertising," and the magazine sold very well. By its third edition, *Formosa Magazine* had a circulation of more than 100,000 copies—second only to the Taiwan TV guide.[29]

Tensions between the magazine and the KMT mounted considerably in December, when two volunteers at the magazine's office in Kaohsiung were apprehended by the police and beaten. On December 10, radicals on the *Formosa* staff, led by Yao Chia-wen and Shih Ming-teh, planned a major demonstration that coincided with International Human Rights Day. After alleged attacks by government provocateurs, demonstrators armed with club-like torches clashed with armored riot police, who launched tear gas on the crowd, resulting in a bloody clash with numerous injuries on both sides.[30]

The Garrison Command, the branch of the military in charge of the secret police, held a press conference on December 11, accusing the *Formosa Magazine* staff of seditious behavior. KMT officials at the Fourth Central Committee Plenum released statements criticizing the demonstration organizers. Other government officials, including all the mayors and county executives in Taiwan, issued a joint statement condemning organizers of the Kaohsiung demonstration as "violent rebels" (*baotu*). Soon, the mainstream press echoed these condemnations.[31] Editorials across the island called for punishing the violent behavior at the Human Rights Day demonstration, which had quickly become known as the Kaohsiung Incident. Two days later, in an islandwide sweep, the magazine's offices were raided and nearly all opposition figures associated with the demonstration were arrested and subjected to lengthy interrogation and, in some cases, torture to elicit confessions of sedition.[32]

Popular support for the jailed Dangwai leaders increased in 1980 when word spread that the mother and twin daughters of the imprisoned provincial assemblyman Lin Yi-hsiung were murdered on February 28, the date associated with an islandwide uprising for self-rule in 1947.[33] The day before the killings Lin's mother had visited him in prison; learning he had been tortured, she attempted to contact a branch office of Amnesty International in Japan. Many people believed the murders were an attempt by the KMT leadership to silence the Dangwai prior to their trial for sedition.

According to historian Denny Roy, most Taiwanese agreed with the official position that the Kaohsiung demonstration had been a threat to public order while sympathizing with the motivations of the rally organizers.[34] Owing to public pressure demanding fair handling of the trial proceedings, the government decided to hold the Formosa trial in a more transparent manner than trials for political offenses in the past.[35] Defendants were allowed a large team of legal representation, family members were permitted to attend court sessions, and journalists were allowed to report openly on trial proceedings. Despite attempts by defendants to overturn confessions signed under the duress, 40 people associated with the Kaohsiung Incident were imprisoned for sentences ranging from three years to life in prison.[36]

In retrospect, the sweeping imprisonment of major opposition figures was not the end of Taiwan's democratization but its beginning. A list of defendants and their defense attorneys reads like a "who's who" of major figures in the Democratic Progressive Party in the 1990s and 2000s. Chen Shui-bian, the defense lawyer for the legislator Huang Hsin-chieh, was elected to two terms as president of Taiwan in 2000 and 2004. Lu Hsiu-lien served as Chen's vice president. Shih Ming-teh, who was sentenced to life in prison, later served as DPP party chairman, as did Huang Hsin-chieh and Lin Yi-hsiung. Defense lawyers Chang Chun-hsiung, Hsieh Chang-ting, and Su Chen-chang served as premiers in the Chen Shui-bian administration. Other defendants, such as Chen Chu, Yao Chia-wen, Chiu Chue-chen, and the writer Yang Ching-chu served in the Legislative Yuan, the National Assembly, and high-level positions in the DPP government. In the 1980s, even the spouses of imprisoned Dangwai leaders were elected to national office owing to the wave of popular indignation and support for democratization and human rights.

President Chiang Ching-kuo responded to popular pressure for democratization by permitting gradual liberalization in the 1980s, tolerating the then illegal establishment of the Democratic Progressive Party in September 1986, and lifting martial law in July 1987, an act that permitted the establishment of freer news media. In addition, Chiang's administration made efforts to increase the participation of native Taiwanese within the KMT, government institutions, and representative bodies. During a meeting with senior officials, Chiang noted: "Times are changing, the environment is changing, the tide is also changing."[37]

Increasing Political Participation in a Multiparty System

At the time of Chiang Ching-kuo's death in January 1988, his successor, President Lee Teng-hui, inherited power without strong support within the party. Following a series of power struggles, however, Lee was gradually able to transform the KMT from an authoritarian political party to a "democratic-type" political party with a strong focus on Taiwan affairs.[38] In the spring of 1990, Lee encouraged democratization in the aftermath of student demonstrations in Taipei calling for elections for all seats in Taiwan's parliamentary bodies and direct elections for all top governmental posts. Following the first-ever elections for all seats in the Legislative Yuan in 1992, the number of mainlanders who held seats in the national legislature was reduced from 60 percent to

22 percent. Moreover, the DPP gained 31 percent of the seats, firmly establishing its position as an alternative voice in parliament.[39]

In the early 1990s, two major factions appeared within the KMT—the mainstream faction headed by Lee and the nonmainstream faction led by mainlanders and their supporters. Dissatisfaction among mainlanders prompted a splinter group of legislators and former high-ranking bureaucrats to form the Chinese New Party in 1993. Drawing support primarily from disgruntled middle-class mainlanders, the New Party promoted itself as a morally responsible alternative to the Kuomintang and DPP and as a strong proponent of reunification with China. Most New Party leaders had enjoyed positions of authority during the Chiang Ching-kuo administration or were mainlander intellectuals. Other young politicians joined the party because it was relatively easy to obtain New Party nomination for public office. According to Tien Hung-mao, by 1994 the KMT was almost completely led by Taiwan-born politicians, with the exception of members of military and veterans associations; 61 percent of all the seats in the KMT's top decisionmaking body, the Central Standing Committee, were held by native Taiwanese.[40]

In 1995 and 1996, efforts by DPP chairmen Shih Ming-teh and Hsu Hsin-liang to collaborate with the KMT and the New Party in the interests of a "grand reconciliation" and a coalition government precipitated the exit of a group of DPP supporters due to disagreements over the sacrifice of ideological positions about national identity for short-term political advantage. On October 6, 1996, several members of the Taiwan Association of University Professors established the Taiwan Independence Party (*Jianguodang*), a party advocating de jure independence and a change of the country's formal name from Republic of China to Republic of Taiwan.[41] Support for the Taiwan Independence Party in national elections was not high; a number of the party's founders, including former party chairman and Academia Sinica member, scientist Lee Chen-yuan, returned to the DPP after Chen Shui-bian's election as president in March 2000 brought an end to five decades of KMT rule.

The loss of the KMT presidential candidate, Vice President Lien Chan, in the election of 2000 was partly due to the fact that the traditional supporters of the KMT divided their votes between Lien Chan and former Taiwan provincial governor James Soong, who had campaigned as an independent and placed second in the election behind Chen Shui-bian. (Lien Chan finished in third place.) Soong's strong showing in the election prompted him to found the People First Party (PFP; *Qinmindang*), a party composed of Soong supporters who favored eventual unification with China and later allied with the KMT in parliament. Days after the founding of the PFP, massive demonstrations by disgruntled KMT supporters forced Lee Teng-hui to resign as party chairman in 2000. Some KMT demonstrators expressed regret that James Soong had not run as the KMT candidate, and others claimed that Lee had secretly supported Chen Shui-bian by choosing a weak successor.[42]

In the summer of 2001, a group of Lee's supporters, many of whom had held positions of importance in the KMT during the period of Lee's chairmanship, founded the Taiwan Solidarity Union (TSU; *Taiwan tuanjie lianmeng*), a party advocating Taiwan independence, the abandonment of the Republic of China as Taiwan's name, abolition of cultural symbols linking Taiwan to China, and the creation of a new constitution. In late 2001, the TSU won a small number of seats in the Legislative Yuan and began to coordinate its policy positions with the Taiwan Independence Party and the DPP in what became known as the "pan-green camp," the color green symbolizing a preference for Taiwan's de jure independence. The KMT and the PFP joined forces in the "pan-blue camp," which was associated with a pro-China orientation and flexibility concerning Taiwan's unification with China. Competition between the pan-green and pan-blue camps increased prior to the 2004 presidential election, which the pan-greens won by a very slim margin, giving President Chen Shui-bian and Vice President Lu Hsiu-lien a second term in office.

In the 1990s, the willingness of Lee Teng-hui to permit electoral competition by the proindependence Democratic Progressive Party and former Dangwai intellectuals associated with *Formosa Magazine* allowed the opposition to win increasing popular support for democratization. In addition, Lee's tolerance was opposed by mainlanders within his party, splitting the party and leading to the establishment of the Chinese New Party. Ultimately, Lee's successor as president was the opposition party politician Chen Shui-bian, whose views on Taiwanese sovereignty more closely resembled Lee's than those of KMT candidate Lien Chan. The price Lee Teng-hui paid for guiding Taiwan's political system toward democratic consolidation in September 2001 was expulsion from the KMT, an outcome that led to numerous defections from the party.

Intellectuals Debate Political Reform

The relaxation of restrictions governing freedom of speech and assembly after the end of martial law in 1987 made it possible to discuss publicly virtually all political and ideological topics. Furthermore, new opportunities became available in the 1990s for disestablished intellectuals to participate in politics, and occasionally antiestablishment intellectuals were welcomed into the political establishment. For example, long-time advocate of Taiwan independence, former Taiwan University political scientist Peng Ming-min, ran as the DPP candidate for president in the spring of 1996, eventually losing to Lee Teng-hui. Following Lee's victory, he invited former Dangwai leaders Huang Hsin-chieh and Lu Hsiu-lien to serve as presidential advisers.

In the 1990s, intellectuals vigorously debated Taiwan's national identity, specifically the question of whether Taiwan Chinese or Taiwanese had a sense of nationhood. According to historian Hsiau A-chin, in the first half of the

1990s the rise in the number of people identifying themselves as Taiwanese grew while those who saw themselves as Chinese decreased sharply, prompting the DPP to expand its conception of Taiwanese identity to include all major ethnic groups: native-born Hoklo, Hakka, and aborigines as well as mainlanders and their progeny.[43] A similar rendering of Taiwan national identity appeared in a briefly used public school textbook approved by the Ministry of Education, *Get to Know Taiwan* (*Renshi Taiwan*). An inclusive Taiwanese national identity entered mainstream political discourse by the late 1990s.

Other debates preceded major reforms of Taiwan's political system. In 1996, academics and politicians debated the merits of abolishing or reducing the scope of the Provincial Assembly and provincial government, owing to the high cost of having an additional tier of government in such a small country. They had sought symbolically to indicate that Taiwan was "more than a province" prior to Hong Kong's retrocession to Chinese rule as a Special Administrative Region on July 1, 1997. A related debate concerned the elected post of provincial governor, which represented a constituency that largely overlapped with that of the president. Eventually, the provincial government was vastly scaled back, and elected offices at the provincial level were eliminated. To compensate the Provincial Assembly members who lost their posts, the size of the Legislative Yuan was increased from 157 to 225 seats.

KMT and DPP politicians and scholars also debated the transfer of powers over constitutional amendments and presidential impeachment from the National Assembly to the Legislative Yuan as well as the merits of swapping Taiwan's semipresidential system of government for a parliamentary system. As of 2000, the KMT and the DPP agreed to a plan to phase out the National Assembly, a body that formerly had served to elect the president and amend the constitution. The National Assembly was dissolved in 2005.

In the 1990s, some politicians found connections with organized crime syndicates to be useful for mobilizing voters, and gangsters found political connections useful as a source of protection from law enforcement agencies. Intellectuals by the mid-1990s expressed concern that elected bodies at all levels in Taiwan had become penetrated by politicians with ties to organized crime. Ma Ying-jeou was one of a succession of ministers of justice who enforced criminal penalties for vote buying. The practice eventually became the exception, rather than standard practice, for politicians seeking office.

On November 16, 1996, Minister of Justice Liao Cheng-hao announced that one-third of city and county councillors and 5 percent of national legislators had *heidao* or gangster backgrounds. Three years later, Taiwan's most famous intellectual, the president of Academia Sinica Lee Yuan-tseh, estimated that half of the elected officials had gangster backgrounds.[44] One outgrowth of rising popular discontent over the poor caliber of elected officials was the consensus in 2004 among all major political parties to reduce the size of the Legislative Yuan drastically and abolish Taiwan's multiple-member district, single nontransferable vote electoral system, which prior to 1994 had also existed in Japan. Reformers associated corruption in politics with the ability of shady politicians to mobilize small, loyal constituencies in multiple-member districts by engaging in "vote buying" or pork barrel spending. Reformers, such as Chiu Yi-ren of the Democratic Progressive Party, argued successfully for the creation of an electoral system with larger single-member districts that have been associated with a two-party system and were expected to reduce the ability of politicians to win seats based on support from narrow constituencies. In addition, plans were made to cut the total number of Taiwan's national legislators nearly in half. Politicians with ties to gangs were thus expected to decrease in number and influence over time.[45]

The Mass Media and Intellectuals

Since the late 1980s, the mass media have drawn deeply on the expertise of Taiwan's educated elite to contribute to policy debates as pundits for a plethora of print, radio, and television media concerning a wide variety of political subjects. Intellectuals, activists, and politicians frequently contribute opinion pieces to major newspapers such as the *Liberty Times, China Times, United Daily,* and the Hong Kong–based tabloid *Apple Daily.* Their opinions have been sought for news features, especially concerning issues about which incumbent politicians are reluctant to talk.

In a popular format that emerged in underground radio stations in the 1970s, "call-in" programs have provided the public with opportunities to vent frustration, voice general concerns, and challenge pundits directly. The 1993 Cable Television Law opened the door to domestic and foreign investment in the television market and gave new television stations the chance to compete with Taiwan's three terrestrial stations once controlled by the KMT. In the 1990s, a robust television industry emerged featuring several 24-hour news channels that hosted dozens of call-in television programs. Anthropologist Alice R. Chu suggests that guests on highly "marketized" ratings-driven television call-in shows are often selected for their extreme positions, resulting in fierce debate on matters of major and minor significance and creating the feeling that Taiwan is in a state of perpetual crisis.[46] Well-known academics have been regularly invited to participate in these programs, provided they are willing to face rhetorical mud-slinging or "saliva war" (*koushui zhan*). The effect of Taiwan's free mass media in combination with Taiwan's passion for political news and media programming has made it possible to disseminate the views of reform-minded intellectuals broadly while creating a political environment in which controversial political issues are debated so frequently as to seem commonplace. No politician (or relative of a politician) is safe from criticism, and no topic is taboo. Where once opposition politicians cried out for access to the mass media for empowerment of their political agendas, there are now cries from intellectuals to rein in the media, which they accuse of misinformation and libelous reports.

Intellectuals After Mao

We turn now to China and its markedly different experience. Under Mao Zedong's successor, Deng Xiaoping, who became China's paramount leader in December 1978, China moved away from a state-planned to a market economy and opened up its economy to the outside world. By appointing his successors, Deng fostered lasting commitment to major economic reforms. He appointed as head of the Chinese Communist Party Hu Yaobang (1980–1987), Zhao Ziyang (1987–1989), Jiang Zemin (1989–2002), and Hu Jintao, who took over the party leadership in 2002. Economic changes accompanied by decentralization of political power, increasing participation in the international community, relaxation of controls over personal activities, and pragmatic leadership produced a more open intellectual environment. Except for the Hundred Flowers period (1956–June 1957) during the Mao Zedong years, the resulting intellectual and ideological pluralism was unprecedented since the 1949 Communist revolution. Yet, in the last two decades of the twentieth century and the early years of the twenty-first century, China has remained a Leninist party-state.

As during most of China's pre-1949 history, de facto intellectual autonomy first developed in academia, the arts, and popular culture. Any attempts, however, to challenge the political leadership or the party's authority in these areas evoked forceful suppression by the government, as during the imperial period and the era of Kuomintang rule (1928–1945). If the intellectuals' interests remained within the limits of their disciplines and outside the realm of politics, however, the government generally did not intervene. Moreover, because by the 1990s China had developed a market economy and the government no longer assigned jobs to college graduates, intellectuals were not totally dependent on the party-state for their livelihood and thus were less deterred from ideological dissent by economic considerations.

After Mao's death in 1976, Deng Xiaoping and his fellow reformers welcomed the intellectuals who had been purged by Mao back into the party establishment. They helped rebuild the government devastated by Mao's campaigns, reform the economy, and open the country to the outside world. Imbued with the tradition of intellectual service to the state, as throughout Chinese history, they were drawn into the policy process through political patronage. Under the auspices of various political patrons, they assumed the leadership of important government policymaking institutes and think tanks and were put in charge of professional federations in place of the party hacks of the Mao era. They also organized associations and societies that, though still under the patronage of the party, had more autonomy than the official professional federations. Only gradually, as their various efforts failed to stop the persistent repression of dissidents and recurring political campaigns, did they move toward the idea of trying to limit political power by developing laws and establishing institutions to prevent political abuses. But they still sought to achieve these goals by working within the existing political system and through their political patrons.[47]

Another new factor in the post-Mao period that helped the establishment as well as the disestablished intellectuals organize on their own auspices and use unorthodox means to make their views known was China's growing contact with the outside world. Through access to the global media, Voice of America (VOA), Radio Free Asia, the BBC, Hong Kong outlets, and the Internet, they could relay news of their activities back to the Chinese public, which, because of domestic censorship, was generally unaware of them. At the same time, greater international interaction not only exerted pressure on the Chinese government to reform but also helped protect those involved in political activities from harsh punishment. Unlike Mao, who did not care what the outside world thought of his actions, the post-Mao governments wanted China to be accepted as a respected member of the international community. Therefore, as with Taiwan, outside pressure could act as a restraint on the government's repressive actions and on occasion could help expand public space for political discourse within China, though less so in the Hu Jintao era.

In addition, the widespread introduction of new communications technologies, including instant messaging and pagers in addition to cell phones and the Internet, by the late 1990s allowed the Chinese people more access to uncensored and independent sources of information and to one another. By 2008, the number of China's Internet users had risen to 210 million people.[48] At the same time, the party was acutely aware of the Internet's potential to undermine its political authority. Thus, it introduced a variety of methods to control Internet content through censorship, surveillance, firewalls, and filtering techniques. Nevertheless, despite the party-state's attempt to limit the content and prevent access to "undesirable" sites, sophisticated users found ways to access the sites they desired through alternative and foreign proxy servers among other methods to evade official controls and communicate with one another through coded speech.[49]

Consequently, China's embrace of the global telecommunications technologies provided the establishment and disestablished intellectuals, as well as the general public, with communication mechanisms to interact among themselves and with other groups outside of government control. They used the Internet not only to carry on debates but also to coordinate meetings, compose petitions, and organize demonstrations, thus further expanding public space for political activities and facilitating unprecedented interaction among different groups and individuals. Yet, without effective institutions and laws to protect political debate and association, efforts to assert political rights in China's expanding public space, particularly when carried out by groups rather than by single individuals, were inevitably short-lived. Nevertheless, a small number of establishment and disestablished intellectuals at the end of the twentieth century asserted their political rights without waiting for the state to grant them. For brief periods, through the media, books, the Internet, and organized protests, they expressed views that dissented from those in authority. Not surprisingly, one of their overriding demands was for freedom of expression and association, which would allow them the opportunity to carry on their political activities.

Perhaps the greatest change in the position of intellectuals in the post-Mao era was a blurring of the separation between intellectuals and ordinary people. This blurring had already begun during the Cultural Revolution, when educated youth were sent to the countryside to learn from the peasants and to work in factories with the workers. It became increasingly apparent by the mid-1990s, when shifting coalitions of establishment and disestablished intellectuals plus workers and small business people took place in a variety of venues, such as in ideological debates, presenting petitions to the government, engaging in collective protests, or commenting on government policy in public letters, online chat forums, and web logs or blogs.

Challenging Official Ideology

Unlike during the Mao era, when intellectuals could only express ideas publicly that Mao had endorsed,[50] in the post-Mao era, particularly by the mid-1990s, groups of establishment intellectuals expressed a variety of ideological views—neo-Maoist, neoconservative, neo-Confucian, new left, nationalist, and liberal. Although freedom of expression was not guaranteed by law, these groups participated in political discourse and debates that challenged the policies of the party leadership. In fact, the role of public intellectuals in the establishment changed from the 1980s to the 1990s. In the 1980s, most of the intellectuals who dominated ideological and political discourse were members of networks associated with China's top party leaders. But by the 1990s, some intellectuals began to speak and act as independent actors and participate in relatively independent ideological groups, They debated, organized, and published articles and petitions that challenged the party's views and policies, as well as one another, even at the cost of being expelled from the establishment and becoming politically marginalized.

Whereas the neo-Maoists and a few of the Marxist humanists were of the older generation, most of the other participants in the political discourse and debates in the 1990s were of the Cultural Revolution and 1989 generations. Unlike the Marxist humanists of the 1980s who, even when they thought the political system was bankrupt (as many did after the Cultural Revolution) did not want to risk severing themselves from the establishment, a small number of the younger generations were willing to become marginalized or disestablished. The establishment intellectuals during the Mao era, and even into the 1980s, were loyal dissenters and upright scholars who, in the Confucian tradition, spoke truth to power and sought to transform the government from within. By contrast, in the 1990s and first decade of the twenty-first century, even intellectuals in the establishment expressed dissenting ideas.

Diverse groups of establishment intellectuals used journal articles, public forums, and books to argue on behalf of a variety of economic and political reforms. Whereas in the 1980s they called for political and economic reforms within a Marxist ideological framework, those calling for change in the 1990s engaged in wide-ranging debates, without official direction or ideological constraints. They debated a broad range of topics—from the relevance to present-day China of the traditional beliefs in Confucianism, Daoism, Mohism, and Legalism to May 4 liberalism and Maoism. In fact, there was more diversity among the establishment intellectuals than among the disestablished intellectuals, whose major demands were for democratic political institutions, human rights, a reevaluation of the 1989 student demonstrations, and the release of political prisoners.

The overriding focus of the debates was on how to deal with the serious social dislocations, increasing inequalities, and rampant corruption unleashed by China's economic reforms. Ostensibly, the 1990s appeared to be the most prosperous period of economic development and relative stability in China's modern history. As the economic reforms took off in the mid-1990s, they brought remarkable economic growth, an expanding market, and increasing international economic integration. Yet, the by-product of these reforms—accelerating social and economic polarization between the faster-growing coastal areas and the interior regions; between the newly rich entrepreneurs and the workers in bankrupt state-owned industries; and between generally prospering urban dwellers and disgruntled farmers, whose economic growth, sparked by the land reform of the early 1980s, had leveled off by the early 1990s, inducing the migration of millions of rural residents into the cities in search of jobs—had the potential of great social instability. A three-year study by the Chinese Academy of Social Sciences (CASS) published under the title *Blue Book on Chinese Society, 2002* found that at the start of the economic reforms in the 1980s, the richest 20 percent of Chinese households were four and one-half times better off than the poorest; by 2002, the richest households had incomes nearly 13 times greater than the poorest, a ratio close to that in the United States and far greater than that of West European countries.[51]

Consequently, despite the economic growth and seeming stability, potentially destabilizing social, economic, and environmental forces unleashed by the economic reforms and growth provoked increasing public anger. This anger was expressed in large-scale demonstrations of workers, farmers, pensioners, and ordinary people against corruption; official abuses of power; burdensome local taxes and fees in the countryside; confiscation of land for factories and infrastructure projects without adequate compensation; unpaid health care, pensions, and wages; layoffs at failing state-owned enterprises; and widespread pollution of the air and water. The continuing repression of old and new unofficial religious believers, such as the Christian home worshippers Falungong practitioners (members of a Buddhist-Daoist sect who sought freedom to worship and meditate without official approval), and ethnic minorities seeking more autonomy also evoked more frequent, confrontational demonstrations in the 1990s.

Consequently, most of the politically engaged intellectuals, whether on the left or the right of the political spectrum and whether inside or outside the establishment, called for a variety of political and economic changes in order to alleviate the grievances induced by the economic reforms or, at least, to channel the growing protests into less disruptive responses. Whereas public discourse in the 1980s was dominated by the efforts of Marxist humanists, in the 1990s and early twenty-first century it was dominated by a more pluralistic discourse than at any other time since the 1949 revolution and was less directed by the top political leadership. What was unprecedented in the People's Republic was the fact that these ideological debates were conducted without party permission and the support of a political patron and, at times, challenged party policies. They were independently generated, following their own trajectories, until the party believed its authority was being threatened and suppressed them and their proponents.

Although the discourse and debates among the various groups and even within each intellectual group are quite complicated, in order to present the broad spectrum of their views and conflicts with the party, it is only possible here to describe their divergence from the views and policies of the party leadership. Others have described the debates within and among the various groups.[52] The neo-Maoists sought to turn the clock back to the pre–Great Leap Forward Maoist era; the new left sought to revive some aspects of Maoist populist economic and political collectivism, such as the egalitarian experiments of the Great Leap Forward and the efforts to establish direct democracy during the Cultural Revolution; the neonationalists and neoconservatives sought a recentralization of political power and less interaction in the global economy; and the liberals advocated the assertion of political rights and the establishment of an institutionalized system of checks and balances.

When these groups debated among themselves, there was generally no interference from the party-state. As Perry Link has described the political atmosphere in the 1990s, "nearly anything can be said in private, which is a big advance over the Mao years. And because academic journals had such modest circulations, they are given somewhat more latitude than other publishing media. As long as scholars don't confront the top leadership head-on, they can write in scholarly journals pretty much as they choose."[53] However, when these debates spilled over into the mass media and became more organized, the party leadership regarded them as a direct challenge and suppressed them, along with their advocates. Nevertheless, for brief periods of time, one group or another was able to get its ideas debated and its views discussed in the public arena.

Exactly 100 years after China's Hundred Day Reforms in 1898 that were ultimately to lead to the beginnings of political changes during the last years of the Qing dynasty, the year 1998 ushered in broad-ranging public discourse on political reforms. And like the Hundred Day reformers, the major exponents of political reform in the late twentieth century were establishment intellectuals—scholars, writers, journalists, and ex-officials—who were not at the center of power. They worked at think tanks, universities, and newspapers, or they were in retirement, but they managed to present their views on political reform in books, scholarly journals, forums, and other channels in the public arena. At times, they even joined with those outside the establishment to call for political change.

Those proposing political reforms represented a broad ideological spectrum, from the older generation of Marxist humanists, who still couched their calls for political reforms in Marxist language, to younger intellectuals from the Chinese Academy of Social Sciences and the universities, who cited a range of Western liberal thinkers from Adam Smith to Karl Popper to support their arguments. Although none of the establishment intellectuals proposed a multiparty system or direct elections of the political leadership by universal suffrage, they did advocate the establishment of other institutions associated with liberal democracy: some emphasized the rule of law; others stressed freedom of expression and association. Some were concerned with inner-party democracy; others with grassroots democracy. Virtually all, however, called for a political system based on some form of checks and balances. What they had in common was a shared emphasis on the need for political system reform in order to deal with the rampant corruption and accelerating economic and social inequalities accompanying China's economic reforms.

Those expressing liberal political views in the late 1990s differed from the Marxist humanists of the 1980s in that they were relatively more independent of political patronage—not only because of China's accelerating market economy and openness to the outside world but also because of their desire to acquire intellectual autonomy. Furthermore, with the collapse of the Soviet Union and the Communist states of Eastern Europe in 1991 and the bankruptcy of Marxism-Leninism, the liberals in the 1990s, unlike their predecessors in the 1980s, did not call for reform within a Marxist framework. Yet, virtually all of the liberals used the Marxist argument that when the economic substructure changes, there must also be changes in the political superstructure. If not, they warned, contradictions will arise that will undermine the substructure. Nevertheless, whereas Marxist-Leninist ideas still influenced some older officials and Hu Jintao called in 2005 for renewed emphasis on study of Marxist ideology and self-criticism, with the exception of the neo-Maoists and a small number of younger intellectuals of the new left, Marxism-Leninism waned as an inspirational force for most intellectuals by the late 1990s, as they drew increasingly from a variety of Western sources to buttress their views. In some respects, the views and activities of the liberal establishment intellectuals at times echoed the views of the disestablishment intellectuals, though only rarely did the two groups join together in political action.

Although the liberals addressed the same problems as the other ideological groups—how to deal with the growing corruption, economic and social polarization, and increasing alienation spawned by the economic reforms—their answers differed from those of the other groups and were regarded by the party as the most threatening to its authority. The liberals' calls for the establishment of democratic institutions of checks and balances, primarily freedom of the press and association, directly challenged the party's dominant political power and the unlimited control of the Leninist party-state on which its power was based.

Disestablished Intellectuals:
The Democracy Wall and 1989 Tiananmen Generations

Although intellectuals in the establishment sought to bring about political change through their positions in the political, economic, and cultural hierarchy, a small number worked from outside official channels to bring about political change. Some of them were members of the generation of urban youth who most likely would have been in the establishment had it not been for the fact that their education was suspended during the Cultural Revolution when Mao mobilized them as Red Guards to rebel against authority, creating chaos, and then sent them to the countryside to learn from the peasants. Far away from their families, teachers, and the party, they formed their own discussion groups in which they began to question party policies. When they returned to the cities after Mao's death in the late 1970s, a number of them maintained contacts with groups that had been formed during the Cultural Revolution and participated in the Democracy Wall movement in late 1978–1979, demanding political as well as economic reforms.

Another group of political activists was composed of the leaders of the 1989 demonstrations, who called for political reforms, along with an end to corruption and inflation. Ultimately both of these movements, Democracy Wall and the 1989 demonstrations, sought reforms to move China in a more democratic direction. The party, however, regarded them as challenges to its authority and suppressed them and arrested their leaders. In the early 1990s, however, most of the leaders of these two movements had been released from prison owing to pressure from the United States and to China's desire to host the Olympics, which it did not get until 2008. Unlike most members of the educated younger generation, who either went into business (*xiahai*) or into the professions,[54] these activists were blocked from the intellectual establishment because of their past political activities. Yet, despite the party's repression, they continued to speak out and try to assert their political rights.

Ironically, it was during the destructive, chaotic Cultural Revolution that the Democracy Wall participants learned to engage in public debates, put up wall posters, publish leaflets, mobilize support, and organize political actions with others without the permission of the authorities. The leaders of the 1989 demonstrations used similar tactics in the six weeks of political action sparked by Hu Yaobang's death on April 15, 1989, until the military crackdown on June 4. Deprived of the opportunity to become members of the establishment, they were forced either to become free-lance intellectuals, workers, or individual entrepreneurs. At times, they made common cause with ordinary workers, farmers, and other social groups. As a result, they turned increasingly to grass-roots political efforts to bring about change and to assert their political rights. Thus, despite the party's repression and its arrest of their leaders, a significant number of the participants in these two movements persisted in their attempts to assert their political rights.

The leaders of Democracy Wall made the issue of human rights a focus of their movement. Although the concept of rights (*quanli*) that entered China by way of Japan in the late nineteenth century had been fervently debated in intellectual circles during the early decades of the twentieth century,[55] after the 1949 Communist revolution it had been denigrated as a Western bourgeois concept, though it was briefly discussed during the Hundred Flowers movement. Nevertheless, a number of the Democracy Wall groups and the journals they published—*April 5 Forum* (*Wusi luntan*), *Explorations* (*Tansuo*), *Beijing Spring* (*Beijing zhichun*), *Human Rights Journal* (*Renquan bao*), and *Seek Truth Journal* (*Qiushi bao*)—although of differing political persuasions, went beyond supporting the economic reforms of the Deng Xiaoping leadership to exploring new avenues of political action and dialogue, specifically focusing on the question of political, civil, and human rights—terms they tended to use interchangeably.

As with other issues, discussions of these rights in the late 1970s were conducted within the Marxist-Leninist ideological framework in which the activists had been indoctrinated. They knew little about the political changes under way in Taiwan but were knowledgeable about Soviet and East European dissidents, whom they learned about primarily in the party's internal news bulletin, *Reference News* (*Cankao xiaoxi*), to which they had access through their parents or associates. The Democracy Wall participants also repeatedly emphasized the rights of freedom of expression, association, and political participation, as guaranteed in China's constitution. In addition, they cited the "four big freedoms"—(1) speak out freely, (2) air views fully, (3) hold great debates, and (4) write big-character posters—that Mao had inserted into the 1975 constitution. The introductory issues of a number of their journals stressed their founders' commitment to political rights. Like the East European and Soviet dissidents in the 1970s and 1980s, they referred repeatedly to the constitution as the basis for their actions.

Although the various autonomous associations that formed during the 1989 demonstrations were dismantled following the June 4, 1989, crackdown, after a lull, a number of grassroots political organizations reemerged in the mid-1990s. They organized petitions, established independent publications, and built new coalitions, culminating in the effort to establish an opposition political party, the China Democracy Party (CDP) in 1998.[56]

Most of the leaders of the CDP were workers or individual entrepreneurs (*geti hu*), who, but for their participation in the Cultural Revolution, the 1978–1979 Democracy Wall movement, or the 1989 Tiananmen demonstrations, would have been establishment intellectuals. The CDP represented what party leaders had feared most since 1980, a coalition of intellectuals, individual entrepreneurs, workers, and some farmers engaged in political activity, reminiscent of Poland's Solidarity movement that had brought down the Polish Communist Party. Unlike the establishment intellectuals who debated and published articles about freedom of speech and association, they took concrete actions to make these freedoms a reality by attempting to establish an opposition party. The multiclass nature of the CDP also reflected another change in China in the 1990s—the issue of political reform was no longer the concern of only the intellectual elites. The diverse class backgrounds of the CDP members demonstrated that the demand for political change had moved beyond an intellectual elite to the population at large. Moreover, this was the first indication in the People's Republic of intellectuals joining together with other social classes in political actions.

Efforts to register local CDPs began during the state visits of prominent foreign leaders in 1998. It started in Hangzhou in June and spread to cities along the coast, and then to the inland provinces, the northeast, and Sichuan until the visits of the foreign dignitaries ended in late 1998. With the shift of the international media elsewhere, virtually all the leaders of the fledgling opposition party were arrested, thus terminating the first attempt to establish a multiparty system in the People's Republic. Nevertheless, the fact that a grassroots political movement to establish an opposition political party was sustained on and off for almost six months was unprecedented in China in the second half of the twentieth century.

In the late 1990s another grassroots movement emerged of cyber-dissidents, who also called for political reforms. It was led mostly by a small number of people from the post–June 4 generation.[57] Whereas the Democracy Wall activists used wall posters, mimeographed pamphlets, and debates in front of city walls and in parks and the 1989 demonstrators used access to public squares, the foreign media, telephones, and copy and fax machines to spread their ideas and to elicit support, this movement was made possible by the introduction of the new telecommunication technologies in the mid-1990s—computers, the Internet, cell phones, and text messaging. These technologies provided the cyber-dissidents and others with the potential to break down further the separation between intellectuals and ordinary citizens and to coordinate and organize a movement on a national scale. The various coalitions that formed to bring about political change at the end of the twentieth century resonated with those of the May 4 movement, when students reached out to form coalitions with workers, merchants, and other social groups, and only then, as Elizabeth Perry points out, did their combined quest to assert political rights become a significant political force.[58] Unlike Taiwan, however, the rising entrepreneurs played only a minor role in these various political efforts as CCP leaders pursued a strategy of co-optation by encouraging entrepreneurs to join the party.

Expanding Citizen Participation

Although most of those who participated in independently organized political activities in the 1990s, whether through political debates, organized protests, public petitions, efforts to register an opposition party, or democratic discourse on the Internet, were somewhat isolated from the population at large and were eventually suppressed, this does not mean that their writings and activities did not have an impact on the general population. Moreover, as political scientist Kevin O'Brien explains, people act as citizens long before they may be fully conscious of their political rights.[59] Equally important, whereas the articulation of a rights consciousness and the assertion of political rights may be attributed to the assimilation of Western concepts, the protests of workers, farmers, and small entrepreneurs against abusive officials and their demands for fair treatment can be traced to concepts that appeared early in Chinese history, such as the legalist advocacy of the impartial administration of the law and Confucianism, particularly Mencius's advice to officials to govern fairly and in the interest of the welfare of those being governed.

Widespread demonstrations by different sectors of the Chinese population—workers, farmers, pensioners, migrant laborers, religious believers, and urban and rural residents who were protesting environmental pollution, loss of health care and pensions, and the confiscation of their homes and land for modern development—thus exploded all over China in the 1990s and accelerated in the early twenty-first century. These demonstrations revealed an increasing popular awareness of the right to associate and organize in order to gain one's due, whether to unpaid wages, pensions, health care, more compensation for one's property, less official corruption, lower rural tax burdens, clean air and water, or freedom of religious worship.

A Redefinition of Chinese Citizenship

Thus, in the post-Mao era Chinese citizens resumed efforts to assert their political rights that had begun a hundred years earlier during the 1898 Hundred Days of Reform but had been interrupted by the 1949 Communist revolution and the Mao Zedong era. Moreover, by the beginning of the twenty-first century, a rights consciousness was spreading from the intellectual elite to other social groups. There were still virtually no institutional or legal protections for such rights, and protest movements were harshly repressed. However, unlike during the Mao period when millions were harshly persecuted for the actions of a few, in the post-Mao period persecution for political dissent does not extend far beyond the accused. Although the repression of political dissenters continues, it does not have the crusading zeal, coerced mass participation, or forced confessions of the Mao era. Further, because of China's move to the market, when those who were persecuted were released from prison, though purged from the establishment, they were able to find means of livelihood. And unlike during the Mao era, they were not completely silenced. Some still tried to function as citizens, either on their own or with others, and they were able to express their political views through nonestablishment publications and groups, on the Internet, and in organized demonstrations.

The pace of political reforms accelerated in China at the turn of the century, not only in terms of party-sanctioned reforms, such as village elections, but also in terms of a variety of political strategies used by establishment and disestablished intellectuals. Unlike the Marxist humanists of the 1980s, whose connections with reformist party officials gave them opportunities to educate people ideologically, most public intellectuals came to believe that it was necessary to establish democratic institutions as well as to educate. They adopted a more activist approach, through publishing books independently, engaging in ideological debates, writing petitions, holding demonstrations, and mobilizing groups. And a small number were even willing to risk their positions and work outside the political and intellectual establishments in order to achieve their goals. At times, they joined with and drew members of other social groups into their political activities.

Nevertheless, the institutions believed to be necessary in Western political thought for democracy and that today exist in Taiwan, such as freedom of expression and association, an independent judiciary, an elected legislature and national leaders, and a multiparty system, do not exist in China at the start of the twenty-first century. The difficulties in establishing such institutions are due not only to the continuing dominance of the Leninist party-state but also to the fact that China, unlike Taiwan, has not yet developed an independent middle class—a bourgeoisie—to support such institutions. With a few exceptions, such as individual small entrepreneurs who participated in the China Democracy Party and the emergence of a small number of defense lawyers, independent journalists, and public intellectuals, most of China's expanding business and professional communities in the late twentieth and early twenty-first centuries have been co-opted into the party and the official establishment. Nevertheless, as we have seen, though unprotected by institutions or laws, various individuals and groups in the post-Mao era continue to contest the policies of China's authoritarian government and attempt to assert their political rights.

Will China Be Like Taiwan in the Future?

Taiwan's small size; its legacy of Japanese colonial rule, which helped build the infrastructure and educate the population; the US pressure to liberalize politics; and the Taiwanese desire to be identified as a democratic polity in order to gain international legitimacy have provided Taiwan with very different incentives than the People's Republic for political reforms. Furthermore, the Taiwanese middle class developed into a genuine bourgeoisie with opinion leaders who sought independence vis-à-vis mainlander leaders. In contrast, China's new entrepreneurial class is being co-opted into the party and often collaborates with local party leaders in business ventures.

Unlike Chiang Ching-kuo and Lee Teng-hui, China's leaders have crushed any effort to establish an opposition party. In fact, China's fourth generation of Communist leaders, led by party head Hu Jintao, have narrowed public space for political discourse that opened up in the late 1990s and stepped up the arrest and repression of editors, journalists, cyber-dissidents, defense lawyers, and public intellectuals. This generation of leaders and their associates were educated primarily at China's top universities—Beijing University and Tsinghua, China's MIT. But unlike Taiwan's leaders, who were trained as lawyers and in the social sciences, they were primarily trained as technocrats, with more resemblance to the party leaders in the former Soviet Union, until Mikhail Gorbachev, trained as a lawyer, launched political reforms in the late 1980s.

China in the early twenty-first century stands in stark contrast to Taiwan in the late 1980s, when the relaxation of restrictions governing freedom of speech and assembly after the cessation of martial law made consideration of nearly all political and ideological topics possible. Furthermore, in the 1990s, new opportunities became available for Taiwan's disestablished intellectuals to participate in politics, and occasionally antiestablishment intellectuals were welcomed into the KMT establishment.

The difference between mass media in Taiwan and China is considerable, even when China of the present is compared to Taiwan in the 1970s. Recent content analysis conducted on media reports in major daily newspapers in Taiwan and China shows that in 1978 Taiwanese media were much freer to criticize the state and debate a wide range of issues than Chinese newspapers in 1980, a year of considerable media openness in the PRC.[60] In Taiwan the media have become freer and more diverse. The "space" available for mainstream Chinese mass media to produce reports and to debate political issues has declined since the late 1990s, whereas the amount of national and local propaganda has increased. Yet, access to alternative and independent sources of information has grown in both polities with the advent of the Internet. Taiwan's greater per capita wealth, however, has allowed a much higher proportion of the population to go online. In Taiwan, 68 percent of the population has Internet access compared to around 10 percent of the population in China.[61] Moreover, the Taiwanese government does not restrict any form of political content on the Internet, whereas online media in China, including blogs, are subject to CCP censorship and filtering.

Unquestionably, the behavior and beliefs of most of China's political reformers at the turn of the century have much in common with the Confucian literati and Marxist humanists of the 1980s. Like their predecessors, they remonstrate with the leaders to change their political ways, and they seek to work within the prevailing structure to achieve their aims. Yet, unlike the Confucian literati and Marxist humanists in the 1980s, a small number of Chinese intellectuals have rejected the need for political patronage and seek to build an independent base for reforms. Similar to their East European counterparts in the 1970s and 1980s, they are willing to work both inside and outside the party and the intellectual establishment to influence and challenge the entrenched regime.

Still, unlike the East Europeans or Taiwanese, Chinese reformers have been unable to bring down the Leninist party-state or to establish diverse political institutions at the start of the twenty-first century. In spite of the loosening up and devolution of party power that accompanied China's economic reforms, China's party-state, though gravely harmed by the Cultural Revolution, is still much stronger than the party-states in Eastern Europe before the fall of Communism in the 1990s and in Taiwan before its democratization in the late 1980s. In contrast to the economic reforms in the 1990s in the former Soviet Union, China's economic reforms in the post-Mao period, despite the resultant increasing inequalities and rampant corruption, have improved the livelihood of most of the population, thereby allowing the party to retain its legitimacy. Furthermore, unlike the East European intellectuals and even their May 4 predecessors in the 1920s, China's political activists did not link up with the emerging entrepreneurial class and workers in political action until after the June 4 crackdown; and even then only a small number of disestablished and marginal intellectuals actually joined forces with other social groups. They did not have the broad-based social support enjoyed by their East European and Taiwanese brethren.

Nevertheless, it would be wrong to discount the impact of these various efforts to assert political rights in China because they were quickly suppressed and the institutions they sought to build have yet to be established. These actions may signify the beginnings of a genuine change in the relationship between China's population at large and the state at the start of the twenty-first century and could lead in time to developments similar to those that occurred in Taiwan in the 1980s. In China, however, democratization will be difficult without an expansion of opportunities for intellectuals to participate in political debate, the establishment of legally autonomous social organizations, greater media openness, and legitimation of other political parties.

Notes

1. Intellectual pluralism, or public debates by individuals and groups, that occurs within party and state organizations can be seen as a subset of what Jerry F. Hough (1977, 24) termed *institutional pluralism*. For references to related literature see Linz and Stepan 1996a, 41.

2. Hamrin and Cheek 1986.

3. Goldman 1994.

4. Fewsmith 2001.

5. Linz and Stepan 1996a, 38–54.

6. Taiwan's period of soft authoritarianism commenced with President Chiang Ching-kuo's decision to use a relatively open manner of holding the court martial for *Formosa Magazine* staff who participated in the December 10, 1979, Human Rights Day demonstration in Kaohsiung. In 1989, Lee Teng-hui was elected chairman of the Kuomintang at the 13th Party Congress; as the top leader of the party-state, he permitted newly legalized opposition parties to compete with the KMT in elections for supplementary seats in the Legislative Yuan as well as in local elections. This ushered in a period of hybrid authoritarianism in which Democratic Progressive Party candidates and independents competed on unequal footing with KMT incumbents, who benefited from party-financed vote buying and other tactics to defeat or intimidate challengers. For an excellent chronology of political events in Taiwan, see Rigger 1999, 220–223.

7. Diamond's regime typology draws upon a rich literature considering nuanced differences in modern authoritarian regimes. Diamond 2002, 21–35.

8. Ching 2001; Kerr 1974, 113–143.

9. Gold 1994, 52–53.

10. Ibid., 52.

11. Hoare and Smith 1971.

12. Dickson 2003, 25.

13. For a summary of the literature on pluralism, see Almond 1983, 245–260; Sartori 1970 makes a spirited defense of the need to retain the concept of autonomy in what has been called "political," "classical," or "representative" pluralism. His narrow

definition is not one that would allow the term to be applied to most Communist regimes. However, subsequent work by Robert A. Dahl 1971, Linz and Stepan 1996a, and others makes a compelling case for the application of the concept of "institutional pluralism" to describe the complex dynamics within state institutions in contemporary China.

14. The differences between social organizations in Taiwan and China are well illustrated in Chapter 4.

15. In Taiwan, over time the concept of "nation" gradually changed from including the Chinese mainland to focusing strictly on territories controlled by the Republic of China (ROC) government.

16. Dickson 1998, 354.

17. In a similar vein, Samuel Huntington has argued that support for liberalization by a country's political leadership was essential for democratization, regardless of a country's preconditions for democratic transition. Huntington 1991, 107–108.

18. Roy 2003, 175.

19. In May 1990, President Lee Teng-hui granted a total of 34 political pardons. The pardons restored political rights to future legislator and vice president Lu Hsiu-lien and released Shih Ming-teh and Hsu Hsin-liang from prison; the two men later served as chairmen of the Democratic Progressive Party. Ibid., 185–191.

20. Hsueh 1996, 53–72.

21. Rigger 1999, 104–105.

22. Ibid., 105–106.

23. Hu Shih personally paid for one year of Peng Ming-min's graduate training at McGill University. Peng 1994, 101–102, 117.

24. Ibid., 127–129.

25. Tien, ed. 1996, 9–10.

26. Rigger 1999, 108.

27. Roy 2003, 167.

28. Lu 2006, 135–148.

29. Ibid., 148.

30. Lu, Reconsidering, 1992.

31. For a clear, and relatively brief, description of the events surrounding the crackdown on the opposition figures associated with *Formosa Magazine,* see Hsu 1997, 48–51.

32. Former Taoyuan County executive Hsu Hsin-liang fled to the United States; Shih Ming-teh, one of the demonstration organizers, initially escaped the police dragnet only to be caught weeks later after receiving plastic surgery (from a dentist!) to alter his appearance.

33. At the time, Lin's house was under 24-hour surveillance. Taiwan vice president and *Formosa* trial defendant Lu Hsiu-lien has said the date was seen as a deliberate attack on the nativist, prodemocracy opposition because it occurred on the same day as the February 28, 1947, uprising by Taiwanese that seized control of the island's largest cities. That uprising was subsequently crushed by KMT troops in a wave of arbitrary violence, imprisonment, and politically motivated murder that eliminated hundreds and possibly thousands of Taiwanese elite. Interview with Lu Hsiu-lien, August 2000; Lai, Myers, and Wei 1991.

34. Roy 2003, 169.

35. Lu Hsiu-lien has attributed the government's decision to President Chiang Ching-kuo's displeasure with the handling of the Kaohsiung Incident investigation. She claimed that Chiang believed his subordinates provoked demonstrators to violence and then blamed the riot that ensued on demonstrators. Personal communication with Lu Hsiu-lien, August 2001.

36. Roy 2003, 168–169.

37. Taylor 2000, 406.

38. Tien, ed. 1996, 12.

39. Nathan 1993, 435–436.

40. Nathan 1993.

41. The Taiwan Independence Party's name in English is not a literal translation of its name in Chinese. A literal translation is "Nation-building Party."

42. Roy 2003, 230.

43. The DPP's widely adopted slogan was "four great ethnic groups" [*sida zuqun*]. Hsiau 2000, 105.

44. Chin 2003, 13–17.

45. After 2008, the Legislative Yuan will be composed of 73 lawmakers elected from single-member districts in a first-past-the-post system and 40 lawmakers from party lists and aboriginal districts. Lin Jih-wen, 2006, 125.

46. Chu 2004, 89–110.

47. Goldman 1994

48. China Internet Network Information Center (CINIC), "The 21st Statistical Survey Report on the Internet Development in China," January 20, 2008.

49. Chase and Mulvenon 2002; Esarey and Xiao 2008.

50. Even during the Hundred Flowers period (1956–June 1957), Mao had ordered intellectuals to criticize the party's bureaucratic methods. When they also began to criticize Mao and the party, he launched the Anti-Rightist campaign against them.

51. Chinese Academy of Social Sciences 2002; Lakshmanan 2002.

52. Wang Hui 2003; Wang Chaohua 2003.

53. Link 2002.

54. Keyser 2003.

55. Svensson 1999, 20–25.

56. Wright 2004.

57. Barme and Davies 2004, 75–108.

58. Goldman and Perry 2002, 10.

59. O'Brien 2002, 225–229.

60. Ashley Esarey, "Chinese Media: A Comparative Perspective," working paper, September 2007.

61. Central News Agency 2006, 12. Broadband penetration in Taiwan has reached 68 percent; 72.11 percent of households have some form of Internet access. In China, 137 million people were going online as of late 2006—10.5 percent of the country's 1.3 billion population.

4

Religion and the Emergence of Civil Society

Richard Madsen

I t is commonly argued that a prerequisite to the institutionalization of an effective democracy is the development of an active, self-regulating civil society. Contemporary discussions of civil society commonly identify it with the realm of NGOs. In the past three decades, there has been a spectacular growth and development of self-described NGOs in both China and Taiwan, and there has been much discussion of the rise of civil society in both places. Can we meaningfully compare the development of civil society in both places? Can we use the rise of NGOs as an empirical indicator of the extent of this development? Can we ask whether the development of civil society in China will support the development of democratic institutions in the way in which this happened in Taiwan?

Definitions and Traits

A problem with carrying out such a project is that basic terms such as *NGO* and *civil society* may carry different meanings on both sides of the Taiwan Strait. An NGO in Taiwan is organized according to different legal principles than an NGO in China. It has, as it were, a different social DNA. The usage of the term *civil society* also differs in both places. So to compare the path leading from civil society toward democracy in Taiwan with social developments in China, we have to get beyond commonly used terminology. We need to determine basic components of civil society and to explicate the theoretical assumptions that would link these basic components to the establishment of democracy.[1]

   In classical political theories, civil society usually denotes the realm of voluntary association—groups formed by people who are free to enter or exit. Such voluntary affiliations are possible with the dissolution of "feudal" social arrangements that fix people within ascribed statuses and with the resultant possibilities for social mobility. The most powerful force for dissolving such ascribed relationships has been the ascendancy of market economies. The main location for the fostering of voluntary associations has been the modern city.[2]

Over the past half century, market-driven economic development in Taiwan has been loosening the corporate bonds that once tied individuals to extended families, and since the 1970s it has created a predominantly urban society. This has made possible a great variety of new voluntary associations that today play a key role in Taiwan's democracy. Although Mao Zedong wanted to modernize China by destroying all "feudal" ties, in China Mao's form of state socialism actually froze many traditional, ascriptive social ties in place. Because of the household registration system, farmers could not leave their villages. This led to the deepening of dependency on traditional family ties. Under the work-unit system, industrial workers could not move around in search of work and were dependent for housing, education, and health care on a hierarchically ordered system. The Maoist attempt to destroy feudalism actually led to what Andrew Walder has called "neo-traditionalism."[3] The market reforms that began after Mao's death in 1976 have led to a gradual—but by no means complete—loosening of ascriptive ties. Farmers now migrate by the tens of millions to the cities for work. Within the cities, workers have been cut loose from the cradle-to-grave dependencies of the work-unit system. This has led to a spectacular growth in new forms of voluntary association.

China and Taiwan differ, however, in the ways in which these voluntary associations are organized and in their relationship to the state. In Taiwan, many voluntary associations become formally organized—with bylaws, elected leaders, and so forth—and call themselves NGOs.[4] In doing so, they call upon a legal system that gives them clearly defined rights to independence from the state. Their legal constitution actually helps to preserve their independence. In China some voluntary associations become formally organized and call themselves NGOs—but this is tantamount to giving up their independence. To become a formally organized NGO requires registering with a government agency (exactly which agency depends on circumstances) and accepting supervision and ultimately control by government officials. Even though many organizations actually carve out a great deal of practical autonomy, this autonomy is contingent on the good will (or inattention) of their supervising institutions and can be taken away at any time.[5] In China, groups that want to take a truly critical stance versus government policies often eschew formal organization and do not seek official registration. In China such groups would not be classified as NGOs. In Taiwan, social movement groups that want to effectively challenge the current government might actively seek formal designation as NGOs, because this would give them a measure of legal protection.

Thus, most NGOs in Taiwan would match basic Western definitions of civil society organizations. They are voluntary associations with liberties that are protected by a rule of law, which restricts them only from encroaching on other people's rights. At the same time, many informally organized groups in Taiwan—which might reject formal organization because they are engaged in illegal activities—would not meet common Western standards for civil society. In China, on the other hand, many self-described NGOs would not meet these standards, whereas many informally organized, officially unrecognized groups might reasonably be considered at least part of an incipient civil society.

Civil Society and Sustainable Democracy

Civil society does not automatically lead to sustainable democracy. It is a necessary but not sufficient condition for such democracy. Civil society can be the basis for citizens to manage their own affairs peacefully, "civilly." Or it can generate bitter social divisions that can lead to anarchy—which might only be overcome by strict authoritarian rule. The qualities of civil society that sustain socially responsible self-governance do not develop independently from the state. The qualities of a civil society depend on their relationship with the state—which depends on how the state responds to problems created in the early development of civil society. There are in Western political theory different visions of how the state should respond to the challenges to social order and good governance generated by the emergence of a civil society.[6]

The classic liberal tradition was very optimistic about the capacities of civil society to regulate itself. Unlimited opportunities for free association would lead to a realm of voluntary associations with overlapping memberships. By enabling citizens to articulate and protect their interests, well-organized groups would block the power of the state and force rulers to be accountable. Moreover, by enabling citizens to regulate themselves and provide for most of their needs, the voluntary associations would eliminate much of the need for a strong state. Meanwhile, the overlapping, constantly shifting membership of voluntary groups would prevent social polarization and enhance social communication, thus producing a naturally peaceful society.

The Marxist tradition, in contrast, focused on the economic polarization made possible by civil society. Those groups that have more resources tend to get bigger, and as they get bigger they gain even more resources and use their wealth to exclude the poor, which leads to violent class conflict. This leads to a need for strong state action to repress civil society.

The civic republican tradition, exemplified by Alexis de Tocqueville, affirmed the positive potentials of civil society but cautioned that these could be realized only within certain cultural and political contexts. A healthy civic group life had to be based on cultural mores, "habits of the heart," that gave citizens moral self-discipline and a concern for the common good; and these values would be difficult to sustain if a society faced external threats to its survival or if it became dominated by a "manufacturing aristocracy."[7]

The corporatist tradition in its various forms offers solutions to the problems of civil society that occur when civil society arises within the wrong kind of cultural and political contexts. If a society is deeply divided along ethnic, racial, religious, or cultural lines, the realm of voluntary associations can become polarized along these lines and lead to an anarchy that can only be quelled by a strong state claiming to act in the general interest. If the society faces severe (real or imagined) external threats, a strong state may legitimize itself by limiting the freedoms of voluntary assembly, by destroying those groups deemed a threat to national security, and by co-opting and coordinating the others to serve the general interest.

None of these approaches to minimizing the liabilities and maximizing the benefits of civil society is likely to be sustainable in its pure form over the long run. Most polities, including the United States, are based on a mix of these approaches. Whatever approach a polity takes to maximizing the benefits and minimizing the liabilities of a civil society, the approach tends to take on a life of its own, resistant to any sudden change. The approach that a polity takes to an incipient civil society depends at least in part on the mix between the integrative and disintegrative qualities of that civil society. Using terminology advocated by Robert Putnam, we might define these qualities in terms of the mix between "bonding and bridging social capital."[8] Social capital is the capacity of members of a society to cooperate in pursuit of common interests. Bonding capital leads to the formation of exclusive, closed groups in conflictual competition with one another. Bridging capital leads to open, overlapping group membership.

Unsurprisingly, in both China and Taiwan one sees societal confusion and government ambivalence about how to handle an inexorably emerging civil society; and one sees an uneasy, often contradictory, mix of policies derived from a number of political traditions. In both places, the proliferation of voluntary associations has rather vividly demonstrated the risks and liabilities of civil society as well as the positive goods that can come from it. In both places, the emergence of civil society coincides with increases in public social conflict: for example, in China between workers and managers, farmers and local officials, religious and ethnic minorities against the dominant Han Chinese; in Taiwan, between Taiwanese and mainlanders or between advocates of confrontation versus accommodation with China. In both places, the legacy of harsh authoritarian rule creates resentments that enflame such tensions. All of this raises the specter of social anarchy and dramatizes the unrealistic assumptions that underpin classic liberal optimism about the beneficial potential of civil society. Meanwhile, alleged threats to national security in a dangerous world lend credibility to some who would argue for the need for a strong, centralized government that can establish stability and protect the people by restricting civil society.

Taiwan and China have, however, followed different strategies to limit the risks and liabilities of civil society while fulfilling its positive potential. The strategies can be understood as mixes (not necessarily coherent) of elements from the Marxist, civic republican, and corporatist traditions—and, in Taiwan, the classical liberal tradition. In each case, the mix is colored by Asian cultural values.

This theoretical framework sees civil society not as a static entity but as a historically developing social process. Let us, then, turn from theory to narrative. We first consider the path taken by Taiwan from the beginnings of civil society to the institutionalization of democracy. Then we will consider the directions that China seems to be taking as it begins a journey along the same path.

Taiwan

On Taiwan, the KMT regime pursued a basically Leninist strategy toward civil society in the 1950s and 1960s. Independent social organizations were not allowed. All social organizations were embedded within a system of "transmission belts" from government to the people and were subjected to constant surveillance and control. To maintain its contrast with the Chinese Communist Party on the mainland, the KMT government could not justify these measures in ideological Marxist terms. The KMT claimed that these measures were necessary not because of class struggle but because of the need to maintain national unity in the face of urgent external threats and to overcome potential ethnic conflict between mainlanders, native Taiwanese, and aborigines—basically a corporatist justification. There was somewhat more room within this system, however, for the incubation of civil society groups than there was in China. Christian missionary organizations, for example, were allowed not only to proselytize and to establish educational institutions but also to organize youth groups, co-ops, women's charitable associations, and even labor organizations. Both US military officers and businesspeople organized local branches of the Rotary Club. Military officers' wives organized groups for helping the poor. Moreover, despite its control of large corporations, the KMT did not own all the "means of production" as the CCP did in China. There was a place for small-scale entrepreneurship within a (constrained) market economy, and this provided opportunities for mobility and association that were nonexistent in mainland China.[9]

Beginning in the late 1960s, however, even though civil society was still being harshly repressed in China during the Cultural Revolution era, some of the repression of Taiwanese civil society was starting to loosen. Part of this was owing to a weakening of the KMT government during the last years of Chiang Kai-shek and the succession of his son Chiang Ching-kuo. Another part came from the rise of the middle classes in Taiwan. By the late 1970s, economic development was producing an increasingly urban society with an expanding middle class composed of independent entrepreneurs, on the one hand, and educated professionals on the other.[10] The mobility of these middle classes produced new opportunities for association and new aspirations for personal independence. At the same time, the increased complexity of urban society produced needs for social welfare that the government had difficulty meeting. Finally, the relative openness of Taiwan to international exchange allowed for the circulation of new ideas about social and political organization.

Despite being stifled in the Kaohsiung Incident in 1979, the *Formosa Magazine* social movements stimulated the formation of other social organizations in the early 1980s. When the martial law that had justified political repression was lifted in 1987, the stage had been set for an explosion of social organizations.[11] Thousands of new voluntary associations sprang up in the five years after the end of martial law, and many took advantage of the new political openness to become formally organized and to gain a global reach.

The Taiwan government employed a weak version of the corporatist strategy for keeping such groups under control. As in China, it required all such groups to be registered with a government agency—a "mother-in-law" agency as they say both in China and Taiwan. But unlike in China, the Taiwan government proved utterly incapable of exercising significant surveillance and control over such groups. In practice, there quickly developed something close to the free marketplace of associations that classical liberalism assumed was the ideal way to make full use of the energies of civil society. The discourse of many of these groups seems to have mimicked the rights-based individualism of many social movements in the United States. They used their freedoms of assembly and expression to forge new identities, express grievances, and demand rapid social change. Hsiao argues that by the mid-1990s, social movements had emerged in Taiwan with four distinct foci: (1) those concerned with new problems such as consumer protection, pollution, rising housing costs, and conservation; (2) those concerned with ethnic groups and minority language rights, land control, and cultural identity and preservation as well as the rights of other disadvantaged groups, such as the elderly, the handicapped, and veterans, and the treatment of certain religious groups; (3) those concerned with the state's corporatist mode of control over key social groups, such as workers, farmers, students, women, and teachers and intellectuals; and (4) those concerned with established rules governing politically sensitive issues such as the ban on contacts between people in Taiwan and China and human rights violations.[12]

The proliferation of such organized, social movement associations created what Hsiao called a "demanding civil society."[13] The risks and liabilities of such a demanding civil society on a fragile, newly emerging democracy are evident. One danger was that the groups would be vehicles for a belligerent mass politics that would render difficult the institutionalization of orderly new rules of political procedure. Another danger was that the social movement groups would coalesce around and inflame the ethnic and language divisions on Taiwan. In Robert Putnam's terms, they generated a great deal of bonding but not much bridging social capital.

Such a proliferation of many noisy demands for the rights of one or another relatively small constituency must be a prospect that would terrify officials in the PRC, a specter of chaos. But Taiwan society has not descended into chaos. To understand why, we have to consider other elements of Taiwan's civil society, elements that produce bridging social capital that counterbalances the centrifugal forces of Taiwan's social movement organizations.

Some of the most effective carriers of bridging social capital are the philanthropic organizations that expanded in size and influence after the end of martial law. A book recently published by Taiwan's Ministry of Foreign Affairs summarizes the range of such organizations.

> Some organizations engaged in humanitarian aid are INGOs [international NGOs] with branches in Taiwan like the long established Red Cross Society of R.O.C., the Chinese Fund for Children and Families/Taiwan (CCF/Taiwan) and World Vision Taiwan, or ORBIS Taiwan established in 2001. Some are religious organizations like the Buddhist Compassion Relief Tzu-Chi Foundation and the Puhsein Foundation. Other NGOs hail from the medical profession such as Taiwan Root Medical Peace Corps, Noordhoff Craniofacial Foundation and the International Action and Cooperation Team. Finally, some NGOs focus on community development and education for disadvantaged groups, such as the Eden Social Welfare Foundation, Compassion International and the Field Relief Agency of Taiwan.[14]

As can be seen from this list, many of these organizations have a foundation rooted in religious and ethical movements among Taiwan's middle classes. Their seeds were planted in the two decades preceding the end of martial law, often as the result of creative transformations in traditional religious belief and practice, transformations that initially seemed to have no political implications. The most visible and influential of the religiously based organizations are animated by the principles of "socially engaged Buddhism" (*renjian fo*). Notable among these are Tzu-chi (the Buddhist Compassionate Relief Association) and the Buddha's Light International Association, which I have studied in a new book on religious renaissance and political development in Taiwan.[15] In the next few pages, I will focus on the contributions of these two organizations to a harmonious civil society, but much of what I say could apply as well to the other philanthropic groups mentioned above.

Tzu-chi was founded in 1966 in Hualien by a Buddhist nun, Dharma Master Cheng Yen. Influenced—so the legend goes—by a conversation with some Catholic nuns about the importance of connecting religious faith with charitable work, Cheng Yen organized a small group of Buddhist laywomen to help care for the poor and the sick. The informally organized association grew steadily but slowly during the 1970s and became a full-fledged NGO. In 1979, Cheng Yen decided that Hualien—at the time a poor, undeveloped part of Taiwan populated heavily by aborigines—needed a modern hospital and embarked on an effort to raise US$20 million to build it. Against all expectations, she succeeded (actually raised close to $30 million) and won renown. In 1987, her organization had a core group of only about 500 lay volunteers. After martial law, the numbers exploded: there are now about 20, 000 core volunteers (two-thirds female, one-third male), a very large network of lesser-engaged affiliate volunteers, and about 4 million regular donors. In 1990, Tzu-chi began to expand into the Taiwanese diaspora around the world. Branches of its organization have been set up on every continent. Tzu-chi uses its money (at least US$150 million in regular donations per year and billions of dollars in total assets), the energy of its volunteers, and its enormous network of connections to carry out a wide variety of charitable and educational works, not only in Taiwan but around the world. These works are organized with a high degree of professionalism.[16]

The Buddha's Light International Association was organized for lay Buddhists in 1992 by Dharma Master Hsing Yun, the founder of Buddha's Light Temple, a monastery established in 1968 near Kaohsiung that has now developed branches around the world. A formally organized extension of the charitable work carried out by socially engaged Buddhist temples, the Buddha's Light International Association claims that it is now the fourth largest service organization in the world. Like Tzu-chi (and perhaps originally in emulation of it), it carries out charitable and educational works around the world, all publicized through sophisticated use of the media.

Although these Buddhist charitable NGOs are popularly identified with certain fractions of the Taiwanese middle classes—Tzu-chi with upper-middle-class professional service workers and Buddha's Light International with small entrepreneurs—and with certain ethnic groups—Tzu-chi with Taiwanese, Buddha's Light International with mainlanders—in practice they are quite mixed. In their effort to expand, the charismatic leaders of each organization tried to make it attractive to as wide a population as possible. Although the popular images are not without a base in reality—the kinds of people contributing to that image are somewhat overrepresented in each organization—each group includes all ethnic groups in Taiwan (ceremonies and lectures are conducted in both Mandarin and Taiwanese) and a wide range of members from Taiwan's broad middle classes.[17]

This gap between what these organizations *represent* and what they *are* is of great importance sociologically and politically. Taiwan's rapid economic development has produced a middle class full of conflicts. Meanwhile, the island's delicate geopolitical position and conflicted history set up potentially devastating conflicts between mainlanders and native Taiwanese. The differences between popular religious organizations could provide a frame of reference for thinking about such social and political divisions. When this happens in other societies, religious groups can become the agents of violent social polarization. But this has not happened in Taiwan. The groups that I have described have encouraged the blending of different segments of the population and facilitated reconciliation between potentially warring factions. Though these two groups, and others like them, reflect divisions among Taiwanese society, they have done so in ways that have kept the divisions from becoming antagonistic. This has been crucial for the consolidation of Taiwanese democracy.

Thus, across a range of Taiwanese philanthropic civil society organizations there are organizations that build bridges between class and ethnic factions and cool the passions of contentious politics. In his first inaugural address, Chen Shui-bian referred to the work of such organizations during the 1999 earthquake: "Amid the fierce power of Nature, we have seen Taiwan's most beautiful compassion, strongest faith, and greatest trust. Our compatriots have been injured or wounded . . . but with the spirit of a 'volunteer Taiwan,' Taiwan's new family will stand up resolutely on its feet once again."[18] It is a civic republican vision of the contribution of voluntary organizations to Taiwan's "new family" (a notion colored with Confucian value) in a spirit of (Buddhist-inspired) compassion.

It is difficult to know whether the bridging organizations that I have mentioned can overcome the destabilizing effects on democracy of some of the factionalizing social movement organizations on the Taiwan scene today. But it is fair to say that the destabilizing pressures would be worse without such bridging organizations.

Where did the bridging philanthropic social organizations come from, and could similar bridging components of a civil society develop in China? Although these groups were established independently of the state and began their development outside of government-approved regulatory frameworks, they did not develop into important carriers of bridging social capital without state assistance. They were beneficiaries of efforts made by the KMT government to co-opt constructive voluntary associations through appeal to classical ethical aspirations toward social harmony.

Take Tzu-chi, for example. Though founded in a remote backwater, away from government scrutiny in 1966, it began to grow into a significant organization in 1976, when President Chiang Ching-kuo, confronted with a rapidly developing urban society that lacked adequate social services, instructed all temples to carry out charity work. Tzu-chi won an award for doing this especially well. Later, in the 1980s, it was the Taiwan provincial government that played a major role in building the Tzu-chi hospital in Hualien. The initiative to build the hospital came from Master Cheng Yen, but when she embarked on her fund-raising effort, she had no land upon which to build it. In 1980, Chiang Ching-kuo himself promised to help her get some land, and public land was eventually donated by Hualien County. Though a product of state corporatist policies of co-opting and guiding civil society, Tzu-chi grew rapidly and undertook considerable independent initiative after the end of martial law. But it grew so rapidly precisely because it had had good, if somewhat detached, relationships with the government before 1987. Participating in it was a safe and respectable way of taking the initiative to address some of Taiwan's social problems. Because of its ideology and its history, however, Tzu-chi still retains a spirit of cooperation with Taiwan's government.

Tzu-chi maintains its autonomy from the state—it refuses, for example, to engage in partisan politics—but sees its job as helping the state provide for the public good. For example, in the aftermath of the devastating earthquake that afflicted Taiwan in 1999, Tzu-chi raised $250 million to rebuild 50 public schools. The logic of this enterprise, and the vision that sustained it, was just the opposite of that which guides "faith-based initiatives" in the United States. Here, private religious organizations seek public funds to support private schools. There, religious organizations seek private donations to build public schools. NGOs like Tzu-chi are no longer like transmission belts linking government and people, but more like belt buckles joining private and public sectors.

In recent years, Tzu-chi and other such bridging philanthropic organizations have developed further because of Taiwan's position in a globalizing world. Unlike NGOs in China devoted to social welfare and education, which often have to rely on foreign financial support to do their work and often incur the suspicion of government for that reason, Taiwan's philanthropic organizations are home grown. Instead of receiving money from abroad, they give money and volunteer aid to people in need around the world, for example, victims of the Southeast Asian tsunami or Hurricane Katrina in 2005.

It is remarkable how many of the religiously based philanthropic organizations—including Taoists and some Christians as well as Buddhists—tend to explain their activities in this world in terms of a Confucian social ethic—but not, as in China, an ethic based an authoritarian state Confucianism. Rather it is a humanistic Confucian vision stressing the value of mutual responsibility found in the book of Mencius. When expressing their social vision, they rely heavily on the metaphor of the family—even a community of strangers can be thought of as a big family, the nation is a family, the world is a family. Imagining the interdependent family rather than the rights-bearing individual as the main component of the social world leads to a vision of mutual responsibility and trust.[19]

The Ministry of Foreign Affairs book on Taiwan's NGOs speaks of the mission of such philanthropic organizations in tones colored with Confucian notions of reciprocity:

> Following World War II . . . the country relied on humanitarian aid from western Christian organizations, which donated food, established orphanages and hospitals, and helped eradicate infectious diseases. Hard times are a thing of the past and Taiwan has been able to help other countries, dispatching emergency relief teams and volunteers in times of natural disasters or providing material, medical and educational assistance in economically disadvantaged regions of Africa, Southeast Asia, Mongolia and South America.[20]

Besides such Confucian moral sentiments, however, the encouragement of such philanthropic organizations is also motivated by pragmatic political purposes. Such organizations project an image of Taiwan's generosity to the global community and in turn earn a significant amount of international goodwill for Taiwan—goodwill that a vulnerable Taiwan greatly needs. This ability to attract international goodwill in turn increases the support of such organizations among the population of Taiwan.

In contrast, some of Taiwan's social movement organizations are more dependent for ideas and even for material support from foreign organizations, such as environmental, labor, or human rights organizations. This may actually put a check on their ability to expand their influence in Taiwan.

Meanwhile, in 2000 the Taiwan government set up an NGO Affairs Committee, not to control NGOs, but to coordinate their activities, help them develop more professional forms of management, and enable them to network more fully with international counterparts. This step encourages the development of those bridging philanthropic social welfare organizations that we have claimed help to soften some of the harshness of a demanding civil society.[21]

Out of an authoritarian government, Taiwan has therefore developed an extremely lively and open civil society. The explosive potential of Taiwan's social movements is more destabilizing than such movements in strongly institutionalized democracies such as the United States. On the other hand, Taiwan's society has nurtured social organizations that generate a great deal of bridging social capital and contribute to social harmony. Taiwan's authoritarian government was wise enough, or lucky enough, to foster the development of such groups before the end of martial law and to co-opt them to the work of harmonizing society. The groups would never have gained the degree of public legitimacy and popular support that they have today, however, if they had been perceived as simply privileged agents of the government. It was important that their membership was based on voluntary commitment and that their leadership freely accepted government invitations for cooperation.

China

In China, since the beginning of the reform era in 1979, a steadily expanding market economy has led to increasing opportunities for citizens to associate freely together. There are now millions of associations of all kinds—commercial, educational, religious, philanthropic, recreational, environmental. The government's inability to deliver needed social services has led to procedures for the formal organization of nonprofit organizations (NPOs) and NGOs. Continuing need for foreign development assistance has also opened a space for international nongovernmental organizations (INGOs).

The proliferation of such forms of a nascent civil society causes real dangers, however—dangers not just to the regime but also to social stability. Some commercial organizations help the rich to get richer and to swindle the poor. Partly because of a legacy of repression, some religious organizations take sectarian forms: they are hostile to the government and hostile to religious rivals. Some groups are potential or real channels for expressing resurgent ethnic identities, whether of national minorities or of Muslims or Tibetans. A pervasive culture of cynicism—itself a legacy of decades of political repression and national trauma—makes it difficult for many groups to see themselves as vehicles for anything but the pursuit of narrow self-interest. Lack of members trained in methods for group management leaves many groups vulnerable to mismanagement. International NGOs sometimes have hidden agendas, pursued with cultural insensitivity and the arrogance of power, that could threaten the Chinese social order.

The Chinese government's response to this has drawn predominantly from its Marxist-Leninist tradition, with Chinese cultural characteristics, mostly based on the East Asian legalist tradition. The attitude is to see civil society as a danger to be solved through political control. During the Maoist era, following Marxist-Leninist principles, the government suppressed all forms of independent social organization and then attempted to fill the gap by providing health and welfare and even quasi-religious services through state bureaucracies and through "mass organizations" organized and controlled by the government. Now, in the reform era, it lacks the means completely to suppress such groups, but it still tries to apply the old methods to keep them under control. All "social organizations" have to be registered with an appropriate government agency or "mass organization." This registration subjects them to official surveillance and control. Organizations that accept such arrangements are often rightly called government organized NGOs (GONGOs). Groups that do not register are subject to suppression by the police, although they can sometimes evade such suppression if they keep a low profile or take advantage of the ineptitude and corruption of the public security forces.

The most authentically voluntary of the new forms of association in China's mobile, market-driven society are those that are informally organized—no membership lists, no fixed constitution, no registration with the government, and no legal protection. Quasi-religious organizations such as the Falungong underwent an explosive growth before provoking the government's all-out campaigns of suppression.[22] Even though the government may have succeeded in decimating Falungong within China, it has not been able to stamp out the wide array of groups with a moral-religious orientation that spread through loose networks inspired by charismatic leadership. Pentecostal Christian networks, for example, have undergone an exponential growth since the early 1980s.[23] Both Falungong and Pentecostal networks exhibit millenarian tendencies and prophesy cataclysmic upheavals that will suddenly bring this corrupt world to an end.

Networks of secular activists committed to redressing the grievances of people victimized by official corruption or government indifference have also grown, despite government efforts at suppression, as have criminal organizations for human trafficking, drug smuggling, and promotion of the sex trade. Some of the most dynamic associations in China are just outside of the government's control and have an oppositional attitude toward authority. If the authoritarian government were to weaken, the result might be an extraordinarily demanding civil society, a society convulsed by social movements more disruptive than those experienced in Taiwan. The prospects for a smooth transition to democracy in China would seem to depend on the presence of harmonizing, bridging voluntary associations that could provide a spirit of reconciliation and responsibility to balance the inevitable and necessary spirit of criticism and promotion of individual and group rights. But although the Chinese government now considers itself on a mission to promote a "harmonious society," it has not yet done much to promote the development of harmonizing voluntary associations.

Some influential Chinese are advocating for a rule of law that would institutionalize a stable space of liberty for social organizations and protect them from arbitrary government interference.[24] It will still be some time before this is accomplished. The approach of the Chinese Communist Party and the government toward the rule of law is ever more deeply colored with the values of the legalist tradition, in which a ruler does not submit to a rule of law that guarantees rights to ruler and subject alike but rather uses regulations to keep the populace under control and can change the regulations at any time necessary to maintain the ruler's power.

Though still employing some Leninist methods, albeit in weakened form, the government can hardly justify its attempted control over civil society in classical Marxist terms. It has, after all, presided over the development of one of the greatest rates of income inequality in the industrialized world. So the justification is increasingly corporatist: a strong state is necessary to prevent social chaos, to coordinate the various social groups so that they work for the common good, and of course to keep them from being infiltrated by foreign enemies of China.[25] Appeals to national pride and patriotism aim to generate some of the moral commitment to the common good that one associates with the civic republican tradition. This too is beginning to be flavored with another strand of East Asian culture, interpreted so as to emphasize respect for authority and suppression of self-interest in the name of a "harmonious society."

Comparisons

There are certain features of these recent developments in China that remind one of the early stages of social organization development in Taiwan in the late 1960s and early 1970s. The mobility of a dynamic market economy is providing opportunities for new forms of voluntary association, many of them informally organized to avoid control by a suspicious government. These groups are addressing emerging social needs, such as needs for mutual support and economic security, that the government can no longer effectively address. Sometimes the government suppresses groups that become too prominent or whose activities seem too challenging. Groups that are relatively small and that do not seem threatening to local or national authorities may experience benign neglect. The Taiwan case suggests that such groups, growing up like wildflowers within the cracks of an authoritarian political system, can provide the seeds of a self-governing civil society.

The Taiwan case suggests also that such groups may be hard to study. They are effective in the early stages of the development of a civil society precisely because they escape the attention of the government—and therefore probably also the attention of outside researchers. Therefore, we can only offer speculative scenarios about their future development. I will first offer a positive scenario and then a negative one.

The positive scenario is that even though such groups become independent from the state, they do not become actively hostile toward the state. Although the government's all-too-frequent arbitrary interference with such groups could provoke them to take up an anarchist path, they retain a respect for authority derived from Confucian cultural traditions, which leads many of them to cooperate with the government voluntarily to maintain social order while pushing constructively for policy changes. As the government's capacities for social control further weaken and as new, more belligerent groups arise to express social grievances, some of the earlier, order-seeking groups also grow to the point where they provide enough social solidarity and promote enough social reconciliation to keep the inevitable social turbulence from descending into chaos. This generates enough public confidence in citizens' capacity to solve their own problems to continue supporting a democratic transition. Although there is a grand "blooming and contending" period in which many schools of political thought flourish and compete in the public arena, nationalistic impulses give an edge to modern adaptations of indigenous public philosophies that favor social persuasion, consensus, and harmony. This leads to a shaky, but gradually stabilizing democracy with a corporatist cast.

A negative scenario is that 50 years of cruel and often incompetent rule by a quasi-Leninist state have generated a much deeper bitterness and much more distrust for authority than was present during early stages of democratic transition in Taiwan. In particular, the Tiananmen crackdown on June 4, 1989, revived and prolonged memories of social chaos and government repression that had begun to fade in the generation after the Cultural Revolution. The intensity of social conflict is increased by the high levels of income polarization and the blatant political corruption that have accompanied the Chinese version of market reforms in the early twenty-first century. Unlike in Taiwan, where many incipient social organizations were nurtured by an irenic version of Confucian cultural traditions, many groups in China become carriers of millenarian, anarchic strands in the Chinese tradition, which once inspired movements such as the White Lotus or Taipings and were revived and translated into Marxist garb during the Great Leap Forward and the Cultural Revolution. Such problems are exacerbated by bad leadership, and China explodes into chaos as the state loses its grip.

It seems likely that the Chinese state will eventually lose its grip. Even if, as Robert Weller suggests in Chapter 6, it is possible to introduce considerable resilience into an authoritarian state, the societal complexity that inevitably comes with deepening connections to globalized communication and commerce will probably strain the limits of any kind of a centralized, one-party state. Which of the above scenarios follows the loss of control will depend in part on measures that government leaders take now to foster a responsible civil society. If they encourage the continued development of social organizations that have already begun to form independently and if they foster a mutually respectful spirit of partnership with such groups, they may send China down a Taiwanese-style path toward a viable, if inevitably shaky, democracy.

Notes

1. The development of this theoretical formulation was helped by the incisive comments of Tom Gold and Chang Mau-kuei on an earlier version of this chapter.
2. Gellner 1994.
3. Walder 1986.
4. NGO Affairs Committee 2006.
5. Saich 2000; Zhang 1995; Weller 1999; Fan 2003.
6. Chambers and Kymlicka 2002; Rosenblum and Post 2002; Madsen and Strong 2003.
7. Tocqueville 2000, v. 1 128; v. 2 247.
8. Putnam 2000, 20–24.
9. Gold 1987; Rigger 1999; Madsen 2007.

10. Hsiao 1993.
11. Rigger 2001.
12. Hsiao 1995a.
13. Ibid., 239.
14. NGO Affairs Committee 2006.
15. Madsen 2007.
16. Huang and Weller 1998; Chandler 2004; Laliberté 2004.
17. Hsiao, ed. 1993.
18. Chen Shui-bian 2000.
19. Madsen 2002; de Bary 1998.
20. NGO Affairs Committee 2006, 64.
21. Ibid., 42–60.
22. Nancy Chen 2003; Thornton 2003.
23. Aikman 2003.
24. Pei 2003.
25. Unger and Chan 1995.

5

Business Groups:
For or Against the Regime?

Dorothy J. Solinger

Conventional modernization theory finds a link among economic growth, the emergence of a bourgeoisie or a middle class, and demands for democracy. Both Taiwan—over the decades from the 1950s through the 1980s—and China after 1980 experienced such growth; both also witnessed the appearance of a newly moneyed class in the wake of developmental change. But can we extrapolate from Taiwan's subsequent democratization that China's authoritarian polity will soon likewise succumb to similar pleas? My claim in this chapter is the following: the case of Taiwan does fit the theory, whereas the Chinese one, so far at any rate, does not. I focus specifically upon the political stances and roles of one particular segment of the middle class in these two societies, that is, the one involved in business.

In Taiwan, though the principal promoters of political transformation were intellectuals, there is evidence that owners of small- and medium-sized businesses stood behind and financed their efforts; in China, conversely, to date the research we have suggests that this is not likely to be the case.[1] A close look at these two cases, moreover, does not just distinguish between them but also offers refinements to the popular prognostication. To support these claims, I will point to the disparate sociopolitical histories and the cultural and economic factors that bear on these cases, all placed within the context of each regime's larger goals and its consequent treatment of the aspiring business sector in the two places (regime aims and behaviors). The comparison is a structured one, in that we have here divergent outcomes in two locales that, at least on the surface, had much in common in the past.

I will argue that the loyalties, allegiances, and grievances/resentments of businesspeople toward their governments can predict their stances toward regime change and democratization in their own polities and, further, that these affective commitments can be modeled as a function of the aims and behaviors of the two regimes, as these regime attributes have affected busi-

95

nesspeople. Thus, stated most simply, my guiding hypothesis is the following: The nature of the social connections (or alliances, or relations of co-optation) that members of a bourgeoisie have experienced with their regime—what is popularly termed in China as their *guanxi*—provides the most succinct and parsimonious explanation for businesspeople's role in the movement toward new forms of governance in China and Taiwan. The key factor in the opportunity for democratization to unfold in both places is capitalists' contacts. Which contact mattered most to them as they launched and developed their firms and their ventures was what counted.

I should emphasize here that I am situating capitalists' concerns within a framework that forefronts their material interests and not their specific ideological preferences for regime type. This approach is necessary for me as I have no access at this point to surveys of the political value preferences of people who were involved in business in the 1970s and 1980s in Taiwan; where possible, I will draw on work of others who have done surveys of these attitudes in China, but, to keep the analysis of the two places roughly comparable, I will draw mainly on material issues. Also, there are divisions within any group of businesspeople, and in neither country did (or do) all capitalists of all sizes (from large-scale to petty) adopt the same political position. Certainly capitalists are not all of a kind, and significant differentiation within the category can have real implications for regime perceptions of and treatment toward them,[2] and, in turn, for the capitalists' views of the state. But a case can be made that by the mid-1980s enough capitalists were disposed to assist in unseating authoritarian rule in Taiwan to bolster the likelihood of that event. This was not the situation in China in the early 2000s.

Theoretical Considerations

Social scientific predictions about the prospects for democratization in authoritarian regimes have often harked back to Barrington Moore and Samuel P. Huntington, both of whom target the business-related portion of the middle class as pivotal to the process. Moore's most regularly cited contribution has been his noted observation, "no bourgeois, no democracy"; he has also asserted that "the bourgeoisie . . . lurks in the wings as the chief actor in the drama [of democratization]." This judgment holds for Moore most notably for the initiation of parliamentary democracy: "An independent class of town dwellers has been an indispensable element in the growth of parliamentary democracy."[3] In the years since Moore composed these thoughts, the installation of an elective legislature has been judged to be an indispensable feature of what is held to be a democratic regime. Huntington has also referred to the business sector as a critical advocate of democracy. In this regard, he has pointed out that "in every society affected by social change, new groups arise to participate in politics";[4] under conditions of economic development and industrialization, an enlargement of a middle class is stimulated, a social category whose components, he holds, become "the most active supporters of democratization."[5]

Huntington's and Moore's analyses about the bourgeoisie as a prerequisite for democratic development have not gone unchallenged, however.[6] But whether they are correct or not, Moore, for one, did not write that every instance in which a bourgeoisie exists is one in which its members will agitate on behalf of and further the introduction of democracy. Rather, Moore proposed that this class was a necessary condition, but not a sufficient one, and that it was not poised to push events along a linear path toward democracy in every case.[7]

I submit that the part played by capitalists in the two societies of concern in this book depends upon the type of *guanxi* (or social connections) upon which these actors have been forced to, and have grown to, rely: Have they been able to work successfully with the current state to do their business, or have they had to turn elsewhere—to social forces outside the state—for backing? Related to this is that the nature and style of interaction that exists between a given regime and its businesspeople need to be examined. This relationship, in turn, is a function of a regime's political goals and its corresponding economic developmental strategy, as seen in the politics of a state's property ownership, plus its class and ethnicity policies. All of these more specific features and projects had and have a great deal to do with outcomes in the China and Taiwan cases, respectively, as we will see.

Huntington has speculated that the response of a regime to its business class, especially to one newly on the rise, is apt to be wary. He warned that in "exclusionary one-Party systems" (a type of regime in which "the Party maintains its monopoly over the political system by limiting the scope of political participation," a label that fits both Taiwan before democratization and the PRC today), the regime will be prone to view a set of people whose wealth has recently increased as a likely menace: "The principal threat to the maintenance of [the system]," he wrote, "comes from the diversification of the elite resulting from the rise of new groups controlling *autonomous* sources of economic power, that is, from the development of an *independently wealthy* business and industrial middle class" (emphasis added, to make a point I will stress as I proceed).[8] Depending upon how rulers choose to handle the moneyed class, the latter will or will not be in a position to build up significant ties with the regime. So I posit the business class as ultimately reactive in its relations with the state.

Huntington's statement alerts us to the importance of asking two questions relevant to business-state connections that have implications for business's bias toward regime change. The first one is: Just how "autonomous" were and are the "sources of economic power" of this portion of the middle class prior to democratization in the locales of our concern here? Second, how will "the system" under review (or, more properly speaking, its elite) elect to respond to the potential challenge posed by these people? Indeed, the polity's reaction to this social force should be a topic for inquiry, not a matter of certainty. Threatened top politicians can meet this challenge in a number of ways, as Bruce Dickson has shown, from complete rejection and exclusion to forms of co-optation and inclusion—from treating businesspeople as outsiders to seeing them as a partner in building up wealth.[9] Where state co-optation of and support for businesspeople have been the mode of response, the capital comprising the ventures in question cannot be considered to be "independent."

The second inquiry, about reactions from above, can benefit from the insight of Charles E. Lindblom that "any government official who understands the requirements of his position and the responsibilities that market-oriented systems throw on businessmen will . . . grant [businessmen] a privileged position."[10] True, during the time when the two states were not democratic, it would be quite inaccurate to label their "systems" pure market ones. But certainly both were "market-oriented" during the years following the early 1980s. Lindblom's reminder is that in general politicians governing a market economy do require the cooperation of capitalists to bolster their rule. The disagreement among scholars over how political leaders might perceive the existence (or, in a newly marketized economy, the advent) of a bourgeoisie—as a threat and adversary, à la Huntington, or as a necessary ally, as per Lindblom—also skirts over the critical issue noted above of the diversity among the businesspeople in any one context. All of these considerations have a bearing on the repercussions that the presence of a bourgeoisie might have for political change.

To summarize, the critical items here are these: the conditions under which a business class is apt to agitate for democracy, the factors that shape a regime's reactions to the existence of businesspeople within its borders, the degree of autonomy from the regime of the economic resources of the moneyed class (or particular sections within it), the relation of economic resources to power in different places, and the extent to which subdivisions (and subdivisions of what sort) within any given capitalist class might have a critical bearing on the interaction between these different subdivisions and the political leadership.

A key to answering these queries is to bring the phenomenon of *guanxi,* the Chinese term connoting social connections, into the equation. According to Mayfair Mei-hui Yang, the term (at least in China) refers to the cultivation of personal relationships and "the binding power and emotional and ethical qualities of personal relationships," including the "obligation to give, receive, and repay."[11] Similarly, for Gary G. Hamilton, the term pertains to "certain sets of ties that are bound by norms of reciprocity." "Most anthropologists and sociologists of Chinese society," he relates, "argue that *guanxi,* which includes relations and relation building, lies at the heart of Chinese society."[12] Certainly, however, these formulations could have broader applications, beyond just the case of China and its style of personal connections, for patron-client–style linkages between business and the state operate globally.

Entailed in the notion of *guanxi* are "networks of mutual dependence" and a corresponding indebtedness. The personal relationships so nurtured are "based implicitly on mutual interest and benefit, and on an expectation that a favor entails a debt to be repaid; they have a binding power and primacy," Yang explains.[13] The phenomenon of committed personal ties of this sort can assist in analyzing the variable linkages between regime and bourgeoisie that obtained in predemocratic days in each of the two polities, and, my argument goes, this type of tie also structured (in Taiwan) and continues to structure (in China) the stances of these classes toward regime change.

The definitions laid out above suggest that the concept of *guanxi* contains within itself the possibility of several oppositions, depending upon its presence or its absence between any two parties (with "parties" understood collectively, such as "the state" and "the bourgeoisie"). For example, in the grammar of *guanxi,* where there is indebtedness, there should be loyalty, and the converse will apply as well; where there are debts incurred, there should not be antagonistic demands. But where there are no debts, such demands may well surface. Moreover, where there have been courtesies and assistance, there should be gratitude; but where there has been none (or, worse yet, where there have been slights and rejection), then grievances, and the potential for opposition, are in order.

Stretching the concept further, within a *guanxi*-governed society, not only gratefulness but also dependency often accompanies indebtedness, whereas autonomy creates space for opposition. The upshot of these propositions is that those who have been beneficiaries—who have ties of *guanxi* with the governors—will tend to feel indebted and thus to act loyally, and so are less apt to call for change, more apt to favor the preservation of the status quo to which they see their own fate (and their privileges within it) as bound. Those who have been neglected or ignored—or even wronged—are, conversely, prone to be proponents of change. And, finally, from the regime's perspective, those who have been patronized can be a source of cooperation, whereas those who are estranged can become a threat. These alternatives are pregnant with implications for the postures toward politics and regime transition entertained by the purveyors of private capital in the PRC (in the present) and in Taiwan (in the past).

In what follows, I start with some similarities and differences between pre-1986 Taiwan and today's China, in order to justify and qualify the comparisons that will follow. Next, I set out several considerations about each regime and its capitalists, in accord with the framework and propositions offered above. First, I look at the goals and behaviors of each polity (and the transformations in these goals over time). Second, I review these two states' treatment of these people in their predemocracy days. Third, I reflect upon the ethnic and class origins of each bourgeoisie. These factors each had important conditioning effects on the type of relationships—and the presence or absence of *guanxi* in them—that unfolded over time between state and bourgeoisie in each location and, in turn, on the consequences for democratization, whether realized (in Taiwan) or theorized (in China). I assess these effects in my last section.

Similarities and Differences

The states both in post-Mao, "reform"-era, China and in pre-1980 Taiwan can fairly be labeled authoritarian regimes, ruled variably dictatorially by a single, Leninist-type political party. In both cases, the party brooked little if any freedom of speech while making wide use of censorship. Also in both, there was no space for the autonomous organization of private interests, as the empowered party aspired to penetrate social groups of all colors. Where corporatism and transmission-belt management were not employed to rein in nonstate communal entities, these regimes endeavored either to repress or to co-opt the members.[14]

Another factor here is something that Chu Yun-han has written of Taiwan in these years, that is, that the party there governed through an "authoritarian equilibrium" that "depended on prosperity"; these words could just as well have been penned in description of its neighbor to the north after 1980.[15] As for economic policy, again there were marked parallel features. In both, state ownership was prominent, and small business stood at a disadvantage, since governmental generosity was bestowed only upon the larger firms, especially those in the possession of the party or the government.[16] In neither case did the owners of the smaller enterprises find it easy to acquire loans from the big banks that operated under the aegis of the state.[17] Both places also continue up to the present to operate with some reference to the Confucian-based principle of *guanxi* and the mutual obligation it entails.

Perhaps most centrally for the purposes of this chapter, both places experienced phenomenal state-led industrialization and modernization—in Taiwan especially from the 1960s through the 1980s, and in China in the 1980s up through the present.[18] And also in both, one outcome of that growth was the birth or rebirth of what could be called a middle class.[19] Whereas in Taiwan in 1949 there has been said to have been only a tiny middle class following the 1895–1945 Japanese occupation,[20] by the late 1980s, somewhere between 25 and 40 percent of the population could be counted as belonging to that category. A recent study of China gives a figure of 35 percent for the early twenty-first century.[21] For Taiwan, a number of analysts link the rise of such a sector within the population to the appearance of democratization.[22] These various similarities justify the comparison between two political entities, both of which govern societies where Confucian values, and consequently traditional notions of *guanxi,* influence the populace. The similarities lay the groundwork for my extension of an insight about Taiwan's bourgeoisie to a prediction about China's.

Yet the differences between the two sites are also pertinent to the story at hand. The most prominent is that, regardless of its hefty share of productive assets, the Republic of China/Kuomintang regime managed an economy that was essentially capitalist. In contrast, after 1979 the PRC's economy was in transition from a socialist, planned economy, and only progressively acquired more and more capitalist elements through the 1980s and 1990s.[23] This means that private business existed in Taiwan for nearly four decades before the breakthrough to democracy occurred, whereas in China private business only gradually achieved the right to operate openly after 1979. For a period in the 1980s it was still officially ideologically suspect, which it again became for a few years after 1989. A second major difference is that the two governments ruled under quite dissimilar external circumstances. In Taiwan, US pressure, with which Taiwan was forced to comply, in light of its heavy dependence on US approval for its weapons supply, market access, and indeed, its very survival,[24] pushed for the existence of a private sector from the start. To the contrary, leaders in China were in no sense beholden to the United States and could select any developmental model they wished.

Third, and most critical, the KMT on Taiwan was ruling the island as outsiders, initially comprising Chinese who arrived there in the late 1940s from China, in a society that considered itself "Taiwanese." What was perceived by the "natives" as an ethnic split became a crucial divide within the business sector in Taiwan, one that mirrored the most flagrant political split within the populace. This ethnic cleavage was a division between the large businesses (mostly either mainland-originated or state-run [read KMT-run]) and the private-sectoral small and medium enterprises (SMEs) (generally Taiwan-owned firms). From my perspective, the most telling tidbit on this theme is provided by Alexander Ya-li Lu, who, writing in the early 1990s, distinguishes an older from a "new" middle class. He holds that the latter group, which comprised intellectuals, professionals, and businesspeople, was the source of both the main members and the activists of the *dangwai,* or opposition movement, and that the majority of the members of this group were of Taiwanese origin.[25] Along this line, in the words of a recent author, the state in Taiwan practiced "coercion and manipulation of the private sector,[26] especially *insofar as its owners were Taiwanese*" (emphasis added).

These insights inform my contention that the "middle class" or, for the purpose of this chapter, the portion of it known as the "bourgeoisie," needs to be disaggregated for political analysis. Correspondingly, such disaggregation is necessary too for my claim that the nature of this part of the middle class's relation to the regime—and therefore its stance toward regime change—may have to do with the specific treatment that group has received from the regime. This variable—in contrast to the rise in income and education that characterized all businesspeople in Taiwan over time—leads me to a more nuanced explanation of the connections between class and political support for or against the regime and, accordingly, for or against regime change.

In China, there neither is nor has there been any such ethnically based separation of any political significance among businesses. On the other hand, vestiges of the former socialist system have fostered *ownership/class-based* distinctions (i.e., small firms tend to be the creations of farmers or previous outcasts such as ex-prisoners, whereas bigger ones often got their start with help from or even leadership by state or party officials) that continue to carve up the capitalists. The Taiwanese state purposefully excluded most Taiwanese entrepreneurs and limited the scale of their ventures, planting the seeds of grievance and anger for decades. In China, alternatively, those with close connections with the state (its officials, its enterprises) prospered, such that an expanding number of those in business could promote their activities unimpeded and even encouraged. The following sections explore these differences in more depth.

State Behavior

In this section, I trace the regime goals and behavior toward entrepreneurs over time in both places. In the following section, I will lay out the origins and composition of the businesspeople in each place, setting the stage for the last section, in which I draw conclusions about the political stances of each set of capitalists in each country, as a function of those goals, behaviors, and types of businesspeople.

When the KMT government first reclaimed and then retreated to the island of Taiwan after 1945, it encountered an alien population, one composed mainly of Chinese people from China's southeast whose ancestors had migrated there over the past several centuries but who—chiefly because of the prior, 50-year colonial overlordship of Japan—had developed a separate identity as "Taiwanese," not just as "Chinese" people. The bifurcation this engendered between two subethnicities within the Han group was only exacerbated by rapacious and violent behavior toward the Taiwanese on the part of the incoming KMT.

Aware that their regime was that of a set of conquering outsiders and that it was, accordingly, weak on legitimacy, the newcomers were desperate to keep down the natives in the hope of preventing or eliminating potential opposition. They therefore worked to attain the following aims: to obstruct any economic rivalry from the locals; to make the economy thrive through their own efforts; and to ensure the security and survival of their own rule.[27] The KMT also prioritized a vibrant economy so that its output would undergird the political project of recovering China.[28] As just stated, an important effect of Nationalist strategy—especially when combined with the KMT's various measures to limit the size of the small Taiwanese firms (to be discussed later)—was to draw a line in the sand between local and outsider/state firms, for the most part privileging the latter and antagonizing the former.[29] Michael Hsin-huang Hsiao remarks on there "always" having been ethnic tension between the KMT state and Taiwanese businesses.[30]

In China after 1978, in the aftermath of the death of the omnipotent Mao Zedong, the situation was similar, yet different in significant ways. There the post-Mao political elite was also bent on (re)constituting authority and bolstering its legitimacy; the recent past there, however, was one in which China's own leaders (not Japanese officials or KMT carpetbaggers) had pretty much alienated the population as a whole with the ravages of the Cultural Revolution, which had just been brought to a halt. For these leaders, there was no question of barring any specific subgroup from participation in its hell-bent drive to boost productivity, jack up the economy, expand jobs, and improve living standards, for the elite was straining mightily to elevate China's national stature and, just as important, to recapture the hearts of the populace.[31] A strong economy could only bolster the chances for these outcomes.

To these ends, the regime resurrected private business as early as 1979,[32] and by early 1984 was recognizing the value of this activity publicly in a central party document.[33] In 1987, the leadership conferred a grant of official legitimacy on private entrepreneurship,[34] and in the following year, Article 11 of the state constitution of 1982 was amended to permit the private sector "to exist and develop within the limits prescribed by law." In 1999, the same article was again updated to read that "the non-public sector of the economy comprising self-employed and private businesses within the domain stipulated by law is an important component of the country's socialist market economy," adding that "the state protects the legitimate rights and interests of the self-employed and private businesses." In March 2004, the constitution was once more revised to include protections for private property, stating that it was to be elevated to an "equal footing with public property."[35]

On many occasions, the party repeatedly affirmed its overriding priority of economic growth, development, and abundance.[36] As Bruce Dickson has astutely described the situation, as the party's mission shifted in late 1978 from revolution to the task of bolstering "socialist economic modernization," people engaged in business were increasingly protected and even courted, as he phrased it, both "to promote the Party's agenda" and to "prevent . . . a challenge to the state."[37] In light of this objective, in July 2001, then party chief Jiang Zemin proposed removing the prohibition against admitting entrepreneurs into the Communist Party, a ban that had been formally in force since 1989 but often honored only in the breach, in any event.[38] This bid served as an offshoot of Jiang's Theory of the Three Represents, an indirect offer of inclusion to various social forces traditionally ranked outside the party's past constituencies, especially businesspeople.[39] True, these formal bows to the bourgeoisie amounted to a tacit acknowledgment that their political status had remained suspect at least into the early 1990s. But even the smaller fry were thriving by then.

In addition to admitting entrepreneurs into the party and creating an environment in which even party members themselves felt free to go into business (*xiahai*)[40]—a trend that picked up considerable speed in and after the early 1990s—in recent years the party has advanced various policies whose effect has been to raise the incomes and improve the lifestyles of a new "middle" segment of society that includes professionals, private entrepreneurs, and state bureaucrats. Behind these steps are the state's hopes of forming a high-consumption component of the population whose buying will invigorate the national economy. Among these moves has been a series of salary increases, along with a program that endowed state firm employees (and other elements of the new middle class who are connected to the state and public employment) with an opportunity to purchase their own housing at very low rates.[41] By the middle of the first decade of the twenty-first century, it was possible for Scott Kennedy to judge—after hundreds of hours of interviews with businesspeople—that these individuals enjoyed "shared goals" with the state; David Goodman similarly speaks of a "community of interest" between the middle class and the party-state.[42]

In sum, both states had issues of legitimacy to deal with, the KMT in 1949 and the CCP after 1978. Both, in the interest of attaining such legitimacy, also chose to enhance their economic prowess, not only in the eyes of their own populaces but also in the international arena. Clearly, for both regimes this would entail taking a position toward the sectors of society poised to contribute economically, and for both this would mean some form of management of groups that the government had more or less marked as outsiders.

Despite similar goals, when it came to these governments' practical stances toward the businesses within their realms, they made different choices. The KMT viewed this as a question of grappling with a populace ethnically distinct from the one that the party itself represented and, consequently, one that could be threatening, from the rulers' perspective. For the CCP, however—which by 1978 had long been dominant and effectively unassailable—it was a matter of simply reversing its prior class standpoint, along with its definition of its foundation ideology of socialism (so that state ownership was no longer to be a necessary feature of that ideology), a new posture it began by 1979 but that took some years to consolidate.

It is possible to cast these respective state choices in the form of a broad contrast: the KMT elected to handle its legitimacy problem by keeping the native Taiwanese at a distance, for the most part, despite some softening of its stance over time, in what amounted to a generally *exclusionary* strategy. So native Taiwanese firms were left out, even as the regime nurtured big business, most of which its own mainlander colleagues monopolized. The CCP, on the other hand, opted after 1979 to enhance its legitimacy by gradually broadening its class base, in particular, by enforcing a project of *inclusion* over time, insofar as the bourgeoisie as a whole was involved. I go on to elucidate this contrast in more detail.

Through what specific policies and measures did these states, respectively, essay to exclude or include their more moneyed citizens in the pursuit of the aims specified above? To answer the question for Taiwan requires going back in time to the late 1940s, when the KMT state was just beginning to entrench itself on the island. In the first days of its rule, the KMT confiscated 1,259 units of so-called enemy enterprise property, which comprised strategically vital financial, transportation, basic utility, and manufacturing assets.[43] As many as 85 Taiwanese industrial firms were also grabbed up by the KMT in the five years between 1945 and 1950.[44]

In the course of these takeovers, local employees were dismissed, and such rancor was engendered by the process as a whole that one of the demands in the famous February 1947 Taiwanese protest movement was for the right to manage public utilities.[45] Meanwhile, mainland-originated capitalists were allocated government resources on the basis of connections established before migrating to the island.[46] Both in the early years when import substitution was emphasized and US aid was generous, and continuing over time, mainlander enterprises got preferential treatment in the regime's economic development strategy.[47] Some 45 years after the installation of the KMT regime on the island, Chu Yun-han was able to term the extent of state assets "huge."[48] Other writers in Taiwan have speculated that two of the chief aims behind these moves were to provide the KMT with autonomy from local society as well as to endow the party with the necessary financial and economic resources to dominate the Taiwanese.[49]

Even in the 1970s, when the KMT leadership was once again struggling to sustain its legitimacy in the wake of its expulsion from the United Nations and the United States' initiation of proto-diplomatic dealings with the PRC—a time when the KMT-led regime began to incorporate Taiwanese people into the party and even to place them in positions within the government—state firms were granted the principal part in major industrial projects, a choice Hsiao maintains was made in order to enhance and sustain the weight of the state-controlled sector. The only opening to the Taiwanese at the time was what has been cast as a ploy to co-opt them through joint investments, plus offering some of them slots on the governing boards of business organizations.[50]

Beyond specifically privileging mainland Chinese and party-affiliated firms, in the view of its critics the KMT also posed barriers that—intentionally or otherwise—acted to limit the growth of private, especially Taiwanese, firms.[51] The small and medium enterprises that the Taiwanese tended to operate and own received scant support from the state; besides, they failed to qualify for state-proffered incentives available just to larger firms.[52] The upshot was to marginalize the native enterprises, keeping them either small or only medium in size.[53] Even when Taiwanese people were admitted into the state economic bureaucracy, Chu notes that they were not in positions that would enable them to handle top-priority policy matters and, what was even worse, were put under close scrutiny, in order to ensure that they did not favor the local private sector.[54] Chu also tells of how the larger, state-connected firms engaged in collusive pricing, which hurt the business of the smaller downstream firms.[55]

These various restrictions to which they were subjected effectively prevented locals from entering the manufacturing sector.[56] The final insult was an imaginary line that cut up the populace ethnically, blocking native people from participating in national politics until the 1970s.[57] This ostracism extended to a refusal on the part of the rulers to incorporate Taiwanese businesspeople's views on policy.[58] In short, in the words of Shiau Chyuan-jenq, "before the mid-1980s, the authoritarian state was powerful enough to retain the upper hand with the business community."[59]

Lacking ties to the ruling party or even to influential channels within the government, the small and medium firms, virtually all of which were Taiwanese-owned, were cast back upon their own personal *guanxi* for capital and other resources and for business networks.[60] Indeed, Gary Hamilton has called Taiwan's a "networked economy" and described what occurs there as a "*guanxi* capitalism";[61] Susan Greenhalgh went so far as to elaborate a model in which "family networks undergird the economy."[62] In the early 1980s, she avers, as many as 97 percent of private industrial firms were structured around families;[63] moreover, she noted at that time, "being Taiwanese" meant that to climb socially and economically it was imperative to draw on family, community, and religious ties.[64] Chu Yun-han found it possible to make the same claim a decade later, pointing as well to the lack of lineage bonds between the native Taiwanese and the power-wielding mainland Chinese that obtained as of the early 1990s.[65] Certainly this relegation to the outside left its sourness among the entrepreneurs who were left out, even as they managed to thrive on their own.[66] This meant that the key to the commercial success of these native firms was their own, nonstate connections, their friends and relatives, and various sorts of "curb-side" or other forms of informal money markets.[67]

In China, to the contrary, though the smallest firms also struggled in a netherworld of bureaucratic predation[68] and an absence of official protection or financing once they were resanctioned after 1979, any capitalist venture, however petty, that was founded by or supported by CCP officials—or by someone with good *guanxi* with party or state officials—routinely became the recipient of an array of rewards and facilitations that smoothed the way toward business success. These benefits could range from access to necessary raw materials, to licenses, or to bank credit.[69] With time, the members of the local bourgeoisie were often courted by petty bureaucrats and officials and admitted into the party itself if they were not already party members, their firms sometimes also absorbed by grassroots governments or their personnel.[70] And already in the 1980s private business in the rural areas expanded its opportunities by building ties with officialdom,[71] or, often, by donning a so-called red hat, that is, hiding its true private essence by arranging with cadres to register as "collective."[72] Such cadres had a clear incentive to take them in, for this increased the chance that the locality could meet or surpass its quota for rapid growth.[73]

By early 1990, it was already possible to speak of the two sides—bureaucrats and businesspeople—as "symbiotic," a description that only grew more and more appropriate with time.[74] By the early 2000s, managers and operators of large firms were involved in direct interaction with government officials in the central government on policy germane to their enterprises, and their organizations—even if created, penetrated, and supervised by the party—could even be said to be influential on matters of concern to the businesspeople in them, whose open lobbying on behalf of their interests was often effective.[75] Whether through co-optation of individuals or through corporatist connections on a collective basis via state-sponsored associations, business—especially larger business—worked in lockstep with the regime.[76] Here then we see a major difference in the locus of the *guanxi* (or business alliances) on which much of the bourgeoisie relied (in Taiwan) and relies (in China) in predemocratic days. I go on to explicate the implications for businesspeople's stance on regime change of this variable location of *guanxi* in the two places.

The Political Stance of the Bourgeoisie

Based on the analysis above, it is possible to draw some conclusions about the governance preferences of the bourgeoisie in China and Taiwan, respectively. The argument up to this point has been that simply being a member of the bourgeoisie does not affect one's political stance in a uniform way regardless of the political context. Instead, I hold, to understand these people's political positions it is necessary to inquire about the site to which businesspeople generally look when they try to succeed in the marketplace. In both places—perhaps as a reflection of the staying power of Confucian customs—excelling at getting wealthy through buying and selling appears to depend upon one's personal support system.[77] In Taiwan, for the native businesspersons, such systems' components have been one's family and friends; in China they are usually party officials, whether in one's home region or in Beijing. To take a closer look at these networks, I turn next to the origins and composition of the bourgeoisie in both places.

A quick review of the sociopolitical backgrounds or origins of the members of these groups will establish the groundwork for understanding from the business side the linkage between state goals and objectives and how the business operators did or did not get to play a role in them. The first step is to distinguish between the owners or managers of firms of different sizes. In Taiwan, the larger firms were usually (though, granted, not in every case) ones that originated from mainland capital and were nearly always those connected to the state or the KMT, and these were the ones that grew large through their proprietors' *guanxi* with and, consequently, allegiance to the state.[78] The SMEs, then, were the ones in the possession of what could be called members of the middle class.[79] Although the big businesspeople came from China after 1949, forged their firms from their compensation after land reform, or were recipients of US aid in the 1950s,[80] most of the smaller ventures (which grew into medium ones with time) tended to be the product of the export trade in which Taiwanese capitalists engaged in the 1960s. What native bourgeoisie existed in Taiwan after the 1960s was largely an extension of these early SMEs.[81]

According to Michael Hsin-huang Hsiao, the good fortunes of these SMEs was not the product of state policy, but instead occurred thanks to their entrepreneurs seizing the opportunity of the world market after the domestic one had become nearly entirely dominated by outsiders, the *waishengren*.[82] The same policies that unintentionally benefited these businesses, Hsiao holds, also attracted foreign direct investment from the United States and Japan, which in turn promoted more SMEs.[83] Another group of outward-oriented SMEs developed out of persisting trade with Japan, a business that Taiwanese merchants carried forward from prehandover times.[84] Apparently those native businesspeople who experienced the growth and prosperity of their SMEs by the late 1960s were in no way beholden to the Republic of China state.

In China, to the contrary, Bruce Dickson has pointed to the "common backgrounds and shared interests of the emerging middle classes and state officials."[85] This situation was distinctively different from what happened on Taiwan; David Goodman, basing his comments on his study of local (mostly rural, it appears) elites in Shanxi Province, has observed that small-scale private entrepreneurs intent upon expansion normally depend upon close collaboration with their local governments or with connections within the party.[86] Among the strategies he cites for becoming a businessperson, Goodman points to some cadres' children capitalizing on their parents' ties within the party; others, he notes, were themselves once village heads or local party secretaries.[87] In a somewhat earlier study, Susan Young found that 60 percent of the rural private entrepreneurs she surveyed had been cadres before stepping into the world of capital.[88] And in a later piece, Bjorn Alpermann also discovered that the majority of those practicing business in the rural areas he researched had once been cadres or were still simultaneously in such a role.[89]

Kristen Parris, Lu Xueyi, Kellee Tsai, and David Wank all trace successive streams of entrepreneurs who established themselves from the late 1970s onward. All of them agree that, in the words of Wank, as businesspeople built up their firms, over time each group, as it surfaced, had "better [social] capital for linking with local state agents."[90] And it has been the late entrants into the marketplace who have succeeded the most handsomely. At the national level as well, the operators of big business have been ever more ensconced within the ranks of officialdom.[91]

On the basis of the foregoing, I turn now to investigate the effects for democratization (or potential democratization) in China and Taiwan of a moneyed middle class. To begin with Taiwan, Cheng Tun-jen, writing in the late 1980s after the democracy movement was overtly launched, called this drive a "middle class movement," one with ties to small business.[92] Likewise, Shiau Chyuan-jenq, more than a half decade later, confirmed this assessment in his statements that "in comparison to large or public enterprises, [exporting SMEs] had much weaker political links to the ruling party and the executive system of the state. . . . It has been said that the opposition Democratic Progressive Party was primarily funded by the contributions of small and medium-sized businesses."[93]

In China, to the contrary, by the late 1990s, as Chen Jie has discovered, private entrepreneurs exhibited a level of "diffuse [or generalized] support" for the regime that pretty much matched that of state enterprise cadres, a level that was also not far from that of government bureaucrats. In terms of their "specific support" (in regard to particular state policies), as an occupational group they ranked second only to the military and to state bureaucrats.[94] Various analysts have offered their opinions as to why this may be the case, ranging from capitalists' fears that political instability, or—worse yet—fundamental change, could undermine their positions; to being hostile to politics; to being pragmatically single-minded about their work in business; and on to being grateful and, thus, loyal to the regime or to officialdom as a whole for specific policies or for individual support.[95] True, it has been found that some big firms' capitalists might favor democracy for some of its features, but they do not work or agitate for its appearance.[96] One indication of this point is the interesting fact that, of the 151 most active members of China's one failed opposition party, the China Democratic Party that emerged in 1998, just three were private entrepreneurs.[97]

Conclusion

This chapter began with the ambition of fine-tuning a major proposition about the likelihood of democratic transformation in China by reviewing the relationship between the growth of a moneyed portion of the middle class in Taiwan, on the one hand, and its support for the end of the authoritarian regime under which it lived, on the other. The idea, as throughout this book, was to see what Taiwan's experience could foretell about China's potential for this kind of change.

Instead of finding that—despite some similarities between the two places—China's recent prosperity will be apt to mimic Taiwan's, socially and politically, I have suggested that more accurate predictions could be garnered by looking more closely at the conditions under which a business class is apt to agitate for democracy. It appears now that the stories of these two cases are different in a crucial way. A principal variable for assessing this result, I found, is the existence or absence of tight, supportive bonds between the business class and its political regime. Where the bulk of the bourgeoisie is very satisfied and well-served by the state, its support for regime change should be much lower than where the reverse is the case.

I also asked about the factors that shape a regime's reactions to the emergence of such a class; it now appears that in Taiwan, where ethnic differences marked a region being conquered from the outside, the incoming rulers were disposed to reserve the sphere of business for themselves and their co-nationals, as a safety precaution against being outmaneuvered by the locals. If, variously, as in China, the rising class has been nurtured by and co-opted into the regime, that regime is unlikely to fear moves toward autonomy from the former. Moreover, the analyst needs to be cognizant of the existence of various segments within a business class, for ethnic and size factors may mean that generalizations that are too broad can be unwarranted.

Political prediction is always perilous. Can we really draw any implications for the case of China from what we know to have happened on Taiwan, just on the basis of the loyalties of their respective affluent classes? To ensconce my hypothesis about connections within a relatively safe framework, I placed it upon the fairly firm terrain of personal connections, which, as a common folkway in the two Confucianist societies of China and Taiwan, made it reasonable to compare the two. But training a spotlight on the similarity of *guanxi*'s necessity for good business in them both only served to highlight the crucial difference of the partners with whom businesspeople have been forced to—or been able to—work in the two disparate contexts. It would seem reasonable to infer that when the political elite is the patron of the capitalists, the latter would be more prone to protect the regime at hand than to work to cause it to collapse.

Notes

1. The best recent study on the topic is Tsai 2007.
2. Tsai 2005.
3. Moore 1966, 418, 422.

4. Huntington 1968, 21.
5. Huntington 1991, 65–67.
6. Collier and Mahoney 1997; Rueschemeyer, Stephens, and Stephens 1992; and Bellin 2002.
7. Stories that counter such a prediction can be found in O'Donnell 1973 and Stepan 1985, both writing on the role of business in Latin America.
8. Huntington 1968, 15, 20.
9. Dickson 2003, 1997. Dickson has mentioned both co-optation and building corporatist links with capitalists' associations as adaptive strategies. Other possibilities are to eliminate capitalists, expropriate their assets, exclude them, or limit their growth.
10. Lindblom 1977, 175.
11. Mayfair Mei-hui Yang 1994, 1, 6.
12. Hamilton 1998, 57.
13. Yang 1994, 8.
14. For Taiwan, Tien 1989, 43, 46, 59–60; Hsiao 1995b, 80–82; and Weller and Hsiao 2003, 174. On China, see White, Howell, and Shang 1996, 27, 31.
15. Chu 1992, 30. For China, Dickson 1997, 154; 2004, 149.
16. Hsiao 1995b, 82.
17. For Taiwan, Wu 2005, 287–288; Greenhalgh 1988, 234, 243; and Hamilton 1998, 70; for China, Tsai 2002.
18. Good sources on Taiwan are Cheng 1989, 481; Myers 1984; Gold 1988; and Tien 1989.
19. For Taiwan, Fan 2004, 166–167; Gold 1997, 166; Alexander Lu 1992, 122–123; for China, Lu 2004, 270–275.
20. Tien 1989, 30; Cheng 1989, 475. Gold 1988, 182, states that the KMT "liquidated or suppressed native elites," and as others have noted, the KMT's February 1947 massacre of locals wiped out the local elite. See Lin Man-houng 2006, which says that some Taiwanese merchants were arrested in the 1947 massacre. Thanks to Julia Strauss for providing this reference.
21. Tien 1989, 33; in a later publication, Tien estimated that the proportion was one-third, as of the early 1990s (Tien 1992b, 36). For China, Lu 2004, 97, 275.
22. Tien 1992b, 35; 1989, 31, 33, 42. Hsiao and Koo 1997, 313, question drawing a simplistic correlation between the rise of the middle class and the advent of democracy. Chu 1992, 125ff, states that democratization heightened business influence in government after 1988 and not the other way around.
23. For Taiwan, see Cheng 1989, 478.
24. Gold 1988, 182; Cheng 1989, 492.
25. Alexander Lu 1992, 122–123. Like Chu and Cheng, this author did his work in the immediate aftermath of the democracy movement's initial victory. Lu 2004, 270, includes in his "new middle class" people who do mental labor, have a higher education, are paid in wages, and are influential in social affairs.
26. Wu 2005, 297.
27. Shiau 1996, 216; Tien 1989, 24.
28. Gold 1988, 200.
29. Ho 2007 refers to "antagonism." Thanks to Julia Strauss for providing the Ho article. A similar distinction among two business classes can be found in Gates 1981.
30. Hsiao 1995b, 82.
31. Parris 1999, 265, 282.
32. Solinger 1984, 201–205; Young 1995, 132–133.
33. Young 1995, 106.
34. Ibid., 110.
35. This is taken from an e-mail sent on March 5, 2004, by Michal Korzec.

36. For instance, in a *People's Daily Online* statement on May 31, 2002, then party general secretary Jiang Zemin proclaimed an order to "make prosperity the national economy."

37. Dickson 2003, 23, 26, 29; Alpermann 2006, 33.

38. Dickson 2003, 1, 103.

39. This paragraph was borrowed from Solinger 2003. See also Fewsmith 2001, 230; Lawrence 2000; and Nathan and Gilley 2002, 116, 167–168. According to Nathan and Gilley, 168, the theorists who developed the concept did so out of a recognition of the growing significance of the middle class.

40. Dickson 2003, 106; Parris 1999, 268; White, Howell, and Shang 1996, 198–199.

41. Rosen 2004, 27–28; Tomba 2004, 3, 5–7, 25.

42. Kennedy 2005, 55; Goodman 1999, 261.

43. Liu Chin-Ching, *Taiwan chanhao chingchi fensi* [An Economic Analysis of Postwar Taiwan] (Taipei: Jenchien, 1992), 24–28, cited in Ho 2007. Chu 1992, 26, states that "the party controlled a complex web of party-run or party-invested enterprises and billions worth of financial assets." Hsiao 1995b, 82, cites unofficial estimates as holding that "about half of the total assets of Taiwan's corporations" were "controlled directly or indirectly by the state and the party." See too Cheng 1989, 476. Chu 1994, 118, lists the economic and political functions of state firms.

44. Wu 2005, 41, 46.

45. Cited in Ho 2007.

46. Wu 2005, 101.

47. Hsiao 1995b, 82; Gold 1988, 70; and Wu 2005, chap. 4, for Taiwan; for China, White, Howell, and Shang 1996, 201.

48. Chu 1994, 118; Hamilton 1998, 44–45; and Wu 2005, 40–41, 46.

49. Ho 2007; Hsiao 1995b, 85; Wu 2005, 81, 297.

50. Hsiao 1995, 82–83.

51. Cheng 1989, 481, claims that this was done in part by not picking out "national champions" to foster from among these firms. See also Wu 2005, 39, and 118–130. On the other hand, Gold 1988, 73, states that the KMT did select cronies, but of course with only a small handful of exceptions, these would not have been people who were ethnically Taiwanese. Wu 2005, 117, makes the same point. Chu 1992, 21, refers to entry barriers, as does Gold 1988, 190, as well as monopoly licenses and government grants targeted at party-controlled enterprises, all instituted to protect favored firms from private competition. Hamilton 1998, 45, 69, charges that since the state monopolized supply infrastructure and basic goods and services (electricity, gasoline, steel, petroleum, and others), it kept such sectors out of private hands.

52. Wu 2005, 285–287, 296.

53. Chu 1992, 132.

54. Ibid., 133.

55. Ibid., 136.

56. Chu 1994, 118.

57. Gold 1988, 184, 190, states that all businesspeople were barred from politics, not only those native to Taiwan.

58. Ibid., 190.

59. Shiau 1996, 219.

60. Ibid., 222; Tien 1989, 37; Hamilton 1998, 43; Gold 1997, 179; Chu 1992, 133.

61. Hamilton 1998, 49, 71, for Taiwan. Parris 1999, 280, on China, quotes an official as referring to China's "connection economy [*guanxi jingji*]." The difference,

though, is that who is connected to whom in each place in order to carry out business successfully varies in a significant way.

62. Greenhalgh 1984, 20; 1988, 234.

63. Greenhalgh 1984, 532.

64. Ibid., 537.

65. Chu 1994, 114, 117.

66. Tien 1989, 37.

67. Gold 1988, 71; Hsiao 1995b, 84, 88–89; Wu 2005, 304–308.

68. This sort of treatment was most severe at first, in the early 1980s, when full ideological and constitutional blessings had not yet been bestowed upon these tiny businesses. See Solinger 1984.

69. Dickson 2004, 144; White, Howell, and Shang 1996, 201.

70. Dickson 2003; Parris 1999, 281.

71. Young 1995, 95ff, describes various forms of informal cooperation between private operators and state or collective firms.

72. Parris 1999, 265, 268.

73. Ibid., 108–109.

74. Solinger 1992; Wank 1999, 69; and Dickson 2003, 107. Another way of putting this is in Goodman 2001, 134, which speaks of "interdependence and accommodation" between the two groups.

75. Kennedy 2005, 27, 32, 54, 164; Pearson 1997, 100.

76. Pearson 1997, 101, 107, 111, 115; Dickson 2003; White, Howell, and Shang 1996, 207.

77. Goodman 2001, 133, has written: "Entrepreneurs [in China] need to network to succeed."

78. Hsiao 1995b, 85–86.

79. Cheng 1989, 474.

80. Gold 1988, 188–189; Wu 2005, 91–98.

81. Gold 1997, 166. The only data I could get that demonstrate to some extent the contribution of smaller firms to Taiwan's economy in the earlier decades come from Surveys on Industry and Commer, the Executive Yuan, Republic of China, for the manufacturing sector, for the years shown here. The manufacturing sector is the mainstay of the economy. Small and medium enterprises' shares of the output value in the manufacturing sector are as follows: for 1971, 26.72 percent; for 1976, 27.32 percent; for 1986, 33.83 percent, and for 1991, 37.67 percent. Thanks to Cheng Tun-jen for these data and explanation.

82. Hsiao 1995b, 78–79.

83. Ibid., 79.

84. Lin Man-houng 2006.

85. Dickson 2003, 12.

86. Goodman 2001, 139.

87. Ibid., 149–151.

88. Young 1995, 115.

89. Alpermann 2006, 40.

90. Parris 1999, 266; Lu 2004, 277–278; Tsai 2005, 1132, 1135–1139; Wank 1999, 116–135.

91. According to an official report, from research conducted by the Research Office of the State Council, the Chinese Academy of Social Science, and the Research Office of the Party School, as of March 2006, at least 3,220 Chinese individuals had assets of 100 million yuan or more, and 2,932 of these people (or 91 percent) were family members of senior officials. See Mo 2006.

92. Cheng 1989, 474; in an e-mail of September 8, 2006, Cheng referred to "those 'invisible' folks who supported their electoral campaigns, financed their journal publications, absorbed their litigation expansion . . . and took care of their families when they were jailed," explaining that "there were aggregate data and enough circumstantial evidence to allow us to at least hypothesize that the opposition movement was socially embedded in the new middle class—owners and managers of small and medium enterprises."

93. Shiau 1996, 222.

94. Chen Jie 2004, 87, 130. Chen draws on David Easton's concept of "diffuse support" to refer to "a person's conviction that the existence and functioning of the government conform to his or her moral or ethical principles about what is right in the political sphere" and of "specific support" to stand for a person's "satisfaction with specific policies and performance of the government" (2004, 4).

95. Dickson 2003, 13, 80, 83; Pearson 1997, 92–93, 100; Tomba 2004, 24; Unger 2006, 29, 30.

96. Kennedy 2005, 180; Pearson 1997, 88; Tsai 2007.

97. Wright 2006, 8.

PART 2

Regime Responses

6

Responsive Authoritarianism

Robert P. Weller

The social sciences offer two very different literatures on resistance. One tends to concentrate on resistance as a rational response to the political and economic environment, often goaded by feelings of relative deprivation. Growing mostly out of political science and sociology, these studies have concentrated on active unrest, especially when it may have significant social consequences. The other literature, which grew more out of anthropology and history, has focused instead on indirect forms of resistance, where consequences for politics or economy may not be so clear. Such "cultural resistance" can be an important lens with which to bring broad structures of power into focus, even though it leads us to examine apparently apolitical arenas—carnival instead of riots, or punk music instead of petition drives.[1]

There is nothing inherently contradictory about the two approaches, and they can sometimes complement each other. An examination of political resistance will be strengthened by including the broad social lines of tension that the cultural resistance literature reveals. The cultural approach in turn would benefit from asking if and when its forms of opposition can congeal into movements with direct political effects. One of the goals of this chapter is to build on the cultural insight that nonpolitical cultural differentiation can be crucially important while continuing to ask when such differences become politically relevant. Without some approach like this, we will continue to be taken by surprise when the political potentials suddenly become clear, as in "people power" in the Philippines, the role of mosques in the Iranian revolution, or even Falungong in China.

A second goal is to begin thinking about these issues in a somewhat different context by asking how resistance can provide important feedback to the state, rather than assuming a simple opposition and antagonism. Good governance under any regime requires some form of popular feedback. We need only look at totalitarian extremes to see the dreadful consequences of losing

117

the mechanisms that allow information to flow up the political hierarchy. This was, for example, one of the crucial causes of the mass starvations that ended China's Great Leap Forward.

Democratic elections are a quick and powerful mechanism to provide such feedback, but they are far from the only one. Information flows up through public meetings, legal cases, Internet bulletin boards, petitions, and even angry demonstrations. Although China has shown no interest in any innovations that could potentially challenge the control of the Communist Party, it also recognizes the structural problems that one-party rule creates in knowing how government is really working on the ground. Its experiments with forms of governance over the last two decades have created space for every single one of these new paths for information flow.[2] China now has a constant stream of protesters to expose the alleged wrongdoing of venal companies or local officials, "letters and visits" (*xinfang*) to bring complaints to the eyes of higher authorities, and even sometimes forms of e-governance that allow direct feedback to city officials.

Although protests pose the problem most clearly, each of these mechanisms creates a tension between the provision of effective feedback and the threat of social breakdown, of the "chaos" (*luan*) that all Chinese governments have long condemned. One requirement of such a strategy of allowing more social space is thus the ability to keep the resulting stresses under control—to keep worker protests over unpaid unemployment benefits from turning into an independent union movement, or religious groups from becoming Falungong. Even though Taiwan made clear that an authoritarian regime can go on for a long time this way, it also reminds us that the inherent pressures in any mechanism that provides sufficient feedback for effective governance are part of the complex of forces that can result in democratization.

This strategy of allowing many forms of feedback short of broad elections is one aspect of China's general move over the reform period to allow far more space for social organization independent of the state. This is where the two goals I have briefly outlined come together: all kinds of nonpolitical ties can be mobilized under these conditions. We can see social relations through kinship, temple, and neighborhood, for example, in a wide range of movements in both Taiwan and contemporary China.

Bruce Dickson took on a similar problem when he examined regime adaptability in Taiwan and China. Based primarily on the strictly political arena, he concluded that the regime in the People's Republic "has not availed itself of the feedback mechanisms that allowed the KMT to adapt incrementally." He therefore concluded that the regimes in the two places are fundamentally different, in spite of their shared Leninist legacy.[3] Publishing in the same year (1997), however, Shi Tianjian instead described a wide range of feedback mechanisms in Beijing as a response to the growing market economy and as a way to enhance adaptability.[4] Andrew Nathan, too, saw a fundamentally adaptable regime in the PRC, whose "resilient authoritarianism" grows in part out of effective response to popular feedback.[5] None of this may lead to democracy, of course, and may even help to dissipate democratic pressure by providing better governance. Expanding the problem of feedback beyond politics proper into society and culture more generally further clarifies how the regime in China continues to adapt successfully but also shows potential lines of tension. My argument here shares these authors' emphasis on the importance of feedback and on the adaptability of some kinds of authoritarian regimes. It differs from Dickson, however, in also seeing those mechanisms at work in the PRC and from all of them in emphasizing realms that are only indirectly political.

This chapter will draw on two disparate (though sometimes interacting) issues for its examples—religion and the environment. I will argue that a wide range of nonpolitical social ties survived under authoritarian rule in Taiwan, in part to solve the problem of feedback, and that this helped promote the island's eventual democratization. Similar forces are at work in China, but the result need not necessarily be the same. Although the dynamics of encouraging social ties and allowing them limited political possibilities are similar, we need to recall that not all society is civil society and that thriving social ties and open pressure on the state are no guarantee of democracy. Responsive authoritarianism can continue for a long time and need not always change for the better when the internal tensions become too great to bear.

Responsiveness and the Environment

Environmental policy is one of the areas where China has been developing a kind of responsive authoritarianism. China recognizes the need for a strong environmental policy, both to prevent the collapse of an environment that is already badly deteriorated and to stake a claim in the international world. It was thus the first country to produce a national Agenda 21 document, outlining its plans for sustainable development as a signatory of the Rio Declaration of 1992.[6] It has upgraded the status and strength of its environmental regulatory bureaucracy, and it has enacted a wide range of environmental laws and regulations. In spite of this, however, very serious obstacles remain in creating and implementing effective environmental policies, and environmental problems continue to be severe.[7] As in some other arenas with economic implications, however, central policy often conflicts with interests of local cadres. One result has been to apply a wide array of techniques to create information flows from below. These include allowing a place for environmental NGOs, lawsuits, petitions to officials, media coverage, hotlines, and even protests.

It is worth noting that very much the same thing happened in Taiwan, but beginning a decade or two earlier, while the island was still under its long-term state of emergency. Let me begin there, drawing on cases of NGOs and of environmental protest.

Taiwan's legal structure for NGOs before its democratization in 1987 had been essentially corporatist—one organization was given a monopoly over each social sector in exchange for loyalty and cooperation with the state. This is quite similar to the structures China has introduced for most of the reform period. In fact, however, both Taiwan and China have allowed somewhat looser practice than the law implies. Taiwan's earliest NGOs were the major international ones, especially in business, health care, and poverty relief (Kiwanis, Rotary Club, Red Cross, Young Men's Christian Association [YMCA], and so forth). Indigenous NGOs tended to develop later, especially during the 1970s. As in many authoritarian situations (including China today), they gravitated toward areas where they could put some pressure on the government while still claiming complete loyalty to central policy. These areas include women's rights, consumers' rights, and the environment.

Taiwan's first clearly environmental organization took form through a magazine called *Life and Environment* (*Shenghuo yu Huanjing*), published by Huang Shun-hsing, a non-KMT member of the national legislature. It began in 1979 and lasted only a few issues. The first formal NGO was Lin Chun-i's (Edgar Lin's) Taiwan Greenpeace, founded in 1982. Lin also ended up in politics, but not until after democratization. Until then, Taiwan Greenpeace provided an important vehicle that allowed him to pressure the government without ever crossing the line into dissidence. It was a more conservative strategy than that of some more radical political figures, but it also let him establish a public forum and genuinely lobby with a government not usually willing to listen to outsiders. Other pioneer NGOs, such as the Consumers' Foundation, also established environmental wings, and some of their leaders also went on to pursue political office after democratization.

The dramatic loosening of control after 1987 in Taiwan led to a huge increase in NGOs of every variety, but the main point for my purposes here is that their early precursors were already part of a critical dialogue with the government. This worked even with an authoritarian and largely corporatist system.

The pattern of local environmental protest in Taiwan has developed in a similar way, even though the people involved were usually aggrieved villagers instead of activist intellectuals. As with NGOs, environmental protests developed about a decade before martial law was lifted, during a time when few saw much hope for genuine democracy on the island. Recall that many leading dissidents had been jailed (most not for the first time) after the *Formosa* incident of December 1979. Nevertheless, environmental protests erupted regularly from the late 1970s on. One of the largest and most influential in Taiwan's history began in 1985—it successfully ended DuPont's bid to build a titanium dioxide plant in Lukang. This was well before Chiang Ching-kuo had announced his intention to lift martial law.[8]

Local protest organizers capitalized on their strong neighborhood roots, appealing rather little to broad environmental argument, and mobilizing instead through lineages, political factions, and sometimes temples to appeal to people's concerns over health, economy, and the long-term continuation of their family line. Protests against construction of Taiwan's fifth naphtha cracker, for example, benefited from the crucial intercessions of a local temple, which provided both money and a pretext for street marches that would otherwise not have been permitted. A deity even appeared through a medium to tell people to vote against construction in a public referendum. In some cases, especially the endless struggles Taiwan has seen over solid waste disposal, local political factions have been the primary players.[9]

Few of these movements achieved their primary goals of closing or preventing the construction of factories. Most of them, however, did have important effects, such as forcing the construction of proper sanitary landfills, getting agreement to install pollution-mitigating equipment, and extracting money for individual compensation and sometimes to establish well-funded community foundations. Local protests and large NGOs thus succeeded, to an extent, in changing government and industrial behavior. Although both provided different kinds of platforms for political opposition, they were as much a kind of cooperation as resistance, a nondemocratic forum that allowed for short-term settlement of disputes and longer-term adjustment of policies.

China in the last decade or so has also allowed a startling increase in both environmental NGOs and local protests. Although the protests remain quite small, more like Taiwan before the anti-DuPont protest, the NGOs are more developed than anything in Taiwan until the huge boom that occurred after martial law was lifted in 1987. The legal structure that China adopted for NGOs developed initially in the mid-1980s and was explicitly corporatist: it allowed for only one organization to represent each sector, with strong political controls on registration. In practice, however, registration was considerably more fluid, with some registering as the law outlined, others as for-profit enterprises (e.g., Global Village Beijing), and still others finding tangentially related units to sponsor their registration (e.g., Friends of Nature). There have been periodic crackdowns on NGOs since then, especially after the Tiananmen and Falungong demonstrations, but numbers have always rebounded quickly afterwards.[10]

The older environmental NGOs stem from the early 1990s. The earliest was the official creation of the environmental bureaucracy in the government—an NGO in name only. The first more independent group was Friends of Nature (Ziran zhi You), founded by Liang Congjie in 1994. This and several other early groups shared some important characteristics. All had an institutional life limited almost entirely to Beijing, although specific projects might take them all over the country.[11] All had leaders with solid connections to some high officials. Perhaps most important, all had genuine but very cautious environmental agendas. None explicitly opposed government policies. They were not involved in protests against the Three Gorges Dam, for instance, or against nuclear power. Instead, they tended to publicize, promote, and press for the enforcement of the central government's environmental policies.

This cooperative attitude stems from the corporatist nature of the system, but it would be a mistake to conclude that such groups are simply creatures of the state. China has many environmental policies that are not enforced. This has been especially true in rural areas, where we continue to see a constant flow of problems such as industrial pollution of drinking and irrigation water, deforestation, and decimation of endangered species. Local governments tend to profit from these activities, through either direct involvement or by receiving taxes or rents from others. Thus when a group like Friends of Nature campaigns to save an endangered species by ending illegal logging, resistance from local officials can be fierce. The central government may understand that local officials have little financial alternative, but they are also caught by their own environmental rules. NGOs have to walk a very fine line between showing their loyalty to central policy and opposing actual environmental behavior as much as they can. The end result in many cases is an effective change in environmental practice. By publicizing local abuses to the central government, and to the population at large, even these very cautious NGOs have some leverage to create a responsive authoritarianism. Even more space has opened up for some kinds of NGO activity in the past few years, as we see many newer and smaller groups sprouting up in other parts of the country and on college campuses. The broad effect is a further expansion in the potential for responsiveness from the state, even as it also creates further potentials for tension with the state.

Like Taiwan in the decade before its democratization, China also has local environmental protest that does not involve any institutionalized forms such as NGOs. This is much harder to document systematically, but we have enough newspaper accounts and academic case studies to get a broad picture. As in Taiwan in the early period, most protests are reactive. They try to ameliorate existing severe pollution rather than prevent possible future pollution, and they usually espouse economic and health goals rather than broader environmental ones. Although some have seen the rise of protests of all kinds in China as an indication of weakening state control, we could also see it as yet another mechanism for getting local feedback without holding substantive elections. In this sense, the rise of protests is consistent with the development of more sanctioned forms of complaint that increased at about the same time, such as petitions and visits to government offices (*xinfang*) or lawsuits.[12]

The case of a rural entrepreneur named Gao illustrates some of the complex dynamics that can result.[13] Gao had contracted to use a pond in rural Anhui Province to raise crabs. In 1999 he discovered most of his crabs dead, the victims (according to him) of pollution from a nearby factory that reprocessed waste from an oil refinery. He immediately informed the county Environmental Protection Bureau office, which investigated but ultimately took no action at all. Gao then proceeded to pursue three avenues at once. First, he filed a suit against the local environmental protection bureaucracy, saying that the county government had ignored the problem because the factory generated an income of about 800,000 renminbi (RMB) for them each year. Second, he went over the heads of the local government by appealing directly to the municipal-level Environmental Protection Bureau. Finally, he orchestrated the villagers to file their own separate petition complaining about damage from the polluted water and asking 1,000 RMB in compensation for each villager. This was the only case of environmental protest I ran into personally, but it fits general patterns in China.[14] There is certainly an element here of antagonism toward the state, but we could see this just as easily as a mechanism for the cooperative resolution of local problems, where these mechanisms of mild unrest allow higher levels of the state to understand local conditions in ways that might not otherwise be possible.

By comparing predemocratization Taiwan and the PRC, I do not mean to imply that the PRC is simply following in Taiwan's political footsteps, toward a transition from authoritarian, single-party control to democracy. On the contrary, one moral we could draw from the Taiwan case is that authoritarian governments can continue for a long time through the benefit of feedback mechanisms such as NGOs, petitions, complaints, and even local demonstrations. With a careful combination of co-optation, encapsulation, and repression, these newly freed social forces can exist symbiotically with the state for a long time.

Creating this kind of social space, I have argued, can provide important benefits for authoritarian states. At the same time, however, such techniques imply an inevitable relaxation of control. They increase the potential that growing social forces may press against the structure of the state itself. Colonialism provides numerous examples of such techniques in a somewhat different context. Both the Japanese colonial state in Taiwan and the British in Hong Kong and India made room for local elections that allowed people some control over the officials who had immediate power over them but who could never challenge higher levels of government. Taiwan under the old KMT and China today, of course, use the same technique. Although I am not focusing on elections in this chapter, this encapsulated democracy is another technique of responsive authoritarianism. Colonial Hong Kong and Taiwan appear to have kept the technique well under control until their regimes ended for quite different reasons. In India, however, we could look to those elections as one of the arenas where a new indigenous leadership learned the techniques of democracy and organizing and as one of the experiences that raised their ambitions to the level of the central state itself. This inner tension probably characterizes all the techniques of responsive authoritarianism.

Difference and Resistance

The discussion so far of improving governance through more responsive authoritarianism has been limited to arenas that address the state directly. It implies that a confrontational model of state-society relations, even in the presence of the sprouts of civil society, may not always be useful. This is even clearer if we expand our scope beyond the political realm to the kinds of social groupings that may have important long-term political consequences but that do not address the state directly at all. They may depart from state agendas, but do so only through the politics of difference rather than resistance.

Let me try to clarify this through a few examples, beginning with identity issues in Taiwan. The KMT had long marked certain aspects of identity in Taiwan, most obviously through the identity cards that indicated place of family origin, so that even people born in Taiwan were recorded as mainlanders if their fathers had migrated. Informal markers of identity were even clearer, especially in language and access to political power. Ideologically, however, they were all brothers and sisters, and anything that might encourage an explicit politics of identity was repressed. For example, no social organization could use the word *Taiwan* in its name, teachers were not allowed to use local dialects, and Taiwanese dictionaries were almost impossible to find. This remained true right up until the island's democratization.

Nevertheless, Taiwan in the 1970s saw the birth of several apparently unrelated nativist movements. None of them expressed any political agenda, but in retrospect all of them were crucial precursors of the identity politics that swept over the island after democratization and that were so important in nearly all later elections. For instance, I went to a restaurant in 1978 that claimed to be the first specializing in "Taiwanese cuisine." Taipei's influx of mainlanders had the side benefit of creating a great diversity of Chinese cuisines in the city, with superb representatives of nearly every regional cuisine. Traditional Taiwanese foods were also widely available, of course, in homes and at the stalls of the ubiquitous street food vendors. Yet there had been no Taiwanese equivalent of Sichuanese or Shanghainese restaurants. There was plenty of Taiwanese food, but the "cuisine" was born in the late 1970s.

A movement to promote homegrown (*xiangtu*) literature, which was not simply written by Taiwanese but rooted in the experience of Taiwan, had begun already in the 1960s. In part this literature posed a sort of local nostalgia against the rapid modernization and globalization of the island, and its insistence on a unique sense of place also affirmed a sense of Taiwanese (as opposed to generic Chinese) identity. Something similar happened in modern dance, where the earliest group was founded in 1973 by Lin Hwai-min, a native Taiwanese. He drew on uniquely Taiwanese dance forms with roots in local opera traditions, along with a broader interest in Japanese and Korean tradition and the modern dance world of New York. The Japanese connection, which was clear in television and pop music through the 1970s, also indirectly valorized Taiwan's colonial past.

Academics during this period also became interested in developing an indigenous (*bentu*) theoretical position. This was in part a critique of the Western notions that they had all learned as doctoral students in Europe and North America, but in part the creation of a uniquely local identity, just as we saw in food, dance, and literature.[15] None of these movements expressed a political agenda of any kind, and all were tied to their specific intellectual and institutional contexts. Looking back, however, it is easy to see how each of them promoted a sense of the historical uniqueness of Taiwan and led to the assertions of a specifically Taiwanese identity that became so important in the postdemocratization politics of the 1990s. They were the result of a combination of people struggling with the nature of their own fields (from anthropology to dance) and the increasing space that the authoritarian government allowed through the 1970s.[16]

None of these movements translates directly to mainland China, but there are nevertheless some similarities. Scholars there are looking for Chinese alternatives to Western discourses, and artists and writers experiment with techniques that draw on both Chinese traditions and global trends. Indeed, the phrase "with Chinese characteristics" has become so commonplace in realms from the environment to fast food that it threatens to draw snickers. The dynamics of the way this can develop, however, are fundamentally different from Taiwan. There is no PRC equivalent of Taiwan's underlying tension between "mainlanders" and "Taiwanese," and these developments in the sense of identity are more likely to affect China's stance toward globalization than its internal politics.

The People's Republic does, however, include multiple forms of local identity, which show up in language, folk arts, cuisine, and many of the other features that the Taiwanese began to foster in the 1970s. Yet because China has so many locals, and because it lacks a political elite defined through its outsider status, it is difficult to imagine these identities becoming as central as they have in Taiwan. It is not unusual to hear some Taiwanese claim that they are Taiwanese and not Chinese, but it is hard to imagine someone claiming to be Sichuanese and not Chinese.[17] The potential is there, of course, but it is only likely to be realized if there is a collapse of central authority. Instead, it is easy to imagine a more general appeal to Chinese identity in the face of global pressures, which might feed the sprouts of the strong nationalist sentiment we can already see there. Taiwan has its own version of this in some people's hope for an independent Taiwan, but the pragmatic pressures of the world situation have so far put brakes on Taiwan's nationalism. Diplomatic pressure from the PRC is crucial in this, but it is also worth recalling that Taiwan was under Japanese rule for much of the period when mainland China first developed a strong, mass-based sense of nationalism, and the entire agenda of nationalism may be less well rooted in Taiwan. In this case, I would thus expect rather similar-looking and avowedly nonpolitical trends to have quite different political implications in the two places.

The survival and resurgence of apparently premodern institutions such as lineages and temples in both Taiwan and China outline another area well outside the usual boundaries of politics, which nevertheless has important political consequences. Taiwan never experienced the Cultural Revolution's level of repression of these institutions, but the KMT and CCP shared a general modernist attitude that these were remnants of an outmoded era. They were wrong, however, and except for the most oppressive years of the Cultural Revolution, rural areas across much of China and Taiwan have maintained traditions of temple worship and sometimes large lineages (although these were never universal across China). They survived in the face of government disapproval primarily because of their small scale, lack of clear political agenda, and strength of local support, which made them not worth the trouble of trying to crush except in China's most totalitarian moments. Contrary to the expectations of many, these institutions have grown ever more dynamic as first Taiwan and then the mainland began to thrive in a market context. There are villages in China that could never afford a temple in the past but have now built one for the first time.[18] Many others, of course, have been rebuilt or converted back to their original use. In Taiwan too, village and temple religion is booming, quite possibly to a degree never seen in the past.[19]

As with modern dance or cuisine, none of this offers any direct political challenge. Even on the mainland, where most village temples are unregistered and technically illegal, and where there is no sanctioned legal place for lineages, this is really more difference from a state agenda than resistance to it. Nevertheless, Taiwan shows how important these institutions—often the most important village social ties beyond the immediate family—would become in the consolidation of democracy. These were some of the crucial ties, for instance, through which candidates mobilized votes. Even now, political candidates at all levels typically put in appearances at temples, and temples have long had close ties to local political factions. These groups were also important in the development of Taiwan's incipient civil society. I mentioned above the vital role a local temple played in the massive protest against construction of the fifth naphtha cracker. Temples have been important in many other environmental protests (on both sides of the issue) in Taiwan, as have appeals to lineages.[20]

China, of course, has not democratized except at the most limited and local level of village committees. Anecdotally, though, we also hear of lineages playing an important role in those elections, and we can see the nondemocratic political importance of lineages in many ethnographies of the PRC, which show the complex ties between lineages (or lineage branches) and local leaders throughout the nation's history. We see it also in Lily Tsai's study of local governance, where she found that villages with lineages and those with active temple committees were more likely to attract government benefits such as roads and schools than villages without them.[21] We see something similar to Taiwan again in cases where these newly reanimated institutions play an important role in local protest, as when fertility temples in rural Gansu helped organize an environmental protest.[22]

This realm of apolitical society can thus become vital for politics under some circumstances. In others, though, it remains apolitical, and that is how it survives. One of the core problems is how to understand when the social interpretation of something like worshipping a deity or eating rice with sweet potatoes changes, since both the god and the food themselves remain unchanged. During periods of repression, people tend not to voice interpretations of such acts, certainly not political interpretations. Remaining in the nondiscursive realm of everyday life is a strategy of relative safety. Realization of the political potential requires a combination of increased social space from a state interested in becoming more responsive (even if still authoritarian) and a social organization from below. Temples and lineages have been generally more important in this than food, for instance, because they already had a clear social base that could authorize a new interpretive frame.

Not All Society Is Civil Society

To rephrase slightly, I argued in the previous section that social capital offers a vital potential political resource, even though at most times it may appear to be apolitical. The potential is realized in moments like the environmental movements I have mentioned and was clear in Taiwan's consolidation of democracy. This claim draws in part on the social capital literature that has thrived since the events of 1989 in Eastern and Central Europe sparked academics to reconsider issues of civil society. Some of the more enthusiastic proponents of that position, however, have tended to equate all society with civil society, arguing—like Putnam in his earlier work on Italy—that any increase in horizontal social ties ultimately helps create a stronger market economy and a more democratic polity.[23] This claim is not true, however, and encourages us to misread the political potentials of such ties.

Let me illustrate this first by returning to the example of popular temples. I have emphasized how important local religion could be in organizing environmental demonstrations. In Taiwan these became precursors of civil society, and although the future direction of China is much less clear, the potential at first glance seems similar. We could add many other characteristics that make temples critical nodes of local social solidarity. They are usually organized as share-holding organizations, with village neighborhoods or lineage groups usually constituting the shares, and run by a committee. The deity usually chooses the committee leaders by lot—a sort of divinatory democracy open in principle to everyone. More recently in Taiwan they are often elected. Temples are important public symbols of village unity and welfare, and villagers of all kinds, from children jumping rope to old men playing chess, tend to spend idle time in their front plazas.[24]

Yet all of this covers over the inherent inequalities of wealth, power, gender, and age in any Chinese village. When leaders are chosen, for instance, only older and wealthier men tend to put their names forward. It is very rare to see a woman on a temple committee. In some cases, temples have ties to the secular underworld as much as to the spiritual one. Avron Boretz, for instance, documents the uncomfortably close ties between temple performance groups and gangsters in southern Taiwan.[25]

Even more generally, we need to recall that Chinese temple religion is fundamentally local in its outlook. Although some deities are national or regional in scope, many others find followers in only very limited areas. Even when the deity is widespread, worship is locally organized, and few ties bridge the gaps between temples. There is thus no Church of Guan Gong or Mazu, but just a lot of local temples to them. It is difficult to see how such a resource could scale up out of local issues to national ones, out of neighborhood society to civil society. It is not impossible, of course, but a huge amount of institutional work would have to be accomplished to allow it. Taiwan's Mazu temples have become an islandwide cult of a sort, but even there the handful of core temples has no effective institutional unity.

Environmental protest has similarly usually been localist. This is true in many places around the world, where a "not in my backyard" attitude serves to protect specific localities by displacing problems to other people's backyards rather than by solving the underlying issues. A study I was involved with in Anqing municipality of southern Anhui Province, for example, found that people felt very little concern for far-reaching effects of their activities, such as acid rain or global warming.[26] On the other hand, they were quite sensitive to problems that affected them or their families directly, such as economic damage to their crops or health problems. The case of Gao and his crabs, which I mentioned earlier, similarly addressed only local economic issues. Although this pattern certainly stems in part from the political impossibility of wider organization in the People's Republic, it remains true of the great majority of protests in Taiwan as well.

This is one reason why temple religion has sometimes been a natural ally for protesters. Deities protect their own turf. They do not mind if the government wants to build nuclear power plants and oil refineries, as long as no harm comes to their particular locality. This probably explains why the national leadership of Taiwanese environmentalism has been uncomfortable: they are universalists in their approach to the environment, whereas both deities and most people living with local pollution care only about their own place.

The problem of society and civility runs deeper than just the difficulty of scaling up from local interests. Social movements, particularly under relatively unresponsive authoritarian regimes that provide few outlets for public opinion, frequently turn to quite uncivil mechanisms. The example of South Korea's violent popular protests under earlier more repressive regimes is well known in Taiwan. One of the central leaders of the protest against Taiwan's fifth naphtha cracker told the story of their blockade of one of the gates of the factory compound. The police had been able to lift the blockade one night by removing the banners and the two men who stood watch. The protesters responded the next morning by arranging a "religious" parade that included a performing group armed with traditional weapons. This is the sort of group often tied to young hoodlums. According to this leader, people also took Molotov cocktails. I was not able to verify this, but the threat of violence was certainly clear even without them.

When I asked this leader about newspaper reports that the company had hired gangsters to intimidate the protesters, he replied simply that it was not a problem because "they have their gangsters and we have ours." We also see a tendency toward violence in many demonstrations on the mainland, especially when local governments prove completely unresponsive. Although the consequences of this can be severe, it is also one of the few possible mechanisms to capture the attention of higher authorities who might rein in local officials. This is the balancing act that responsive authoritarianism requires. It rests on the confidence that such movements can reveal problems but can also ultimately be kept in check.

Democratization often transforms the nature of protest and resistance. Although a handful of NGOs helped lead the way in many cases of peaceful transformation, the real boom in numbers of NGOs in East Asia and elsewhere has occurred as a result of democratization, not as its precursor.[27] At the same time, the social movement sector has faded in places like Taiwan or South Korea, as leaders often find the NGO form or direct participation in politics a more useful way to pursue their goals. Most civil society groups in democratized East Asia now see themselves as working peacefully with the state, rather than in opposition.

There may even be transformations in religion. The government in Taiwan now encourages temples to organize as a sort of an NGO. Large temples have long had boards of directors or managing committees, but memberships are now chosen by registered "believers" in democratic elections rather than by divination. This is still quite a new development, and the consequences for religion are not yet clear. At the very least, however, it seems to be increasing pressure for transparent management. The trends toward an islandwide cult of Mazu and a new globalizing Buddhism also show religion scaling up in a way that it rarely has before.

Thick social capital is no guarantee of democracy, but it does play an important role in providing feedback to the state. Responsive authoritarianism and democracy channel this in quite different ways, as we have seen in the transformation of social movements to NGOs, or the current changes in Taiwanese religion. The authoritarian option benefits power holders, who feel safe from the constant threat of electoral overthrow. Yet it also requires living with the constant possibility that social ties may overrun their feedback function and begin to pose a larger threat.

The Limits to a Taiwan Model

Taiwan's peaceful and largely successful transition to democracy is the third of Taiwan's "miracles" that is sometimes offered as a model to the rest of the world. The first was the land reform of the early 1950s, which succeeded in getting land to the farmers and doing away with large landlords. The change was peaceful and the landlords were compensated. As a model, however, it never traveled very well and was borrowed unsuccessfully from Vietnam to El Salvador. Taiwan's experience depended on the unique combination of several favorable factors: an earlier Japanese reform had created clear ownership records that rarely exist elsewhere; US aid and enormous nationalized assets left over from Japanese colonial rule made compensation much cheaper for the government than would normally be the case; and the government came from outside, with no strong ties to local landlords and a huge military force that had already showed its willingness to crush any local resistance with deadly force. The second miracle—Taiwan's economic transition from developing to developed nation—also turned out not to generalize well in places like Latin America and even to differ significantly from nearby South Korea or Japan, because of its differing political and cultural history. This does not bode well for the globalization of a possible Taiwanese democratization model, or even just its transfer across the Taiwan Strait.

On the other hand, we can still learn a great deal by comparing the two situations. In this chapter I have primarily been concerned with information feedback mechanisms that good governance requires. The techniques of responsive authoritarianism that I have been discussing attempt to create such feedback without endangering the single party's hold on power. All of them require the government to allow some limited development of social forces that it does not directly control—NGOs, environmental protests, carefully limited local elections, even village temples or lineages. In both China today and Taiwan before 1987 (and quite probably in all such cases), this creates an inherent tension between social groups and the state, even as it opens up an interactive space between them.

This was one of several factors tipping Taiwan from an authoritarian equilibrium to democratization. Just where this tipping point lies may be unique to each case—that is, I do not think there is a Taiwan model. Still, the comparison with the mainland may at least help us understand the dynamics and ultimately to clarify the lines of variation and causation in the broad correlation between wealth and democracy that several of the chapters in this book note. There are some obvious similarities: the largely shared cultural history, the state's conscious embrace of local-level elections, its opening of a space for NGOs (even if they are controlled under a corporatist framework), its open permission for petitions and visits to voice complaints, and its apparently tacit permission for small-scale demonstrations.

The differences, however, may be just as important. Responsive authoritarianism in China and Taiwan may have many similarities, but they were born into different worlds. Taiwan in the 1980s saw many recent cases of democratization and of authoritarian regimes that had come to ugly ends. Iran's revolution had just been a few years earlier, and the collapse of Ferdinand Marcos in the Philippines and the general unrest that would soon unseat South Korea's government were current news as Taiwan moved to democratize in the mid-1980s. Two decades later, however, China continues to congratulate itself on not having followed the Soviet Union's path in 1989. Taiwan's awkward diplomatic position gave it the added incentive of shoring up global support and sympathy by democratizing, but China does not have the same kind of need.

The two also differ in the possible role that nationalism might play. It is not clear that strong feelings of nationalism are necessarily problematic for democracy, but certainly they frequently occur under quite undemocratic regimes. Here, as I mentioned earlier, China has a much stronger tradition of nationalism than Taiwan could, and its frequent accompaniment of antiglobalization and self-strengthening language does not suggest a tip toward democracy. China's much larger scale and the relative intractability of its problems—growing inequality, vast and increasing differences in wealth and education, the enormous regional variation, the depth of poverty in some areas—may discourage a voluntary move to democracy compared to Taiwan, which was in a better position to afford the political costs. Unlike the broad modernization literature showing some statistical correlation between wealth and democratization, this more controlled comparison between China and Taiwan suggests that not all middle classes are the same. The comparison makes us aware of the powerful influence of different histories and of the robust adaptability (but also underlying tensions) of authoritarian regimes.[28]

China may be able to maintain a sort of equilibrium across the tensions inherent in responsive authoritarianism for a long time to come. Certainly many other places, including Taiwan for several decades, have managed it. Those tensions may create a certain push toward pluralism and perhaps democracy, but history has shown that the push can often be resisted. When and if democracy does arrive, however, the social dynamics that already existed will be among the crucial resources. We can see this in the ever increasing centrality of NGOs, temples, social movements, and all the other social descendants of Taiwan's version of authoritarian rule. Understanding this dynamic, as I have tried to suggest, requires looking at social resources that appear utterly apolitical as well as those that address the state directly, because all of these shape the mechanisms of responsive authoritarianism and the shape of democratic transition.

Notes

1. The quite different works of Mancur Olson (1971) or Charles Tilly (1982) are classic examples of the first approach, which concentrates on direct, political resistance. For a very influential example of the second, more cultural and indirectly political approach, see Jean Comaroff's (1985) work on South African Zionism.
2. For a related way of thinking about this, see Oi 2004.
3. Dickson 1997, 14.
4. Shi 1997.
5. Nathan 2003.
6. This was the major agreement, signed by 178 governments, resulting from the United Nations Conference on Environment and Development.
7. See Economy 2004.
8. On the anti-DuPont movement, see Reardon-Anderson 1992. On environmental protest in Taiwan, see Weller 1999, 115–126.
9. Weller 2006, 106–115.
10. Weller 2005.
11. In a study of NGOs in Guangzhou and Xiamen in 1999, my collaborators and I found no significant environmental NGOs.
12. Oi 2004.
13. I discuss his case in more detail in other work (Weller 2006, 118–119, 147–148). For a more general discussion of similar cases where people pursue multiple avenues of resolution, see O'Brien and Li 2004.
14. The best-known recent example was the June 2007 protest against construction of a chemical plant in Xiamen. Thousands of people took to the streets, diffusely organized by text messaging. The government halted construction, although it also took steps to discredit the protests (Economy 2007).
15. Much of this was first pointed out in Hsiao 2005.
16. For documentation of this increasing openness in art and cultural policy within the authoritarian context of the time, see Winckler 1994.
17. The dynamics among China's ethnic minorities, however, may be quite different. This is especially true in the northwest, but statements of divergent identity are more common generally among minorities than among any Han outside of Taiwan.
18. Gao 2005.
19. For documentation of this change, which became clear in the 1970s and 1980s, see Chiu and Yao 1986.
20. I develop this argument in detail in Weller 1999.
21. Tsai 2004.
22. Jing 2000.
23. Putnam 1993.

24. More elaborate versions of such argument can be found in Dean 1997 and Feuchtwang 2003.

25. Boretz 2003.

26. Alford et al. 2002.

27. For evidence of this, see the essays in Weller, ed. 2005, especially the introduction.

28. This argument resembles some of the others in this book, most clearly those of Dorothy Solinger in Chapter 5 and of Merle Goldman and Ashley Esarey in Chapter 3. Bruce Gilley's introduction in Chapter 1 summarizes some of the arguments from the modernization side.

7

Developing the
Rule of Law

Randall Peerenboom and Weitseng Chen

Five East Asian countries or jurisdictions rank in the top quartile on the World Bank's Rule of Law Index: Singapore, Japan, Hong Kong, South Korea, and Taiwan. East Asia remains the one regional exception to the otherwise rather disheartening attempts to establish rule of law in developing countries. Apart from North American and Western European countries, Australia, and Israel, the only other countries in the top quartile are Chile and French Guiana from Latin America, Slovenia as the lone representative from Eastern Europe, and a handful of small island states and oil-rich Arab countries.[1] What accounts for the success of East Asian countries? Will China follow them into this elite group? What, if anything, can other countries learn from the success of East Asian countries?

Although Taiwan and China are currently at different stages of development, both have followed a similar path in establishing rule of law, a path that other successful East Asian countries have also followed to a considerable extent. In the first section, we set out the East Asian Model (EAM).[2] Next we take up Taiwan's development in light of the model. In the third section we look at China's development, and we conclude with a discussion of what the experiences of Taiwan and other Asian states suggest might lie ahead for China, as well as some general observations about what Taiwan, China, and the EAM tell us about modernization theory, democratization, the implementation of rule of law, and good governance.

This chapter challenges standard views of legal system development in Taiwan and China. Many histories of legal development in Taiwan tend to present a predominantly, if not uniformly, bleak portrait of law during the martial era. This is then contrasted with a predominantly, if not uniformly, sanguine view of law in the postdemocratization period. Democratization was no doubt a pivotal event, leading to rapid and dramatic improvements in the legal system. Nevertheless, Taiwan's legal system obviously did not just suddenly leap from the bottom quartile into the top quartile on rule of law indexes upon the start of democratization in 1986. The legal system had developed steadily during the martial law era, albeit subject to restrictions in some areas. At the time of democratization, judicial and governance institutions were relatively strong. There was a competent and professional corps of judges, prosecutors, lawyers, and other legal system actors. The legal system was able to handle most cases fairly and impartially. The judicial system was therefore poised for rapid improvement once certain political fetters were removed. At the same time, democratization did not resolve all of the tensions and problems in the legal system or in governance. As in all countries, the legal system remains a work in progress, with rule of law an inspirational ideal to be struggled for if always imperfectly realized.

As with Taiwan prior to democratization, portraits of the legal system in China are often exceedingly bleak, with many commentators questioning China's commitment to rule of law. Much of the popular and scholarly focus is on deficiencies in the handling of politically sensitive cases.[3] The torrent of reports condemning China for human rights abuses tends to overshadow slow but steady progress in strengthening institutions and building a corps of professional judges, lawyers, prosecutors, and police. Yet it is on the basis of these incremental, often politically contested, institutional changes that the rule of law is built.

The East Asian Model

The EAM—a notion that admittedly serves a useful purpose only at a high level of generalization and conceals considerable diversity when subject to closer scrutiny—involves the sequencing of economic growth, legal reforms, democratization, and constitutionalism, with different rights being taken seriously at different stages in the process. The EAM can be described in terms of six main facets.

First, there is an emphasis on economic growth rather than civil and especially political rights during the initial stages of development. A period of rapid economic growth occurs under the authoritarian regime.

Second, a pragmatic approach is taken to reforms. The government follows some aspects of the Washington Consensus and rejects or modifies others. In particular, the government adopts most of the basic macroeconomic principles of the Washington Consensus for the domestic economy, rejects or modifies the neoliberal aspects that would drastically reduce the role of the state through rapid privatization and deregulation, and remains active in reducing poverty and in ensuring minimal material standards to compete in a more competitive global economy.[4] The government also modifies the prescribed relationship between the domestic and global economy by gradually exposing the domestic economy to international competition while offering some protection to key sectors and some support to infant industries.

Third, as the economy grows and wealth is generated, the government invests in human capital and in institutions, including reforms to establish a legal system that meets the basic requirements of a procedural or thin rule of law.[5] Over time, as the legal system becomes more efficient, professional, and autonomous, it comes to play a greater role in the economy and society more generally.

Fourth, democratization in the sense of freely contested multiparty elections for the highest level of office is postponed until a relatively high level of wealth is attained.

Fifth, constitutionalism begins to emerge during the authoritarian period, including the development of constitutional norms and the strengthening of institutions. Social organizations start to emerge and civil society begins to develop, albeit often a civil society with a different nature and political orientation than in Western liberal democracies. Organizations with a political agenda are often subject to limitations. Citizens enjoy economic liberties, rising living standards for the vast majority, and some civil and political rights, although with limitations especially on rights that involve political issues and affect the control of the regime. Judicial independence remains limited, with the protection of the full range of human rights and in particular civil and political rights suffering accordingly.

Finally, there is greater protection of civil and political rights after democratization, including rights that involve sensitive political issues, although with ongoing abuses of rights in some cases and with rights frequently given a communitarian or collectivist interpretation rather than a liberal interpretation.[6]

This summary of the EAM very roughly describes the arc of several Asian states, albeit with countries at various levels of economic wealth and legal system development and with political regimes ranging from democracies to semidemocracies to socialist states.[7] South Korea and Taiwan have high levels of wealth, largely rule of law compliant legal systems, democratic government, and constitutionalism. Japan does as well, although it is a special case given its early rise economically and the postwar colonial influence of the United States on legal and political institutions. Hong Kong, Singapore, and Malaysia are also wealthy, with legal systems that fare well in terms of rule of law, but either are not democratic (Hong Kong) or are nonliberal democracies dominated by a single party (Singapore and Malaysia). Thailand, less wealthy than the others, has a weaker legal system and, under exiled prime minister Thaksin Shinawatra, adopted policies that emphasized growth and social order rather than civil and political liberties. Its most recent attempt at democratization, which began in 1992 when Thailand was a middle-income country, resulted in the eighteenth coup since 1932. China and Vietnam are at an earlier stage. Although China is a lower-middle-income country and Vietnam is a low income country, both have legal systems that outperform the average in their income class but are still weaker than the rest. They remain effectively single-party socialist states, with varying degrees and areas of political openness.

There are also examples of less successful paths in Asia (and elsewhere). Some involve countries that democratized at lower levels of wealth: Indonesia, India, the Philippines, Bangladesh, and Cambodia. Others involve authoritarian systems that failed to invest in human capital and institutions: North Korea, Laos, and Myanmar.[8] The latter tend to have the weakest legal systems and are mired in poverty, with all of the human suffering that it entails. When authoritarianism fails, it fails badly.

Taiwan's Rule of Law Transition

Taiwan's experience comports closely to the East Asian Model, albeit with certain distinctive features including ethnic conflicts, Taiwan's unusual international status, and limited but lively elections at both local and central levels, all discussed at length by others in this book. Prior to democratization, Taiwan followed a dual-track path, with many legal reforms in the commercial law area and tight restrictions on political and civil rights—at least when the exercise of such rights threatened social stability or the control of the ruling regime. The legitimacy of this restrictive legal order was bolstered by Taiwan's uncertain international status; the KMT's intention to counterattack the mainland; an economy suffering from inflation, shortage of foreign currency, lack of resources, and unemployment; the yearning for social stability; and the need to restructure after the devastating war. After assuming control of Taiwan in 1945, the KMT established a martial law regime. Much of the regime, which was centered on resource mobilization and economic control to reallocate resources for use by the military, was developed on the mainland during the war with Japan and transplanted to Taiwan.

The Temporary Provisions Effective During the Period of Communist Rebellion (1948), the Martial Law (1949), and other laws nullified many aspects of the 1936 constitution, which had provided significant protection for human rights. The Martial Law delegated immense authority to the executive branch to enact administrative ordinances restricting citizens' civil and political rights, including privacy, property rights, the right to strike, and freedom of expression. Taking advantage of this power, the KMT promulgated many ordinances to tighten control over the society in the early 1950s, including ordinances that regulated radio stations, mail, and other telecommunications as well as newspapers, magazines, and other print media.[9] Chiang Kai-shek also relied on the Temporary Provisions and Martial Law to halt parliamentary elections. A 1960 amendment of the Temporary Provisions nullified the constitution's term limit for the president, paving the way for Chiang to be reelected more than twice.

During the "era of White Terror" from 1949 to 1987, there were around 29,000 political cases involving 140,000 persons and another 3,000–4,000 cases in which people were executed.[10] Although most cases in the 1950s involved accusations relating to support for Communism, most cases after 1960 involved the suppression of democratic and rule of law movements.

In addition to the contrast between support for economic reforms and the crackdown on political dissidents, the dual-track nature of development is apparent in the operation of the Control Yuan. The Control Yuan focused on supervision of public servants in the financial and economic sectors. From 1948 to 1996, financial and economic impeachment cases accounted for 44 percent of all cases, whereas police administration cases accounted for just 4 percent, judicial affairs 10 percent, land administration 3 percent, and social administration 0.6 percent.[11]

The effect of the dual-track system is also evident in the operation of the administrative litigation system. Although the Administrative Litigation Law was enacted in 1933 and the administrative court began operating in Taiwan in 1950, the system imposed few constraints on the state. By 1960, there were only 109 cases per year, with plaintiffs prevailing on average in only 14 cases annually. By contrast, there were 9,196 cases in 2004, with plaintiffs prevailing in 1,034 cases.[12]

There has been considerable discussion of Taiwan's economic policies as an example of an East Asian development state.[13] Suffice it to say that Taiwan fits the EAM, particularly from 1960 to 1980 when it implemented an export-oriented policy and protected state-owned enterprises (SOEs) and certain infant industries. In comparison to China, Taiwan's economy was less open and remains less open in many respects. To be sure, much of Taiwan's growth preceded the World Trade Organization (WTO) era. Overall, however, the trend has been toward greater openness.

Economic reforms and increased interaction with the international economic order and foreign investors generally reinforced legal reforms under the dual-track approach. However, some economic policies had negative consequences. Special laws to protect SOEs and large private companies or to attract foreign investment led to inconsistent legal interpretations.[14] With the piecemeal approach working reasonably well, the KMT lacked the incentive to cope seriously with the structural problems of the legal system until the 1980s, when such a complicated legal regime threatened market efficiency.[15]

In addition, these special laws and statutes gave rise to policy discriminations within the legal system, because they aimed to protect and nurture large companies rather than small and middle-sized firms, which accounted for 98 percent of business enterprises in Taiwan.[16] These policy discriminations led to a backlash in the late 1970s and 1980s. In response, the KMT enacted a number of laws addressing the grievances of labor and small and middle-sized firms. However, these measures could not fully dissolve the rising tensions resulting from long-lasting policy discrimination.

With the government focused more on economic development than social justice, the legal system proved inadequate to address rising social tensions. As a result, the number and the size of social protests increased rapidly. The reported frequencies of protests rose from 175 in 1983 to 1,172 in 1988, with the average size of protests increasing from 73 people to 267 people. All incidents of large-scale protests with more than 5,000 participants took place in the three years prior to democratization.[17]

As in the EAM model, Taiwan invested heavily in human capital and institutional development during the economic take-off period. On the whole, government institutions, including the legal system, grew steadily stronger. At the same time, Taiwan's experience suggests some nuances with respect to the development of legal institutions, particularly the legal profession.

First, judges and prosecutors in Taiwan have been selected through a unified examination system, as is now also true in China. They were also required to undertake more rigid training than other public servants.

Second, the basic structure of an administrative law regime was established in the 1940s. Laws modeled on modern civil law countries such as Germany were passed to regulate legislative procedure, taxation, the financial system, the civil service, professional license examinations, customs, international trade, administrative reconsideration, and administrative litigation. Compared to China, which entered the reform era with a legal system severely weakened by the Cultural Revolution, these laws provided a more solid foundation for, and lowered the transaction costs of, subsequent reforms.

Third, the Control Yuan provided an internal mechanism for checks and balances throughout the period. In comparison to the prosecution of corruption in China, where lower- and middle-level officials have been hit hardest, the Control Yuan was fairly even-handed toward officials of different levels when it enforced the law, with impeachment of middle-ranked officials accounting for 45 percent and that of high- and low-ranking officials accounting for 34 and 21 percent respectively.[18]

Fourth, local elections provided another means of accountability and channel for public participation. Local elections started when Japan colonized Taiwan in 1935. The KMT expanded local elections for instrumental reasons when it took over.[19] Although the KMT could manipulate these elections, elections were one of two major channels for reformers and members of the political opposition to have their voices heard. The other channel was publications, although the KMT frequently outlawed journals and magazines that dealt with issues deemed too sensitive, such as Taiwan independence or attacks on Chiang Kai-shek.

Local elections provided the political cover for the survival of a limited civil society during the White Terror era. Taiwanese used to describe the election period as "election holidays" from the KMT's tight control over the freedom of expression. Local elections became an alternative mechanism for imposing on rulers legal restraints regarding civil and political rights that were not enforced in courts. Many lawyers who had represented political and human rights cases also jointly participated in elections in the 1980s.[20] Over time, candidates and activists who cited laws to challenge the KMT found more receptive audiences among an increasingly articulate and economically secure electorate.[21]

In contrast to efforts to strengthen the ranks of judges, prosecutors, and administrative officials, the KMT tightly controlled the legal profession. Lawyers were defined as playing a supplementary role in assisting judges and prosecutors in efficiently resolving disputes.[22] The chief prosecutor supervised bar associations. Furthermore, the KMT limited the numbers of attorneys through a very strict bar exam with a passing rate of 1–2 percent.

Even though it tightly limited the passing rate, the KMT provided a back door for its political supporters or more controllable people. As a result, most attorneys were mainlanders who came to Taiwan after 1949 and tended to support the KMT. In 1960, 96.4 percent of the board members of the Taipei Bar Association were mainlanders, even though the mainlander population accounted for only 14 percent of the total population. By the late 1990s, however, the ratio was about 1 to 4, close to the 1 to 6 ratio of the two ethnic groups. Along with this transformation came a change in the political orientation of the bar association. Whereas the Taipei Bar Association used to take a similar stance to the KMT, the Bar proposed its own political reform agenda in the 1990s.[23]

Although extensive local elections started in 1946 when Taiwan's nominal GDP per capita was less than $140, multiple party elections for the highest level of office were postponed until a relatively high level of wealth was attained. When the KMT ended martial law in 1987, Taiwan's nominal GDP per capita was $4,839 and was $8,016 based on purchasing power parity (PPP). To be sure, wealth alone is insufficient to predict when a country will democratize, although it is a better indicator of whether democracies are likely to survive and consolidate.[24] In Taiwan's case, other factors played a role in the decision to democratize, including international pressure and the need for Taiwan to gain international support, President Chiang Ching-kuo and the KMT's toleration of political opposition in the 1980s, ethnic politics, and increased domestic pressure on the government to make good on its commitments to rule of law and democracy.

As in the EAM model, constitutional norms began to take root in Taiwan well before 1987. The KMT claimed early on that Taiwan was a democratic country with rule of law and equal rights protection, as opposed to Communist

China. Such claims allowed reformers to challenge government actions by invoking the same discourse. As a result, over time, the KMT's legitimacy became increasingly tied to legality, rule of law, constitutionalism, and democratic reforms. For instance, Presidents Chiang Ching-kuo and Lee Teng-hui announced a number of critical legal reforms soon after taking office to enhance their administrations' legitimacy in the eyes of a populace that did not have much say during the election process.

Institutionally, the Grand Justice Council played a critical role in the development of constitutionalism since the 1950s.[25] Although the KMT intervened in the nomination process of grand justices in early years, the council was able to ensure that most parts of the legal system functioned well through its interpretations of the constitution.[26]

Civil society also emerged. Many groups presented no challenge to the government. Those that did were often treated harshly. However, over time, opposition groups grew in number and strength and were less easily deterred by harsh punishments. The *Free China* journal incident in 1960, for instance, had a great impact on a rising democratic movement. In the late 1950s, some elite members of the KMT who were prestigious liberal scholars and reformers promoted liberalism and democracy in the journal. When they tried to establish an alliance with native Taiwanese political activists, the KMT cracked down. The crackdown essentially put an end to the collective opposition movement until the late 1970s.

By contrast, the KMT's repression of the *Formosa Journal* incident in 1979 had only a short impact on democratic movements. In 1979, political dissidents, under the umbrella of the *Formosa Journal,* extended political activism to street protests and mass rallies in an attempt to foster a national network.[27] After a rally that led to violent confrontations between the police and the participants, 41 political dissidents were subsequently sentenced to various prison terms. However, soon after that, opposition movements revived their street activities.

It is interesting to note that the KMT allowed a completely open trial for the arrested dissidents to show its commitment to rule of law, a politically motivated decision to preempt domestic and international pressure. Ironically, this trial inspired many legal professionals to broaden their social participation and even embark on a political career.

Finally, human rights protection, the autonomy of courts, and judicial efficiency improved significantly in Taiwan after democratization. The constitution was amended six times from 1991 to 2005 to enhance accountability through free elections of the national legislative body (1991), direct election of the president (1996), reform of the parliamentary system (2000, 2005), electoral reforms (1991, 1999), local self-government (1992), and restructuring of the central governmental (2000). After the lift of media control, various social and political movements also gained new momentum.

Prior to the democratization, the KMT's strategy to establish rule of law without democracy successfully created the necessary conditions for economic growth. However, one core feature of rule of law—putting the state under the scrutiny of the judicial system—was not fully achieved until after democratization. As a result, for instance, the administrative litigation court, referred to as the "dismissal court" in early years, only became effective in the late 1980s. The number of administrative litigation cases in 1987 was twice that of 1980, 12 times that of 1960, and 138 times that of 1950. Similarly, both the number of state compensation cases and the percentage of cases won started to increase in the mid-1990s. The average number of cases per year from 1990 to 2005 was three times that of the 1980s, while the plaintiff's winning rate during the same period was nearly four times higher than during the 1980s.

The judiciary as a whole has been greatly strengthened. Between 1980 and 1997, the number of court personnel doubled.[28] Beginning in 1986, the Grand Justice Council also adopted a more activist approach, contributing to rapid constitutional development. The council did not strike down any law based on a human rights violation before 1972. From 1972 to 1985, the council at times indicated that certain laws were unconstitutional, but in most cases only required that the laws be amended rather than nullifying them.[29] In contrast, from 1985 to 2003 there were 367 interpretations, 97 of which struck down laws for infringing human rights. The council has even gone so far as to strike down constitutional amendments as unconstitutional, as in Interpretation no. 499 in 2000.

Moreover, empirical studies suggest that corruption within the judicial system has been reduced in recent years.[30] In a 2006 survey of practicing lawyers, just 3.8 percent of respondents expressed dissatisfaction with the integrity of judges and legal staff, and only 4.7 percent questioned the independence of the judiciary.[31] Human capital improvement appears to be one factor. Since the late 1980s, law schools have been able to attract the best students. In addition, political intervention has become rare. Increased external supervision from bar associations, NGOs, political parties, and the media has also raised the cost of corruption. For instance, the Judicial Reform Foundation (JRF), one of the most active NGOs promoting legal reforms in Taiwan, has been conducting a nationwide evaluation of judges since the mid-1990s. JRF recruits volunteers to sit in on court trials to evaluate each judge's performance and then issues an annual report.

In 1999, the Judicial Yuan held a national Judicial Reform Conference following an unprecedented Judicial Reform Rally led by lawyers.[32] This conference resulted in a series of institutional reforms in early 2000 involving judicial personnel; the judges' evaluation system; attorney regulation; legal aid; human rights protection; judicial efficiency; reallocation of judicial power among judges, prosecutors, and the police; and the adoption of features of the adversarial system into the existing inquisitorial system. These reforms gave rise to comprehensive amendments of the Criminal Procedure Law in 2002 and 2003 and of the Civil Litigation Procedure Law in 2003.

Although democratization has enhanced rule of law in Taiwan, it is no panacea. Nor can all improvements or persisting problems be attributed to democracy. Corruption remains a problem. According to Transparency International, in 2005 Taiwan ranked thirty-second, behind Singapore (fifth), Hong Kong (fifteenth), and Japan (twenty-first) but better than South Korea (fortieth), Malaysia (thirty-ninth), China (seventy-eighth), and Indonesia (one hundred and thirty-seventh).[33] In many areas legal norms still do not adequately constrain bureaucratic implementation.[34] Moreover, freedom of speech and assembly continued to be subject to a variety of restrictions until further reforms were implemented after numerous social and student movements in the 1990s.[35] Public confidence in the court system is also questionable. A survey in 1999 found that trust in the courts was still low even after democratization, with 34 percent of the respondents questioning the fairness of courts.[36]

However, recent surveys suggest improvement, at least among those with actual experience in the courts.[37] A survey of plaintiffs, defendants, and all related persons involved in civil and criminal trials in 2005 shows that the satisfaction rate is 70 percent for civil trials, 65 percent for civil appeals, 59 percent for criminal trials, 49 percent for criminal appeals, and 69 percent for juvenile trials.[38] In addition, the overall satisfaction rate for judicial services is 88 percent, including open information, court facilities, legal aid, the efficiency of the trial process, and transparency.[39] In 2006 and 2007, the indictments of both the DPP's and KMT's highest officials with some of their family members—including President Chen Shui-bian's son-in-law and wife, the KMT's chairman Ma Ying-jeou, Vice President Hsiu-lien Annette Lu, the former prime minister Yu Shyi-kun, and secretary-general to the president Chen Tang-shan—also demonstrates a high degree of judicial independence.[40]

China's Emergent Legal System

China is a lower-middle-income country. As such, and in accordance with the EAM, it has not yet democratized in the sense of open competitive elections for the highest offices. China is following the EAM in other respects as well, as demonstrated at length elsewhere.[41] In this chapter, we will limit our discussion to key similarities and differences between Taiwan and the mainland and highlight the major challenges China is facing in establishing rule of law.

As has occurred in Taiwan, China has followed some aspects of the Washington Consensus and rejected or modified others.[42] There has been a general transition to more open markets. However, the process has been much faster and deeper than in Taiwan. China is now one of the most open developing economies in the world. Its average tariff rate of 10 percent is much lower than that of Argentina (32 percent), Brazil (31 percent), India (50 percent), and Indonesia (37 percent). Its ratio of imports to GDP is almost 35 percent, compared to 9 percent for Japan.[43] Similarly, China has been more open, and relied more heavily on foreign direct investment, than Taiwan, South Korea, or Japan. In 2003, the ratio of the stock of foreign investment to GDP was 35 percent in China, compared to 8 percent in Korea, 5 percent in India, and 2 percent in Japan.[44]

China, like Taiwan, passed special rules for foreign investors and state-owned enterprises. The overall trend has been for the foreign and domestic regulatory systems to merge, although there are still significant differences. Preferential treatment for foreign investors, including lower tax rates, and for state-owned enterprises has given rise to resentment among disadvantaged domestic companies. As in Taiwan, such preferences gave rise to tensions over the lack of a level playing field.[45]

Unlike the situation in Taiwan, growth in China has been extremely unequal. There are, however, two variants of the EAM, which differ with respect to inequality and public expenditures on health and education. Japan, South Korea, and Taiwan have paid more attention to equitable growth, whereas Singapore and Hong Kong have tolerated greater inequality.[46] China's Gini coefficients, in the .40 to .45 range for the past several years, are also in line with more general development patterns. The average Gini coefficient for countries with a real per capita income of less than $1,000 is .34. The average rises to .46 when per capita income is between $2,001 and $3,000, and then falls to .33 when per capita income exceeds $6,000.[47]

In both Taiwan and the mainland, the legal system has played a greater role in economic growth than often suggested by those who belittle the importance of rule of law for development.[48] The excessive focus on property rights, and in particular the obsession with the courts as the enforcer of property rights, has blinded observers to the many other functions of the legal system in facilitating economic growth. The legal system also performs an enabling function by creating the basic infrastructure for transactions, including markets, security exchanges, mortgage systems, accounting practices, and so on.

Between 1978 and 1982, the emphasis was on the reconstruction of the basic institutions of a socialist legal system. The 1982 constitution incorporated the fundamental rule of law principles of a government of laws not men: the supremacy of the law and the equality of all before the law. In March 1999, the constitution was amended to incorporate the new policy formulation *yifa zhiguo, jianshe shehuizhui fazhiguo*—rule the country in accordance with law, establish a socialist rule of law state. In 2004, the constitution was again amended to expressly provide that the state respects and promotes human rights.

Nevertheless, there continue to be debates (often conceptually confused and empirically weak) similar to those that occurred in Taiwan about whether the legal system is best characterized in practice as rule of law or rule by law.[49] The role of the party with respect to the legal system remains largely undefined as a matter of law and contested as a matter of theory. As the ruling party, the CCP will inevitably have a significant role in determining the direction of legal system development. As the ultimate authority, only the party is able to break deadlocks among state organs. However, as in many developing countries, many of the problems have less to do with ideology than with economic resources and institutional capacity. In addition, the fragmentation of power often results in local governments ignoring central government laws and policies, as does an implicit political compact whereby the center requires local officials to achieve economic growth and maintain stability with little support from the center, and thus affords local officials considerable leeway in how they meet those goals.

The government's efforts to establish a socialist rule of law state have resulted in major changes affecting virtually all aspects of the legal and political system. Reforms have led to significant changes in party-state relations and state-society relations and to major governing institutions, including the people's congresses, the procuracy, police, and the legal profession.[50] Judicial reforms fall into three broad categories: efforts to make the adjudicative process more efficient and just, reforms aimed at enhancing the quality and professionalism of judges, and attempts to increase the authority and independence of the courts. As in Taiwan, reforms have involved considerable foreign borrowing, including from common law systems, to the point where China is now a mixed system. There has been considerable progress in increasing the educational level, competence, and professionalism of judges, prosecutors, legislators, administrative officials, police, notaries, and other judicial system actors.[51] However, China is a very large country. Within the court system, there is wide variation by region and by level of court.

Reforms have increased the authority and the independence of the courts and the presiding judges that hear cases.[52] Thus, it is an overstatement to claim that the lack of independence precludes the possibility of a fair trial in all cases. Different types of cases present different challenges.[53] For instance, the funding of courts by the government, and the appointment of judges by the people's congress at the same level, leads to local protectionism and undue influence in some cases, especially in lower-level courts. Moreover, politically sensitive cases continue to be handled without much regard for due process and basic rule of law principles.

Administrative law has been one of the most active areas of reform. The wide-ranging reforms to the administrative law regime include acceptance of a new conception of governance based on the principle of administration according to law; strengthening of the administrative law regulatory framework; improvements in the quality of the civil service; the limited, albeit not insignificant, efforts at deregulation; recent measures to increase transparency and public participation; and last but not least, the attempts to strengthen the various mechanisms for reining in state actors.

In comparison to Taiwan at a similar stage of economic and legal development, Chinese citizens sue government officials, and win, more often. Indeed, Chinese plaintiffs prevail more often than their cross-Strait counterparts do even today. Whereas Taiwanese plaintiffs prevail in 11 percent of cases, Chinese plaintiffs prevail in 15–20 percent of cases where the court quashes or modifies the agency decision and approximately 40 percent of cases if one includes the 20–25 percent of cases where the plaintiff withdraws the suit after the agency changes its decision.[54]

Unlike Taiwan, China has actively sought to promote the rapid expansion of the legal profession, particularly in the first two decades of reform. The pass rate for the national bar exam was approximately 7.9 percent in 2002, 11.1 percent in 2003, 12.3 percent in 2004, and 14.39 percent in 2005, considerably higher than in Taiwan.[55] As in Taiwan, the role of lawyers has changed over time. Whereas 1980 regulations depicted lawyers as "workers of the state," the 1996 Lawyers Law redefined lawyers as legally certified practitioners who provide legal services to society. The legal profession undoubtedly has gained in independence and autonomy, although lawyers are still subject to supervision by the Ministry of Justice (as they are in many countries). Moreover, some activist lawyers have been harassed, subjected to sanctions, or arrested on trumped-up charges, although the number of such cases is small and often overstated in the media.[56]

Nevertheless, the government clearly is concerned about the potential for activist lawyers to increase social instability. In 2004 alone, there were 538,941 multiparty suits, up 9.5 percent from 2003.[57] In response, the national bar association issued guidelines, much criticized in the media. As the regulations point out, many multiparty suits involve land takings, relocation of residents from their homes, state-owned enterprise system reforms, and social welfare claims from farmers. These cases raise a number of complex social, economic, and political issues. They also often lead to social disturbance and protests, which increasingly are turning violent. To avoid adverse consequences, including possible harassment of lawyers involved in such cases, the bar association's regulations seek a balance between social order and the protection of citizens and their lawyers in exercising their rights.

In sum, China's institutional development has been impressive for its level of wealth. China outperforms lower-middle-income countries in political stability, government effectiveness, and rule of law; it does slightly worse in control of corruption, and is about average in regulatory quality.[58] Nevertheless, as is typical of middle-income countries, there is still a need to strengthen institutions.

At this stage, the main role of the constitution has been to provide an initial distribution of power among state organs, and thus the background against which legal reforms, many of which affect the balance of power among key state actors, are negotiated. For example, the constitution now gives the procuracy the power to supervise the courts. In recent years, the procuracy has interpreted this power to mean that it has the authority to supervise final judicial decisions. As expected, the judiciary has argued that the procuracy's power of supervision should be eliminated, or at least limited to general oversight of the court or investigation of particular instances of judicial corruption. According to most judges, the procuracy should have no power to supervise individual cases. The courts have also come into conflict with the legislative branch over similar powers of individual case supervision and with administrative agencies over the power of judicial review of agency decisions. For the time being, most of these conflicts can be solved only through party intervention.

The constitution for a variety of reasons has played a limited role in litigation to protect individual rights. Except for one recent civil case involving the right to education, the constitution has not been considered to be directly justiciable, and even that case did not involve enforcing the constitution against the government.[59] As in some civil law countries, courts in China do not have the power to strike down abstract acts in administrative litigation suits; in other words, courts may not overturn a generally applicable administrative regulation or rule simply because it is inconsistent with the constitution or higher-level court decisions. Although the court may apply the higher-level law in the particular case, the conflicting lower-level regulation remains in place.

The absence of an effective constitutional court or review entity has further reduced the importance of the constitution as a source of rights protection. Even if there were a constitutional court or similar entity, it is doubtful that the constitution would be interpreted in a liberal way given the prevailing statist socialist conception of rule of law, the existing threats to social order combined with support from both the ruling regime and broad public for stability, and the nonliberal orientation of the majority of Chinese citizens.

Nevertheless, the constitution has served those inside and outside government as a source of empowerment for legal actors and the development of constitutional norms.[60] In particular, the constitution has played a role in establishing broad grounds of legality, accountability, and justice, which activists and reformers have then drawn on to push for reforms.

For example, activists, including several law professors, based their calls to eliminate detention and repatriation (where migrants without residence permits could be held in administrative detention centers or sent back to the countryside without a right to appeal before a judge) on general constitutional principles of equality and freedom of movement. They also pointed out the faulty legal basis for this practice. Whereas national laws required that all limitations of personal freedom be based on national laws, lower-level administrative regulations provided the only legal basis for detention and repatriation.

The constitution has also provided the normative basis for a series of discrimination cases. In one case that combined the right to education with a discrimination claim, three students from Qingdao sued the Ministry of Education for its admissions policy that allowed Beijing residents to enter universities in Beijing with lower scores than applicants from outside Beijing. In another case, a person infected with Hepatitis B recently won an administrative litigation suit when he was denied a post as a civil servant because of his disease. Other employment discrimination cases have challenged height, gender, and age restrictions.

To be sure, some of these cases have been dismissed on technical grounds. Nor do these cases involve political dissidents or the right to free speech. Parties who invoke the constitution to criticize the government or call for greater democratization have been notably unsuccessful.[61] Nevertheless, these cases signal an increasing willingness on the part of plaintiffs, lawyers, and courts to look to the constitution as the basis for norms and principles that may be applied in particular cases to expand protection of the rights of individuals, subject to current doctrinal and jurisdictional limitations.

Representatives elected to office have also begun to show a greater concern for the demands of their constituents, with some representatives emerging as populists and social activists.[62] Some have developed a name for themselves by advocating rule of law, democracy, and civil rights. Others are known for their advocacy on behalf of particular interest groups such as migrant workers, laid-off workers, or people whose houses have been taken by the government as part of the process of urbanization and development of city centers or industrialization in the countryside. Many of the populist legislators receive assistance from NGOs and lawyers.

Taken together, the various changes demonstrate an ongoing transformation in social, legal, and political culture.[63] To be sure, the government has moved cautiously on political reforms, much like other successful Asian states. The government clearly does not want to lose control.

One of the biggest limits on constitutionalism, however, is that there are wide disputes at a fundamental normative level about the type of society China should be. The differences between the new left and the new right and between statist socialists, soft authoritarians, communitarians, and liberals preclude the type of supermajorities needed to legitimate major constitutional reforms. As a result, even though the constitution has been amended four times since 1982, the changes have either been minor or have served to provide a greater role to market forces and the private economy—an area where there is already a sufficiently dominant view among the various groups to legitimize these changes.

China's rule of law and good governance rankings were all lower in 2005 than in 1998, with the exception of regulatory quality. Although the lower rankings may be a statistical anomaly or due to subjective biases, there are signs of reform fatigue and diminishing returns.[64] China is not unusual in encountering obstacles and opposition to the implementation of rule of law and good governance at this stage of development. Many countries are able to make some initial progress and show improvement in terms of economic growth, institutional development, and good governance given low starting points. However, once they reach the middle-income level, they get bogged down. Powerful interest groups capture the reform agenda, opposing further reforms or pushing for reforms that do not benefit the broad public.[65] Economic growth slows or reverses. The reform momentum is dissipated. Some states settle into a stable but dysfunctional holding pattern, and others sink into chaos and become failed states.

Economic reforms have led to a more pluralistic society. Economic reforms and the government's efforts to promote rule of law and rights-consciousness among citizens have also led to greater demands on the legal system. State organs are expected to handle matters in a just and efficient way, to be more transparent, and to allow more public input in the decisionmaking and supervision processes, and the establishment of rule of law is meant to provide a more rule-based method for handling the increasing tensions, conflicts, and disputes. Unfortunately, as typical in middle-income countries, China lacks adequate resources to satisfy all demands, and the current mechanisms and institutions for handling the rising tensions are too weak and ineffective.

Lacking effective channels for resolving the conflicts generated by economic, social, and political reforms, citizens are taking to the streets to seek justice—or at least to vent their anger. The number of protests has risen sharply in recent years, leaping from 58,000 in 2003 to more than 74,000 in 2004 alone. Such protests, many of them violent,[66] are a threat to social stability and thus to sustained economic growth.

Whether the future is likely to see more repression or greater protection of civil and political rights depends in part on the outcome of deeply contested debates about how to respond to the increasing social tensions, the sharp rise in demonstrations, and the specter of a popular uprising such as the color revolutions in the former Soviet republics. Among the three dominant competing perspectives, one extreme emphasizes repression of dissent and tight limits on social organizations and the exercise of civil and political rights that threaten political stability, combined with an ideological battle to win the hearts and minds of Chinese citizens, government officials, and party members by revamping socialism and explaining the reasonableness of the current reform agenda. Signs of this approach include the increased restrictions on the press and the Internet, the arrest of lawyers and human rights activists, the closure or close monitoring of social organizations, the crackdown on public intellectuals, and the cancellation of academic conferences on constitutionalism and political reform.

At the other end of the spectrum are those who argue that rapid and broad-ranging reforms are necessary to prevent the reform process from stalling, to meet the rising demands from the citizenry, and to avoid a political crisis. Rather than tightening restrictions on civil society and the exercise of civil and political rights, the government should relax restraints.

A third, moderate perspective acknowledges that the country is confronting a variety of serious challenges to social stability, as is typical for middle-income countries. Hence, there is a need to maintain restrictions on civil and political rights. However, at the same time, there is an equally pressing need to continue to invest in human capital, to strengthen institutions, to pay more attention to social justice and the wealth effects of economic reforms, and to gradually expand civil and political liberties. In short, stick to the East Asian Model. Repression alone does not provide a long-term solution. It simply increases the likelihood that at some point there will be some sort of political crisis or that China will end up like other stable but dysfunctional middle-income countries.

At the moment, the moderate approach appears dominant. Despite the tightening in some areas, reforms have continued in other areas. The State Council's 2005 Democracy White Paper is generally reflective of this approach, with its invocation of classical ideas such as democratic centralism resting somewhat uncomfortably with calls for greater public participation and description of new institutions such as social consultative committees.[67]

The moderate approach inevitably will give rise to criticisms from both those who think the government is being too repressive and moving too slowly on reforms and those who take the opposite view. Almost everyone will object to some specific policies or the results in particular cases. The renewed emphasis on democratic centralism seems to be an attempt to manage diverse views without allowing conflicting views or discontent to undermine political stability. Citizens are allowed to express their views on controversial issues and thus to blow off steam, but only up to a point. Once the various viewpoints are debated, and the authorities reach a decision, public discussion is curtailed. However, maintaining a balance will be difficult. The short term is likely to be rocky.

Conclusion: China, Taiwan, and Beyond

In Taiwan prior to democratization, government legitimacy rested heavily on economic growth and nationalism, as it does in China today. Rule of law was widely perceived as necessary for economic growth, leading to substantial legal reforms. Over time, however, these bases for legitimacy proved insufficient in Taiwan and may prove so as well in the mainland. Rule of law, greater freedoms, and ultimately democracy or at least greater participation in the political process are likely to be required to maintain legitimacy, particularly if the economy fades.

China, like Taiwan, has pursued a dual track for legal reforms. Improvements have been most notable in the commercial area. On the other hand, the governments in both Taiwan and mainland China have been quite capable of repressing threats to political or social order and have imposed numerous restrictions on civil and political liberties. Nevertheless, over time, there were spillover effects in other areas, including changes in the fundamental norms of governance.

The transition from the lower-middle ranks to the upper-middle or high income ranks is a particularly difficult period for countries, Taiwan and China included. The East Asian Model suggests that some combination of controls on potential sources of instability and continued investment in human capital and institutional reforms is necessary. Bueno de Mesquita and Downs have shown that authoritarian regimes may sometimes be able to achieve economic growth while postponing democracy by providing standard public goods— such as public transport, public health, and primary and secondary education—while controlling public goods necessary for political coordination, such as civil and political rights and a free press.[68] An authoritarian regime that ensures economic growth and restricts coordination goods has a substantially higher chance of survival, whereas allowing freedom of the press and civil liberties decreases the regime's chance of survival by 15 to 20 percent. The experiences from Asian countries suggest that this strategy produces better results than democratization at low levels of wealth. Of course, authoritarian regimes may unjustifiably delay the transition to democracy or be too restrictive in particular cases. Thus, to the extent that some form of democracy is the preferred regime type for developed countries, the dilemma for middle-income countries is that premature democratization may not lead to rule of law or democratic consolidation; on the other hand, postponing democracy may ultimately result in higher-quality rule of law and democratic consolidation, but the chances are greater that the authoritarian regime might survive indefinitely or at least postpone democratization longer than necessary.

What lessons will PRC leaders draw from the Taiwan experience? On the one hand, Taiwan may be seen as a positive example of a transition with little blood shed and little impact on social stability or economic growth. On the other hand, Taiwan may be seen as a negative example where NGOs and activist lawyers were able to challenge the legitimacy of the state and drive the reform agenda. Moreover, Taiwan was much wealthier and the legal system much more developed when courts began to hear a wide range of controversial cases.

An examination of Taiwan, China, and the East Asian Model more generally sheds light on several important issues regarding modernization theory and democratization, the implementation of rule of law and good governance, and their relationship to wealth. There are two broad variants of modernization theory. The first emphasizes economic development as the motor for other reforms; the second puts freedom and democracy first. Taiwan and the other successful Asian countries, and China thus far, are examples of the former approach.

There is a high correlation between wealth and rule of law and good governance, as well as human rights and other indicators of human well-being.[69] All of the countries in the top quartile of the World Bank Rule of Law Index, including the East Asian countries, are high or upper-middle-income countries. This is consistent with the general empirical evidence that rule of law and economic development are closely related and tend to be mutually reinforcing.[70] The experiences of Taiwan, China, and other Asian countries lend support to the general proposition that economic growth leads to institutional development, and vice versa.[71] Taiwan's legal development since 1949 occurred against a backdrop of a transformation from a low-income country with a nominal GDP per capita of US$145 in 1951 to a high-income country with a nominal GDP per capita of US$15,203 in 2005. The relationship between GDP and rule of law is actually stronger in the Asian region (r = 0.91) than for countries overall (r = 0.82).[72]

The experiences of both successful and unsuccessful Asian countries also lends support to the general proposition that countries that democratize at higher levels of wealth are more likely to consolidate democracy than those that democratize at a lower level. The Third Wave of democracy called into question the view that there are preconditions for democratization. Empirical studies also demonstrated that there is no magical tipping point at which countries become democratic.[73] Unfortunately, most Third Wave democracies have turned out to be disappointing. The number of cases of successful consolidation of liberal democracy is small and dwarfed by the number of failures. In his revised 2003 edition of *Democracy in the Third World,* Pinkney strikes a decidedly more pessimistic note than in the 1994 edition: "While virtually all of Latin America and the vast majority of countries in Africa and Asia are now living under elected governments, breadth has been achieved but not depth, quantity but not quality, transition but not consolidation."[74]

As in the previous waves of democratization, several Third Wave democracies have reverted back to various forms of authoritarianism or have become mired in highly dysfunctional states of formal democracy. Many if not most democracies among developing countries today are illiberal democracies that are formally democratic but fail to adequately protect human rights, among many other shortcomings.[75] It is often difficult to tell them apart from authoritarian regimes except for the holding of periodic elections where the outcome is tightly controlled. The vast majority of democratic governments remain corrupt and inefficient. Few have managed to achieve sustained economic growth or to improve human well-being.

In light of the poor empirical record of many democracies in terms of economic growth, human development, and consolidation, the dominant view through the 1960s, 1970s, and early 1980s that there are preconditions to successful democratization is now making a comeback—although no one is sure what the necessary preconditions are or how to satisfy them.

The example of Taiwan also sheds light on the relationship between rule of law and democracy. Empirical studies have shown that electoral democracy (in the sense of competitive multiparty elections in which citizens vote for leaders at all levels of government) and rule of law tend to be reinforcing, albeit weakly.[76] However, electoral democracy is neither necessary nor sufficient for rule of law. Within Asia, Hong Kong and Singapore are examples of jurisdictions that rank high on rule of law indexes but are not democratic (Hong Kong) or rank low on the Polity IV Index (Singapore's 2002 ranking on the 0–10 point Polity IV Index was 2). Among Middle East countries, Oman, Qatar, Bahrain, Kuwait, and the United Arab Emirates are in the top quartile on the World Bank Rule of Law Index but have a 0 ranking on the Polity IV Index. Conversely, just as nondemocracies may have strong rule of law-compliant legal systems, democracies may have legal systems that fall far short of rule of law. Guatemala, Kenya, and Papua New Guinea, for example, all score highly on democracy (8–10 on the Polity IV Index) and yet poorly on rule of law (below the twenty-fifth percentile on the World Bank Rule of Law Index).

Nevertheless, the experiences of Taiwan and other East Asian countries, including China to date, also suggest that there are limits to how fully rule of law can be implemented in the absence of democracy. Most notably, courts are likely to lack adequate independence and authority to handle certain politically sensitive cases impartially. Taiwan and South Korea fit the EAM in that after democratization the courts emerged as independent and authoritative forces capable of handling even politically sensitive issues involving controversial constitutional amendments and the criminal liability of past presidents impartially.[77] In contrast, other countries fit the pattern, but in a negative way in that democratization at lower levels of wealth has exacerbated or at least failed to resolve shortcomings in the legal system, including problems with the authority and independence of the judiciary. In Indonesia, corporatist ties between judges and the political, military, and business elite have undermined the authority and independence of the judiciary.[78] In the Philippines, the courts continue to be so heavily influenced by the politics of populist, people-power movements that basic rule of law principles are threatened.[79] Democratization alone is clearly not sufficient to ensure an independent and authoritative judiciary.

Asian countries that have followed the EAM have been remarkably successful in achieving sustained economic growth, establishing rule of law, and implementing some form of constitutionalism that respects human rights. Nevertheless, even assuming the soundness of the EAM, other countries may not be able, or may not want, to follow it. Having democratized, most developing states will not be able to restrict civil and political rights in the name of social stability and economic growth in the way China and other East Asian states have. Citizens of other developing countries may also object that the tradeoff is unnecessary in their case or not worth it. In addition, other countries may not have the political or economic power to resist external pressures to open the domestic economy to foreign competition in the way China has.

More fundamentally, as this comparative study of Taiwan and China demonstrates, each country faces unique challenges and opportunities. Along the way, many particular choices are made. Some institutions gain power, some lose power; some segments of society are made better off as a result of reforms, others are made worse off. Accordingly, the story of modernization or law and development in any given country is inevitably a story of *politics*— and largely local politics at that. Thus, it is not likely that any single model will apply everywhere. At minimum, the model would need to be adapted in light of local conditions. Indeed, the key to the East Asian success has been the willingness to be pragmatic.

Notes

1. Peerenboom 2007a.
2. We have reservations about whether there is a single model. The main reservations are that the common features are stated at a high level of abstraction, there is considerable diversity with respect to specific issues and policies, and the essence of the East Asian approach has been pragmatism—which emphasizes flexibility and adaptation rather than dogmatic adherence to specific guidelines. That said, there are significant "family resemblances" (to borrow Wittengstein's phrase) or patterns among East Asian states. Thus, the World Bank (1993, 367), although denying that there is a single model or recipe for success, then turns around and summarizes a number of principles and lessons for other developing countries. In the end, not much hinges on whether these principles, lessons, and patterns are referred to as a "model" or as "suggestive guidelines that must be interpreted and adapted to fit local circumstances." Given the absence of any methodological or substantive standards for distinguishing between a model and suggestive guidelines, we will continue to refer to the EAM or the model.
3. US Department of State 2004; Congressional-Executive Commission on China 2005.
4. China has learned this lesson the hard way. Although China has done reasonably well in addressing poverty, the focus on aggregate economic growth has led to rising inequality. In addition, the relatively low amount of public spending on education and health, combined with a turn toward market forces in the health sector, has increased social tensions. In recent years, to remedy these problems, the government has begun to increase public spending on education, health, and welfare services. Peerenboom 2007a.
5. Briefly put, a thin theory stresses the formal or instrumental aspects of rule of law—those features that any legal system allegedly must possess to function effectively as a system of laws, regardless of whether the legal system is part of a society that is democratic or nondemocratic, capitalist or socialist, liberal or theocratic. Although proponents of thin or procedural interpretations of rule of law define it in slightly different ways, there is considerable common ground, with many building on or modify-

ing Lon Fuller's (1964) influential account that laws be general, public, prospective, clear, consistent, capable of being followed, stable, and enforced. In contrast, thick or substantive conceptions begin with the basic elements of a thin concept of rule of law but then incorporate elements of political morality such as particular economic arrangements (free-market capitalism, central planning, etc.), forms of government (democratic, single-party socialism, etc.), or conceptions of human rights (liberal, communitarian, Islamic, etc.).

6. On human rights in Asia, see generally Peerenboom et al. 2006.

7. See generally Peerenboom 2004 and the individual country chapters therein.

8. Laos and Myanmar had average growth rates of more than 6 percent between 1991 and 2001, and government officials may be beginning to realize the virtues of the EAM. Even North Korea shows signs of change.

9. Chen Weitseng 2000.

10. The restrictive martial laws were widely abused. Li 2001.

11. Control Yuan 2006.

12. Judicial Yuan. Republic of China, Taiwan. 2006. The counterintuitive fact that the prevailing rate in the early years is higher than in the postdemocratization years suggests that prevailing rate alone is not necessarily an effective indicator to observe the extent to which the administrative litigation constrains state power. People in the early years who resorted to litigation rather than alternative dispute resolution usually had strong cases, along with more financial resources, information, and the necessary *guanxi* (connections) to win their cases in court. Given the low number of cases during that period, a small number of successful cases filed by these well-informed plaintiffs results in a high prevailing rate. Nevertheless, the total number of successful cases is so small that the threat of losing in administrative suits does little to constrain state actors.

13. See, e.g., Johnson 1987; Wade 1990.

14. Chen Weitseng 2002, Chen Weitseng 2000, 100–102, 119–122.

15. The KMT government established a task force—the Commission of Economic Reform, constituted by officials and scholars as well as entrepreneurs—in 1985 and for the first time examined the regulatory legal regime in great detail. Chen Weitseng 2000, 134–136.

16. The KMT implemented various favorable policies for foreign investors and select private firms, such as easy access to land, tax exemption, purchasing guarantee, and cheaper price of raw materials through a dual-price system. Subsidies were provided for firms in strategic industries such as steel, textile, plastics, and polyvinyl chloride. Chen Weitseng 2000, 71–79.

17. Chu 1992, 101–105.

18. Control Yuan 2006.

19. As leader of "free China" and liberator from Japanese colonialism, the KMT had to provide Taiwanese a better version of polity than Japan and Communist China (PRC). Further, as an immigrant regime, the KMT sought to ally native Taiwanese elites by allowing room for political participation. Wang et al. 2006, 144–147.

20. Most of the key leaders in the current DPP administration were lawyers involved in the 1979 *Formosa* trial, including President Chen Shui-bian, Vice President Lu Hsiu-lien, and Prime Minister Su Tseng-Chang.

21. See Chu 1992, 49–51; Lin 1998; Chapter 3 by Merle Goldman and Ashley Esarey and Chapter 8 by Tun-jen Cheng and Gang Lin. However, as Cheng and Lin observe, the level, scope, and degree of competition in local elections remains limited in China. Moreover, many of the factors that led to more competitive and widespread elections in Taiwan are lacking or less applicable in China's case. Ethnic tensions are

less severe, China is an emerging superpower less susceptible to international pressure, and the central leadership is less tolerant of political pluralism and dissent. Further, as Goldman and Esarey note, China has not yet developed an independent middle class to support liberal democracy. The CCP has successfully co-opted much of the business and professional community.

22. Wang and Tseng 2005, 133;Winn and Yeh 1995, 580–581.

23. Wang and Tseng 2005, 192–194, 270–271, 283, 341–343.

24. See Przeworski et al. 2000; Acemoglu and Robinson 2006.

25. Chang 2001; Chen Tsung-fu 2000, 2001.

26. Nominees for grand justices had to be approved by the KMT Standing Committee before they were officially announced. It was not until 1984 that the KMT stopped its direct intervention in the nomination process for the justices of the highest court. Judicial Yuan 2005a, 79, 132.

27. See Tien Hung-mao 1992a, 3.

28. Liu 2002.

29. Yeh 2003; Chen Tsung-fu 2002.

30. Judicial Yuan 2005c.

31. Judicial Yuan 2006.

32. Wang et al. 2006, 200.

33. Transparency International 2005. There is no simple relationship between corruption and political regime type. Without further reforms, corruption may become worse during the political and economic restructuring after democratization and transition to a market economy. See generally Rose-Ackerman 1999.

34. Cooney 2004, concluding that "Taiwanese are much less liberal than they are democratic."

35. Frederick Lin 2006. By 2007, however, Taiwan ranked 32nd on the World Press Freedom Index, higher than Japan (37), United States (48), Hong Kong (61), Singapore (141), and China (163). Reporters Without Borders 2006.

36. Chen Tsung-fu 2002, 14–16.

37. The general public tends to hold a more cynical view than lawyers toward judicial corruption, reflecting their information sources (e.g., the media rather than personal experience), their own experiences and sense of justice (e.g., concerns about lawyers fees and court costs), and their perception of the impact of the overall political climate on the judicial system (i.e., the politicization of judges and their legal decisions). For instance, according to Transparency International's 2007 report on judicial corruption, around 64 percent of survey respondents in Taiwan described the judiciary as corrupt, compared to 53 percent in the United States, 49 percent in Korea, 26 percent in Japan, and 22 percent in Hong Kong. In the case of Taiwan, a survey suggested that more than 67 percent of the respondents received their impression of the court through mass media and newspapers, whereas merely 14 percent based their impressions on their own experience. Transparency International 2007; Judicial Yuan 2004.

38. Judicial Yuan 2005b.

39. Judicial Yuan 2005c.

40. Except for the case of President Chen's son-in-law, who has been charged with insider trading, the underlying issue in all other cases concerns the customary use of soft budget funds in light of a rigorous anticorruption law that was rarely enforced against high-ranking senior officials in the past.

41. For a more extensive discussion, see Peerenboom 2007a and the cites therein.

42. See ibid. and the cites therein.

43. Branstetter and Lardy 2005, 12.

44. Wolf 2005.

45. Huang 2003.

46. See Peerenboom 2007a.

47. Przeworski et al. 2000, 120.

48. See Peerenboom 2002, 450–512; 2003. See also Clarke 2003; Clarke et al. 2006; Pistor and Wellons 1999.

49. See Peerenboom 2002, 9–10, 64–65, 130–145, and the cites therein.

50. See Lubman 1999; Peerenboom 2002, 2007a; Office of Legislative Affairs 2008; Tanner 2005; Yang Dali 2004; Dowdle 2002.

51. See Lubman 1999; Chen, Albert 2004; Peerenboom 2002, 2007a.

52. See Peerenboom 2007b; Liebman 2007.

53. For a discussion of the factors that have led to problems in implementing the criminal law, see Peerenboom 2007a, and for environmental law, see van Rooij 2006.

54. Plaintiffs prevail in about 12 percent of cases in the United States and only 4–8 percent of the time in Japan. Peerenboom 2002, 400, 440. How often plaintiffs *should* prevail in each system is a separate issue and would require a detailed substantive review of a large number of cases from each system. Nevertheless, the high rates in China show that there is more accountability and that the courts are stronger than often suggested.

55. "The Bar Pass Rate Should Be Greatly Raised," available at http://www.dffy.com/sifakaoshi/xx/200512/20051205072719.htm (accessed January 15, 2007). See also news reports of *Fazhi Ribao,* September 18, 2005, and December 24, 2006.

56. Fu 2007; Fu and Cullen forthcoming; Pils 2007; Hand 2007.

57. PRC Supreme Court 2005.

58. Kaufmann et al. 2005.

59. Shen 2003.

60. Dowdle 2002; Cai 2005.

61. Peerenboom 2007a.

62. Cai 2005.

63. See also Chapter 2 by Yun-han Chu.

64. Kaufmann et al. 2005 concede the difficulties of assessing trends in a particular country indicator given the large margins of error. The decreases may be attributable to the addition of new data sets and large margins of error (standard deviation of .12 for rule of law), with the latter the more important factor. Peerenboom 2007a.

65. Daniels and Trebilcock 2004 group obstacles to rule of law into three general categories—resource and institutional capacity shortcomings, social-cultural-historical problems, and political-economy barriers—and argue that political-economy obstacles, including opposition by key interest groups, have been the biggest barriers in Latin America and in Central and Eastern Europe. See also Hellman et al. 2003.

66. According to the state media, more than 1,800 police were injured and 23 killed during protests in just the first nine months of 2005.

67. State Council, White Paper 2005.

68. Bueno de Mesquita and Downs 2005. The study found that restricting coordination goods does not prevent economic growth, except at the highest levels of per capita income.

69. The correlation between GDP and rule of law is $r = .82$; government effectiveness $r = .77$; control of corruption $r = .76$; civil and political rights (as measured by the World Bank's voice and accountability indicator) $r = .62$; social and economic rights (as measured by the Human Development Index of the United Nations Development Programme [UNDP]) $r = .92$; and women's rights (as measured by the UNDP's Gender-related Development Index) $r = .93$. Peerenboom 2004, 148.

70. Based on time series data, a study has found that the causal relationship

between institutions and economic growth runs in both directions, although the impact of greater growth on institutional development is stronger than the impact of institutions on growth. Chong and Calderón 2000. See also Rigobon and Rodrik 2005. A World Bank study agrees with the finding that wealth matters to some extent but concludes that the causal impact of income on governance is small and that most of the correlation reflects causation from governance to per capita incomes. Kaufmann et al. 2005.

71. Peerenboom 2002; Pistor and Wellons 1999; Clarke et al. 2006.

72. Peerenboom 2004, 148.

73. Przeworksi et al. 2000.

74. Pinkney 2003, 232. McFaul 2002 notes that 22 of the 28 former Soviet republics are either dictatorships or unconsolidated transitional regimes. See also Carothers 2002; Diamond 1999.

75. Zakaria 2003.

76. Rigobon and Rodrik 2005.

77. Wang 2002; Hahm 2004; Ginsburg 2003.

78. Dick 2006. For a discussion of judicial independence in China that challenges several standard assumptions, see Peerenboom 2007b.

79. Pangalangan 2004.

8

Competitive Elections

Tun-jen Cheng and Gang Lin

The genesis and early organizational development of the Kuomintang (or the Chinese Nationalist Party) and the Chinese Communist Party displayed striking similarities. They were formed in the early twentieth century, about a decade apart (1912 and 1921, respectively) to rebuild the nation and society out of the ashes of imperial China.[1] Both parties won power through the pivotal roles they played in two different revolutions, a nationalist one for the KMT that gave birth to Nationalist China in 1911 and a socialist one for the CCP that delivered the People's Republic in 1949 and drove the Nationalist regime to Taiwan. Upon their birth, both quickly adopted a Leninist configuration—secretive, cell-constituted, vanguard-led, presumably mass-based, and with a decision rule called democratic centralism. With self-appointed historical missions, both parties superimposed themselves onto the state and society, permitting them to exercise untrammeled political power.

At some point, however, the developmental paths of the two parties diverged in both time and nature. The KMT in the past two decades has been transformed, willingly or not, from the ruling party into a regular political party facing competitive elections and coming to accept "institutionalized uncertainty." In the year 2000, following a historic electoral defeat, the KMT even had to hand executive power over to its archrival political party in Taiwan, the Democratic Progressive Party. Only through an electoral victory can the KMT now regain power, a test it failed in 2004. As a strategy for political recovery, the KMT as an opposition party has begun to democratize itself.

The institutional dynamics that Taiwan has experienced have yet to be replicated in China. Although China is experimenting with somewhat competitive elections at the village level, it is unclear whether local election will become a prelude to higher-level elections. The CCP may be considering the use of "limited and controlled elections" to "promote" intraparty democracy, but interparty competition remains an alien concept to a ruling party that is not

161

(at least not yet) receptive to the notion of an electoral mandate. Does Taiwan's historical experience with a competitive election and party system provide us with a road map to analyze and predict the course of institutional change in China? To address this question, this chapter first delves into the two parties' authoritarian past, especially their similar organizational attributes and the political hegemony they possessed. The second section then examines the conditions under which competitive elections emerged as the driving force for the transformation of the hegemonic party in Taiwan. In the third section, the chapter identifies recent and current developments in China and uses Taiwanese experience to shed light on possible developments there. The chapter concludes that historical legacies are far more entrenched in China and that party transformation there will be more incremental, uneven, and episodic than in Taiwan.

The Two Hegemonic Parties as Political Twins

The KMT and the CCP were twins: both acquired political hegemony, both claimed entitlement to governance, and both developed into organizations with the capacity to guard their political power.[2]

The KMT founded republican China in 1911 out of a collapsing Manchu empire, bridled the unruly warlords, and consolidated political authority in the 1920s. It laid a foundation for the modernization of the economy in the 1930s and regained Chinese control of tariffs from Western powers in the 1940s. The CCP founded itself in 1921 in the wake of the modernizing May 4 movement of 1919; developed its power bases in rural China after 1927, particularly during the period of anti-Japanese war; and finally drove the KMT out of the mainland in 1949. While still on the mainland, the KMT aimed at national construction. Once it retreated to Taiwan, the KMT regime vowed to recover the mainland.

This "historical project" justified the KMT's monopoly of power in Taiwan. The perpetual control of political power created a strong nexus between the party and the state. The KMT defined "the people" as their social base, developed an encompassing and inclusive corporatist structure that strove to be a "catch all" party that cut across various social cleavages. This ideological underpinning excluded extreme ideologies—such as Communism—from the political realm and severely limited the space for societal opposition to develop. Two small parties that also retreated to Taiwan in 1949 were allowed to exist but were not allowed to compete fairly or to win elections. Indeed, the KMT treated the two "official" opposition parties more as friends than rivals, advancing subvention rather than dishing out punishment to them.

Instead of espousing any ideology, the KMT advanced a political doctrine that was eclectic in nature, was based on rather vague principles (which easily could be reinterpreted), and was without platforms for social transformation (which avoided designating winners or losers for class conflict).[3] The doctrine did possess a socialist hue, expressing a lofty commitment to social welfare and a distaste for classical liberalism—although the KMT broadly occupied the ideological middle ground that, in turn, permitted policy to vacillate between social redistribution and liberal Darwinism. The KMT party was active in, but did not in any sense dictate to, the economy. The market was distorted and controlled but not displaced, and it remained the principal institution for economic activities. Private property rights were maintained, although they were not fully respected or guaranteed.

In contrast, after taking power in China in 1949, the CCP managed to penetrate the society through a corporate structure, continuous social mobilization, and thought transformation. The party had a strong sense of purpose to reach Communism, a tightly knit ideology with a utopian goal. However, in recent decades, the CCP has begun to look more like the KMT of the 1950s and 1960s. Although the CCP still commits itself to Communism, it has been envisioned as a remote ideal goal rather than a feasible social system for the foreseeable future. Its "socialism with Chinese characteristics" is a paradoxical mixture of economic utilitarianism and social egalitarianism.[4] The CCP is no longer obsessed with class struggle but emphasizes economic development and social harmony via economic marketization and interest coordination, respectively. Private property rights are constitutionally protected, but individualism is yet to become a legitimate value orientation. Despite the political centrality of economic and social elites in China, the party has tried to display itself as a vanguard for all Chinese people. The Chinese party-state has stopped running state enterprises directly while maintaining significant and less productive state-owned enterprises that enjoy preferential policy and financial privileges. Like the KMT in predemocratization Taiwan, the CCP works with "democratic parties" in a very coordinated way. Like the KMT, the CCP also passed the torch from revolutionaries to technocrats, becoming a ruling party using technocrats to effect economic development.

Although the imperatives of domestic legitimacy and control drove both parties to move away from radical goals, this was not enough to force them to forgo political dominance altogether. After all, the potential loss of such a change would be substantial: their claims for institutional privileges based on their roles in revolution, their control of state resources and immense career opportunities for their cadres, as well as their partisan influence on the judiciary and coercive power. In relinquishing authoritarian control, the KMT and the CCP, as hegemonic parties, would have to become ordinary parties and compete in the political market. As hegemonic parties, the KMT and the CCP thus had less incentive to launch or consent to democratic change than former military regimes in South Korea, Thailand, and many Latin American countries.

Yet this relinquishment of political dominance is precisely what happened to the KMT. How did this "second transition" come about?

The KMT's Transformation

Cumulative Effects of Local Elections

We contend that the introduction of local elections—meant to co-opt grass-roots elites—entrapped the KMT in a protracted process of organizational change that eventually prepared it for full-blown electoral competition. A national-level election under the auspices of the KMT regime was first held in 1946, a year after World War II ended. Upon its defeat by the CCP on the mainland and its relocation to Taiwan in 1949–1950, the KMT suspended national elections indefinitely on account of national emergency. Local elections—held in pre–World War II Taiwan on a very limited scale under Japanese colonialism—were not only allowed to resume but were actually expanded to the provincial level. Why did the KMT regime not suspend local elections altogether?

First, local elections were a nice way for an émigré regime to govern an unfamiliar society. Elections provided local elites with an arena in which to compete among themselves, indeed a safety valve to vent whatever grievance they might have harbored after a highly redistributive land reform. Local elections were a mechanism for the KMT to divide and rule and to co-opt local elites. The electoral system adopted was the single nontransferable vote (SNTV) system, a perfect design that allowed the party organization to serve as coordinator among competing local elites.[5] Second, local elections allowed the KMT to put up a democratic facade, helping to keep Taiwan's affiliation with the liberal democratic camp and secure US support, especially during the first two decades of the Cold War era.[6] Capped at the provincial assembly level, local elections could not possibly dislodge the KMT from the provincial government, not to mention the national government. Still, subnational elections on Taiwan were enough of a showcase when compared to the other side of the Strait.

Local elections in Taiwan were comprehensive, institutionalized, and quite real. They have been regularly held for both executive and representative elections at the township and county levels since 1950 and for the provincial assembly since 1951. They were real in that they were fairly competitive, and non-KMT candidates could and did win. The candidate-to-seat ratio was a consistent ratio of 2:1 for the county councillor election and the provincial assembly election. The ratio was about 3.5:1 for the contested seats for county magistrates and city mayors, and the uncontested seats for this kind of executive elections decreased significantly in the first decade of the elections. Prior to 1986, political opposition consistently won between 30 and 40 percent of votes in all local elections and seized between 10 and 30 percent of seats.[7]

Local elections were, however, under the KMT's close watch so as not to exceed its "comfort level" or cross an unspoken red line. The KMT could live with a political opposition collecting up to 40 percent vote share, but beyond this high water mark, rules would be altered and coercion might even be used to prevent further advance of the opposition. Why did the opposition's 40 percent vote share seem to denote the KMT's comfort limit? First, thanks to the SNTV electoral system, 40 percent of the votes generally meant 30 percent of the seats for political opposition. Under the SNTV system, the individual-based, ill-integrated opposition typically suffered around a 10 percent "seat deficit" (the discrepancy between the vote share and the seat share), whereas the highly organized KMT generally reaped a 10 percent "seat bonus." Second, if the opposition could not break the 40 percent level of vote shares, seat deficits or bonuses were likely to remain as an "organization" and "tactical" issue. Had the vote share of opposition approached the 50 percent mark, winning half of the votes and yet receiving a minority share of seats, the fairness of the electoral system would have become an issue and the legitimacy of local elections would have been undermined.

The hypothetical red line was that political opposition would not be tolerated if via electoral competition it captured key executive offices with high national status. Precluding the Taiwanese provincial governorship—which had only some personnel power and little budgetary power—from electoral competition abundantly revealed the KMT regime's aversion to any elected official with an electoral mandate from the whole island, which is geographically coterminous with the national territories that the KMT regime effectively controlled. An electoral mandate in the hands of political opposition validated in Taipei (the capital and the hub of northern Taiwan), in Kaoshiung (the second-largest city and the hub of southern Taiwan), or in both places would come close to overshadowing the KMT's outdated mandate that was based on the 1947 election on the mainland that it no longer controlled. When the Taipei city mayoralty fell into the hands of the opposition at the turn of the 1960s, the KMT initially tolerated the situation, but after the opposition enjoyed a few terms, this elective office was turned into an appointive one. When the mayoralty of Kaoshiung was within the reach of opposition at the beginning of the 1970s, the city of Kaoshiung was elevated to the status of municipality, turning its elective chief executive office into an appointive one.

Nonetheless, local elections steadily and subtly impacted the KMT party organization and the nature of political competition. First, by institutionalizing local elections, KMT leaders came to rely more and more on voters' voices than on the party's internal disciplinary and auditing units to monitor and assess their cadres.[8] Voters' choices became a useful feedback mechanism for party leaders. For instance, voters' rejection of local faction candidates pampered by the KMT cadres in the 1960s in the Kaoshiung and Pintung area led the party to field more technocrats in the 1970s.

Second, local elections nurtured the managerial types of cadres within the party and gave them political clout. These "election managers" were not necessarily liberal reformers, but their intraparty careers were vested in the KMT's performance electoral processes, unlike the conservative ideologues who were primarily mindful of maintaining political stability so as to focus on the grandeur of a national mission such as retaking the mainland. The more competitive the KMT candidates, the better election results the KMT could achieve, and the better off these managerial cadres would be. They were not necessarily for political liberalization and full-fledged interparty competition, but they were not averse to moving incrementally toward that direction. As local elections expanded in scope and as national-level elections began to open up, the KMT elite bifurcation became more and more pronounced, allowing the democratic opposition to exploit the potential internal division within the KMT.

Third, local elections created what we may call the trickling-up pressure for the ruling party to expand the scope of electoral competition. The comprehensive nature of a local election made it possible for a person to pursue an election-driven career, bidding sequentially for a hierarchy of elective offices that began with the village council, then the township council, the county council, the provincial assembly, and ended up with the county magistrates. In one decade only, local elections had already given rise to a political class—the office seekers and their close associates. Given the pyramidal nature of the political office, the higher the rung one attempted to reach, the more competitive the pressure one would experience. By the end of the second decade of local elections (the late 1960s), the funneling pressure was intensifying, as crops of electoral office bidders—mostly too young to retire—were clogging the narrow and, at that time, terminal gates of electoral officialdom. The KMT party-state could only recruit a very few of these seasoned election bidders into its national government or its own party bureaucracy. Beginning in the early 1970s, a limited and slowly growing number of seats at the national-level representative bodies were opened up for electoral competition. Most scholars surmised that this expansion of electoral space was meant to replenish the rapidly aging and decaying lifetime members of these bodies. However, there was no denying that the introduction of limited national-level elections alleviated the elite circulation pressure built up by two decades of local elections. Most office seekers for central level elections were trained or groomed in local elections. Many, if not most, of the opposition leaders who spearheaded the democracy movement from the mid-1970s on were initially KMT members groomed by the party managers in charge of local elections to be "vote-getting" talent in provincial assembly elections. Had the KMT not opened up some space for national-level elections, more local political elites of its own would have joined the opposition movement.

Fourth, local elections eventually made interparty competition more imaginable and less repulsive to the KMT leaders. The party initially only allowed individual-based, unorganized dissent, and the party indeed used coercion to prevent the formation of a new party at the turn of the 1960s. However, it did not take too much effort for various dissidents to find a way to coalesce. Initially this was accomplished by way of dissident journals; later on, by study groups during nonelection times and by informal grouping during election times, all this without presenting themselves as an organized political party. But clearly they were indeed coordinating their actions. The second effort to smash the opposition took place in 1979, resulting in a famous trial of the leading members of the opposition movement, a trial not only drawing attention from abroad but also unintentionally forging the opposition into an even more cohesive group. The trial publicized the common namesake of the leading wing of the opposition and integrated various generations of the opposition movement. From that point on, the opposition functioned like a party, except in name, taking concerted action all of the time. KMT election managers, for their part, also treated the opposition as a de facto rival political party, fine-tuning nomination and campaign strategies as if functioning under a two-party system. In due course, the election tally also listed the democracy movement people as a separate group right next to the KMT, rather than as part of an unorganized nonpartisan category. The separate listing and the fact of being listed on par with the KMT gave the opposition a distinct identity. Thus, before lifting the ban on the formation of a new political party in 1987, the KMT was already facing the reality of organized opposition and de facto interparty competition.

To compete with political opposition, the KMT did make efforts to hone its skills and co-opt local elites. Although the party center had previously had the final say about candidate selection, it experimented with various methods of identifying the potential nominees, including opinion surveys of party members, cadres' evaluations, closed primaries, and public opinion polls. Grassroots criticisms typically led the party to alter the candidate selection method. With the expansion of competitive elections, the KMT then set out to further indigenize and pluralize itself, as reflected in the changing composition of party members and leadership ranks. By 1986, the year that the KMT leadership agreed to let Taiwan embark on its democratic transition by lifting the bans on new parties and new press and by moving toward full-scale, competitive elections, the KMT had long become an essentially Taiwanese party with two-thirds of its rank-and-file members recruited from the local society, though its leadership stratum was not yet localized. And by 1986, the KMT had had 34 years of experience in running local elections and 11 years of experience in running limited, but increasingly competitive and continually widened central elections.

The rise of competitive elections from 1950 to 1986 and the trend from one-party domination to multiple-party competition were not necessarily linear. Although the electoral space continued to expand, the progress toward political liberalization followed a more halting pattern. As contended above, the KMT was not comfortable if the opposition reached 40 percent of votes and approached the red line. Twice, the opposition was suppressed, once in 1960 when the *Free China Journal* attempted to coalesce and once in 1979 when the new generation opposition attempted to massively mobilize the public. As the new opposition gained momentum using the journal publications as a proxy for party organization in the 1980s, the suppression accentuated. Indeed, even though one can certainly contend that 34 years of local elections prepared the KMT to face competitive, multiple-party competition, one cannot argue that the democratic breakthrough in Taiwan in 1986 was historically inevitable.

The Damoclean Sword of Political Promise

The praxis of local elections was not the only factor contributing to the rise of competitive elections and the transformation of the KMT. The political promise that the KMT made to introduce constitutional democracy after a period of tutelage was also instrumental to political institutional change on Taiwan.

From the day it assumed political power in the early twentieth century, the KMT promised to eventually give the society a constitutional democracy in the form of full-scale competitive elections among parties. (This was a promise that the CCP did not make, as the CCP never recognized the need for advancing liberal democracy in due course.) Democracy would have to be delayed, however, given national exigency and a sequence of tasks that presumably should precede the introduction of liberal democracy. The KMT had advanced at least four major projects to postpone the advent of liberal democracy: namely, military operation against warlords, political tutelage for the public, counterinsurgency for retaking China, and economic development. The warlords were reined in during the 1920s, but the KMT continued to dominate political power as it trained the people for democracy, a task severely disrupted and sidetracked by a protracted and acute war fighting with the invading Japanese military from 1937 through 1945. The KMT was said to be ready to honor its promise to usher in a liberal democracy when it convened a constitutional assembly in 1946 and, upon the promulgation of a new constitution, held a nationwide election to compose a new government. However, the KMT quickly put that promise on hold after it was defeated by the CCP during the 1946–1949 civil war and forced to relocate to Taiwan. To cope with the CCP insurgency and to recapture the mainland, democratic elections at the national level were suspended, martial law was imposed, and the formation of new media organizations and political parties was banned. Given that Taiwanese society was put into military mobilization mode, democratic elections could only be given a chance at the local level. As the hope for returning to the mainland via military operation dimmed at the turn of the 1960s, developing the Taiwanese economy and building Taiwan as a model for the mainland became the new, urgent tasks used to justify the KMT's hegemonic power and to defer the "restoration" of constitutional democracy with which the party had briefly experimented in the late 1940s.

Given that the KMT was able to invent one project after another and that the party had no audience cost (i.e., punishment coming from the affected public), it would seem odd to argue that the political promise made by the KMT helped to bring about interparty competitive elections and transform the KMT from the hegemonic party to a regular party. It appears that the political promissory note issued by the KMT might not be worth the paper itself. What the king gives, the queen can take back. Audience costs were difficult to generate in a nondemocratic setting, as voters were not able to punish the ruling party by throwing it out like a rascal.[9] The question becomes, How did the KMT's political promise contribute to the rise of a democratic institution in Taiwan? We advance four arguments.

First, to an authoritarian regime, an unfulfilled promise is arguably more costly than a denial, hence a promise is typically postponed rather than broken. A promise arouses expectation, whereas a denial does not. If a regime has always denied the need for establishing a liberal democracy, the public may disagree with or despise the regime, but they do not form an expectation for democratization. However, if a political promise has been given but not lived up to, the expectation will be frustrated, and the party giving the promise will lose credibility. Making a credible commitment is a highly intractable problem for authoritarian rulers, as their power is neither constitutionally restrained nor effectively overseen by opposition.[10] It follows that authoritarian rulers often painstakingly attempt to delay and defer, rather than break, promises. Delaying and deferring mean that a regime lives on borrowed time and in the shadow of the future (in financial terms, this is akin to rescheduling a loan payment rather than resorting to default or repudiating the payment obligation). The KMT's historical promise (but not denial) to deliver a constitutional democracy is like the sword of Damocles hanging above the issuer of a promissory note.

Second, political projects used to defer the promise for delivering a liberal democracy have to be credible and are, by definition, temporary. At some point, therefore, an authoritarian regime can conceivably run out of projects and, willingly or not, return to that promise. The military operation was completed in 1928 when the last warlord agreed to succumb to the political central authority. The political tutelage project had been dragged out far too long and was undertaken too perfunctorily to remain credible. By the time that World War II came to an end, even the KMT's own party had doubts about the necessity and indeed feasibility for continuously embracing this project. When the military return to the mainland became a pipe dream at the turn of the 1960s, resources initially earmarked for military mobilization lost their justification. The task of building a prosperous Taiwan as a model for China became a new goal or new justification for the KMT party-state to continue political domination. After two good decades of rapid economic growth, continuous export success, educational expansion, and other achievement, socioeconomic development no longer seemed to be a viable project that could deflect the public attention away from the good old KMT promise for delivering democracy. As all these historical projects were either made irrelevant or accomplished, democracy—the political promise that the KMT enunciated in the 1910s— emerged as the most awaited political project in the 1980s.

Third, the unfulfilled promise put the KMT as the ruling party always in a defensive position while allowing the opposition to define and frame the issue of the day. Prior to 1986, the KMT was always absorbed in downplaying and ducking the issue of political liberalization and democratization and in justifying the imposition and maintenance of the martial law decree in Taiwan. As the standard arguments for postponing democracy—Communist insurrection on the mainland and economic development on Taiwan—increasingly lost their marginal utility, the opposition had become more innovative and audacious in making a case for democratization on Taiwan. Going through journalists' articles penned by democracy activists, one can easily find these activists' astute uses of reference societies, measurable yardsticks, and seemingly reasonable timetables to make their case. The political discourse they initiated was permeated with a refrain like the following: If an election were not a good idea for a divided nation, why was West Germany a full democracy? If voters were permitted to choose local officials, why should not they be entrusted to select national-level officials? If elites could compete at the provincial level, why were they not allowed at the national level? If authoritarian Spain with a per capita income of US$1,000 was ready for multiple-party competition, why was Taiwan not ready for it when its per capita income was way beyond that threshold? If elections were not possible for the mainland area, why were elections for the national-level representatives in Taiwan not allowed, especially when the class of 1946 representatives was wilting? The list could go on, but the point is clear: in deferring to political promise, the KMT in effect gave the opposition a political high ground to frame the issue, specify the necessary conditions, and draw a timetable for Taiwan's democratic transition.

Fourth, an audience cost is not entirely lacking in an authoritarian regime, especially if this regime is susceptible to external pressure. Although domestic voters might not be given a chance to throw the rascal out for broken or unfulfilled promises, external actors may be able to punish an authoritarian regime for not living up to its promise if this regime is dependent on foreign aid or security protection and if the external actors are willing to exercise aid and other leverage. This leads us the next factor that we think was instrumental to institutional change in Taiwan in the 1980s.

International Expectations and Pressures

The most immediate reason for the KMT leaders to embrace democratic transition was probably the mounting expectations and pressures coming from the international community, especially from the United States, at a time when the KMT's democracy-deflecting political projects were exhausted and its self-confidence in competing in the political market was still strong. The international security environment was most benign to the KMT's political domination in the 1950s, allowing the party to be an Asian showcase of the liberal democracy camp by merely holding local elections (and doing so under the martial law decree). In due course, however, the strategic landscape on the systemic level changed for the worse for Taiwan: détente set in and, as China noticeably pursued economic reform and adroitly turned outward, Taiwan quickly lost its presence in major international organizations and the bulk of diplomatic ties to China. Moreover, on the state-to-state level, China (the main source of threats for Taiwan) and the United States (Taiwan's security provider) were developing parallel interests vis-à-vis the Soviet Union, a development that had serious fallout for Taiwan. One way to prevent Taiwan from being totally isolated by the Western community and from being victimized by Sino-American rapprochement was for Taiwan to turn into a full liberal democracy.[11] Native Taiwanese opposition movement activists, especially those advocating Taiwanese independence in the United States, were most astute in exploiting this situation and in informing the US policy community, especially on Capitol Hill, about Taiwan's human rights and democracy issues. As a security consumer, the KMT regime was most sensitive to US congressional hearings on these issues either in general terms or over specific cases (such as the murder of Taiwan's political dissidents on US soil).

It seems fortuitous that external pressures and expectations for political liberalization and democratization peaked precisely in the 1980s, the decade during which the KMT, as the ruling party, was in the best position to cash in its political capital provided by two good decades of stellar development. A comparison with South Korea, Taiwan's most competitive economic rival, shows that although they were widely regarded as the two most successful newly industrializing economies, Taiwan had more robust macroeconomic performance than Korea, and the distinction between the two was most pronounced in the 1980s. The KMT technocrats managed the two energy crises (1973–1975 and 1979–1980) better than their Korean counterparts. Furthermore, in the second half of the 1980s, Korea suffered overcapacity, hyperinflation, and increased income gap between the *chaebol* sector and the rest of the society. Taiwan was improving income distribution and accumulating more trade surpluses than South Korea and was soon able to liberalize its import markets to move from a primarily investment-based economy to one that was also consumption based.

A survey on the perception of social stratification shows that far more of the public in Taiwan—more than 70 percent of them—self-identified as the middle of the middle class. The middle class was not averse to democratic change per se, but it was wary of any change that might undermine its achievements.[12] Given the risk-averse nature of the middle class, the opposition found it hard to break the 30 percent barrier of votes (and hence the 20 percent barrier of contested seats, thanks to the seat bonus that constantly went to the KMT). The glass ceiling over the head of the opposition suggested to the KMT that it could continue to expand the scope of electoral space and even agree to proceed with democratic transition without losing political power, especially if it could steer the course, pace the process of democratic reform, and transform itself into a dominant political party.

The ideational and exemplary effect of three dominant-party systems, in Japan (the Liberal Democratic Party), Italy (the Christian Democratic Party), and Sweden (the Social Democratic Party), loomed large in the KMT's political calculus in the mid-1980s. All told, the call for democratization came in the midst of economic prosperity and in the wake of three good decades of local elections and one good decade of supplementary elections at the national level. External pressure and expectation, economic prosperity, and its own organizational capacity led the KMT leadership to calculate that opening up a multiple-party, competitive political market was a calculated risk that the party could afford to take.

The CCP's Experiments with Controlled Elections

Spillover Effects of Village Elections

The most significant political reform in the post-Tiananmen era of Chinese politics was the emergence of village elections. Before the new Organic Law on Village Committees was issued in 1998, about 60 percent of villages had conducted democratic elections.[13] By the end of 2003, 28 of the 31 provinces in China had made or revised regulations on implementing the Organic Law on Village Committees, 25 provinces had made regulations on village committee elections, and 80 percent of farmers had participated in the elections. Despite regional variations, the trend is in the direction of increasing village self-governance and electoral competition. In 1999, 34 percent, 36 percent, and 50 percent of the incumbent village cadres in Henan, Ningxia, and Guizhou provinces/regions, respectively, lost elections. During 2000, more than 40 percent of incumbent village cadres in Shanghai, Inner Mongolia, and

Shanxi lost elections, and the percentage in Heilongjiang was even higher (53 percent).[14]

Electoral procedures have opened public space at the village level for local elites. Many private entrepreneurs compete in village elections. As Robert Pastor and Tan Qingshan predicted earlier, new economic forces and groups are demanding outlets to defend their interests or espouse their views of the public good as China's economy grows.[15] According to a study by the Zhejiang Provincial Civil Affairs Bureau in 2004, 65 percent of 421 democratically elected village chiefs were wealthy entrepreneurs in the province.[16] During the same year, 30 percent of 132,000 newly elected village committee members in the province were rich people (*xianfu qunti*); in several counties (e.g., Yiwu and Yongkang) of the province, the percentage was as high as 60 percent.[17] Increasingly rights-conscious villagers also cite the corrupt electoral process when they press claims against local officials on social and economic issues.[18]

Electoral momentum has encouraged elites favoring liberal reforms to expand the scope of political competition beyond villages. One example was the first direct election of a township head (*xiangzhang*) in Buyun Township, Sichuan Province, in 1998.[19] In 2001, the Central Committee circulated a decision of the Party Group of the Standing Committee of the National People's Congress, which reiterates that the township head should be indirectly elected by the people's congress at the same level, rather than being elected by voters directly. To resolve the tension between national legal regulations and local electoral momentum, some remedies were invented. At the end of 2001, the Buyun Township leaders allowed voters to directly nominate candidates by votes for the township headship; the candidate was then formally elected by the township people's congress. This formula of "public nomination and election" (*gongtui gongxuan*) for selecting township leadership (referring to the township head or the township party committee secretary) had been employed in 47 percent of the townships in Sichuan by the end of 2002.[20] In a slightly different way, Jiangjiashan Township of Zhejiang Province allowed voters to directly elect *two* candidates for township headship in December 2004. Similar experiments were practiced at the township level within the domain of several cities (Jingmen, Xiangfan, Xianning, Huanggang) of Hubei Province, Yubei District of Chongqing Municipality, and Suqian City of Jiangsu Province. In the case of Zhangguan Town of Yubei District, *two* candidates for the town head were provided to the local people's congress for election. It is even more significant that seven townships in Yunnan Province directly elected their township heads successfully in 2004.[21]

Another experimental model of township electoral reform is to subject the party committee secretary to direct election by party members. "Public election" (*gongxuan*) or "public nomination and election" of township party committee members and secretaries has been increasingly practiced in some provinces or municipalities such as Sichuan, Chongqing, Jiangsu, and Hubei on a trial base and further institutionally formalized. Suqian City of Jiangsu Province has since the end of 2004 promoted direct election of the town and township party committees in its subordinate districts and counties on a comprehensive scale. Other provinces involved in this reform practice include Zhejiang and Yunnan.[22] Based on these experiments, the fourth plenum of the Sixteenth Central Committee passed a resolution on strengthening the party's governing capabilities in September 2004. According to this resolution, the scope of the direct election for leading groups of grassroots party organizations should be expanded gradually.[23]

Public nominations and elections of local officials have also been experimented with at the county level, though on a limited scale, such as with the heads of Pei County of Jiangsu Province and Baixia District and Yuhuatai District of Nanjing City.[24] In these areas, party organizations above the county level do not determine candidates for county heads. Instead, potential candidates can nominate themselves or be nominated by other people. Through a series of procedures, including recommendation by people (*minzhu tuijian*), piloting studies (*zhudian diaoyan*, which means cadres staying at a selected grassroots unit to gain firsthand experience for guiding overall work), speech delivery followed by a question-and-answer session, public survey, and party examination (*zuzhi kaocha*), the final candidates are submitted to the county people's congresses for elections. In 2004, the organization department of the Sichuan Provincial Party Committee decided that candidates for cadre selection and promotion in the province should first be approved by the majority of people concerned through the procedure of democratic recommendations. In other words, ordinary people have gained the "preliminary decisionmaking power" (*chujuequan*) in selecting cadres.[25] Direct elections for deputies to local people's congresses have been experimented with in a few municipalities above the county level. The institutional roots of these elections can be traced back to the relatively competitive village elections for village committees initiated in the late 1980s. These innovations, however, have not been officially endorsed by the central government.

Different Political Promises

Like local elections in Taiwan, village elections in China are comprehensive, and they have begun to create a sort of trickling-up pressure for the ruling party to expand the scope of electoral competition. Although local elections in Taiwan nurtured a group of election managers within the KMT whose careers were vested in the party's performance in elections, party cadres in China have also developed an interest in gaining popular support for their designated candidates for grassroots party and government positions. One significant difference between the two parties, however, is that the KMT would allow the opposition to compete for local governmental posts as long as they did not exceed the red line of 40 percent of votes, whereas the CCP would be uncomfortable to see their designated candidates be challenged by nonparty members. This brings us to the second factor that was instrumental to Taiwan's democratization in the 1980s but that is absent in China: the KMT's political promise to introduce multiparty democracy after a period of tutelage.

Constitutionally, the CCP has never committed itself to the project of liberal democracy with multiparty competition. Although the party has promised to promote "people's democracy" based on the practice of "inner party democracy," its priority at this stage is socioeconomic development, a project that, in the party's view, may not be finished until 2020. Moreover, the party's definition of people's democracy contains the flavor of socialist democracy and presupposes the superiority of the one-party rule. Post-Mao leaders defined village committees as *nongovernmental* mass organizations and encouraged villagers' autonomy to demonstrate the party's enthusiasm at promoting socialist democracy. With the passage of the new law, all of China's one million villages are mandated to elect their leaders from multiple candidates by direct, secret ballot vote. However, the village election is extragovernmental by nature. Theoretically, it cannot work as a formula for developing electoral competition for government positions from the bottom up. Two institutional factors have logically limited the degree of genuine democratization in rural China.

First, the line between nongovernmental organizations and government agencies is blurred. Although the village committee is defined as an "autonomous mass organization," it is actually subject to the control of the township government. According to the law, governments at the township level should not intervene in matters within the legal limits of village self-governance. Many township governments, however, regard the village committee simply as a tool for policy implementation. In other words, village authorities in China primarily function as a convenient policy-implementation arm for higher governmental authorities. As far as village elections are concerned, the crucial stage of candidate nomination and selection is greatly controlled by party and state administrations at the upper level. A survey of village elections in Zhejiang Province conducted by He Baogang and Lang Youxing shows that even though township cadres widely took a suspicious attitude toward village elections, they have also increasingly manipulated such "democratic practices" to rid themselves of villager committees that they deem not cooperative enough.[26] Several reports by the Carter Center show that village elections do not meet the requirements of multiple candidacy, transparent nomination process, and the use of secret ballots or voting booths.[27] The initial pool of nominees is usually narrowed down to only one more candidate than the number of available positions, ballot distribution is irregular and open to interference by interest groups, few voters choose to vote in private, and a secret voting system is not required in elections of delegates to township people's congresses. According to Zhong Yang, higher governmental authorities depend primarily on two authoritative powers available to them to control village officials and their behavior: power over the village cadre personnel and the village officials' financial compensation. Such institutional constraints have prevented the villagers' committee in rural China from being a genuine democratic and autonomous organization, even though it is procedurally elected. Village democracy is therefore, according to Zhong, seriously hindered by the undemocratic nature of Chinese township/town governance.[28]

Second, without a promise of multiparty democracy in the future, the control of local politics by the party is inexorable. The 1998 law states that the party's village-level organization serves its role as the core of leadership without indicating which organization, the party branch or village committee, should decide important village affairs. Just as at every level of formal government the party's organ has ultimate control over the corresponding state organ, the party secretary of the village has more de facto power than the village committee that is directly elected by villagers.[29] According to Zhong's survey in southern Jiangsu, many villagers believed that the person who had the final say in their village was the village party secretary, not the head of the village committee.[30] Other studies confirm that village elections have not been effective in empowering the village committee head. This has contributed to the low turnout rates (less than 60 percent) in some regions.[31] As Zhong and Chen point out, those who tended to vote in village elections were people with low levels of internal efficacy and democratic values and high levels of life satisfaction and interest in state and local affairs. Anticorruption sentiment does not seem to play any role in village elections; peasants with higher levels of internal efficacy and democratic orientation stayed away from village elections due to the institutional constraints on these elections.[32]

The institutional conflict between the "autonomous" village committee, elected by villagers, and the village party branch, appointed by the party leadership at the higher level, has not led to the withdrawal of the party from grassroots affairs. Rather, it has resulted in the strengthening of the village party organization via electoral reform. In 2002, the party mandated that all who want to be village party secretaries must first stand for election to the village committee, subjecting party cadres to the electoral process.[33] This reform was developed from an experiment of the so-called two-ballot electoral mechanism in electing village party branches in some regions.[34] Over the past years, the two-ballot system has been further developed in Sichuan Province, in which 90 percent of village party secretaries are elected by party members among candidates recommended by party members *and* ordinary people in the formula of *liangtui yixue* (two recommendations and one election).[35] The rationale for nonparty members to have a voice in the party branch election is that party secretaries in China's grassroots actually manage most village affairs, not merely party affairs.

Given that the village party branch, rather than the elected village committee, has the final say in many villages, two models of reform experiments are being explored. The first model is that the village party secretary serves concurrently as village committee head, thus being subject to elections by villagers. Following this way of thinking, the village party branch and the village committee have been integrated into one institution with two names (*liangkuai paizi; yitao renma*) in some places. Another model is that the village party secretary serves concurrently as chair of the village representative association, which is authorized to elect the village committee, make decisions on important village affairs, and supervise the work of the village committee.[36] In either case, the party secretary remains influential in village affairs, but his or her authority rests upon either the village committee or village representative conference and is subject to election by villagers.

The significance of this practice is to prevent those most disliked from being elected. However, as the township party committee determines official candidates, this system cannot guarantee that those elected are the most liked by ordinary party members or villagers. In other words, villagers do not have a real *selecting* power, but only a *veto* power to rid themselves of useless and corrupt rulers. It is interesting that villagers' veto power is not only employed in the preelection stage but is also extended into the postelection stage in the case of recall. It is noteworthy that in Western democratic societies, the right to recall elected officials is seldom used. In the Chinese situation, the right of recall may work to supplement the imperfect electoral system at the village level.

Although the party seems to have an ideological preference for democratic policymaking (*minzhu juece*), democratic administration (*minzhu guanli*), and democratic scrutiny (*minzhu jiandu*) of village affairs, populism does not have much practice at the grassroots level, not to mention at the higher levels. Rather, the two-ballot system, as well as the practice that the party branch secretary serves concurrently as the village committee director or village representative conference chair, has enhanced the legitimacy of the village party branch as the core of leadership in China's grassroots and continues to cultivate the spirit of elitism. Introducing a democratic mechanism into the preexistent one-party system demonstrates that China's political reform follows the path chosen by the Chinese many decades ago. Because the reform was initiated and promoted by the insiders, one should expect a gradual, developmental trajectory, rather than a dramatic change in China's political system.

Deflecting International Pressure

Unlike Taiwan, China's great power status, immense market potential, and strong nationalist sentiment have all made it easier for the CCP to withstand the global democratization wave. This does not mean that the CCP is immune to international pressure for democratic change. Indeed, Chinese reformers realize that China's entry into the WTO requires that the country play by the international rules of the game (*yu guoji jiegui*), transform traditional government functions, and speed up the process of establishing a socialist legal state. In a related fashion, Chinese political culture must also be rejuvenated (*zhengzhi wenhua gengxin*) to adapt to a new international order supported by political mutual trust, economic cooperation, and cultural exchange.[37] In the past, the CCP always denounced liberal democracy as either a hypocritical showcase of the bourgeoisie or as irrelevant to China's unique national circumstances. In the new era of globalization, the party has declared that diverse civilizations and social systems in the world should coexist and that peoples under different social systems could learn from each other.[38] In his May 31, 2002, speech at the Central Party School, former party general secretary Jiang Zemin called on the party to develop socialist political civilization (*zhengzhi wenming*) in China.[39] According to Chinese official interpretation, the new concept of "socialist political civilization" contains several points. First, political civilization is part of the civilization of humankind; advanced political civilization includes progressive political ideas, such as democracy, liberty, equality, fairness, justice, political transparency, and human rights, that are shared by all human beings. Second, in promoting political development, China can learn from the achievements of political civilization of other peoples, including *some elements* of Western democracy in terms of theoretical principles, institutional design, and political process. Third, the development of socialist democracy in China should correspond to the country's economic and social development as well as its political tradition, and China should never copy any "Western political models."[40]

The bottom line is that the CCP has not committed itself to the idea of multiparty democracy, either domestically or internationally. The party never rejects democracy as a good idea but maintains its autonomy in theoretical interpretation and political practice. Although some ideas, such as a limited government, checks and balances of powers, rule of law, and constitutionalism, have gradually been embraced by Chinese leaders, the core value of liberal democracy—multiparty electoral competition for political leadership—is still absent in China's academic discourse, not to mention its political agenda. The CCP no longer challenges liberal democracy with socialist democracy in the global arena but still considers the latter as the best choice for the Chinese people. It believes that one-party rule can accommodate other democratic elements, such as electoral competition, public participation, the rule of law, and even the ideal of deliberative democracy (ironically understood broadly in mainland China as consultative democracy, an idea underlying the institution of the Chinese People's Political Consultative Conference). The perceived domestic problems of US democracy, the perceived disasters suffered by former Eastern European socialist countries after dramatic regime change, and the negative perceptions of Taiwan's democratic processes have all contributed to the Chinese ruling elite's vigilance against "peaceful evolution" and enhanced its confidence in searching for a "third way" between one-party authoritarianism and multiparty democracy.[41] Even though the Chinese regime tends to regard itself as a stakeholder of the current world community, it also dreams of building a new international economic and political order and democratizing international relations. Such a view of the world, plus the growing nationalism informed by China's economic power, has helped the CCP regime to deflect international pressure for a democratic transformation.

Conclusion

From the above comparisons, one can see that village elections in China, starting from the late 1980s, have become increasingly competitive, but that the level, scope, and degree of competition remain narrower than what Taiwan first practiced in the 1950s. One unique mechanism, which was innovated during the process of electoral reformation in China, is to merge party authority with popular endorsement. As a village leader concurrently serves as party branch secretary and village committee director or village representative conference chair, elections have turned out to be a mechanism for political cooptation of social elites into the CCP, therefore sapping outsiders' opposition and dampening democratic competition. At the same time, as ordinary villagers are more or less involved in the election process at the grassroots, the party organizations have to make sure the candidates they nominated meet people's expectations and will not be rejected by the voters. At the township level, the party's organizational elite also need to take into account ordinary people's opinions when nominating candidates for people's congress delegates, congressional chairperson, and township government head, in order to align voter or congressional delegate preferences with that of the party. To match the party's decision with people's opinions may be more formalistic than substantive, but it does add a new dimension to the regime's organization work at the grassroots.

Just like the KMT's organizational elite whose job it was to ensure that the party's candidates be elected in pre-1986 Taiwan, the CCP's grassroots organizers also have a keen interest in finding a "general will" between the party and the people. In addition to prenomination and preelection coordination and mobilization, the party's organization elite intentionally maintains a narrow margin between the number of posts and competing candidates to limit people's selecting options. Although the two-ballot system and public nomination procedures seem to require candidates to win the hearts of ordinary villagers, such trickling-up effects are neutralized by penetrating-down influence from the party organizations at the upper level. Without strong competition from outside against the party's nominees, the organizational elite's job of collecting people's opinions is much easier when compared with their counterparts in Taiwan (e.g., Li Huan, former KMT general secretary, and John Guan, former director of the KMT's organization department) during the 1970s and early 1980s. Even if the CCP expands its controlled competition for government posts at the higher level, political co-optation might still preempt potential challengers from the party's monopoly of the grassroots politic. Whereas the KMT regime under Chiang Kai-shek began to significantly recruit native social elites into the party during the 1970s, the CCP has experienced a compositional change since the beginning of this century, when intellectual and private entrepreneurs were officially and rigorously co-opted into the party. As the party has become more heterogeneous and inclusive, the traditional way of democratic centralism does not work as well as in the earlier period.

At this stage, the CCP seems determined to rule indefinitely; the political market—where different political parties compete for the right to govern a polity—is arguably still closed. There is no political promise for liberal democracy, as in the case of the KMT; instead, the CCP has literally affirmed the superiority of socialist democracy. Ironically, the party also promises to realize people's democracy through the initial step of intraparty democracy, which suggests that China is not democratized yet. Since 2000, the CCP has been assiduously trying to advance new discourse on "political civilization" that may accommodate some universal democratic values and mechanisms. Although the Four Cardinal Principles remain in the PRC constitution, the terms of democratic governing and legal ruling have been used more often than the traditional democratic centralism and people's dictatorship in the party's documents and discourse. A promise of democratic governing is a promise, and the CCP may eventually find it hard to eat its own words.

Like the KMT, the CCP has invented a lot of political projects to deflect the issue of democracy, such as economic development, cultural rejuvenation, and the building of a harmonious society (the key theme of the recently concluded sixth plenum of the Sixteenth Central Committee). If the KMT's experience is any guide, political rights may be a topic that the CCP will have to confront once the current projects have been somehow attained. In fact, the establishment of a harmonious society relies not so much on the doctrine of the rule by virtue as on a democratic mechanism for interest articulation and aggregation. The CCP's preoccupation with "social construction" (*shehui jianshe*) and social harmony at this stage, however, may deflect people's attention from the more fundamental issue of political reform. Apparently, the party prefers political coordination and organizational co-optation to free competition.

It is worth noting that the CCP's motivation to promote intraparty and people's democracy in general and local elections in particular has been derived from its concern with widespread and institutionalized corruption. The decision to improve the collective policymaking of the party committees was first pronounced upon in 1996 by Wei Jianxing, director of the party's Central Discipline Inspection Committee, attesting to the fact that the more immediate and direct pressure for expanding power sharing among the ruling elite stems from the need to fight against corruption. Former premier Zhao Ziyang realized the linkage between corruption and lack of democracy more clearly and much earlier. As Zhao's brain trust, Chen Yizhi, revealed, Zhao stated in the 1980s that if the CCP could not resolve the problem of corruption, then a multiparty system would have to be introduced.[42] China's hope for democracy relies more on the ruling elite's initiation than on social opposition. In contrast with Taiwan, ethnic division cannot be a contributing factor for democratic change on the mainland. Even though underdog organizations or groups heavily engaged in petition movement—supported by human rights activists—or even some underground associations with a variety of agendas might pose a formidable challenge to the Chinese regime, the party remains dominant owing to its successful co-optation of social elites.

It is difficult for China to replicate the Taiwanese experience in forging democratic institutions. Local elections in China are extremely limited in scope, neither nurturing political opposition nor creating trickling-up effects. Indeed, local elections have provided the CCP with a mechanism to co-opt the local elite, and the current trend is for elected officials and party leadership at the grassroots level to merge. Although the CCP has been advancing a new discourse on "political civilization" and flirting with democratic values and mechanisms, the persistence in upholding democratic centralism, socialist democracy, and the people's (hence the CCP's) dictatorship remains the fundamental political canon. There has been no explicit commitment to delivering any democratic institution that would permit competitive election among political parties. Promoting intraparty democracy within the CCP is more of an alternative to, rather than a prelude to, interparty competition, a notion that is still beyond the imagination of the CCP leadership. China's great power status, immense market potential, and strong nationalist sentiment make the CCP leaders less susceptible to external pressure for democratization, a pressure that, if coming from the United States, KMT leaders could not really deflect, given Taiwan's dependence on the United States for national security.

The Taiwanese experience does suggest that local elections in the long run can have unintended consequences that might enhance the chance for democratic transition. Elections can be additive and seductive. Social elites can be glued to the electoral process, as can party cadres. As long as elections are allowed to continue, a political class may emerge. A hegemonic party cannot possibly co-opt all of this class for all time. The political elite can be co-opted, but they can also defect. Many political opposition elites in Taiwan were initially groomed by the KMT to be winning tickets.

The Taiwanese experience also suggests that the ability to keep the electoral results within the comfort zone may well be a precondition for a hegemonic party to allow competitive elections at the local level, to expand gradually to higher levels, and eventually agree to open up the political market altogether. Periodic suppression of opposition and the manipulation of electoral systems may well be an unavoidable cost for the advent of democratic institutions.

The CCP has been more assiduous in claiming its historical entitlement and less generous in giving electoral space to local elites than has the KMT. On the mainland, the cumulative effects of local elections on the rise of political opposition and the transformation of the CCP will be less evident and perhaps not self-reinforcing. External pressures for China's democratization will be less direct or effective. China is less likely to let electoral processes gain momentum than Taiwan was. However, the discrepancy between the two sides of the Strait does not allow us to conclude that democratic institutions are unlikely to emerge in China. We are only sure that the trajectory of institutional change will be different.

Notes

1. The Revive China Society, the KMT's forebear, was established in 1895.
2. Historically the twins mostly felt animosity toward one another but occasionally were in a tactical alliance. The two parties collaborated briefly around 1926 against various warlords and in 1937 against Japan, and today they seem to be discovering some "parallel interest" vis-à-vis the Democratic Progressive Party, the current government party in Taiwan that seeks to permanently separate mainland China and Taiwan.
3. To paraphrase Juan Linz, the KMT is akin to other authoritarian organizations in their "mentality" or "eclectic doctrines" but not in their transformative ideology that aimed at restructuring the society along with a utopian goal as in the case of Communist and fascist parties.
4. This attempt is highlighted by the party's goal of establishing an egalitarian society (*gongtong fuyu*) by allowing some people to become rich first.
5. Under the SNTV system, a voter can cast only one ballot, but a candidate cannot transfer any votes to help fellow party candidates to be elected. Nomination of an optimal number of candidates and an extremely even allocation of votes among fellow party candidates are utterly essential to a party's fate in this kind of race. See Tien and Cheng 1997, 14.
6. Cheng 1989, 478.
7. Computed by the authors based on Central Election Commission statistics, collated in Lei 1992, 169–171.
8. Dickson 1997, 23–25.
9. Audience cost enhances a political actor's ability to make a credible commitment. Essentially, if he or she or his or her party reneges, the audience (voters or market players) can vote the rascals out or flee from the local market as a form of punishment. For audience cost, see Fearon 1994.
10. Stephan Haggard and A. McIntyre contend that the credibility problem is inherent in political authoritarianism, whereas the decisiveness problem is pervasive in democratic regimes where the check and balance mechanisms and the presence of

many veto groups make it almost impossible to take timely and decisive action. See Haggard and MacIntyre 2000.

11. Mann 1990.
12. Cheng 1990.
13. Zhao 1998.
14. Cong 2004.
15. Pastor and Tan 2000.
16. Cited in Kulm 2004.
17. Cong 2004.
18. Chi 2000.
19. Although this election was described by the official newspaper, *Fazhi Ribao,* as illegal, it was at the same time cited in positive terms as proof that democracy was not the sole preserve of the West. See Laris and Pomfret 1999.
20. Li 2003.
21. Shi 2006.
22. Ibid.
23. Central Committee, Chinese Communist Party 2004.
24. The two districts in Nanjing City administratively are at the deputy bureau level (*futing ji*). See *People's Daily*'s report, "Gedi ganbu zhudu gaige de ba da liang-dian" ["Eight Spotlights in Reform of Local Cadre System"], *Renminwang* [People's Website]. Available at www.people.com.cn (accessed September 9, 2004).
25. Cong 2004.
26. He and Lang 2002.
27. See for example Carter Center 1998.
28. Zhong 2006.
29. Chi 2000.
30. Zhong 2000.
31. Li 1999, 106; Dickson 1998, 358; Oi 2003, 136–141.
32. Zhong and Chen 2002, 686–712.
33. Oi 2003, 7.
34. Li 1999, 107.
35. Shi 2006, 74.
36. Ibid.
37. Ye 2002.
38. Jiang 2001.
39. Jiang 2002.
40. Yang 2002.
41. Page 2002.
42. Based on our interview with Chen Yizhi, August 10, 1997, New York.

9

International Pressures and Domestic Pushback

Jacques deLisle

The relationship between the international context (including cross-Strait relations) and Taiwan's democracy has been a U-curve. From 1949 into the 1980s, the Republic of China's external environment mostly helped sustain authoritarian rule on the island. During much of the 1980s and 1990s, changes in Taiwan's international context created incentives and pressures that reinforced domestic factors favoring democratization and democratic consolidation. Around 2000, the relationship between Taiwan's international context and democratic development became less positive again because of changes in domestic politics and external conditions.

Taiwan's experience has limited implications for democracy's prospects in the People's Republic of China. The PRC's international environment exerts weaker force and provides less compelling models than has Taiwan's during its democratic transformation and consolidation. Still, Taiwan itself is an especially salient, although ambivalent, aspect of China's democracy-relevant external context.

Taiwan's Shifting International Contexts

From the Kuomintang regime's flight from the mainland at the end of the Chinese civil war until the 1980s, the ROC's international context helped sustain authoritarianism and retard democratization. Like later periods, this long phase was neither uniform nor static. Nonetheless, several factors in Taiwan's external environment consistently were unconducive to democracy in Taiwan.

The Cold War context meant little pressure on Taiwan's rulers to democratize. The Communist victory on the mainland, the establishment of the People's Republic, and the Korean War contributed to a bipolar order in which US policy regarded the Soviet Union and China as the greatest powers in a

185

monolithic and expansionist Communist bloc. Washington brought Taiwan within the US security perimeter and made the Taiwan Strait a front line of the Cold War.

Although the contest was posed in ideological—even Manichean—terms as a struggle between Communism and the free world, US policy tolerated democratic shortcomings among its allies, particularly those at the fault lines between the superpowers' spheres of influence and in the contested terrain of the postcolonial and developing world. Democracy was a value, but anti-Communism counted for more.[1] Repressive leaders were tolerable, so long as they were "our scoundrels." Chiang Kai-shek's regime thus could count on no significant demands from its indispensable protector to democratize, given the generalissimo's indisputably fervid anti-Communism (amply reflected in his implausible goal of recovering the mainland from the "Communist bandits" and Washington's empty threats to "unleash Chiang").[2]

Hostile cross-Strait relations and diplomatic rivalry between Beijing and Taipei were part of this Cold War setting and inimical to pressures for democracy in Taiwan in other ways as well. Although China made no effort to take Taiwan, did little to articulate its legal claim to the island, and sometimes expressed willingness to wait indefinitely for the territory's return, the threat from across the Strait helped legitimate the KMT's authoritarian rule. Struggle with the Communists before the founding of the PRC had prompted formal suspension of the ROC constitution's democratic provisions. Official positions on both sides of the Strait maintained that Taiwan's external context included an unfinished civil war to control all of China, including Taiwan. Cross-Strait military crises in 1954–1955 and 1958, desultory shelling of Taiwan-controlled islands, and chronic concern over PRC spying and infiltration contributed to an atmosphere of imperiled national security. These conditions made coherent and supported the KMT regime's asserted need for martial law and indefinite postponement of elections for legislative bodies that were to represent all of China.[3]

Beginning in the early 1970s, changes in US-PRC relations and related developments altered Taiwan's international environment but did not initially make it conducive to democratization. By the late 1960s, the Sino-Soviet split and belligerent bilateral relations had created fears among China's leaders about a threat from the north that exceeded any from the West. With the passing of the Cultural Revolution's radical phase, the PRC faced international isolation that "revolutionary" foreign policy and radicals' attacks on China's foreign policy apparatus had wrought. These developments opened the way to Sino-American rapprochement.[4]

Warming US-PRC relations and China's diplomatic ascension made Chiang's Taiwan more beleaguered and besieged. Key milestones suggest the steep erosion of the ROC's position. In 1971, United Nations General Assembly Resolution 2758 reassigned the Chinese seat in the United Nations to the PRC and stripped the ROC of UN representation.[5] In 1972, the Shanghai Communiqué expressed mutual commitment to building US-China relations and pursuing cooperation on each side's high-priority foreign policy interests, US acknowledgment of the Chinese position that Taiwan was a part of China (which gave a different and, for Taiwan, troubling tone to an orthodoxy accepted by both the PRC and ROC), the formal agnosticism of the United States about the terms (although not the methods) of possible unification, and Washington's long-term intention to reduce its military presence in Taiwan (provided that regional tensions eased).[6] In 1979, the second Joint Communiqué accompanied normalization of US-China relations and brought the end of recognition, formal diplomatic ties, and the mutual defense treaty between the ROC and the United States.[7] In 1982, the third Communiqué foresaw near-term limits and longer-term reductions in US arms sales to Taiwan.[8] It is telling that Henry Kissinger—the principal US architect of the initial steps—saw Taiwan as an obstacle or irritant in US-PRC great power politics and that US policy proceeded on an expectation that Taiwan likely would not long survive as a separate entity.[9] Although the impact of this deterioration in the ROC's international position would prove more complicated, in the near term at least, it sustained national security rationales for undemocratic rule in Taiwan and legitimated aversion to democratizing reforms that might risk political instability and, in turn, national vulnerability.

From the end of the 1970s on, some US policies and laws softened these blows to Taiwan. Congress passed the Taiwan Relations Act (TRA), mandating informal quasi-diplomatic relations, arms sales, and US opposition to coerced changes in the status quo.[10] Ronald Reagan supplemented the third Communiqué with the "Six Assurances to Taiwan," which reaffirmed the US commitment to the TRA, pledged not to set a date to end arms sales and not to consult with Beijing about arms sales, and promised not to recognize Beijing's claim to sovereignty over Taiwan and not to mediate cross-Strait disputes.[11] More generally, the foreign policies of Jimmy Carter and Ronald Reagan were more concerned than were their predecessors with "values" issues, such as human rights and democracy-promotion, and, therefore, with other states' internal politics.

Still, the dominant political logic of the transformed US-PRC (and US-ROC) relationships remained Kissingerian, realist, and balance-of-power– or triangular-diplomacy–based. Such labels convey indifference to other states' internal orders and skepticism—even hostility—toward promoting democracy abroad. Carter- and Reagan-era policies did not alter fundamentally this authoritarianism-tolerant aspect of Taiwan's external environment. The TRA's human rights section was in legislation forced upon the Carter administration and was a small and backhanded provision (confined to the "declaration of policy" section and stating that nothing in the TRA "contravene[d]" US interests in Taiwanese human rights, which remained an "objective" of US policy). It paled in comparison to the legislation's focus on diplomacy and security.[12] Amid the quest to normalize and strengthen US-PRC relations, Jimmy Carter's human rights policy was muted on Chinese abuses and thereby eschewed incentives to the ROC to sharpen contrasts with the regime across the Strait to win favor in Washington. Reagan-era democracy-promotion (particularly in Latin America) and criticisms of human rights abuses (particularly in Soviet-dominated areas) had little resonance for the policy the United States had for China (and, in turn, Taiwan), perhaps not surprisingly given Beijing's dislike (albeit for dissimilar reasons) of the Soviet regime that Reagan branded an "evil empire."[13]

Factors beyond the security environment also contributed to the lack of pressure for democratic change in Taiwan. In the 1970s and into the 1980s, Taiwan stood alongside South Korea, Singapore, Hong Kong, and historical Japan as examples of an East Asian Model of an authoritarian developmental state. Some analysts saw the model as reflecting cultures that emphasized collective values and cared little for liberal democracy. Others saw a functional logic in which authoritarian rule allowed industrial policy, state capitalists, technocrats, or business elites to pursue growth-promoting strategies without the redistributionist pressures and political instability that plagued Latin America and Africa.[14] The success of the East Asian Model made credible the view that democratization was unnecessary or perilous to economic progress in Taiwan.

In this democratization-unfriendly international environment, authoritarian rule survived on Taiwan from the late 1940s into the 1980s, punctuated by instances of harsh repression. The period opened against the backdrop of the February 28 incident of 1947, which brutally helped consolidate the mainland-based KMT regime's control on the island.[15] Near the era's end, the 1979 Kaohsiung Incident and the 1984 killing in California of journalist Henry Liu I-liang (also known by his pen name Jiang Nan) showed, respectively, intolerance for prodemocracy activism alongside growing journalists' attacks on Chiang family rule.[16] But the regime-criticizing actions by the victims in the Kaohsiung Incident were partly the product of incipient liberalization under KMT rule. Foreign reaction—especially in the United States—to the violence at Kaohsiung, the ensuing military prosecution of prodemocracy intellectuals associated with *Mei-li Tao* magazine, and revelations of government officials' roles in Liu's murder also reflected the waning of international contexts that had supported authoritarianism.

From the middle 1980s through the 1990s, Taiwan's international environment became much more conducive to democratization and democratic consolidation. Reform-era developments in China and their impact on US policy transformed Taiwan's external context. Changes under Deng Xiaoping and Jiang Zemin brought political liberalization and engagement with international legal and political norms that made China seem less adversarial and ideologically unpalatable to key US audiences. Such developments supported strategies under George H.W. Bush and Bill Clinton that sought to integrate China into the international order (rather than contain China and approach it primarily as an aspiring rival power) and to justify engagement policies by their contributions to benevolent political change in China—both directly and indirectly (through promoting China's economic modernization).

Of course, the pace and direction of political change in the PRC were far from uniform during this period. The 1989 Tiananmen Incident and its aftermath, the earlier Campaign Against Bourgeois Liberalization, the still-earlier embrace of neoauthoritarianism, the recurrent repression of political dissent and nascent democratic and other heterodox groups throughout the 1990s, and other instances of retrenchment were interspersed among developments that produced significant net liberalization, political reform and some progress toward "inner-party democracy," limited electoral contests for local offices in the countryside, and some increases in transparency and accountability.[17]

The US engagement strategy was hardly immune from domestic challenge. Warnings and protests from interest groups, policy intellectuals, and members of Congress were supplemented by denunciations of the incumbent administration's "soft" China policy from the opposition party's candidate during presidential elections throughout the 1980s and 1990s. Such efforts, however, failed to reorient policy.

US perceptions of Chinese reforms and their implications for US policy endured. The first Bush administration—with a president reportedly much influenced by his time as US liaison in China—resisted strong responses to the military crackdown at Tiananmen, including renewing most-favored-nation trade privileges in the face of congressional opposition and grudgingly offering asylumlike benefits to Chinese students after Tiananmen to avoid an override of the president's veto of similar but more expansive legislation. Although the Clinton administration briefly and ineffectively linked China's trading privileges to human rights improvement and continued to raise human rights concerns at summits, its core policy remained "constructive engagement," including, in the end, supporting China's WTO bid.[18]

Also contributing to this aspect of Taiwan's changing external context were transformative economic reforms in China that abandoned the planning, autarky, and policy instability of the Mao years. Rapid, market-oriented development and deepening international economic engagement gave US and other foreign interests unprecedentedly large economic stakes—and larger perceived ones—in China. This generated support in the United States (and elsewhere) among business constituencies and policymakers for cooperative relations with the PRC. The most prominent reflection of this culminated just after the end of this period, when the United States backed China's WTO accession and Congress passed legislation granting the PRC permanent normal trading relations, ending the friction-generating annual review of China's human rights practices.

Throughout this period, Taiwan's economy grew impressively, entered more advanced sectors, and integrated more thoroughly into the global economy.[19] Taiwan remained an important trading partner and investment destination for the United States and other advanced economies. It was prepared and eager to enter the WTO and would do so once the barrier imposed by China's nonmembership fell in 2001. None of this, however, could stop China's rise from sharply diminishing Taiwan's economic importance and eroding Taiwan's political standing in the world and, crucially, in Washington.

China's two decades of near-double-digit annual growth funded a massive modernization program for the People's Liberation Army.[20] Much of it focused on Taiwan missions or would be useful in a cross-Strait conflict. Prominent measures included deploying a large missile force in southeastern provinces (which became the subject of a Taiwanese referendum in 2004), enhancing the navy's coastal capabilities (but not yet "blue water" ones), and undertaking war games and missile tests near Taiwan in the middle 1990s (timed to influence Taiwan's first direct presidential election). This inexorably shifting cross-Strait military balance jeopardized Taiwan's security through China's greater ability to threaten the island and the inevitable reassessment of the United States of the rising costs of military intervention in a crisis in the Strait.

During this period, Chinese leaders also began to turn to the long-postponed Taiwan question. Ye Jianying's 1979 New Year's Day message to "Taiwan compatriots" and Deng's articulation of the basic "one country, two systems" model (originally conceived for Taiwan rather than Hong Kong) heralded a new era in which Beijing sought movement toward resolution of the Taiwan question and promised terms that would tolerate Taiwan's different political order and a high degree of autonomy.[21] In the early 1990s, Beijing's agenda of seeking progress and offering accommodation entered a more active phase, most notably in high-level talks between Taiwan's Koo Chen-fu and the PRC's Wang Daohan in 1993. China's 1993 White Paper on the Taiwan question brought an unprecedented clear and formal articulation of China's nonnegotiable claim to sovereignty over Taiwan and fleshed out the proposed model for peaceful reunification.[22] Jiang Zemin's Eight Points in 1995 reiterated established positions, sought to strike a benign tone (including a professed ardent desire to achieve reunification peacefully), and called for reunification talks.[23] After a mid-1990s hiatus during a period of especially poor cross-Strait relations, Beijing resumed this agenda, including another round of Koo-Wang talks in 1998.

Thus, in security matters, cross-Strait diplomacy, and economic affairs, China's abandoning its former version of socialism created an international environment that pressed Taiwan's leaders to find ways to restore, protect, and elevate Taiwan's standing abroad, particularly with the United States. Although US and other governments' quiet approaches to China's continuing lack of democracy and protection for human rights indicated limits to such matters' importance in foreign policy, improvement of Taiwan's standing on "values" issues became a compelling strategy for the ROC.

The roots of these external factors in spurring Taiwanese democratization date back to President Chiang Ching-kuo's apprehension that US derecognition of his government meant that his regime would have to open the door wider to democratic reforms. During the 1980s, particularly in the wake of the Kaohsiung and Henry Liu incidents, Washington increased pressure on Chiang to democratize. US initiatives here dovetailed with developments in Taiwan, including the rise of the *dangwai* opposition, which began largely as a prodemocracy and government reform movement and had begun to enjoy limited success in the highly constrained elections that the KMT regime had begun to permit.[24]

Although the democratic opposition in Taiwan was principally a domestic phenomenon, it also reflected another subtler aspect of Taiwan's international context, especially in the earliest phases of Taiwanese democratization. As parts of the post-Soviet experience demonstrated, an international order in which democratic states, including the United States, provided sanctuary to exiled dissidents could help foster democratic transitions when those who had sought refuge went home. Although some who became leaders of the *dangwai* and its later incarnation, the Democratic Progressive Party, had remained in Taiwan, others had found shelter abroad to avoid imprisonment at home or after release from incarceration by the pre-reform KMT regime. On the other side of Taiwan's political divide, some younger members of the KMT elite who had studied in the United States during the 1970s returned bearing attitudes that were more sympathetic to democratic reform and thereby helped lower barriers to democratization in the late Chiang Ching-kuo years.[25]

During the 1980s and beyond, Taiwan's international economic linkages brought developments that, on many analyses, favored democratic change. Reliance on export-led growth and growing openness to foreign investment entailed denser connections to the international economy. This brought greater exposure to foreign ideas, including liberalism in economics and democracy in politics. Especially by the later 1980s, the dissatisfaction of the United States and other trading partners (born of trade imbalances and related concerns) brought calls for economic liberalization in Taiwan. Ensuing reforms to Taiwan's developmental state and loosening the nexus between political authorities and large enterprises weakened barriers to broader reform—including potentially democratizing reform—of government institutions and politics. More broadly, Taiwan's economic integration with the outside world fueled Taiwan's rapid economic development during this period. This progress raised per capita incomes to levels correlated with sustainable democracy and a middle class that is, on many accounts, a key foundation for democratization.[26]

Democratization also became a central feature of Taiwan's international environment. Taiwan democratized in the thick of what Samuel Huntington famously dubbed the Third Wave. Chiang Ching-kuo's moves to end martial law, legalize opposition parties, allow contested elections for more significant offices, and so on came amid a tide of democratic change in many countries, including the Philippines, Korea, and even to some extent Hong Kong.[27] By the 1990s, Taiwan's external context included the wave of democratization that accompanied Communism's global decline. The collapse of the USSR and regimes it had supported brought democratic governance to some fragments of the former Soviet empire, most durably at its affluent and Westward-looking European fringe.[28] This democratic renascence, especially the post-Soviet cases, brought renewed concern in Washington, European Union (EU) capitals, and elsewhere with their diplomatic partners' internal political orders. Promoting democracy (along with the rule of law) became a more prominent theme in many democratic states' foreign policies. It was embodied, among other places, in Clinton's "democratic enlargement" agenda. The EU and the United States deemed domestic governance and democracy-related norms relevant in recognizing new states that emerged from the rubble of the former Soviet bloc. International law and international relations commentators began to speak of a universal "democratic entitlement."[29]

This aspect of Taiwan's external environment made Taiwan's democratization more normal, both normatively and statistically. It also made democratization a more pressing concern in Taiwan's external relations, given the perennial need to cultivate support from the United States and to secure greater acceptance in potentially amenable segments of the international community—audiences that increasingly demanded or at least claimed to value democracy.

Although China remained insulated from international democratic trends and—except briefly following the Tiananmen Incident—foreign sanctions for its repressive politics, China's less-than-democratic reforms bolstered democratic reform trends in Taiwan. In addition to a significant impact on Washington's China policy, Beijing's softening authoritarianism and rapid development of cross-Strait trade and investment undercut venerable rationales for authoritarian rule on Taiwan. During much of the 1980s and into the 1990s, anti-Communism and vigilance against subversion or invasion from across the Strait became less persuasive as Taiwanese became familiar—many through first-hand experience on the mainland—with a China that seemed less aggressive, overwhelmingly focused on economic development, and committed to winning acceptance in the international order. Although cross-Strait political relations were volatile during this period (and soured for most of the final few years), and the "one country, two systems" model received a consistently chilly response in Taiwan, there was overall a less immediately threatening and sense-of-emergency-creating quality to a PRC regime with which the ROC could engage in the Koo-Wang talks or reach the now-disputed

"1992 Consensus" (which, on Taiwan's reading, allowed each side its own interpretation of "one China").[30]

The post-Soviet strand in the international democratic trend included another phenomenon that ultimately, if ambivalently, supported democratic change in Taiwan. The USSR and Soviet-style states in Eastern Europe had kept ethnic nationalism in check. With the collapse of those regimes, and the fragmentation of the states they had ruled, came a resurgence of post–World War I Wilsonian and post–World War II decolonization notions that primordial and political boundaries should coincide, and a renewed emphasis on international legal rights of "peoples" to self-determination, including in some cases the right of a people to its own state. The 1990s revival of these ideals, unsurprisingly, emphasized that democratic processes were the legitimate means for exercising self-determination.[31]

This aspect of Taiwan's external environment resonated with domestic political developments in which a rising Taiwanese identity was entwined with prodemocracy, as well as proindependence, sentiments.[32] Demands for democratization partly reflected the view that the minority "mainlanders" or *waishengren* who arrived with Chiang Kai-shek's retreating armies, and their progeny, should not rule—at least absent democratic validation—over the majority "Taiwanese" or *bentu* population. From this increasingly salient perspective, the Taiwanese people should choose their own government and shape its policies, including foreign policy—a view most strikingly embodied in the opposition DPP's call, in the 1991 version of its platform, for a referendum on independence.[33]

The democratic imperative for Taiwan that seemingly was immanent in the revitalized international norms of self-determination was problematic to the extent that communal division became the defining feature of Taiwan's politics. Relevant international legal and political principles addressed the right to democracy—and a high level of international status—for coherent "peoples" who were distinct from other, typically neighboring, groups. With the DPP drawing its core support from those most strongly identifying as Taiwanese and the ruling KMT remaining a relative (though evolving) bastion of mainlanders, and with identity politics splitting the island's population and tying the mainlander minority to Chinese across the Strait, self-determination-related prodemocracy norms might engage Taiwan's domestic political development only obliquely. If communal cleavage predominated politically, Taiwan's populace and electorate would map poorly onto the most plausible candidates for peoplehood, being overinclusive (taking in more than the "Taiwanese" majority in Taiwan) or, worse, underinclusive (encompassing only a small portion of a "Chinese" people that, especially in Beijing's view, included everyone on both sides of the Strait).[34]

During Taiwan's democratic transition and early years of democratic rule, however, several developments helped keep an identity-based political schism in check and preserved the relevance of prodemocratic international principles of self-determination. The KMT was undergoing "Taiwanization," bringing more nonmainlanders into its ranks. A Taiwanese, Lee Teng-hui, was selected as vice president and successor to Chiang Ching-kuo. In 1996, Lee won reelection in Taiwan's first direct balloting for president, ensuring a more protracted transition from a more Taiwanized KMT rule to any future DPP administration. That election also came after a campaign during which the PRC's war games and missile tests had backfired, increasing support for Lee and confirming that all Taiwanese lived together under the shadow of Chinese threats. As president, Lee articulated notions of a Taiwanese *Gemeinschaft* and a "New Taiwanese" who included all people on the island. He undertook constitutional amendments and foreign policy initiatives that embraced—albeit not as fully as he would near the end of his presidency and after he left office— elements of "proindependence" agendas that had been primarily the domain of the predominantly "Taiwanese" DPP. Also, in Taiwan's increasingly democratic politics, although the KMT and DPP had to play to their electoral bases, they also faced a common need to avoid alienating the relatively moderate median Taiwanese voter whose sense of identity (Taiwanese, Chinese, or both) was notoriously complex.[35]

During this period, Taiwan's political leaders learned to engage effectively with an evolving international environment that both pressured them to build democracy in Taiwan and afforded them opportunities to use Taiwan's democratic and related accomplishments to advance Taiwan's interests internationally. Throughout the 1990s, Taiwanese leaders and official statements understood, and pressed, the point that Taiwan's democratization could or should confer upon Taiwan higher, more fully statelike international status. They argued that the ROC's political transformation put it in step with the values shared by all "civilized" countries and should allow Taiwan to "assume a more important" and statelike role internationally.[36]

Such sources also emphasized the gap between Taiwan's vibrant new democracy and the authoritarian regime across the Strait. This played to the negative side of the emergent international norm linking international status to a state's (or aspiring state's) democratic character and pedigree (or lack thereof). Thus, the Lee Teng-hui–era Guidelines for National Unification highlighted the contrast (and set forth conditions that were sure to remain long unfulfilled) in declaring that unification could occur when the PRC became as prosperous, democratic, human rights–protecting, and law-governed as the ROC.[37] Other official statements underscored differences in the political systems and the betrayal of international democratic values that would occur if the world were to acquiesce in unification on Beijing's terms.[38]

Taiwanese statements and policies also asserted Taiwan's satisfaction of the domestic preconditions (including democratic ones) of international self-determination norms to support the ROC's claims to state or statelike international status. For example, as Lee later explained the significance of the early 1990s constitutional amendments limiting the ROC's exercise of jurisdiction to Taiwan and providing for direct presidential elections, only "the Taiwan people"—and no one on the mainland—could "authorize" state power and be represented by state institutions of the ROC.[39]

Although a feedback loop or virtuous circle cannot be established definitively, the growing emphasis on the "democracy card" in Taiwan's foreign policy strengthened the reasons for Taiwan to accelerate and deepen democratization. Democratic backsliding or shortfalls at home would threaten the quest for stature and security abroad. Democratic consolidation and development would strengthen the domestic institutional and behavioral foundation for the argument that Taiwan should enjoy higher and more secure international status. In a telling sign of this complicated and reflexive relationship between Taiwan's democracy and the external environment, official statements during this period began to play a two-level game, invoking constraints that Taiwan's robust and legitimate democratic politics imposed on the government's actions abroad, requiring it to press for Taiwan's greater acceptance and standing in the international system.[40]

Connections between Taiwan's external environment and domestic politics became more complex—and less salutary for Taiwan's democracy—beginning near the end of the 1990s. This period saw remarkable milestones of democratic consolidation. A peaceful transfer of power occurred after the opposition DPP's candidate, Chen Shui-bian, won with less than a majority in a three-way race in the 2000 presidential election. Taiwan's democratic constitutional order survived sharp challenges to the legitimacy of Chen's narrow reelection in 2004 (and skepticism about the attempt on Chen's life that likely brought him votes), years of divided government, and corruption scandals tainting both major parties. The 2008 presidential election heralded a peaceful transition back to the KMT. Still, Taiwan's international environment—and the politics of engaging it—distorted Taiwan's democratic development.

At a macrolevel, Taiwan's international context became less supportive of democracy. By the end of the 1990s, a "democratic recession" had set in. Democracy became less clearly the ascendant or dominant mode of governance as an authoritarian resurgence rolled back recent gains (including in Russia and its neighbors) and hope for further democratic progress ebbed elsewhere (including in Taiwan's near-neighbor, now-Chinese-ruled Hong Kong). Democratization became a less compelling foreign policy goal as the "clash of civilizations" supplanted "democracy waves" as a central concern in international relations, especially after 9/11.[41]

Developments in China and Chinese policy greatly shaped the international environment for Taiwan's democratic evolution during this period. Beijing increased its capacity and often asserted its will to counter Taiwan's quest for international "space," check Taiwan's drift toward formal independence, and maintain pressure and increase leverage for eventual reunification.

China's rapid ascension as an economic, military, and diplomatic power put Taiwan in increasingly dire straits, especially given the ROC's dependence on the United States and other members of an international community that had ever more compelling reasons to be solicitous of the PRC's position on issues that Beijing deemed vital, including Taiwan. Accelerating cross-Strait economic integration gave China unprecedented economic leverage as more Taiwanese manufacturing, capital, exports, and people moved to the mainland. Rising nationalism in China encouraged a strident line on foreign policy issues—including Taiwan, given the "unrecovered territory's" status as Chinese nationalism's great unhealed nineteenth-century wound.[42]

Other aspects of PRC foreign policy, however, gave Taiwanese leaders opportunities to pursue enhanced international status, including by methods invoking or employing democratic institutions. Despite modestly redistributionist readjustments under Hu Jintao, China's strategy for economic development still relied heavily on the policy of opening to the outside world, the already-developed coastal regions, cosmopolitan entrepreneurs and enterprises based there, and good relations with Taiwan as a major investment source and trading partner. Beijing's quests for economically beneficial good relations with the United States and other developed countries, acceptance as a normal state and great power in the international community—and hosting a successful Olympics in 2008—weighed against open bellicosity and intransigence toward Taiwan and its democracy.[43]

Beijing's approach to cross-Strait relations and Taiwan's international status during this period was similarly complex and either adeptly layered or reflected ongoing policy conflicts. On basic principles, China was uncompromising. In 1999, Beijing derided Lee Teng-hui's most significant foray on the status question as the act of an unredeemable separatist bent on splitting the nation.[44] For the 2000 Taiwanese presidential election, Beijing issued a second White Paper on the Taiwan question to reassert strongly and formally China's sovereignty over Taiwan, the unacceptability of Taiwan's pursuit of independent statehood, and China's threat to use force under circumstances that included Taiwan's indefinite delay in discussing reunification.[45] China responded to Chen's victory by adopting a "wait and see" attitude, reaffirming that Taiwan must accept Beijing's "one-China principle" as a precondition to progress in cross-Strait negotiations and, ultimately, opting to wait out Chen's presidency.[46] In 2005, China's Anti-Secession Law reasserted, in a singularly formal medium, Beijing's claim that Taiwan was already a part of China, that China could not tolerate independence for Taiwan, and that the PRC would use military force if necessary to prevent separation.[47] Just before the law's passage, Hu's "four-point" foray into Taiwan policy reiterated Beijing's unwavering commitment to the "one-China principle" (and the "1992 Consensus") and resolute opposition to "Taiwan independence."[48]

In its more concrete approaches to Taiwan and its democratic elections,

Beijing's methods grew more accommodating, subtle, and effective. From the 1996 to the 2000 to the 2004 Taiwanese presidential campaigns, China moved from missile tests, to Premier Zhu Rongji's warning against "dire consequences" of voting for Chen (along with the second White Paper), to tactics that included relying on the United States and other foreign powers to rein in Chen's boldest independence-implicating gambits, using a judicious combination of carrots and sticks to cultivate support for the KMT-led ticket among mainland-investing Taiwanese business interests, and asserting that Beijing would hope for improved cross-Strait relations with whoever was elected, although the prospects would be brighter without Chen. Although this approach suffered in 2004 from the distrust in Taiwan created by China's handling of severe acute respiratory syndrome (SARS) and its characterization of cross-Strait transportation links as "domestic," notwithstanding the 2005 Anti-Secession Law, Beijing generally extended the strategy for the following round.[49] Between the 2004 and 2008 elections, China continued to rely on Washington and others to restrain Chen's "secessionist" drift; warmly welcomed the losing candidates from 2004, Lien Chan and James Soong, on visits to the mainland; offered pandas, purchases of Taiwanese fruit, and prospects of other economic gains that could follow if the incumbent lost; and remained largely on the sidelines in the contest between the DPP's Frank Hsieh and its favored candidate, the KMT's Ma Ying-jeou.[50]

Throughout this period, Beijing reiterated its preference for "peaceful reunification" and adjusted its "one country, two systems" model for reunification, expanding promises to accommodate Taiwan's ways and preferences, including its democratic political order. The "one-China" precondition was cast in more flexible terms, with seemingly equalizing language stating that Taiwan and the PRC both "belonged" to one China.[51] The Anti-Secession Law coupled its hard line on sovereignty with an accommodating position on the cross-Strait status quo, proscribing only further moves toward independence and underscoring differences from a Reunification Law that would have entailed a commitment in principle to reverse a separation that the Anti-Secession Law asserted did not yet exist.[52] Hu's "four points" and report at the Seventeenth Party Congress in 2007 similarly joined familiar commitments on reunification with a conciliatory tone, expressing desire for peaceful reunification, asserting confidence in the people on Taiwan, and suggesting a possible cross-Strait "peace agreement."[53]

In responding to several Taiwanese moves that implicated sovereignty or statehood, Beijing relentlessly cast Chen and other Taiwanese as the parties imperiling a stable status quo.[54] This pattern was especially prominent when Taiwanese leaders evoked or sought democratic foundations for status-related agendas. Beijing's vigilance and adroitness in using this tactic, along with relatively accommodating aspects of its approach to Taiwan, affected another aspect of Taiwan's international context: US policy. Although "strategic ambiguity" often is used to describe US policy, it became increasingly clear during this period that Washington's support for Taipei varied with the degree to which Beijing or Taipei appeared to be responsible for difficulties in cross-Strait relations. Lee's assertions in the later Clinton years of Taiwan's statelike status eroded US support, but Chen's pledge of restraint on status-related issues in his first inaugural helped repair ties.[55] After much stronger support for Taiwan during George W. Bush's first months in office, US backing for Taipei eroded as the administration grew impatient, as Chen turned to such democratic processes as election campaigns, popular referenda, and constitutional reform to press assertive positions on Taiwan's international status and cross-Strait relations.[56] From before the 2004 Taiwan elections through Chen's second term, US positions moved closer to Beijing's in criticizing Chen for challenging the status quo and imperiling stability.[57] This trend reflected Washington's need to accommodate Beijing, given China's rise as a regional and potential great power and given Washington's pursuit of Beijing's cooperation in the war on terror, nuclear proliferation, and bilateral economic issues.

At the same time, an international environment that seemed to be turning inexorably against Taiwan's quest for statelike status and China's increasingly clear (if uncertainly durable) acquiescence in a de facto, but not de jure, independent Taiwan encouraged Chen and other Taiwanese politicians to push the envelope while not crossing the Rubicon (by making a formal declaration of independence). Taiwan's successful democratization and the continued—if diminished—stature of democracy as a value in international relations and US foreign policy meant that these efforts sensibly relied on democratic mandates and processes. This power of democratic means is illustrated by Washington's difficulties in responding to referenda and constitutional reforms that engaged questions of Taiwan's status. US officials walked a fine line in expressing opposition to the substance while defending Taiwan's right to use such procedures.[58]

As this suggests, particularly since the late 1990s, Taiwan's democratic institutions have focused on, and been formed by, addressing Taiwan's problematic international context and the challenges and opportunities it has presented for Taiwan's drive for international standing. The most defining and controversial initiatives from Taiwan's first fully democratically elected presidents—Lee in his final term and Chen—addressed the status question. Although the roots lay in earlier 1990s moves,[59] Lee opened a new phase in 1999 when he declared that cross-Strait relations were "state-to-state" relations (albeit of a "special type") and that the ROC had "no need to declare independence again" because it had been an independent, sovereign country since its foundation nearly a century earlier.[60] As Beijing saw it, Lee promulgated a "two-state theory."

As president, Chen—the leader of a party often labeled "proindependence" and grouped by Beijing with "secessionist" forces on Taiwan—extended his predecessor's agenda. In his inaugural addresses, Chen emphasized his democratic election by the people of Taiwan and derived from it an obligation and mandate to safeguard the "sovereignty, security, and dignity" of the "nation" or "country."[61] Under Chen, it became commonplace to substitute "Taiwan" for "ROC" in many contexts, including referring to the entity that was already an "independent sovereign country" with no need to declare independence again. Chen added a signature phrase in August 2002, declaring that there was "one country" on each side of the Strait.[62] During this period, Lee, Chen, and others invoked parallels between the cross-Strait situation and the divided states of Korea and Germany (for which democracy was or would be the postreunification order) and nations of the European Union (all of which were democracies).[63]

In the constitutional reform drive during Chen's reelection campaign and second term, provisions on the national name and territory were controversial and remained intact, partly because they were closely connected to statehood, given that international law's definition of statehood explicitly includes territory and implicitly demands a formal assertion of state status.[64] Chen suggested that changing the national name to Taiwan or more clearly specifying that the national territory was limited to Taiwan might be undertaken in future constitutional reforms because such matters could not be immune from change in a democratic system if a popular consensus emerged for revision.[65]

In 2006, Chen announced that the National Unification Council and the Guidelines for National Unification—which had maintained an in-principle commitment to the possibility of unification and had appropriated international democracy and human rights norms—would "cease to apply."[66] In the 2004 presidential election and later campaigns, Chen and DPP politicians stressed status-related issues to energize their core voters, and their opponents responded in kind. The DPP charged that giving power to the KMT would endanger Taiwan's de facto independence. Their opponents claimed DPP rule imperiled Taiwan's international support. Such clashes overlay commonality on key cross-Strait issues and recognition that any president on Taiwan must assert sovereignty and status.[67]

This channeling of democratic Taiwan's political energies to status issues has been still greater because of the complex requirements of not transgressing Beijing's "red lines" or excessively alienating Washington. Lee's state-to-state formulation was masterfully muddled in its discussion of sovereignty. Chen's inaugural addresses offered "four noes and one not": no declaration of independence, no change to the national name, no constitutionalization of Lee's "state-to-state" formulation, no referendum on unification or independence, and not eliminating the unification Guidelines and Council. When Chen discarded the "one not" or made statements that cast doubt on any of the "noes" (as when Lee offered up "state-to-state"), much effort was expended to explain how this did not overturn prior pledges or change policy.[68]

A new democratic institution—the referendum—has been closely entwined with, and shaped by, international status questions. Its first use came in two failed referenda in 2004. By asking whether Taiwan should enhance its defense capabilities if China did not end threats to use force and move Taiwan-targeting missiles, the first question implicitly invoked Taiwan's right to self-defense and China's obligation not to use or threaten force. Those international legal rules apply clearly (and, arguably, at all) only among states. The second referendum, calling for a "peace and stability" framework for cross-Strait relations, assumed and asserted that Taiwan had the capacity to conduct relations on a basis of equality with the PRC.[69]

For the 2008 elections, a pair of referenda addressed Taiwan's international status. They asked whether Taiwan should join the United Nations. Like a contemplated 2004 referendum on representation in the UN-affiliated World Health Organization (WHO), these referenda sought a democratic mandate supporting Taiwan's joining an organization widely regarded—including in Beijing and Washington—as restricted to states. Chen went further, claiming the referendum would allow the Taiwanese people to express opposition, in a politically binding way, to unification and to press Washington to alter its "one-China" policy. Such assertions echoed, in muted tones, referenda that politicians from the proindependence Taiwan Solidarity Union had urged, quixotically, after China's Anti-Secession Law: declaring Taiwan to be an independent sovereign state or asking whether Taiwan was part of China.[70]

Taiwan's international context has also distorted Taiwan's democratic development since the late 1990s because constitutional and institutional reforms that might deepen democracy and improve democratic governance inescapably resonate with questions of Taiwan's international status. Reforms that otherwise might be ordinary exercises of democratic prerogatives have proved costly or impossible partly because they have raised concerns abroad about their implications for status issues and suspicions that Taiwan's leaders pursue such reforms because of those implications. The constitutional revision debate that began late in Chen's first term produced the most important examples.[71]

Chen and others sought a "new constitution" rather than constitutional revision. Although defended as an appropriate description of the major changes envisioned, the label has been controversial—and doubtlessly held added appeal for key proponents—because of its connection to independence: adopting a new constitution is something that new states (though not only new states) do, but a merely "revised" constitution assumes continuity of the preexisting state.[72] Even revision—and the in-between proposal of a Second ROC Constitution[73]—presented the same conundrum, in milder form. Chen and other advocates maintained, plausibly, that a revised constitution would be "indigenized" and recast as a "contract" between Taiwan's people and government and would satisfy the desire of "twenty-three million people of Taiwan . . . to have a constitution that really belongs to them."[74] Such reformation also inevitably—and surely intentionally—distanced the constitution from its mainland origins and original pan-China reach. It also implied a self-governing polity and people separate from the PRC's—points that resonated with political claims of independence and international legal requirements for statehood.

The pattern extended to the specific amendments adopted in 2005. Halving the legislature, altering legislative electoral rules and districts, eliminating the National Assembly, and mandating referenda to approve future constitutional amendments could be, and were, characterized as remedies for structural infirmities such as unwieldy or duplicative institutions, excessive partisanship, insufficient responsiveness to constituents, and underdeveloped mechanisms for democratic participation in constitutional reform and governance.[75] Still, the amendments also implicated status issues in ways that proponents doubtless appreciated and that alarmed Beijing and, therefore, Washington. The features that purportedly made targeted institutions bloated or outmoded reflected their design for a larger country with fundamentally different circumstances—China in 1947. With the National Assembly earlier stripped of independent meaningful roles, its abolition was easily construed as a symbolic repudiation of mainland ties. Amendments to strengthen democratic accountability and participation evoked factors that matter for state or statelike status, both politically and legally, including a distinct and self-governing Taiwanese populace and territory, a government that answers to no higher political authority, and democratic governance.[76] Referenda—constitutional (as the 2005 amendment provided) or ordinary (as 2003 legislation authorized)—resonated richly, and therefore problematically, with international norms of democratic governance and self-determination and the history of the referendum idea in Taiwan, which was long associated with a plebiscite on independence (including in the DPP's platform before it came to power).[77]

The focus on international status–relevant issues and the correlative need to anticipate and address reaction abroad have diverted Taiwan's developing democratic politics toward the most polarizing issues and diminished attention to more ordinary and domestic issues, such as economic policy. This skewing of politics toward external issues and retarding of the development of "normal" democratic politics—and ordinary, competent governance—have fed popular disillusionment with Taiwan's democracy.[78]

China's International Context and Democratic Prospects

External factors have less impact on the PRC than they have had on Taiwan. The outside forces that were favorable to Taiwan's democratization in the 1980s and 1990s are weaker and face more formidable resistance in contemporary China.

China is not immune to the concern of the United States and other Western powers with states' internal political orders or global norms born of democratization waves in the 1980s and 1990s. Although Washington's China policy has remained one of engagement, "domestic order" issues perennially color debate and constrain policy: human rights conditionality for trade until China's WTO accession; two congressionally mandated watchdog commissions that followed conditionality's demise; annual reports from the State Department on China's human rights record; support for rule of law and civil society programs in China; efforts to press Beijing on civil, political, and religious rights at presidential summits and through more routine channels; and the constant need to justify engagement to US audiences by touting its potential to change China.[79]

Reform-era China's strategy of opening to the outside world has given external factors greater capacity for influence. Attracting trade and investment, joining major international institutions, and winning acceptance as a responsible power have required Beijing to engage international norms and expectations. Although this engagement has not demanded democratization, it has entailed changes that, especially in contrast to Mao-era baselines, create conditions often associated—if only weakly or in the long run—with democratization: formal acceptance of universal human rights, some degree of rule of law, and extensive engagement with democratic states that include democracy among their foreign policy aims.[80] To an extent unimaginable three decades ago, China's rulers care about the PRC's image abroad. As the world has come to apprehend China's newfound power, China has struggled to present a benign image—an effort reflected in Hu-era doctrines of China's "peaceful rise," "peaceful development," and "harmonious world."[81] So long as democracy remains an important (albeit not preeminent) value and views akin to the "democratic peace" thesis remain influential among key states, intransigent rejection of democracy would be costly for Beijing, particularly with the United States and China's nervous neighbors.[82] Although hypocrisy is hardly unknown in Chinese foreign policy, it requires especially thoroughgoing cynicism to assert that this vice is unconstrained and all moderating changes in Chinese policy are meaningless.

"Unofficial" China has opened to democracy-friendly ideas from abroad, flowing through many channels: PRC nationals educated overseas and returning to China; foreigners resident in China; more information from abroad through more open Chinese media and access to foreign media and the Internet; liberalization at home creating space to criticize some of the regime's democratic shortcomings and to argue for modestly democratizing reforms; and a burgeoning and increasingly influential class of affluent and educated urban Chinese, some of whom find democratic or liberal ideas appealing.[83]

Such forces, however, are not as formidable as they were in Taiwan during its democratic transformation and consolidation. During the late Jiang and Hu eras, moreover, PRC susceptibility to democratization-supporting influences from abroad has plateaued or declined in some respects.

Beijing has consistently chafed at foreign efforts to promote democratic reform. China has perceived and denounced a US strategy of "peaceful evolution" that seeks to alter China's political system without using the force that such an end might otherwise require.[84] Such complaints echo broader criticisms of US "interference" that Beijing raises in response to complaints about human rights and other issues. As this suggests, US predictions of, and pressures for, democratic change in China can have complicated, even perverse, consequences. When US proponents most strongly claim that engagement will move China toward a benign, even democratic, political order (as in the 1999–2000 debate on WTO accession and, defensively, in the 1989 debate over post-Tiananmen sanctions), they cannot maintain acoustical separation from messages that reach China, fueling ripostes to "US hegemonism" and interference. When critics of engagement are ascendant or especially strident (as after Tiananmen and amid post-2000 alarm over China's implementation of WTO commitments, outbound investment practices, and currency and trade behavior), their arguments for a harder line also elicit pushback from Beijing, stalling bilateral cooperation, increasing skepticism about the wisdom of acceding to US requests (including on potentially democratization-fostering issues), and fueling calls for a China that "can say no" to US demands.[85]

China's ascension as a global economic power and major regional power and its growing self-image as a great power have reduced Beijing's need and willingness to accept the international status quo. As Chinese sources routinely point out, many of the rules and norms of the international system are products of processes in which China had little say, and many are not to China's liking. Now firmly ensconced in most major global and regional institutions, Beijing is no longer the supplicant trying to gain acceptance. With its considerable economic importance and political clout, Beijing can insist that its interests and preferences be taken seriously in multilateral organizations and international relations. China thus has been moving from regime-taker toward regime-shaper.[86] Among the areas vulnerable to increased Chinese influence are international norms that the PRC finds unpalatable or threatening, that are new or weakly established, or that are tepidly backed by other major states—such as prodemocracy norms.

Recently, Chinese foreign policy has become more assertive and unfriendly to those norms in ways that go beyond familiar arguments opposing international democracy-promotion for infringing on target states' sovereignty. Here, China has cultivated and deployed growing "soft power" resources. Especially in its dealings with resource-rich nations in Africa, China increasingly holds itself out as a model for development without democratization as well as a source of aid that does not demand democratic reforms from recipients. Through the Shanghai Cooperation Organization and bilateral initiatives, China has fostered a new form of solidarity among

Eurasian authoritarian states and implicitly asserted the normalcy of nondemocratic rule.[87]

Moreover, China's external environment has become less supportive of democracy during this period of China's increasing openness to foreign influence and increasing resistance to international pressure. After the 1980s political reforms died at Tiananmen, any undertaking to democratize China has had to occur against the backdrop of the international democratic recession. Chinese critics of democracy can point to disappointment, failure, and retrenchment in once-democratizing states. Although the "color revolutions" offer counterexamples of pushback against resurgent authoritarianism, they are as unacceptable to China's leaders—or in permitted Chinese discourse—as the original people power revolution in the Philippines.[88]

US pressure on China to adopt potentially democratic reforms has decreased after 9/11. US policies promoting democracy have been secondary to other goals and have addressed regimes other than China. The war on terrorism and wars in Iraq and Afghanistan have pushed concerns about a "China threat"—and policies that might address it by trying to change China's politics—to the background. The US quest for Chinese cooperation on terrorism, and on North Korean and Iranian nuclear programs, and China's acquiescence in the heightened US military presence in Central Asia have muzzled policies that could cause friction by seeking—or being perceived as seeking—democratization in China.

Recent political developments in the PRC point to limited and decreasing openness to democratization-promoting influences from abroad.[89] Jiang Zemin—his rise intimately linked to suppression of the 1989 democracy movement—presided over only very modest democratic reforms: uneven development of village elections, experiments with very local-level elections in the cities, fitful expansion of inner-party democracy, and rhetorical support for socialist democracy. The Jiang-era strategy for dealing with dynamic and wealthy groups that, on many analyses, are most likely to embrace democratic and foreign ideas—the rising capitalist stratum in coastal cities—was co-optation, both economic (leaving them free to pursue riches) and political (giving them legitimacy and access under Jiang's signal ideological contribution, the Three Represents). Preemption of democratic pressures and sustaining authoritarian rule have been the principal aims of political institutional reforms that have borrowed little from foreign democratic models.[90]

Under Hu, there has been no more room for democratic ideas and ideals. The post-Jiang leadership has largely continued the strategy of co-opting entrepreneurs and strengthening the party-state. The climate has been chilly for liberal intellectuals and media outlets that had become purveyors of democratic or democratization-conducive ideas. The Hu leadership is often described as "populist," but that is a far cry from "democratic." Indeed, this populism is partly adverse to democracy, especially in a form consistent with international democratic norms. To be sure, the Hu leadership has in many ways extended Jiang-era policies (which themselves had built on Deng-era precedents) of ruling the country by laws, including the constitution. And the rule of law is associated with political democracy (and market economics as well) in the imagination of the United States and other key sources of support for democratic reform around the world. But, in reform-era China, rule by law and socialist legality appear, often quite plausibly, to be alternatives to—or at least delayers of—democratization (whether from below or from abroad). Influential intellectuals in China are strikingly divided over whether democracy and the rule of law are substitutes or complements.[91] Hu and Premier Wen Jiabao have prominently asserted that Chinese democracy is a long way off and that China will not adopt Western-style democracy.[92]

Moreover, economically disadvantaged groups whose interests Hu-era populism embraces include the masses whom many intellectuals and affluent urbanites regard as not ready for democracy and threatening, if given the vote, to their interests. This populism also plays to hinterland constituencies that are more inclined to anticosmopolitan nationalism than are residents of China's gold coast, where outside ideas receive a warmer welcome. Under Hu, increased attention to interregional and class inequality and achieving a "harmonious society" and "human development" has moderated the previous periods' development-focused and outward-looking agenda, which is increasingly seen as having brought, along with many benefits, economic pain and social dislocation that may grow worse with further integration with the global economy. To the considerable extent that Deng- and Jiang-era strategies of ever-greater openness and marketization built broader pathways and constituencies for external prodemocracy influences, Hu-era readjustments limit their impact.[93]

One key dimension of China's external context is Taiwan itself. Although Beijing pointedly deems Taiwan matters to be internal affairs, Taiwan is functionally an aspect of China's external context and one that has comparatively important—if ambivalent—implications for China's democratic prospects. Taiwan's democratization offers an especially relevant model for smooth and gradual transition from authoritarian rule should the PRC become open to that option. Taiwan offers the Chinese Communist Party leadership an intriguing scenario for a soft landing: the originally Leninist-structured KMT presided over a democratization process that left the KMT and its allies winning majority support in most elections.[94] Taiwan also provides examples of democratization and democracy in what Beijing officially—and many Chinese (and others) in practice—regard as a "Chinese" context.[95] If Beijing were to make progress on a cross-Strait accommodation that formally links Taiwan more closely to the PRC while preserving Taiwan's political system, Taiwan would become a more politically orthodox and legitimate model for PRC reform advocates.

Taiwan already has become a principal source of ideas about democracy and political change and has the potential to play a larger role as cross-Strait ties deepen and if mainland political discourse becomes more open to democratic reform. The common language, historical connection, perceptions (or at least assertions) of Taiwan's Chineseness, and the outsized portion of China's economic, societal, and intellectual connections to the outside world that flow to, from, or through Taiwan mean that many ideas about democracy and political change reach China from Taiwanese sources (including Taiwanese residing in or visiting the mainland). These features also have made Taiwan a major (if often incompletely acknowledged) source for reform-era PRC laws and policies. Although few of these have addressed directly democracy (or even politics), they are part of the broader liberalizing, marketizing, and internationalizing transformation that many theoretical and comparative accounts see as ultimately conducive to democratization.

At least in the near term, however, the Taiwan factor includes much that is unfavorable for democratization in China. Despite its democratization, Taiwan remains for China an exemplar of an East Asian Model of development without democratization. Although much-less-democratized Singapore and Hong Kong are now more congenial models for China's rulers, predemocratization Taiwan still provides an example of prolonged rapid economic development—to a level that still far exceeded what China as a whole has reached today—without effective challenge to authoritarian rule under a party with Leninist origins that delivered rising prosperity. The Taiwan model thus still offers comfort—whether or not misplaced—that the PRC regime might successfully resist democratization for a very long time.[96]

PRC accounts portray contemporary Taiwanese democracy in distinctly unflattering terms. Corruption scandals, flawed elections, and street protests that verge on political chaos are staples of Chinese depictions.[97] In attacking perceived Taiwanese moves toward formal independence or secession, official and orthodox Chinese sources condemn Taiwanese democratic processes and institutions, including constitutional reform and referenda (which often have implicated status issues) and presidential elections (which have retained in office or brought to power Beijing's arch villains of separatism, Lee and Chen).[98] Although the post-Chen era promises improvement, this PRC approach reflects official chilliness toward Taiwan as a democratic model, limits and distorts information available to Chinese about Taiwan's democracy, and shrinks political space in China for addressing the Taiwan model's possible merits. Democracy more broadly is at risk—in China and Chinese discourse—of guilt by association with the officially discredited Taiwan example.

The Taiwan question also presents a major impediment to China's incorporation as a normal power into the international system and the broadened opportunity for the influence of international norms (including democratic norms) that such integration could bring. Taiwan remains the most durable problem in China's relationship with the United States. Beijing's efforts to undermine Taiwan's stature and status also have distracted and disrupted the PRC's engagement with the WTO (where attempts to downgrade Taiwan have been among China's more visible undertakings) and China's pursuit of a non-threatening and economics-focused agenda abroad, especially in Southeast Asia (where Beijing's diplomatic pressure to exclude Taiwan has undercut China's "charm offensive" and fed concerns that the PRC's motives are political).[99] More fundamentally, Beijing's approach to, and focus on, the Taiwan question has helped trap China in a revanchist, nineteenth-century-style notion of sovereignty. This conception puts China at odds with trends in international law and the international order that play down or erode state sovereignty. And it commits China to a "black box" conception of states that are, and should be, largely impervious to external influences, including democracy norms.[100]

The effect of international contexts on China's prospects for democratization is thus limited, possibly declining (in some respects), and ambivalent. For China, the capacity for influence of external factors is more limited than has been the case for Taiwan, and the implications of external factors for democratization are more mixed than they were for Taiwan, especially during Taiwan's 1980s and 1990s democratic transformation.

Conclusion

External factors have been variously unfavorable, conducive, and distortive to Taiwan's democratic development. They facilitated postponement of democratization until the 1980s. From the 1980s through the 1990s, international contexts generated pressure and support for democratic reform and consolidation. Since then, the relationship between the external environment and Taiwan's democratic development has become more complex and ambivalent.

For the PRC, reform-era trends in the external environment—and China's engagement with that environment—have increased the impact and prodemocratic content of foreign factors. But their effect and potential for influence on democratic change remains far less for China than it has been for Taiwan. As in Taiwan, the implications of the international context for democracy in China have become more complicated and, in some respects, less positive in recent years. On both sides of this mixed PRC story, Taiwan's experience—including Taiwan's democratic development and its interaction with issues of Taiwan's international status and Beijing's and Washington's Taiwan policies—has been and is likely to remain a key element of the external environment affecting China's democratic prospects.

Notes

1. See generally, Hoffmann 1978; Packenham 1973; Gaddis 1997.
2. See generally, Cohen 1990, chap. 6; Zhang 1992.
3. On legal and constitutional issues, see Chen Tsung-fu 2003, 374–385; see generally Peter Wang 2007, 320–325; Roy 2003, chap. 4.
4. These developments have been the subject of many accounts. See Mann 1998, chaps. 1–4, 6; 2000, chaps. 3–6; see also Kissinger 1979; Jian 2001, chap. 9.
5. United Nations General Assembly Resolution 2758 1971.
6. "Joint Communiqué of the United States of America and the People's Republic of China" 1972.
7. "Joint Communiqué of the United States of America and the People's Republic of China" 1979.
8. "Joint Communiqué of the United States of America and the People's Republic of China" 1982.
9. Cheong 2003; Sciolino 2002.
10. Taiwan Relations Act, 1979, 22 U.S.C. secs. 3301–3316.
11. "Six Assurances to Taiwan" 1982; Feldman 2007.
12. Taiwan Relations Act, 1979, sec. 2(c), 22 U.S.C. sec. 3301(c).
13. Reagan 1982, 1983.
14. Vogel 1991; Haggard 1990; Berger and Hsiao 1998.
15. Phillips 2007, 275–319; Myers 1991, chaps. 3–6.
16. See Jacobs 1981, 21–44; Bush 2004, 73ff; Wachman 1994, 140–143; *Liu* v. *Republic of China* 1986; 1989.
17. See Baum 1996; Lam 1999.
18. Mann 1998, chaps. 9–12, 15–16; Tyler 2000, chaps. 7–9; Republic of China 1990, Executive Order No. 12711; Farnsworth 1980; Republic of China 1993, Executive Order No. 12850; deLisle 2006a; Lieberthal 1995, 35ff.
19. See generally Howe 1998, 127–151; Cheng 2001, 28–36.
20. See Council on Foreign Relations 2007; Lilley and Shambaugh 1999; Tucker ed. 2005, chaps. 6–8.
21. Ye 1979; *Xinhua* 1981.
22. Taiwan Affairs Office of the State Council of the PRC 1993.
23. Jiang 1995.
24. Hu Cheng-fen 2005, 26–44; Dickson 1998, 361–362; Bush 2004, chap. 3; Richard Bush 2005, 346; Nathan and Ho 1997.
25. Yahuda 1996, 1319, 1322; Dickson 1998, 361; Buruma 1996.
26. See Chu, Hu, and Moon 1997, 267–294; Haggard 1990, 138–146; Howe 1998; Tien 1989.
27. Huntington 1991. Several works have examined the application and implications of Third Wave analyses to Taiwan. Diamond et al. 1997.
28. McFaul 2002; Bunce 2003.
29. See Franck 1991; European Community 1991; deLisle 1999; Brinkley 1997.
30. See Shih 2006, which recounts original accounts of 1992 consensus and current disputes about its existence, meaning, and KMT and Chen administration interpretations; *Renmin Ribao* 2001.
31. See Orentlicher 1998; Buchanan 2004; Hannum 1990.
32. On identity issues and democratization in Taiwan generally, see Wachman 1994; Rigger 1999.
33. See also Rigger 2001, chap. 2.
34. See deLisle 2000b, 55–57; Chen 1991, 1287–1310.

35. Lee 1996; Mainland Affairs Council, Republic of China 1994, sec. IV; see also Tu 1996; Tien and Chu 1998, 97–126; Garver, 1997; Lee 1999; Hughes 1997, chap. 5.

36. See generally, deLisle 2000b, 57–60; *Chung-yang Jih-pao* 1996, which contains the text of a speech by Lee Teng-hui; Mainland Affairs Council, Republic of China 1994, sec. III; Siew 1997; Lee 1999; Lee 1995.

37. National Unification Council and Executive Yuan, ROC 1991.

38. Mainland Affairs Council, Republic of China 1993, 3–8; 1994, secs. II–III; Lee 1999; Kristof 1998.

39. *Chung-yang Jih-pao* 1999; deLisle 2000b, 55–57.

40. Government Information Office, ROC 1994, 3; Mainland Affairs Council, Republic of China 1994, sec. IV; Lee 1995; Liu 1997.

41. Chang, Chu, and Pak 2007; McFaul, 2001; Diamond 1996; Huntington 1996.

42. Richard Bush 2005, chap. 8; Chao and Hsu 2006, 41–67; Jacobs 2006, 84–109; Gries 2004, chaps. 6–8; Goldstein 2005, chap. 7.

43. Li 2005; Goldstein 2005, chap. 8; Fewsmith 2004; Sutter 2005, chap. 3.

44. *Jiefang Jun Bao* 1999; *Renmin Ribao* 1999.

45. Taiwan Affairs Office and Information Office of the State Council of the PRC 2000a.

46. Taiwan Affairs Office of the State Council of the PRC 2000b; Tai 2000; *Ming Pao* 2000; Agence France Presse 2001, which quotes PRC vice premier Qian Qichen.

47. *Xinhua* 2004a, which quotes National People's Congress chair Wu Bangguo.

48. Hu Jintao 2005.

49. Robinson and Brown 2000; Lo 2004; deLisle 2004a; Richard Bush 2005, chap. 8; Lam 2004; deLisle 2003b.

50. Ross 2006; Fell 2007; Christensen 2007; Negroponte 2007.

51. Qian 2002.

52. See, for example, Wang 2004; see generally, deLisle 2007b, 101–138.

53. Hu 2007; Lai 2007.

54. Li 2007, which quotes Taiwan Affairs Office head on UN referendum; Zhong 2004, which describes 2003 CCP Propaganda Department report condemning Chen's referendum and new constitution plans.

55. Christensen 2002, 2000; Ross 2000.

56. See generally, Goldstein 2005, 183–193; Harding 2005, 36–43; Pollack 2005, 104–107.

57. This pattern included President Bush's remarks in front of Chinese Premier Wen Jiabao, criticizing Chen's apparent attempts to alter the cross-Strait status quo, and warnings from high levels at the State Department that "bad" policies, including the UN referendum, were not immune from criticism simply because they were pursued through "democratic means." "Remarks by President Bush and Premier Wen Jiabao at Photo Opportunity" 2003; Buckley 2004; Kessler 2004; *Taiwan News* 2004; Christensen 2007; Swaine 2004.

58. DeLisle 2004b, 17–18.

59. These included such things as constitutional amendments to restrict ROC jurisdiction to Taiwan, a diplomatic shift to pursuit of other governments' "dual recognition" of the PRC and ROC, and a controversial presidential speech at Cornell University. Negroponte 2007.

60. *Chung-yang Jih-pao* 1999.

61. Chen Shui-bian 2000; Chen 2004a.

62. *China Post* 2002; Central News Agency 2004.

63. DeLisle 2000b, 53–55; 2002.

64. League of Nations 1933, art. 1; American Law Institute 1987, sec. 201; deLisle 2000b, 50–53.

65. This lack of consensus or political infeasibility, rather than a prohibition in principle, is the central feature of Chen's explanations of why such matters (and even formal independence) would not be addressed then. Ko 2006; Crody and Faiola 2006.

66. Senior officials were tasked to explain that this move did not alter the status quo or abandon the pledges in Chen's inaugural addresses because nothing was abolished and because China's threat to use force undermined their stated precondition. *China Post* 2006; Bradisher 2006; Agence France Presse 2006.

67. Rigger 2005; deLisle 2005, 2004a; *China Post* 2008; Ma 2008.

68. Lilian Wu 1999; Sophia Wu 2007; Chi and Low 2006.

69. For texts of the referenda, see Office of the President of the ROC 2004; for analysis, see deLisle 2004b.

70. Ruth Wang 2007; Ong 2007; Central News Agency 2005; Low 2005.

71. The following discussion draws on deLisle 2004b.

72. *Taiwan News* 2003; Office of the President of the ROC 2003 (in this *New York Times* interview, Chen expresses impatience with terminological debate); Chen 2004a, which criticizes the piecemeal nature of prior rounds of constitutional amendment and expresses continuing hope for a new constitution); Chang 2005, which covers Chen's proposals for second-phase reforms and his continuing desire for a new constitution; Crody and Faiola 2006.

73. Chen 2007.

74. Chen 2004a; Office of the President of the ROC 2003.

75. For the substance of the amendments, see National Assembly, ROC 2005, arts. 1, 4, 12. See also, Government Information Office, ROC 2005; see also Referendum Law of the ROC 2003, art. 1 (law enacted pursuant to the "principle of popular sovereignty" and to provide for "direct exercise" of citizens' civil rights); Office of the President of the ROC 2003 (in this *New York Times* interview, Chen describes the holding of a referendum as a "milestone in our democratic consolidation and deepening of Taiwan's democracy" and an exercise of a "human right").

76. See League of Nations 1933, art. 1; American Law Institute 1987, sec. 201; deLisle 2000b.

77. Referendum Law of the ROC 2003, art. 1; see in Chen 2004a the section of the inaugural address concerning constitutional reform; Chen 2004b; Office of the President of the ROC 2003.

78. See Chang, Chu, Hu, and Shyu 2004; Fell 2007.

79. For a recent trenchant critique of such benevolent transformation of China arguments, see Mann 2007.

80. See generally, Economy and Oksenberg 1999; Nathan and Ross 1997; Council on Foreign Relations 2007; Lardy 2002.

81. Zheng 2005; Jiang 2005; Hu 2007; Glaser and Medeiros 2007.

82. Brown, Lynn-Jones, and Miller 1996; George Bush 2005; Rice 2005.

83. One study of these channels is Zweig 2002; see also deLisle 1999.

84. *Renmin Ribao* 1991; *China Daily* 2001.

85. Clinton 2000; *Xinhua* 2000, 2004b, 2006b; Song et al. 1996; deLisle 2006a.

86. Goldstein 2005, chap. 9; Mearsheimer 2003, chap. 10; deLisle 2000a.

87. Kurlantzick 2007; deLisle 2007a; Li, Cheng, and Wang 2007.

88. Lam 2006.

89. On these issues, see Li 2005; deLisle 2006a.

90. Dickson 2003; see also Nathan 2003; Huang 2006.

91. On these legal issues, see Peerenboom 2002; Zhao 2006, which focuses on Pan Wei; deLisle 2003a, 2008; Yu 2002.

92. Deutsche Presse-Agentur 2006, which is an interview with Wen Jiabao; Yu 2007, which covers a speech by Hu Jintao; Hu Jintao 2007.

93. Li 2005; Waldron 2004; Friedman 2006, 97–134.

94. Dickson 1997; Cheng 1989; cf. Peerenboom 2007a, chaps. 2, 7–9.

95. The point is contested, of course, but is central enough to make it into the titles of proponents' works. See Chao and Myers 1998; Christensen 2000.

96. DeLisle 2003a.

97. Kyodo News Service 2004b; *Xinhua* 2006b; *China Daily* 2006.

98. Wu 2007; Kyodo News Service 2004a; Li 2007; Zhong 2004.

99. DeLisle 2006a, 287–289; 2006b; Cho 2007; Ba 2006; *Straits Times* 2004, which covers an interview with a PRC Foreign Ministry spokesman.

100. DeLisle 2000b, 1998.

PART 3

Looking Forward

10

Taiwan's Democratic Transition: A Model for China?

Bruce Gilley

Every democratization has its annus mirabilis, and that year in Taiwan was 1986. Eleven years after the death of former Chinese president Chiang Kai-shek, his son, Chiang Ching-kuo, decided that the time was ripe for full democratic change. The decision to lift martial law and tolerate a new opposition party came after a decade of scandals, falling electoral support for the ruling Kuomintang, and growing international pressures. Over the next ten years, leading up to the first free and fair presidential election in a Chinese society in 1996, Taiwan went through a decisive democratic transition. Nonetheless, the transition itself was not a mere continuation of what had come before. The timing and nature of the transition were to some extent autonomous of the past, and the transition in turn had its own autonomous effects on the democracy in Taiwan that followed.

Three years after Taiwan's democratic 1986 breakthrough, the Chinese Communist Party was faced with a similar decision. In the face of nationwide student protests, leaders huddled together in the Zhongnanhai leadership complex, or at the home of senior leader Deng Xiaoping, to decide what to do. Party general secretary Zhao Ziyang argued for radical political liberalization that, on many accounts, would have ushered in the same sort of democratic transition that occurred in Taiwan. But Deng voted *against* democratic change. As in Taiwan, this outcome in China was not a foregone conclusion and could have easily gone the other way. As in Taiwan, this event also had consequences for the regime that followed. Ironically, one of these consequences was a period that looked remarkably similar to that of Taiwan in the 1960s and 1970s. For this reason, there are wide expectations that in the foreseeable future, China will face another moment of choice when a transition will be attempted.

Given the partially autonomous causes and consequences of transitions, it is worthwhile then to consider how a *successful* transition might come about in China, looking at the Taiwan example for clues. What would a democratic transition in China look like and how might policies adopted by international actors affect its chances of success? I begin by highlighting two main aspects of democratic transitions theory—long-term structural factors and short-term agency factors—before applying each to the Taiwan and China cases respectively. I then consider the ways that actors in China have viewed the Taiwan transition and conclude with some relevant policy advice.

Democratic Transitions Theory

The theory of democratic transitions can be roughly divided into two parts: the structural or path-dependent aspects (how the transition is determined by long-term causal factors) and the contingent or autonomous aspects (how the transition is shaped by short-term causal factors). Both parts are necessary in order to understand how a democratic transition comes about and the fate of the democracy that results.

The key structural or path-dependent factor that shapes the nature of a transition is the relative strength of state and society on the eve of transition. That factor is, in turn, shaped by a host of internal and external structural conditions—hence the reason why for many years there was no distinctive theory of democratic transitions at all. Studies of democratic transition were simply extensions of studies of the breakdown of authoritarian rule. However, beginning with the work of O'Donnell and Schmitter,[1] greater specificity emerged in outlining the various types of transition that were possible and how each related to different types of state-society relations under the authoritarian regime.

For simplicity's sake, the *relative* strength of the authoritarian state compared to society can be represented along a spectrum, from weak to strong. This gives us three broad transition scenarios—society-led democratization, state-led democratization, and reformed or resilient authoritarianism—and the risks associated with each. Each of these three categories can in turn be further specified (see Table 10.1).

A first point is that not all regime transitions lead to democracy. Of the 106 regime transitions between 1974 and 1999 studied by Geddes, only 51 (48 percent) led to full or partial democracies. Another 17 led to failed democracies and 38 to new authoritarian regimes.[2] Where social forces are weak relative to the state, as in China in 1989, ruptures may lead to a re-institutionalized authoritarian regime rather than to a democratic transition.

A second key point is that it is the relative, not *absolute,* strength of state and society that matters. The absolute strength of a state will depend upon its various capacities—fiscal, coercive, regulatory, and legitimacy/ideological—as well as its internal integrity—especially the degree to which is it character-

Table 10.1   Democratic Transition Types

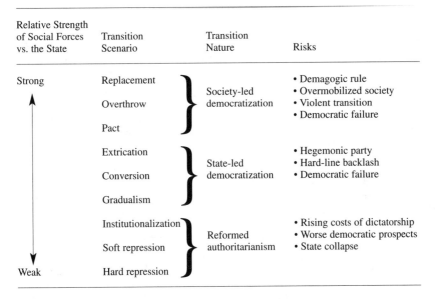

Relative Strength of Social Forces vs. the State	Transition Scenario	Transition Nature	Risks
Strong ↑	Replacement	Society-led democratization	• Demagogic rule
	Overthrow		• Overmobilized society
			• Violent transition
	Pact		• Democratic failure
	Extrication	State-led democratization	• Hegemonic party
	Conversion		• Hard-line backlash
	Gradualism		• Democratic failure
	Institutionalization	Reformed authoritarianism	• Rising costs of dictatorship
	Soft repression		• Worse democratic prospects
↓ Weak	Hard repression		• State collapse

ized by internal pluralism and dissent. The absolute strength of society will depend upon the degree to which social forces are unified, organized, resourced, and effectively led. Yet the *effective* strength of each depends upon the other. A partially factionalized state may remain dominant if social forces are even more factionalized. A highly organized state may be weak in the face of an even better organized opposition.

The other half of democratic transitions theory concerns the contingent or autonomous aspects of the transition that are only indirectly related to the structural conditions that precede transition. Once the winds of change arrive at the doorstep of an authoritarian regime, new factors emerge that are distinct. Experience from the 60-odd democratic transitions in Latin America, Southern Europe, sub-Saharan Africa, Eastern Europe, and East and Southeast Asia between Portugal's Revolution of Carnations in 1974 and Ukraine's Orange Revolution of 2004 allows us to describe democratic transitions in terms of an ideal-type sequence of events, noting the possibilities of failure at each stage (see Table 10.2).

There are important theoretical debates about each stage in this sequence. Are the crises that begin democratic transitions usually economic in nature?[3] What role is played by social mobilization and protest?[4] What determines whether elites will split?[5] What determines whether the inevitable backlash by hard-liners is successful?[6] How do we know if a decision is democratic?[7] What determines institutional choice (in particular to what extent is the

Table 10.2   Democratic Transition Stages

Stage	Meaning	Transition Failure If . . .
Crisis	Particular events that force the regime to consider plans for democratization	The crisis is attributed to nonsystemic factors
Mobilization	Evidence of social mobilization in support of democratization	Mobilization is suppressed
Elite split	Emergence of a reform faction in the regime that favors democratization	Regime unity is maintained
Hard-line backlash	Attempts by regime hard-liners to defeat the reform faction	Hard-liners gain support of swing members
Democratic decision	Announcement of plans to institutionalize democracy	Decision is blocked
Institutional choice	Selection of a democratic institutional design	Survival of "second-tier" actors who subvert democracy
Interim regime	Empowerment of temporary regime prior to first election	Interim period is extended indefinitely
Founding election	Holding of first national election	Incumbent party steals the election

process driven by the rational calculations of actors and to what extent by contingency, fads, and emotion)?[8] What determines the stability and effectiveness of interim regimes?[9] And finally, is a founding election the right marker for a successful transition, or should we include more substantive criteria such as the acceptance of uncertainty by all major actors?[10]

Democratic transitions theory has been developed largely through the study of transitions in Latin America and Southern Europe and to a lesser extent those in post-Communist Europe. The 10 major democratic transitions of Asia—in particular those of Taiwan, South Korea, Indonesia, the Philippines, and Thailand—have received far less attention. The Taiwan and China cases are perfectly suited for the application, and perhaps revision, of democratic transitions theory. Taiwan's 1986 transition succeeded, whereas China's 1989 transition failed. Yet a future transition in China may succeed. In studying these three transitions—one successful, one failed, and one prospectival—we should consider not just the conventional wisdom about democratic transitions but also the theory of democratic transition itself. How do the two dimensions of transitions theory, as outlined above, look when applied to the cases of Taiwan and China?

Transition Types in Taiwan and China

Authors in this book find both similarities and differences in state-society relations between Taiwan prior to its democratic transition and China prior to Tiananmen and today. Dorothy Solinger (in Chapter 5 on business groups) and Merle Goldman and Ashley Esarey (in Chapter 3 on intellectuals) see society in China as much weaker vis-à-vis the state, whereas Richard Madsen (in Chapter 4 on religious groups) and Robert Weller (in Chapter 6 on religious and environmental groups) see more parallels. Yet state-society relations on the eve of transition can also be read backwards from the nature of the transition itself. Doing this suggests that the Taiwanese state was still quite powerful compared to society in 1986, given that the subsequent transition was largely state-led. Looked at in this way, the differences between the relative power of state and society in late authoritarian Taiwan and present-day China narrow, not because society in China is stronger than we thought but because the state in Taiwan was stronger than we thought.

The Taiwan transition is a good example of why it is the relative, not absolute, strength of state and social forces that is determinative. An organized opposition had begun to form and contest local elections in the 1960s in Taiwan. But the KMT-led state, especially with the passing of Chiang Kai-shek, strengthened its own internal character, reemphasizing Leninist democratic centralism, constructing new regulatory institutions, and enjoying the fruits of Taiwan's booming economy. Moreover, the KMT continued to enjoy reasonably strong levels of support from society.[11] Thus when the transition came, the state was the dominant actor.[12] In terms of Table 10.1, the Taiwan transition is probably best described as a conversion, in which the state undertakes a deliberate, planned move to democracy under only moderate pressure from social forces. Chiang Ching-kuo announced the formation of a 12-member panel to consider political reforms in 1986. That unleashed a process that would result in 1992 in the first democratically elected legislature in the Chinese world since the 1911–1912 elections in China and then four years later in the first free and fair presidential election in the Chinese world.

To be sure, there were elements of extrication (a more hurried or crisis-driven conversion) or even of pact in the Taiwanese case. Indeed, some accounts have gone so far as to describe the transition as mixed state/society-led.[13] For instance, following student demonstrations in March 1990, KMT chairman and national president Lee Teng-hui held talks with 52 student representatives and then in April 1990, for the first time, with representatives of the Democratic Progressive Party. Most important, 16 DPP members as well as many prominent regime critics and liberal scholars were invited to join the June/July 1990 National Affairs Conference (NAC) of 150 prominent Taiwanese, called by Lee Teng-hui to deliberate on options for political reform. DPP members, including party chairman Huang Hsin-chieh, were even given three of the conference's 15 chairs, responsible for guiding the deliberations. The consensus reached by this pluralistic body and endorsed by Lee was a plan to make the national legislature and the presidency directly elected. Chi'u argues that the NAC marked the beginning of Taiwan's transition.[14]

To some extent, these invitations were forced upon the president by demonstrations in March and May 1990 in favor of political reform. But the ability to pick and choose who would join the NAC, plus evidence that Lee was already in favor of a directly elected legislature and president, suggests that the KMT remained in charge. Even though the increasingly organized opposition had a significant impact on internal debates within the KMT, at no point did opposition actors become determinative of the timing and nature of the changes. First Chiang Ching-kuo and then, after his death in 1988, Lee set the tone for the reforms that eventually led to Lee's victory in a free presidential election in 1996. The mere fact that the transition was spread out over a 10-year period—from 1986 to 1996—implies a state-led process. The Taiwan case is a reminder that transitions with pacts are not necessarily pacted transitions.

China's failed transition of 1989 was a mixture of soft and hard repression (Table 10.1). Following the ouster of reformist CCP leader Zhao Ziyang, martial law troops fought their way into Beijing on June 3–4, killing an estimated 2,000 citizens. In the year after the failed transition, 127,000 party members were expelled and another 166,000 punished.[15] Hundreds of dissidents and protesters sought refuge in foreign countries, and hundreds of thousands of students were sent to factories to *duanlian* (self-temper). To the extent that there is anything theoretically interesting about this failed transition, it is how quickly it gave way—after patriarch Deng Xiaoping's tour of southern China in early 1992—to a renewed liberalization of the regime. The long-term causes of regime ruptures endure, even when those ruptures are temporarily repaired. Looked at from today's perspective, Tiananmen appears to be merely a blip in the continued liberalization of the CCP regime that began in the late 1970s.

What sort of outcome should we expect the next time that China faces a similar crisis? From the standpoint of this structural or path-dependent theory of transitions, a successful transition in China next time would be more likely if social forces have become more powerful relative to the state than they were in 1989. Certainly there is ample evidence to this effect. Not only does China have a significant middle class today—probably 25 percent of the population in the year 2008[16]—but the liberalization of the media, private business, the legal system, and nongovernmental organizations since 1989 has created a much stronger society. It is simply not possible to imagine a repeat of the 1989–1991 repression in China. Despite significant and far-ranging reforms and rebuilding, the CCP state has become *relatively* weaker than society since 1989 on most accounts. Although fiscal, regulatory, and coercive capacities have been rebuilt or maintained, the CCP's ideological control over society has weakened[17] while its own internal pluralism has increased.[18] Just as Chiang Ching-kuo's recommitment to Sun Yat-sen's populist Three Principles of the People after 1978 opened the way for democratic reformers to rise through the ranks of the KMT, so former CCP general secretary Jiang Zemin's espousal of the populist Theory of the Three Represents in 2001 has opened the way for democratic reformers to rise within the CCP.

This suggests that the structural conditions for a democratic transition have improved in China. Yet it is still unlikely that such a transition would be society-led. There is no successful opposition movement in China—the last attempt to create one in 1998–1999 in the form of the China Democracy Party was successfully crushed. One of the only political activists who ever seriously articulated and planned for a society-led overthrow of the Communist state in China is Peng Ming-min: he was arrested by Myanmar authorities while setting up a political base in that country in 2004 and is now serving a life sentence in China. Meanwhile, many of the new social forces have been in various degrees co-opted by the party-state, as Dorothy Solinger and Merle Goldman and Ashley Esarey note in Chapters 5 and 3. Internal CCP pluralism, meanwhile, has limits. Even reformers inside the party argue for the maintenance of CCP rule.[19] Although social forces are stronger, they are by no means so strong as to render the state ineffective.

This means that the most likely scenario for a future democratic transition in China is a successful but state-led transition. Dickson's belief that "China's democratization, if and when it occurs, will likely be a discontinuous transition"[20] ignores the possible, indeed empirically most common, outcome, which is a democratic transition with significant continuities with the past. Such a prediction is hardly novel. It has been the mainstream view of students of China's politics throughout the reform era, and both Chapters 7, by Randall Peerenboom and Weitseng Chen, and Chapter 6, by Robert Weller, suggest that the regime will stay in control of the pace of political change. Indeed, its roots may go beyond structural factors: Guo shows that "top-down political change" represents a confluence of Confucian, Leninist, and neoauthoritarian intellectual threads in the political culture of contemporary China,[21] a point made more generally about Asian democratizations by Chan.[22] As scholar Sun Yan, an advocate of the state-led approach, argues: "[China's people] likely will continue to rely on the state as the engine of change."[23]

That leaves us with three possible scenarios for democratic transition in China—the three state-led variants of extrication, conversion, and gradualism. From a normative standpoint, many scholars have argued for the merits of the gradualism model of state-led transition in China. Since the failure of Tiananmen, a wave of writings has arisen on "constitutionalism"[24] or "the rule of law"[25] as gradualist tactics for democratic transition. At present, there is little evidence that the CCP is engaged in such a transition. The expansion of direct elections from the village to the township and city level, although endorsed by Jiang Zemin in his speech to the Fifteenth Party Congress of 1997 and then again by Hu Jintao in his speech to the Seventeenth Party Congress of 2007, has been blocked. The reasons for this are obvious: the CCP believes that it would rapidly lose control of any such gradual opening. Given the post-1989 strengthening of social forces, it does not believe it could direct a gradual democratization. In the 1980s, the CCP was both willing and able to begin gradual democratization and thus it passed the 1987 village elections law. But after 1989, it rejected this option. The CCP cannot institutionalize political competition even if it can institutionalize other aspects of the state. Indeed, since the mid-1990s there has been a distinct regression of political contestation at the national level in China, an "end of politics" syndrome that reflects the state's inability to manage political openness without inducing instability.[26]

Peerenboom and Chen's East Asian Model described in Chapter 7 implies that state actors intentionally move their countries to democracy when social pressures arise. But this seems unlikely in China in the absence of some sort of crisis. That means that a more hurried conversion or extrication is the most likely scenario for China. In the case of conversion, the regime takes the initiative at a time of growing social pressure but *before* change is forced upon it and when its legitimacy is still high. This was the case in Taiwan. Yet, as Dickson argued and as Tun-jen Cheng and Gang Lin argue in Chapter 8, the KMT had *already* committed itself to becoming more responsive to social demands. Although the Three Represents and a rising concern with legitimacy[27] show a similar drift in China, the CCP has not yet made democracy an explicit goal of national development. The result is that the CCP will likely require a more pressing crisis to convince it to launch major reforms.

That leaves extrication as the most likely denouement.[28] At this point, the parallels between Taiwan and China break down. The KMT was able to effect a 10-year conversion to democratic rule because it took the initiative *before* it was forced to do so. The CCP, at least from the current vantage point, looks unlikely to move preemptively. Although it would likely retain control of the process, it would be acting in a more crisis-ridden environment. A democratic transition in China will look more like the Soviet case than the Taiwanese case. This is a reminder that prior institutions may trump developmental pressures in shaping transitions. Being a Communist state with an explicit aversion to electoral democracy is more salient to China's future than being a rapidly developing Chinese society.

Transition Processes in Taiwan and China

This then takes us to the second part of transitions theory—the short-term process of transition—and the lessons to be learned from the Taiwan case. Although China's transition is likely to be more rapid than that of Taiwan, the predicted extrication in China is sufficiently close to Taiwan's conversion model, and the stylized stages of every transition of whatever type are sufficiently similar and autonomous of structural conditions, to push the comparison beyond structural questions to questions of process. By tracing the eight-stage process of transition (see Table 10.2) across the three cases—Taiwan in 1986, China in 1989, and China in the future—we can see how structural differences do not translate necessarily into transition process differences.

Crisis

Democratic transitions usually result from a particular crisis that occurs against a backdrop of authoritarian delegitimation. The assassination of Franco's successor, Admiral Luis Carrero Blanco, by Basque terrorists in 1973 or the financial collapse of the Bosnian state trading company Agrokomerc in 1987 could not be more different. But they share one essential feature: they were crisis events that raised the question of the legitimacy of authoritarian regimes. In the case of Taiwan, the 1986 breakthrough was preceded by a long string of crises that, in Tsang's words, "were pushing Chiang [Ching-kuo] to a major review of policy."[29] These included, inter alia: Nixon's 1971 visit to China and Taiwan's subsequent loss of its United Nations seat; the 1977 local elections where the newly formed opposition camp won 35 percent of the seats in the Taiwan provincial assembly (the body charged with running subnational affairs) and 20 percent of the gubernatorial posts at the county level; a mass protest during those same 1977 elections over perceptions that the KMT had stolen the local mayoralty race in Chung-li; the police crackdown on opposition protests held on International Human Rights Day in Kaohsiung in 1979 that led to the injury of 40 civilians and the subsequent jailing on subversion charges of eight of the protest leaders (and 33 other participants); the murder of opposition journalist Henry Liu I-liang (pen name Jiang Nan) in south San Francisco in 1984 by alleged KMT agents; and finally the bankruptcy due to fraudulent loans in 1985 of the Tenth Credit Cooperative, whose chairman was a KMT legislator, that led to the resignation of the KMT ministers of both economy and finance.

This string of crises galvanized a growing opposition to KMT rule through actors such as the wives and lawyers of the Kaohsiung protest leaders or the depositors of the Tenth Credit Cooperative. More important, they realigned power within the KMT, strengthening the hand of reformers such as Lee Teng-hui. A little luck did not hurt as well: Sun Yun-hsuan, the dithering premier, collapsed from a blood clot in the brain in 1984, further strengthening Lee's hand.

The Tiananmen Square movement of 1989 was also preceded by a string of crises, most notably the rise of inflation from 1985 to 1988 due to price decontrols; mounting evidence of official profiteering, including that by Deng

Xiaoping's son Deng Pufang; and finally the death in harness of the popular and officially mistreated former party general secretary Hu Yaobang in April 1989. The regime was facing a temporary legitimacy crisis, and reformers in the senior leadership knew it.

What is notable from contemporary China is how many similar crises have *not* started the wheels of democratic transition. One can enumerate any number of stolen elections; health, environmental, or financial scandals; or mass protest incidents that might have constituted a crisis in the regime. The SARS crisis of 2002–2003, the $550 million in losses made by state trading company China Aviation Oil in 2004, and the chemical factory explosion that threw 100 tons of carcinogens into the Songhua River in 2005 are all examples of the sorts of crises that, mishandled by an unaccountable and secretive regime, have led to panic and protest. The reports on the desk of former party general secretary Jiang Zemin, as described by his wife in an official memoir, offer a neat summary: "Explosions here, rioting there. Murders, corruption, terrorism—little that was nice."[30] That these crises have *not* led to transition processes shows how ill-defined the theory of crises is: without a theory of what makes a crisis salient, we can identify crises only ex post.

The examples of Taiwan in 1986 and China in 1989 show that crises are only crises when the regime is *already* predisposed toward launching major political reforms—as were Chiang Ching-kuo in 1986 and Zhao Ziyang in 1989. That the string of events in contemporary China has not led to crisis is owing to the fact that this crucial element is missing. The reason, of course, is that senior leaders do not perceive that their regime faces a legitimacy crisis, and they are probably right.[31] Short of a major catastrophe, crisis-watching in contemporary China is thus premature. Until there is evidence of a predisposition toward major political reforms within the senior leadership, driven by a perception of dwindling public support, disasters will come and go in China with minimal consequences.

Mobilization

Crises are important because, when coupled with knowledge of support, or at least tolerance, within the regime, they lead to the next stage, social mobilization. Social mobilization represents a mass manifestation of the crisis of the regime—the moment when attention shifts to politics. Mobilization on a sufficiently large or organized scale is important because it is the first *public* indicator that a transition process may be under way. The tolerance of mobilization signals the predisposition toward major political reforms among some elements of the leadership that may hitherto have remained obscured: Soviet leader Mikhail Gorbachev's unexpected tolerance of protesters in Sakhalin Province in 1988 or of the memorial movement of Stalin's victims are two oft-cited examples from the Soviet case.

As noted, Taiwan's opposition movement had been gradually mobilizing since at least 1977. The importance of this mobilization cannot be overestimated even if it is in turn dependent upon regime toleration. Without it, the explicit split in the regime on the question of political reform would be less likely. In the summer of 1986, before the ban on opposition parties had been lifted but after Chiang's empowerment of a 12-member committee to consider this move, the DPP announced its creation. The KMT took no action against the illegal party, which eventually won 13 members in the legislative election of December 1986. This "sudden tolerance of organized opposition,"[32] as Dickson called it, was a good example of how mobilization signals, and in turn accelerates, changes at the top. For this reason, some have pointed to mobilization as having critical causal status in Taiwan and other cases. Tsang, for example, argues that "the vitality and, in the circumstances, the responsible manner in which the opposition and the general public pushed for further democratization ought to be recognized as the more important force [compared to internal KMT pluralism] that built up the momentum for democratization."[33]

China's 1989 social mobilization was the largest in the history of the PRC. Protests occurred in 341 of China's then 434 cities, taking in an estimated 100 million people.[34] Protest groups in Beijing included representatives from the *People's Daily,* the People's Liberation Army Navy, and the National People's Congress staff association. Workers were organized under the newly established Beijing Autonomous Workers' Federation, and students dominated the movement's leadership. One could not have asked for a more substantial mobilization. Retrospective critiques of the movement's factionalism or its failure to embrace the peasantry miss the essential point of mobilizations in state-led democratic transitions: their role is to empower reformers, not replace them. The reasons for the failure of China's 1989 transition must lie elsewhere.

A future mobilization in China need not be as large as Tiananmen in 1989. Moreover, technology and information spread make the possibilities even greater. A growing regularization of popular protest, moreover, is creating norms that make it more likely that citizens would take to the streets given signals of toleration from the top at a time of regime crisis. The very fact that the Ministry of Public Security has, since 1993, made annual reports on the number and scale of public protests shows the normalization of this form of political participation in China. When there is a predisposition toward major reforms in the leadership, mobilization will be rapid and effectual.

Elite Split

The division of an authoritarian regime over the question of major political reforms is the crux of any democratic transition.[35] Indeed, Bunce argued in

2000 that the *only* real generalization of two decades of research on democratization is that "when elites divide, the probability of democratic outcomes increases substantially."[36] What is important to note from the cases here is that elite split is a two-stage process. The first stage is part of the long-term factors that form the predisposition to major political reforms among some elites. The second stage involves the explicit shift from a *predisposition* to an *intention* to launch major political reforms in the face of crisis and mobilization. The split involves those reform-minded elites dividing from resisters on the question of political reform by making their intentions clear internally and, soon enough, externally. Elite splits are important because they are the second public indicator that an attempted transition is under way.

The elite split became evident in Taiwan as early as 1983 with the exile of hard-line KMT Department of Political Warfare director Wang Sheng to be ambassador to Paraguay after his attempts to accumulate power during Chiang Ching-kuo's lengthy illness. His defeat signaled the ascension of the reform faction within the KMT, centered on the Youth Corps of Lee Huan, who became KMT secretary-general in 1987. The emergent split was widened by the fact of growing local electoral competition between KMT and de facto opposition candidates. As Langston argues, and as Tun-jen Cheng and Gang Lin argue in Chapter 8, local elections provided incentives to KMT reformers to break with hard-liners because they believed they could regain power through elections even if they lost power in internecine struggles.[37]

The subsequent democratic breakthrough, according to Dickson, "was dependent primarily on changes in the composition of the party elite, ending a stalemate that had existed for years."[38] As Cheng and Haggard noted: "Internal political debates within the KMT were the crucial factor shaping the transition."[39]

The fact that Chiang himself moved to the side of the reformers as his death neared was obviously of central importance. The reasons for this remain clouded in debate—whether he was a genuine democrat or was acting for strategic reasons. The truth is probably both—as is the case in most democratic transitions.[40] He was Soviet-trained and schooled in strengthening the party and in recovering China. But he also took seriously the Three Principles of the People and believed deeply that legitimacy in the eyes of both history and the people was the ultimate aim of government.[41] The two motivations were in fact complementary. After all, it was not the technocrats but the party affairs personnel who were on the side of reforms in the KMT. Although the party affairs personnel were often seen as conservatives, they were conservative only in a romantic sense—they *believed* in the ruling party. But this belief led them to embrace reforms that they predicted would benefit the party itself. As Scalapino noted: "Chiang Ching-kuo was no democrat. . . . [His] reforms were designed to protect his power and that of the party to which he was fully committed."[42]

The elite split in China in 1989 became public in Zhao's speech to the

Asian Development Bank meeting in Beijing on May 4 in which he sided with the students and said that the party needed to respond to their demands. On his side were such powerful elders as Bo Yibo, who commented in an internal meeting: "We should grab the initiative by launching democratization now, while the leadership role of the Party is relatively strong."[43] The emergence of this split was by no means inevitable: most of the "liberals" taking part in Zhao's political reform study group set up in 1987, including Zhao himself, were opposed to the introduction of multiparty democracy.[44] One factor, obviously, was the role of the Tiananmen protests in encouraging this split—just as protests in Tiananmen in 1976 had encouraged party elders to overthrow the Gang of Four.[45] But, like the Taiwan case, strategic considerations seem insufficient to explain Zhao's bold gambit. At this point, individual leadership and a commitment to popular rule at some normative level seem indispensable. What is obvious from his discussions with a close friend after the incident is that Zhao believed passionately in pluralistic politics, arguing later that a "Western" democratic system was the best one yet developed even if its implementation in China was premature.[46] Although the adage that "democrats do not produce democracy; democracy produces democrats" is certainly true at a general level, it is also true that *some* predisposition or sympathy for democracy is necessary for elites to split. Prudential concerns or rational calculations cannot explain the risks that reformist elites take to initiate democracy.

That is why there is so little optimism about a similar split emerging in China in the future: there is little evidence that any significant elite political actor in China has a commitment to major political reforms, much less democracy.[47] However, as in Taiwan in 1986 and in China in 1989, the revelation of such a commitment may come very late in the game. Mikhail Gorbachev, for example, was promoted to head the Soviet Communist Party in 1985 precisely because he was seen as a party stalwart *opposed* to political liberalization. To understand the potential for elites to embrace democratization, then, we must look back one stage to see whether there are elites who are (1) tolerant or pragmatic in their approach to political organization, (2) risk-taking in their individual behavior, and (3) populist in their political inclinations.

Looked at from this perspective, the Chinese leadership seems no less predisposed to splitting on the issue of democratic reforms than it was in 1989 or than Taiwan's was in 1983. A process of technocratic transformation of party cadres began in China in the early 1980s, mirroring a similar process in Taiwan in the 1960s.[48] Pragmatism, populism, and opportunism, and with them the buried seeds of democratic commitment, are certainly not in short supply in the current Chinese leadership. Designated future premier Li Keqiang, for example, is a Leninist romantic of the "inland" faction who told fellow students at Beijing University in 1978 that he wanted to "change the party from the inside." Designated future party general secretary Xi Jinping, meanwhile, who is due to assume power in 2012, is a results-oriented and nonideological leader whose father, party elder Xi Zhongxun, suffered at the hands of Mao.

In the Taiwan case, Chiang Ching-kuo's convening of a National Construction Conference in 1972 in which scholars aired bold plans for political reform might be seen in retrospect as signaling his predisposition to change. Similar conferences held by Hu Jintao at the Central Party School since then can likewise be seen as signaling an emerging interest in "audacious"[49] political reforms within the Chinese leadership.

Meanwhile, the groundwork for populism has been laid in the CCP. The CCP's populist Three Represents parallels the KMT's populist Three Principles of the People (and Khrushchev's "party of all the people" of 1961, a policy that led in the Ukrainian region of Sverdlovsk to a young man named Boris Yeltsin's joining the Communist Party of the Soviet Union). Hu Jintao's "harmonious society" parallels Chiang Ching-kuo's policy of seeking "political harmony" in late-authoritarian Taiwan.[50] And the emergence since 2002 of distinctive "coastal" and "inland" factions on policy issues in the CCP,[51] both claiming to represent popular views, parallels the emergence of KMT factions through electoral politics in Taiwan in the 1960s.[52]

The only missing element is a predisposition to major political change. At present, that does not exist, and that alone must explain why transition processes have not begun in China. Put simply, an interest in audacious reforms will not become a predisposition toward them until there is evidence of a legitimacy crisis that gives urgency to such plans.[53] The prospect of legitimacy crisis may sweep the CCP off its feet because the CCP is already oriented to being moved with social demands.

Hard-line Backlash

Retrospective accounts of Taiwan's transition tend to downplay, or wholly ignore, the very real attempts by hard-liners to defeat the reformers who had emerged in charge of the KMT. But from the perspective of the 1986 to 1992 period, Taiwan's transition looked very uncertain. Dissidents continued to be thrown in jail for sedition in this period, and the KMT stepped up its control of the national media. Wu describes a "surging tide of conservatism" inside the KMT after Chiang announced his 12-member committee in 1986.[54] The fact that Chiang then fell gravely ill until his death two years later foreboded trouble for the nascent democratic transition.

The conservative backlash in Taiwan was at first aimed at preventing the Taiwan-born Lee Teng-hui from succeeding Chiang. Ironically, it was Chiang's mother, 90-year-old Madame Chiang Kai-shek, who first came forward in January 1988 and then again in July 1988 to prevent the KMT from appointing Lee as party chairman. Having failed, conservatives then attempted in February 1990 to prevent Lee from being nominated as the party's presidential candidate for the following month's National Assembly vote. In this case, the conservatives broke with democratic centralism and nominated a rival presidential candidate, judiciary minister Lin Yang-kang, with Chiang Ching-kuo's younger brother, Chiang Wei-kuo, as his vice president. In all three cases, only careful persuasion and politicking by reformers in the KMT saved the day.[55] KMT reformers such as Jaw Shao-kang, James Soong, and Kuan Chung "were able to convince hardliners of the necessity of reform," notes Hood.[56] Stirred by rising student and DPP protests against the role of National Assembly hard-liners—protestors numbered more than 20,000 in the Chiang Kai-shek Memorial Hall Square on March 19–20, 1990—the National Assembly eventually dutifully elected Lee as president on March 21, 1990.

Having failed to unseat Lee, conservative efforts then shifted to thwarting the planned elimination from the three main political bodies—the Legislative Yuan, National Assembly, and Control Yuan—of the "China seats" elected in 1947 and 1948 that accounted for three-quarters of the total membership in those bodies. In its session that opened in February 1990, the National Assembly tried to pass a law extending its term of office and arrogating to itself the right to initiate and veto laws and to meet annually. This was in direct contradiction of Lee Teng-hui's announced plans of February 1989 to reform the body. Rumors circulated in Taipei about an imminent People's Liberation Army (PLA) invasion of Taiwan in collusion with KMT hard-liners, underlining the seriousness of the situation and signifying the beginnings of a long period in which Taiwan's democratization would become the main issue in cross-Strait relations.

The decision to elect Lee was in part a sign that National Assembly resistance was crumbling. But the backlash was finally defeated only in the high court—a reminder that prior institutionalization of the rule of law can have positive impacts on democratization, as Randall Peerenboom and Weitseng Chen (in Chapter 7) as well as Tun-jen Cheng and Gang Lin (in Chapter 8) argue in this book. In June 1990, the court ruled that Lee's law on "China seats" retirements of February 1989 was constitutional, and all mainland-era representatives must retire by the end of 1991.

It is also noteworthy here to stress the critical role played by Lee Teng-hui in sticking to plans for reforms: although Chiang is often cited as the father of democracy in Taiwan, Lee's critical role in preventing the hard-line backlash and then carrying through the full democratization was arguably just as important.

At the same time, the role of social mobilization, much of it motivated by a rising sense of separate Taiwanese identity, cannot be ignored: the massive protests against the Old Thieves (*lao zei*) of the National Assembly and Legislative Yuan, as the pre-1949–era members were derisively called, by tens of thousands of people in Taipei in March 1990, made Lee's conciliatory style seem moderate. The generous payouts for each retiring legislator and assemblyman—the equivalent of US$170,000 per person in 2008 prices—may have helped as well.

This point helps to explain the successful hard-line backlash in China in 1989 that ended the attempted democratic transition there. That there were hard-liners in the Chinese case opposed to democratic reforms was not the critical point. Hard-liners attempting to sabotage democratic transitions are always in plentiful supply, especially in Leninist or quasi-Leninist systems such as Taiwan and China where the ruling party is organized precisely to ensure such a backlash. As in Taiwan, those hard-liners had a historical pedigree in China that gave them an elevated status within the party—in both cases they were the veterans of the KMT-CCP civil war of 1946–1950 who had "saved the nation." In China in 1989, they were represented by the Eight Immortals (*ba lao*), led by Deng Xiaoping, who still held the position of chairman of the Central Military Commission, and Yang Shangkun, who was president.

Why did the Eight Immortals succeed in China while the Old Thieves failed in Taiwan? In light of the Taiwan case, the answer is that there were no internal moderates in the CCP who could remonstrate with the hard-liners, convincing them to side with Zhao and his reform plans. Whereas this pluralism had developed within the KMT as a result of local electoral competition, such pluralism was deeply insufficient within the CCP in 1989. Premier Li Peng was as hard-line as the immortals themselves. The moderate National People's Congress chairman Wan Li was detained at the Shanghai airport by the local party secretary, Jiang Zemin (who would replace Zhao), as Wan attempted to return to Beijing from an ill-timed overseas trip. The result was that when the Eight Immortals moved against Zhao, there was not a peep from the CCP elite.

What about next time in China? One advantage of the passage of years is that the Eight Immortals are now all dead (the last, Bo Yibo, died in 2007). Meanwhile, Li Peng's last representative, Luo Gan, stepped down from the Politburo Standing Committee in 2007. The PLA, meanwhile, has been almost entirely removed from the realm of politics and its internal policing duties handed over to the civilian-controlled People's Armed Police (PAP). The hard-liners in today's China do not have the pedigree of those of the past. They are peers, not elders, of the current leadership. One can also find a greater degree of moderate opinion within the party today. Nonetheless, there are still serious doubts that these moderates exist in sufficient numbers to overcome a hard-line backlash against an attempted reform-led split. Until the CCP has a longer period of social engagement as a result of the Three Represents, the moderates' ability to wrest control of the party from conservatives must remain in doubt.

Democratic Decision

With the June 1990 high court ruling against the conservatives and the July 1990 NAC consensus on a directly elected presidency, the way was open for a democratic decision in Taiwan—the point at which the regime made an explicit and clear commitment to democratization. After the NAC, Lee appointed a 13-member KMT panel headed by Vice President Li Yuan-zu to study the conference's proposals for a fully elected legislature and National Assembly. In February 1991, the panel voted in favor of those proposals. At that point, the KMT's decision to implement democracy was clear, even if it was not until 1992 that the proposals were fully enacted. Lee had accepted the NAC consensus and made the decision to move forward. In May 1991, martial law was lifted.

China's failed transition of 1989 never made it to such an explicit official commitment to democracy. The hard-line backlash had already overtaken it before then. However, we know for all intents what that initial decision would have looked like. The General Framework for Political Reform produced by Zhao's Working Group on Political Reform in 1987 included plans for expanded local elections, constitutional limits on the CCP's powers, and genuine press freedoms.[57] In the following two years, those proposals were widely debated inside the party. The Tiananmen protests of 1989 brought them to the brink of success, but sent them instead to failure. When Zhao made his dramatic appearance among the protesters in the square in the early hours of May 19, 1989, his plain words were reflective of the fact that the chance for a democratic decision had passed: "We have come too late."[58]

Assuming that a future transition in China makes it past the inevitable hard-line backlash, what might a democratic decision look like? A common finding of democratic decisions in state-led transitions is that they are often couched in the language of continuity, stability, and ruling-party interests. This was the case in Taiwan and would have been the case in 1989 China. In a future transition in China, there will be an even greater variety of ways to couch a democratic decision in the language of continuity, given institutional developments in the post-1989 period. A reformist leadership could, for instance, make good on the 1997 and 2007 party congress promises to expand direct elections to the township and county/city levels. "If the Chinese people can manage a village, I believe in several years they can manage a township," Premier Wen Jiabao, who was at Zhao's side as his chief-of-staff in 1989, said in 2005.[59] Or a reform leadership could announce plans to implement the legal requirement that township-level people's congresses be directly elected, just as Gorbachev's initial reforms were centered on making local soviets genuinely elected and genuinely powerful. All this could be more broadly phrased within the context of post-1989 doctrines such as "political civilization" (*zhengzhi wenming*), "the development of the rule of law" (*fazhi jianshe*), or "constitutional government" (*xianzheng*). Outspoken democratic advocate Yu Keping, who is head of the CCP's Central Translation Bureau and, more important, is director of the government's Center for Chinese Government Innovations that rewards "audacious reforms" at the local level, has proposed a phased democratic transition in the name of "incrementalism." As in Taiwan, a democratic decision in China could result from a little-noticed vote by an obscure CCP committee studying political reform options.

Institutional Choice

In general, state-led transitions adopt new democratic institutions that build upon existing ones.[60] In the Taiwan case, the only major revisions required to transform an authoritarian system into a democratic one were to make the legislature and National Assembly fully elected. The DPP's failure to win the necessary 25 percent of seats in the first popular National Assembly elections in December 1991 (it won 20 percent of the seats up for election, ending with 16 percent of the entire body) ensured that institutional choice remained in the hands of the regime (since the National Assembly had powers to revise the constitution in addition to choosing the president). This was a case where popular mobilization (in this case the National Assembly election) actually legitimated the regime-led nature of the transition: most Taiwanese seemed to prefer that the KMT remain at the helm of the transition. The National Assembly meeting of March 1992 then harmonized legislative and presidential terms at four years each and established a strong-presidency model of executive-legislative relations (again, consistent with state-led transitions). KMT divisions on the question of a direct presidential ballot led the issue to be postponed, but Lee indicated his support of a direct poll in March 1992: "Direct election is the trend of democracy," Lee said.[61]

The degree of leeway for institutional choice in Taiwan was further constrained by an external factor: Beijing, ironically, was opposed to major constitutional revisions that would undercut the KMT's claim to rule all of China, since that was seen as a concession to Taiwanese independence. An oblique constitutional revision passed in 1991 limited the area covered by the constitution to Taiwan but did not give up on the claim to rule all of China. Not until its democratic transition was over did consideration begin of further major constitutional reforms such as the abolition of the Taiwan provincial government, the National Assembly, and the National Reunification Council.

The predicted state-led extrication in a future transition in China likewise implies that it will build upon existing foundations. Indeed, the popular "constitutionalist" proposals for political reform in China today call for an implementation of the existing constitution with only minor revisions, most notably the elimination of the CCP's "leading role" in the political system.[62] The National People's Congress would live up to its official billing as "the highest organ of state power," and the consultative Chinese People's Political Consultative Conference would retain an advisory role, perhaps giving greater representation to regional and minority groups. The current weak president and strong premier would be retained. Although such continuist transitions create later problems for democratic consolidation, as we will discuss below, they are easier to agree upon at the critical moment.

Interim Regime

Interim regimes are those charged with carrying through the democratic decision. In the terminology of Shain, Linz, and Berat, those in state-led transitions benefit from having both "backward legality" (they inherit state power from the outgoing regime) as well as "forward legitimacy" (they are leading the country to democracy).[63] From the lifting of martial law in March 1991 until the first legislative election of December 1992, Lee Teng-hui's cabinet served as the interim regime, guiding the deliberations of the National Assembly and planning its own first electoral battle. Indeed, so continuist was the Taiwan transition that Lee's government was never really recognized as having a "caretaker" capacity at all. Taiwan's transition is seen as having gone directly from authoritarian rule to democratic rule. Yet in those 21 months, it was neither. That the interim regime was so short-lived shows the momentum and support that the transition had developed by early 1991.

If the predicted extrication scenario is a better description of a future transition in China, then the interim regime in that case will be more prominent. Yet it also means that such a regime would be just as short-lived, perhaps even more so given the more pressured nature of the transition. Extrication reduces the likelihood of a permanent interim regime that never makes good on its democratic promises.

Founding Election

Founding elections are good indicators of the completion of a democratic transition where the elections are reasonably free and fair and where the results are widely accepted. In the Taiwan case, legislative elections in 1992 and 1995 and the first direct presidential election in 1996 all met those criteria. This raises the question of *which* election should be taken as indicative. The KMT's sweep of 60 percent of the legislative seats in 1992 gave it its first democratic mandate, which in turn gave Lee's presidency a popular basis it had hitherto lacked. Yet Lee himself was not directly elected until 1996, which in formal terms is a better date to end the transition. What is remarkable is that the results of all three elections were widely accepted by all major groups (save perhaps China, which launched belligerent missile tests off Taiwan's coast in the run-up to the 1996 poll). Just two election outcomes in 1992, in Hualien, were protested, and the 1995 legislative election and 1996 presidential election were free of major controversies.

An election in China would involve some 900 million eligible voters, making it the single biggest event in world history. India's 2004 national election (where 368 million people, or 55 percent of the 670 million eligible voters, voted) showed the benefits that China will derive as a latecomer. India employed electronic voting for the election, which passed off virtually without electoral fraud and defects and with minimal violence. There is today also a vast resource of international groups that help with the administering of elections on which China could draw. Given its size and diversity, issues of contested local polls and disgruntled conservative forces would remain more potentially spoiling in China than they were in Taiwan. Indeed, democrats in China are already wisely warning that this will be part of the country's passage to democracy. Former Zhao adviser Yan Jiaqi, for example, predicts:

> China will likely have to go through several more nationwide protest, strike, and student movements before it achieves mature democracy. It will have to get through several short-lived military coups, many local-level armed conflicts, many cases of major political scandal, the entry of bribery and violence into elections, and maybe a couple of cases where the national election results in a great dispute that brings constitutional government to the brink of collapse. Even so, China can surely march through the various stages of democratic development.[64]

Even at this final stage, then, democratic transition in China will be immensely more complicated, and risky, than in Taiwan. Still, other large countries, such as India, Indonesia, and Brazil, have successfully completed those stages. China's chance to try again, when it comes, will offer evidence of exactly how much has changed since 1989.

Transition Implications in Taiwan and China

Both aspects of democratic transitions—the structural or path-dependent aspects and the contingent or autonomous aspects—have an impact on the degree and nature of the democracy that follows. Table 10.1 shows the risks associated with different structural types of transitions. A similar list could be drawn up for Table 10.2, showing the implications of the various stages for the democracy that follows.

In terms of the structural aspects, the most common finding is that the greater is the social involvement in the transition, the faster tends to be the progress toward liberal democracy in the years that follow.[65] In a study of 64 democratizations from 1972 to 2005, Freedom House found that society-led or mixed state/society-led transitions had dramatically better outcomes than state-led transitions (see Table 10.3).[66]

Taiwan's democratic progress was unusually good, gaining 3.5 points on the 7-point scale shown in Table 10.3 between 1986 and 2005. Although Freedom House classifies Taiwan as a mixed state/society-led transition, it

Table 10.3   Democratic Gains by Transition Type

Transition Type	Cases	Gains (7-point scale)
Society-led	18	2.78
Mixed	32	2.58
State-led	14	1.10
All	64	2.31

Source: Karatnycky and Ackerman 2005.
Note: Gains indicate the change in combined average rating of political and civil liberties scores from year of transition to 2005.

could just as well be classified as a state-led transition, in which case its performance would be all the more remarkable. Looked at from the perspective of the late 1980s or early 1990s, it is important to remind ourselves that this result was wholly unexpected. Cheng and Haggard, for example, wrote in 1992 that "the electoral performance of the DPP in 1989 may well be a one-time gain. . . . The KMT clearly has the capacity and opportunity to transform Taiwan's one-party authoritarian regime into a one-party dominant democratic system."[67] Meaney argued similarly in the same year that there was "potential for the emergence of a hybrid regime, neither fully authoritarian nor democratic, that may persist for a protracted period" and that it was uncertain "whether the [KMT] will stick to its plans for electoral reform if it appears that they might actually result in an opposition victory."[68]

That the Taiwanese transition did *not* give way to a feckless democracy is a testament both to the importance of social pressures and to the normative commitment to democracy that Lee Teng-hui brought with him into office. Once the inevitable pressures arose for a "second revolution" to end KMT rule, the KMT itself had become sufficiently imbued with democratic norms that the rapid march toward a liberal democracy was inevitable. In this sense, Taiwan's democratization enjoyed the best of both worlds: the stability and continuity of a state-led transition and the rapid gains in democratic quality of a society-led transition.

China will not likely be as fortunate. In the Freedom House study, eight countries classified as "not free" prior to transition experienced state-led democratizations (as we predict for "not free" China). Four of them (Kazakhstan, Tajikistan, Uzbekistan, and Zimbabwe) remained not free by 2005, and the others (Ethiopia, Gambia, Mozambique, and Paraguay) were classified as only partly free. Dickson argues that the most likely result of a democratic transition in China would be a stalled transition, a new regime "much like the old regime, minus the Leninist elements. . . . The CCP would likely dominate its societal partners and . . . the outlook for democracy in

China is not good under those circumstances."[69] The prospect of a new People's Republic of Chinastan broods over a future democratic transition in China.

China, then, must aspire to achieve a transition consistent with the latter four examples in the Freedom House study and with the Taiwan case. To do this will require greater social pressures and a sharper division within the CCP—process factors that mitigate the structural ones. The "myth of moderation" as Bermeo calls it,[70] is to assume that all that is moderate and gradual is necessarily good for a democratic transition. This may not be the case. A similar "myth of state strength" is that all forms of state strength are good for democracy. Again, this may not be the case, as Way has argued of post-Communist Europe.[71] The Taiwan example shows that social protest, destabilizing elite divisions, and a divided state may be necessary for a successful posttransition consolidation phase. Similarly, Paraguay's remarkable 3-point gain on its Freedom House score beginning with a state-led democratic transition in 1989 resulted from an internal coup against the repressive rule of General Alfredo Stroessner. The transition was state-led, but the state itself had changed colors prior to the transition. To succeed, China's transition must aspire to be socially mixed, internally divisive, and a challenge to some forms of state strength.

Empirical, Theoretical, and Policy Conclusions

The Taiwan-China comparison is both apt and useful in the case of democratic transitions. It shows both the similarities and differences between the two places, pointing to a better understanding of what was special about both Taiwan's successful transition of 1986 and China's failed transition of 1989. This leads to a better understanding of the forces that will shape a future transition in China.

Several key lessons emerge about the Taiwan case. One is that there was nothing that made the string of scandals and incidents of the 1970s and early 1980s necessarily crises. Only the predisposition of Chiang Ching-kuo to a liberalization of the regime, coupled with a sudden gambit in 1986, made those events critical in nature. Crisis in Taiwan was subjective, not objective.

Second, although it has rarely been mentioned, there *was* a serious hardline backlash in Taiwan that might have derailed the transition there. That backlash was fought in the courts and in the National Assembly and so lacked the drama of a military confrontation. But it was no less serious for all that.

Third, given that the defeat of the hard-line backlash was achieved by Lee Teng-hui rather than Chiang, Lee arguably has a better claim to being the father of democracy in Taiwan than Chiang. His gentle persuasion and unwavering democratic commitment saved what might have become a stillborn, or more violent, transition. Hard-liners complained of "the Lee Teng-hui syndrome" in defeating their plans for sustaining authoritarian rule, perhaps the greatest compliment he could have earned.

Finally, even though social mobilization critically shaped the transition, its main role came *after* 1996, ensuring that Taiwan did not drift toward a feckless electoral democracy dominated by the KMT but instead moved quickly into the ranks of the world's liberal democracies. In other respects, social mobilization and opposition politics played an adjunct role alone. To repeat, Taiwan's transition contained a pact, but it was not a pacted transition.

In light of the Taiwan case, the main lesson that emerges about China's failed transition of 1989 is a simple one: nothing made the 1989 defeat inevitable, or even likely. Virtually all of the preconditions necessary for a successful transition were in place in 1989, save one: sufficient internal pluralism in the CCP to support Zhao Ziyang against the inevitable hard-line backlash of early May 1989. Yet that condition might have been remedied by better luck— a few of the Eight Immortals deceased before 1989 rather than shortly after it, for example, or National People's Congress chairman Wan Li in Beijing rather than traveling abroad. Just as it is important to avoid retrospective views of Taiwan's 1986 transition as bound to succeed, so too it is important to avoid retrospective views of China's 1989 transition as bound to fail. Contingency was critical to the outcomes in both cases.

A second lesson from the China case is that institutions matter. Being Communist is more important to China than being Asian, Confucian, or developing. Internal pluralism was weak in the CCP in 1989 because Leninist institutions conspired to keep it that way. The great question that must be raised in the context of a future transition in China, then, is whether post-1989 reforms have shifted the CCP to a quasi-Leninist party, where Leninist principles are challenged by emergent pluralist ones. Authors in this book are divided on that issue—Ten-jen Cheng and Gang Lin indicate in Chapter 8 that they believe elections have *not* been sufficiently important in China to achieve the same pluralism that they did in Taiwan, but Randall Peerenboom and Weitseng Chen's work in Chapter 7 suggests the emergence of competing legalistic norms inside the party.

To what extent does this analysis force us to reconsider aspects of democratic transition theory itself? Two points deserve mention. For one, the idea that one can objectively measure the crisis-potential of an authoritarian regime is undermined by these two cases. Taiwan's 1986 transition and China's failed 1989 transition both occurred in times of rapid growth, low unemployment, and healthy financial systems. Although we can, and must, study the objective conditions that might be defined as "crisis-type" in nature, ultimately there is only a probabilistic connection between this analysis and what relevant actors will subjectively *perceive* to be a crisis. Purely objective crisis theories in general and objective *economic* crisis theories in particular have only a probabilistic relation to democratic transitions. To understand their potential, one must understand the predispositions of would-be regime reformers and their subjective views of what constitutes a crisis.

More generally, "political economy" approaches to democratic transitions fail on both substantive and methodological grounds. Objective economic conditions have little predictive value in explaining transitions for the same reason that "rational choice" theories of elite choice fail as well: what matters is not some objective set of rules and interests that can be studied as an exercise in interest-maximization but rather the ideas, moral commitments, and subjective perceptions of actors that make an everyday event suddenly appear as an objective crisis or that make unnecessary and self-defeating choices appear as "rational." Like so much of political life, democratic transitions represent a triumph of ideas over interests, or more accurately a redefinition of interests in terms of prevailing ideas. "One person with a belief," wrote Mill, "is a social power equal to ninety-nine who have only interests."[72]

A second general finding for democratic transitions theory, following the above, is that some level of normative commitment to democracy by key elites is necessary for a successful democratic transition. Even though no democracy is ever created by a card-carrying liberal democrat, it is also true that without *some* commitment to the ideals of political equality and popular control, the risk taking and staying power needed from reform elites is unimaginable. Chiang Ching-kuo's rediscovery of the populist Three Principles of the People after his father's death and Zhao Ziyang's explicit commitment to popular rule (but not multiparty democracy) in China both show this. Chiang's successor, Lee Teng-hui, was even more morally committed to democracy. We cannot explain democratic transitions as merely a "fortuitous byproduct"[73] of struggles for domination and clashes of interests, however appealing such formulations are to the cynically inclined. Such clashes could only result in civil war, new authoritarian regimes, or hegemonic electoral regimes. Transitions to democracy must arise from some level of commitment to the normative principles of democracy. Democratic transitions may be contingent, but they are by no means fortuitous. As Gill has written, "If the transitions literature does not recognize this normative aspect of democracy, it cannot explain the appeal of this form of government."[74]

What does this imply for the making of policy toward China? There are many policies that might help to create the structural conditions for a democratic transition in China. Consistent with that, the implications here are that international and domestic actors should strive to strengthen social forces in China as much as possible prior to the transition. The more "mixed" is China's transition, the better prospects the new democracy will have. That the CCP recognizes the dangers of growing social pluralism and has taken steps to limit it—such as by vetting the civil society groups that the European Union is trying to cultivate in the country—is an argument for *more,* not *less,* effort in this regard. Likewise it is important to encourage internal regime pluralism through programs that seek to educate the senior leadership to the widest possible number of democratic societies, both in Asia and abroad.

In this regard, a deeper understanding of the Taiwan experience may aid transition in China. In a 2006 article in the popular journal *Yanhuang Chunqiu,* for example, Wang Yeyang of the Chinese Academy of Social Sciences offers a glowing assessment of Chiang Ching-kuo's far-sighted decision to initiate a democratic transition in Taiwan as social conflict and KMT-DPP conflicts began to rise.[75] The article, entitled "Chiang Ching-kuo and the Kuomintang's Democratic Transition," is important because, as this book has emphasized, it is the intersubjective lessons of the Taiwan experience as much as their objective lessons that will matter to political outcomes in China. Chinese Academy of Social Sciences professor Zhang Boshu's stunning 2007 essay on the lessons from Taiwan's transition for China similarly highlighted not only the importance of organized social forces in pushing for transition but also the role of leadership: "The Taiwan experience reminds us that CCP reformers will meet with all sorts of resistance. Thus reformers inside the CCP must be courageous and wise. They must break out of their organizational state of mind in order to fly towards the shores of freedom."[76]

Do key actors in China share these perceptions of reformist scholars that Taiwan is a model transition for their country's future? Certainly, the official line is that a repeat of Taiwan's democratic transition, like all democratic transitions, is to be avoided. Chiang's initiation of democratic reforms, like Gorbachev's, is represented as a serious violation of Leninist organizational principles. However, outside of this official rhetoric, which is not expressed with much conviction by any scholar in China, there has emerged a counter-discourse, of which the works by Wang and Zhang are good examples. On this view, the Taiwan transition shows the benefits of a preemptive political opening. "By exploiting his powerful leadership position, Chiang Ching-kuo pushed reforms to a breakthrough while also maintaining the overall stability of the political situation. . . . Inter-party relations became more tolerant and social protest was kept within the bounds of the law," wrote Wang.[77] Similarly, in his 2003 book *China's Economic Development and Democratization,* Wang Yanlai argues that the Taiwan transition has lessons for elites in China.[78] In particular, he argues, it shows that there can be much continuity with past political and economic systems and that the eventual loss of power by the ruling party can be minimally disruptive.

A 2005 article by Lin Zhen of Putian University in Fujian Province argues that the key reason for Taiwan's democratic transition was Chiang Ching-kuo's wish to be the "father of democracy" in Taiwan, coupled with a series of regime crises that disarmed internal opposition.[79] Although mainstream in its interpretations—indeed, it draws upon the scholarship of this book's coeditor Larry Diamond—Lin's article is important for what it does *not* say: that democratic transition in Taiwan was, for instance, a result of nefarious "independence" forces in Taiwan or of Cold War strategists in Washington, both official interpretations. Taiwan's transition is instead portrayed in naturalistic, developmental tones. Meanwhile Zhang—who *does* make clear and strong parallels between Taiwan's past and China's future—categorically rejects the notion that losing power in a democratic election would represent a disaster for the CCP. "Losing power would provide a powerful impetus for internal party reforms, allowing the party to seek to return to power within a constitutional framework. Calling this a 'disaster' for the party is deceiving the people and deceiving themselves."[80] Such subjective learning from Taiwan may shape the political future of China.

The revival of KMT electoral fortunes in Taiwan after the second presidential term of DPP president Chen Shui-bian (president from 2000 to 2008) could further emphasize the attractions of the Taiwan transition for actors in China. Although the analysis here has emphasized that a successful transition in China will likely be *more* disruptive to the CCP than the Taiwan transition was to the KMT, that objective lesson does not stand in the way of subjective interpretation that sees the CCP as having all the advantages of the KMT. In this regard, Taiwan has a special policy role to play. To encourage democratic change in China, Taiwan needs to insert itself into the subjective perceptions of society and elites alike in China. In this sense, the establishment of the Taiwan Foundation for Democracy (which supported the conference on which this book is based) is an important step. However, more could be done that would reflect the confidence of Taiwan in its own democratic experience. Why not invite Chinese lawmakers and electoral officials to come to Taiwan to observe and even monitor elections in Taiwan? Why not provide extra funding to Chinese scholars of political reform to study in Taiwan? Why not convince the DPP to show more respect and honor for Chiang Ching-kuo and Lee Teng-hui as democratic heroes of Taiwan?

Given the contingency and autonomy of transition processes, it is also worth thinking in advance how the world community might support a second attempted transition in China. Bunce and Wolchik argue that much more attention should be paid to transitional policies, given that longer-term structural policies are difficult to implement.[81] This means that policies should be in place to create "ratchet effects" during a future transition in China—factors that will ensure the attempted transition does not unwind. Greater on-the-ground scrutiny and reporting of social mobilization will reduce the likelihood of repression, for instance, and immediate promises of economic assistance to a newly democratic state (and economic sanctions on a resurgent authoritarian state) will undermine support for hard-liners.

Democratic transitions are stories of social emancipation with particular local histories. But they also share certain forms, and the relatively universal form taken by the Taiwan case makes it a useful template with which to study

China's past and future transitions. What actors in China will do with that template is a critical question for the future of Asia, and the world.

Notes

1. O'Donnell and Schmitter 1986.
2. Geddes 1999, 115–116. I include the 21 states that resulted from the breakup of larger authoritarian states.
3. Haggard and Kaufman 1995; Hollifield and Jillson 2000; Lee 2002.
4. Collier 1999.
5. Dogan and Higley 1998.
6. Huntington 1991, 137–139.
7. Linz and Stepan 1996a.
8. Benoit and Schiemann 2001; Easter 1997; Horowitz 2002.
9. Shain, Linz, and Berat 1995.
10. Carothers 2002.
11. Chao and Meyers 1998, 124.
12. Cheng and Haggard 1992; Dickson 1997, 1996.
13. Karatnycky and Ackerman 2005; Tsang 1998.
14. Ch'iu 1995, 121.
15. Lam 1995, 156.
16. As estimated for 2008 by Li 2006.
17. Bakken 2004.
18. Li 2005.
19. Nathan 2007, 2006.
20. Dickson 1996, 73.
21. Guo 2003.
22. Chan 2002.
23. Sun 2005, 261.
24. Nathan 1996.
25. Peerenboom 2007a.
26. Gilley 2004b.
27. Holbig 2006.
28. Gilley 2004a, 2006a.
29. Tsang 1998, 12.
30. Robert Lawrence Kuhn 2004, 266.
31. Gilley 2006b; Shue 2004; Wang 2005.
32. Dickson 1996, 63.
33. Tsang 1998, 14.
34. Nathan 2001, 724.
35. See Arendt 1958 on the 1956 Hungarian uprising.
36. Bunce 2000, 707–708.
37. Langston 2006.
38. Dickson 1996, 65.
39. Cheng and Haggard 1992, 12.
40. Vanhanen 2003.
41. Tsang 1998, 14–15.
42. Scalapino 1996, xi.
43. Zhang, Nathan, and Link 2001, 108.

45. Fan 1990, 132–133.
46. Zong 2005, 2007.
47. Nathan 2007.
48. Li and White 1990.
49. Grindle 2000.
50. Moody 1992, 90.
51. Li 2005.
52. Huang 1996.
53. See Gilley 2008.
54. Wu 1995, 37.
55. Ch'iu 1995, 105–108.
56. Hood 1997, 85.
57. Wu 1997.
58. Zhang, Nathan, and Link 2001, 217.
59. "China's Wen Says Moving Towards Democracy," Reuters News, September 5, 2005.
60. See for example Jones Luong 2002.
61. Tammy Peng, "Three-year Delay in Vote on Electing President," *The Free China Journal,* March 27, 1992, p. 1.
62. Cao 2003; Huang 1998; Yan 1996; Yang Jianli 2004; Zhou 2006; Zhuge 1998.
63. Shain, Linz, and Berat 1995, 14.
64. Yan 1996, 228.
65. McFaul 2002.
66. Karatnycky and Ackerman 2005.
67. Cheng and Haggard 1992, 23–24.
68. Meaney 1992, 96, 105.
69. Dickson 2006, 42, 44.
70. Bermeo 1999.
71. Way 2006.
72. Mill 1861/1958, 13.
73. Rustow 1970, 351.
74. Gill 2000, 88.
75. Wang 2006.
76. Zhang 2007.
77. Wang 2006, 27.
78. Wang Yanlai 2003, 226–227.
79. Lin 2005.
80. Zhang 2007.
81. Bunce and Wolchik 2005.

11

Why China's Democratic Transition Will Differ from Taiwan's

Larry Diamond

This book has sought to compare the social, cultural, and political dynamics of democratic transition in Taiwan with the way those same variables are operating in China today. The ultimate question we have sought to answer is huge in scope and consequence: Will political change in China follow (more or less) the logic of Taiwan's transition? My answer to this question is: No.

There are, to be sure, some striking similarities between the two political systems. To begin with the obvious, both the societies share common language, culture, and history, and as Gilley notes, both political systems have their origins in the revolutionary politics of early-twentieth-century China. Both evolved and adapted under new forms of authoritarian rule after profound political traumas—for Taiwan, the retreat of the KMT to the island after its 1949 defeat by the Chinese Communist Party; for China, the mass bloodshed, political turmoil, and revolutionary upheaval of Mao Zedong's years. Following those periods of political turmoil, each system launched into a remarkable period of rapid economic growth that transformed society in Taiwan and is in the process of doing so in China. Rapid economic development had in Taiwan and is having in China many of the effects predicted by modernization theory: the growth of civil society and social and intellectual pluralism and the emergence of more liberal values, which place more of an emphasis on freedom and personal autonomy. These changes generated powerful internal pressures in Taiwan for democratic change, and they are beginning to do so in China, despite the continuing freeze on large-scale institutional reform ever since the demonstrations of 1989.

However, the differences between the two transitions of Taiwan historically and China in the future are more decisive than the similarities. To appreciate this, I suggest taking a different slice in time than the economic development trajectory (1951–1986 in Taiwan, 1977–2012 in China) that Bruce Gilley examines in Chapter 1 of this book. If we wish to understand the effects of socioeconomic development on politics, we have to factor in a generational lag of about 20 years. This requires us to compare the quarter century of political change in Taiwan—from the beginning of the US tilt toward China in 1971 to the holding of Taiwan's first direct presidential election, in 1996, which completed the transition to democracy—with a similar period of change in China's history. Following the same logic of generational delay, I will date that period from the start of China's most recent double-digit growth boom, around 1997, to the as yet unknowable situation in 2022.

To appreciate what lessons Taiwan's experience may hold for China's future, we must compare not only the internal dynamics of these two systems in these two periods but also the world historical situations that each confronted and, in the case of China, will confront. Here, I argue, the comparison is of a relatively small and insecure society that needed to democratize to refashion its international legitimacy and maintain the support of its most vital ally, the United States, as compared with a rising global power that finds itself in tension (and potentially some day at war) with the United States. The two situations could not be more different, and as I will explain, these are far from the only differences in historical context and international environment surrounding the democratization of Taiwan, 1971–1996, and the political evolution of China during the early decades of the twenty-first century. These differences do not imply that China will not become a democracy. They do imply that China's transition to democracy will take longer, be driven by somewhat different logics, and be more fraught with internal and, potentially, international peril than was Taiwan's.

A Tale of Two Modernizations

The most striking parallel between Taiwan and China, graphically depicted in Figure 1.1 in Chapter 1 by Bruce Gilley, is the nearly identical profile of the growth trajectories in per capita income of the two systems, separated by a 26-year lag in time. As Gilley shows, China has so far replicated, virtually identically, the soaring ascent in per capita income achieved by Taiwan during more than a quarter century from 1951. During this period, Taiwan's per capita income increased more than eightfold, from roughly $1,000 (in constant year 2000 price equivalent or purchasing power parity dollars) to nearly $8,500 in 1986. By 1996, when the transition to democracy was completed, Taiwan's per capita income had nearly doubled again, to about $16,000.[1] By 2004, Gilley shows, China's per capita income of $5,333 was almost precisely that of Taiwan in 1978. If China maintains this pace (which was Taiwan's torrid pace in the miracle years of the 1970s and 1980s), then it will reach Taiwan's 1986 level of per capita income in the year 2012.

How does this look from a broader comparative perspective? If we examine per capita income, then we see that China has already entered what Samuel Huntington called the "zone of transition," that is, the range of economic development levels in which transitions to democracy are more likely to take place.[2] According to the World Bank, China's per capita gross domestic product (in constant year 2000 PPP dollars) had reached $6,621 by 2006. That is slightly higher than the level ($6,515) at which Brazil made a transition to democracy in 1985, and not much below the levels of Korea during its democratic transition year (1987, $7,420) and of Chile when it voted to end the Pinochet dictatorship (1989, $7,041). A recent World Bank revision based on new PPP calculations has reduced that level to $4,091 in 2005—in effect lopping about five years off of China's growth trajectory. Moreover, Henry S. Rowen predicts—using conservative projections of future growth due to slower workforce growth and decreasing gains from "catch-up"—that China will reach a per capita income of about $12,000 (in year 2000 dollars) by 2025. Projected against average international trends in the relationship between economic development and freedom, Rowen predicts that China will move into the "partly free" category of Freedom House by 2015 and will become a "free" country, in other words an unambiguous democracy, by 2025.[3] If growth is faster, China's democratization would happen sooner. Of course, as I will explain below, things could go badly wrong, and China's economic growth could implode in a financial, environmental, or political crisis. Then, a different type of transition logic would take hold. But if the momentum of economic development is sustained, China will be within a generation about as rich as Taiwan was *when it completed its democratic evolution.*

It is vital to look beyond the aggregate income figures to consider the social impact of growth. One of the principal means by which economic development has fostered democratization—in Taiwan, Korea, Spain, Chile, and many other societies—is by raising levels of education and information, thereby creating a much more aware and empowered citizenry. In this respect, China—surprisingly for a "socialist" country—has lagged somewhat. In 2000, the country's entire over-25 population had an average of only 5.74 years of schooling, less than the averages for all developing countries (5.89) and for the Asia-Pacific region (6.50).[4] But the pace of educational expansion is fast. Rowen predicts the figure will increase to eight years by 2025.

There are other signs of the social empowerment that follows from rapid economic growth. By 2004, there were 258 cellular phone subscribers for every 1,000 people and an estimated 140 million Chinese Internet users (including some 34 million Chinese bloggers). Life expectancy had risen to 72 years, nearly the equal of countries with much higher human development levels. In the 25 years following Deng Xiaoping's accession to power in 1978—when per capita income in China increased sevenfold and some 250 million people were lifted out of poverty—the circulation of newspapers tripled, and the number of book titles published increased elevenfold. By 2006, there was more than one television set for every two households, compared to one in 330 in 1978.[5] As a result of the dizzying pace of market reform and expansion over the past two decades, China's rulers now have to contend with a much larger, more resourceful, and better networked civil society than existed during the democratic uprising in 1989.[6] "China is now awash with information that would have been considered seditious as recently as the early 1990s."[7] The number of NGOs officially registered with the government had risen from 4,500 in 1988 to more than 300,000 in 2006, and some estimate the actual number is 10 times that.[8]

As Yun-han Chu shows in Chapter 2, there is early evidence that economic and social modernization is being accompanied, as it was in Taiwan and has been in so many other developing societies, by democratic value change. As China continues to become more educated and more urban, and as the younger generations socialized after the 1949 revolution and after the Cultural Revolution replace the older generations, democratic value orientations can be expected to increase markedly—precisely as modernization theory would predict, as Chu affirms, and has happened in Taiwan (as well as Korea). It is even possible that the pace of democratic value change in China could accelerate in the coming years as the country becomes more interconnected internally and more intensely wired to the rest of the world, via cell phones, the Internet, and travel.

The Dark Side of China's Development Path

All of this assumes, however, that China will continue, albeit possibly at a somewhat less torrid pace, its extraordinary economic development and that its benefits will be reasonably broadly distributed. There are many reasons to expect that China, with the world's largest market and financial reserves and with a new generation of more skillful policy technocrats at the helm of government and the economy, will do so. But there are also reasons to question this scenario of continuity and thus the assumption that Taiwan's relatively smooth rise to modernity will be replicated in China. Any social science projection of China's developmental future must at least consider the possibility that deepening contradictions in China's model of growth are not sustainable and that even the current much better educated, more pragmatic and skillful generation of Communist Party leaders cannot manage them much longer without democratizing changes in China's system of government. For some analysts of contemporary China, such as Pei, the party and the state lie at the core of the problem (to a much greater degree than was the case in Taiwan). Pei sees China's authoritarian regime not any longer as "developmental" but as a "decentralized predatory state" in which "the individual interests of its agents"—to cash in on the boom while it lasts and to get rich as quickly as possible by any means—are slowly dismantling political stability. The result is unsustainable economic growth, "achieved at the expense of rising inequality, underinvestment in human capital, damage to the environment, and pervasive official corruption."[9]

Many cities and counties have seen organized crime gain control of business with such collusion and protection from the authorities that they have become "local mafia states."[10] Local rulers prey on poor peasants, levying illegal taxes and fees and then selling off their land for lucrative developments.[11] A 2006 government report "claimed that over 60 percent of recent land acquisitions for construction were illegal."[12] In September 2006, "the country's top auditor warned that looting and misuse of government-held property were wrecking the value of many assets and constituted the biggest threat facing the nation."[13] There have been some high-profile crackdowns, but these have been selective—to neutralize rivals—and fail to address the vast scale of the crisis. Pei and other critics predict that the system will be unable to correct itself in more than superficial ways; sooner or later it will succumb to "the self-destructive dynamics found in nearly all autocracies: low political accountability, unresponsiveness, collusion and corruption."[14]

Like previous Chinese dynasties, the Communist regime could lose its "mandate of heaven" as pathologies of bad governance reach critical mass. Crime, corruption, cronyism, bank fraud, local tyranny, national unresponsiveness, and a host of other ills threaten the stability of Communist Party rule more than may be captured by the chapters in this book. The dramatic rise in economic inequality, to levels that now "rival some of the most skewed countries in Latin America or Africa," could increasingly undermine social stability and in particular the legitimacy of Communist rule, not only locally but at the center.[15] The gap is widening fast between income strata and between the cities and the countryside. With development lagging and unemployment soaring in the rural areas, young men have moved to the cities and constitute a huge pool of rootless migrants, ready to be mobilized in protest. "At any given moment, there are over 120 million rural migrant workers roaming the streets of Chinese cities looking for jobs."[16]

Sustained underinvestment in health and education, which makes the country vulnerable to pandemics such as acquired immunodeficiency syndrome (AIDS) and avian flu or outbreaks such as SARS, has deprived the poor of even the limited access to health care they enjoyed under (real) Communism. Chronic disease is exploding, with reported cases of human immunodeficiency virus (HIV) increasing by 30 percent in 2006 while hepatitis affects 10 percent of the population.[17] A third of China's land is severely eroded; a third of China's 33,000 dams (including 100 large ones) are deemed defective; and three-quarters of its lakes and half its length of rivers have been polluted. The results are spreading deserts (to the edge of Beijing), crippling pollution, and devastating floods.[18] Then there is the state of road and work-place safety: more than a hundred thousand road fatalities in 2002, a hundred thousand illnesses in a year from rat poison seeping into the human environ-ment, a level of mining deaths thirteen times that of India.[19] Any one of these ills, not to mention the complex interaction of them, could explode into crisis in the coming decade—or what Gilley in an earlier work called "metastatic crisis," when dysfunction spreads beyond its initial boundaries to affect other functions and the country as a whole.[20]

These statistics tell a different story of China's modernization, one that cannot continue indefinitely to propel itself forward but suffers increasingly systemic drags on its sustainability that Taiwan did not have to contend with and that China lacks the institutional means or the will to correct. It is certain-ly conceivable that, in the coming decade, these pathologies will inhibit eco-nomic growth, intensify popular discontent, and further grind down the legit-imacy and capacity of the state until a specific crisis metastasizes into some-thing systemic. Pei does not anticipate the fall of Communism any time soon. Rather, the system could remain "trapped in prolonged economic and political stagnation" before it ultimately collapses "in the political equivalent of a bank run."[21] Another possibility is that economic growth could continue, but with widening inequality, corruption, and injustice, until "the radicalization of the poor" reaches truly explosive dimensions and political change comes through an upsurge of social protests or a crisis catalyzing a nationwide wave of protests more intense and possibly more violent than in 1989.[22]

If Pei and other critics are right that political change in China is not going to be evolutionary (as in Taiwan), with more or less steady growth, but rather will be abrupt and disruptive, in the face of some large-scale social, econom-ic, or environmental crisis, there are two directions in which this could lead. One, which Pei believes is just as likely as anything else, is a new form of authoritarianism, possibly a nationalist right-wing one, to hold the country together. The other, which Bruce Gilley envisions in his provocative book, *China's Democratic Future,* is a transition to democracy.

If the scenario of social and political crisis does unfold, then which way China goes politically—to dictatorship or democracy or some hybrid regime—will not be determined solely by events and forces inside China. It will also depend on the regional and international environment in which China finds itself at the time. These are only some of the dimensions on which China's situation today is quite different from that which Taiwan faced in the 1970s, 1980s, and early 1990s. I consider first other contrasting features of the two cases internally and then turn to the markedly different international and historical contexts.

How China Today Differs from Taiwan Historically

China today differs dramatically from the historical example of Taiwan in some obvious ways. Perhaps the most obvious is scale: China's population today is more than 60 times that of Taiwan's during its transition. Almost all of its provinces are much larger than Taiwan's. Indeed, about nine of China's provinces have three times the population of Taiwan, equaling or exceeding the roughly 60 million population of sizable European countries such as Britain, France, and Italy. Sichuan Province has a population of more than 80 million people, Henan and Shandong Provinces more than 90 million. Even most smaller Chinese provinces, such as Fujian, just across the Strait from Taiwan, are larger (in the case of Fujian, about 50 percent larger) than Taiwan in population. Physically as well, China dwarfs Taiwan, with a land mass more than 250 times the size of Taiwan. Indeed, about the time Taiwan completed its transition, when it still commonly referred to itself as the Republic of China and made reference to its being a part of (and the legitimate government of) China as a whole, the official yearbook of the Republic of China acknowledged that "Taiwan is the smallest province of the Republic of China."[23]

Scale matters politically. During several decades of limited political competition, and especially during the 10-year process of transition from 1986 to 1996, Taiwan's ruling party was able to penetrate the local level more effectively and maintain more confident command of the process because of Taiwan's relatively small size geographically and demographically. Of course, the Chinese Communist regime represents one of the world's biggest historical experiments in centralized administrative control and ideological and political penetration of a very large territory, as Tun-jen Cheng and Gang Lin note in Chapter 8 on competitive elections. But even though the Beijing leadership still exercises effective authority over China's vast continental territory, it is not the kind of monolithic and ideological control of Mao's era. Increasingly, there are vast differences among the provinces (particularly between the coastal provinces and the interior) in income levels and political outlook, and the implementation of central governmental initiatives, such as village elections, varies widely not only across provinces but also within them. Although China is much more ethnically homogeneous than was the former Soviet Union, China's political leaders worry about losing control. With so many provinces having populations larger than most nations (other than China, there are only 21 countries in the world with populations of more than 60 million), many of China's provinces have the ability to wrest governing autonomy from the center.[24] And it is much more difficult for the central authorities in Beijing to know reliably what is really going on at so many local levels. The authorities in Taiwan never had to confront anything like this as they loosened central government control, phased-in competitive local elections, and tolerated the rise of an opposition party.

A second enormous difference has to do with the timing and pace of introducing competitive elections. As Tun-jen Cheng and Gang Lin explain in Chapter 8, this happened very early on in the establishment of the KMT regime on Taiwan, virtually from the beginning of its retreat to Taiwan after its defeat in China in 1949. In this case, the ethnic and political cleavage between the China émigrés and the local Taiwanese created an imperative for legitimation of KMT rule and incorporation of local leaders, which the KMT leadership—unable to afford a second political calamity—recognized. Moreover, these elections conferred some real power to govern and manage developmental resources, at the township and county levels after 1950, and at the level of Taiwan's provincial assembly after 1951. Nothing like this has happened in China; there, the only level of political authority where electoral competition has been introduced systematically (and even there, unevenly) has been villages, a tiny microlevel that is largely powerless.

This difference has enormous political consequences for the likely transition trajectories of the two systems. Taiwan was able to, and indeed driven to, negotiate a gradual "soft landing" to real democracy, in part because of the intricate web of pressures and reassurances generated by several decades of local elections. Although the members of China's new generation of party elites are also less ideological and better managers, they owe their positions to the party, not the people, and thus lack the incentive to press for a continuous expansion of the scope of electoral competition that prevailed in Taiwan. This is a major reason why competitive elections in China remain stuck at the largely inconsequential level of the village and why the prospect of real electoral competition at the township or county level—not to mention the provincial one—remains a distant dream. Coming back to the problem of scale, it is also hard to imagine how a province of 40 to 90 million people could organize, as Taiwan Province did for decades, competitive elections without competing parties to organize the competition. The impetus to form at least underground opposition parties to structure the choice and signal the voters would become more compelling as well as more threatening to the Chinese Communist Party.

There was also a strong element of reassurance or political confidence-building in the repeated practice of competitive elections over several decades in Taiwan. The KMT developed a strong political machine and a confidence that they could continue to win elections, even with the legalization of opposition parties and the democratization of the key levers of central government power between 1986 and 1996. As the opposition committed to playing by these rules, each side experienced what Dankwart Rustow calls "habituation," in which the norms, procedures, and expectations of democracy (or in this case, initially, an increasingly competitive authoritarian system) gradually become internalized among contending political actors, so that these politicians place their faith in and learn to conform instinctively to the rules of the game.[25] Part of this process involves the growth of trust among competing political actors, as each side gains confidence that the victory of the other will not mean its elimination or victimization, and thus what Robert Dahl calls a "system of mutual security" takes hold between government and opposition.[26] Although the process was far from perfect or smooth, something like these changes in political norms and expectations was able to unfold over several decades in Taiwan, beginning at a very early point in its economic development. By contrast, as China races out of poverty toward Taiwan's mid-1980s development level, nothing like this process of political contestation and confidence building between ruling party cadres and at least loosely organized opposition forces *has even begun*.

Of course, one should not dismiss altogether the significance of China's experiment over the last two decades with competitive village elections, which, as Cheng and Lin observe, have gone reasonably far toward institutionalization and have seen the defeat of a fairly high percentage of incumbents (e.g., over 40 percent) in at least some provinces. There is even a certain parallel with Taiwan, in which the model and momentum of competitive village elections have encouraged a "trickling-up" to the township level, for election of the township head and in some cases the township party committee and secretary. But this has been a trickling-up at a snail's pace, still limited and experimental. The village committee remains a largely powerless, policy-implementation body, under the thumb of the township authorities, and even the township is well below the level (relative to authority at the center) at which Taiwan had permitted electoral competition decades before its transition. Moreover, a crucial missing element, as Cheng and Lin stress in Chapter 8, is the promise of eventual multiparty democracy, which bound the KMT to a democratic reform agenda at some point but which the CCP has so far steadfastly eschewed. In this respect, as Gilley notes in Chapter 10, the ideological and institutional difference between the two settings—the authoritarian pluralist regime in Taiwan under the KMT versus the (still) Communist regime in China—should not be minimized.

Finally, it is worth noting another striking difference between the two internal settings of Taiwan historically and China today. During the 1970s and 1980s, Taiwan was reaching the stage of an industrialized country with a relatively egalitarian growth pattern (like other East Asian Tigers, such as Singapore and Korea). It is true that during the 1980s income inequality widened in Taiwan, from a Gini coefficient of .277 in 1980 to .303 in 1988, with a majority of Taiwanese listing the gap between rich and poor as a serious social problem.[27] But in China today, inequality is already considerably worse, with the Gini coefficient estimated at somewhere between 0.45 and 0.50, and possibly even higher.[28] Moreover, this more extreme level of inequality than Taiwan ever experienced comes in a Communist country that has trumpeted an ideology of equality, and the party as the defender of mass popular interests, for six decades. It also comes in a context of more visible and extreme corruption and misrule than was evident in Taiwan during its transition. Thus, the longer the Chinese Communist Party waits to open up political power to electoral competition at higher levels, the more it risks an unraveling of its authority, since its cadres have less experience at competing in elections and more burdens of social and economic problems than did the KMT cadres in Taiwan.

The International Contexts

As Jacques deLisle notes in Chapter 9, the international context of the early Cold War and the Communist threat across the Strait was hardly conducive to democratization in Taiwan. But beginning in the late 1970s and accelerating in the 1980s through the completion of the transition in 1996, that context changed dramatically. Taiwan's top leaders—first Chiang Ching-kuo and then Lee Teng-hui—came to recognize that democratization was vital to Taiwan's quest for continued geopolitical and military support from the United States, and thus literally to its survival. It is important to recall that when Chiang Ching-kuo made the decision to initiate the political transition in 1986 and then tolerated the formation of an opposition party, East Asia was seized with democratic ferment. In February 1986, the Philippine "people power" revolution toppled the dictatorship of Ferdinand Marcos through peaceful mobilization, after a stolen election. The 1980s had been a time of rising student, worker, and other civil society mobilization against military rule in South Korea, and in 1987 (when martial law was formally lifted in Taiwan) the Korean military dictator, Chun Doo Hwan, was forced to yield to massive public pressure and allow a direct popular election for his presidential successor. In both cases, timely pressure from the United States had helped to foster a peaceful transition to democracy, and both the Reagan administration and the US Congress were becoming increasingly active in pushing to advance human rights and democracy abroad. Not long after Chiang Ching-kuo died in 1988, Thailand crossed the murky line from a military-dominated semidemocracy to an electoral democracy when Chatichai Choonhavan became the first elected member of parliament to become prime minister since the breakdown of the country's previous democratic experiment, in 1976. Also in 1988, the Pakistani military dictator, General Mohammad Zia ul-Haq died (or, some believe, was assassinated) in a plane crash, and there quickly followed a transition to electoral democracy that brought the democracy advocate and opposition party leader, Benazir Bhutto, to power as prime minister.

During the 1980s, most Latin American countries were also making or had already made transitions to democracy. Between the beginning of the Third Wave of democratization in 1974 and 1988, the number of democracies in the world increased by more than 50 percent, from 40 to 67, and the proportion of democracies in the world rose from 27 to 40 percent. Then in 1989, the Berlin Wall fell, Communism collapsed in Eastern Europe—and nearly so in China itself—and a second burst of the Third Wave erupted. Between 1989 (as Taiwan's transition was moving ahead) and 1996 (when Taiwan's transition to democracy was completed), the number of democracies worldwide exploded, from 67 to 118, and the proportion of democracies among the world's states increased from about two-fifths to three-fifths.[29]

In other words, Taiwan made its transition to democracy during a unique moment in world history, probably the most rapid expansion in the number and proportion of democracies we will ever see. China, by contrast, is unlikely to benefit from such a democratic global zeitgeist. By 1996, the expansion of democracy in the world had leveled off. Although more countries in the world have since become democratic and overall levels of freedom have risen, the proportion of democracies in the world has essentially remained static in the last decade (oscillating around 60 to 62 percent of all states). Moreover, a new burst of democratic breakthroughs in the near future will be more difficult and unlikely, for several reasons. First, most of the most fertile countries for democratization from a developmental standpoint have already made transitions. Second, the majority of the remaining authoritarian regimes are hard cases, because of very low levels of development or unfavorable regional contexts (especially in the Middle East). Third, the difficulties surrounding the US interventions in Iraq and Afghanistan, combined with the increased self-confidence and resolve of authoritarian states such as Russia, China, Iran, Egypt, Kazakhstan, and Venezuela (many of which are major oil exporters at a time when the price of oil globally is hitting $100 a barrel), have generated an authoritarian backlash against democratic mobilization and democracy promotion that makes it more difficult for civil societies and political oppositions to adopt the techniques that led to democratic breakthroughs in the 1990s and early 2000s (in the so-called color revolutions). Cooperation among authoritarian states (for example in the Shanghai Cooperation Organization that draws together Russia, China, and many Central Asian dictatorships) further diminishes the prospects. Add to this the new cold war that has emerged in the form of a US-led "global war on terror" and the difficulties of many of the new democracies in controlling corruption, achieving broad economic development, improving political institutions, and therefore consolidating democracy, and there emerges a much less favorable global context for democracy in the world.

Indeed, China may have more of an effect on global democratic trends than vice versa. Certainly no development in Asia would more powerfully tip the odds in favor of democratization in authoritarian countries as disparate as Burma, Vietnam, Singapore, and Malaysia than a breakthrough to electoral democracy in China. In contrast to Taiwan, then, China will be much more of a shaper than a receiver of regional and global political pressures and demonstration effects.

There is one ironic twist to this generalization, which deLisle notes in Chapter 9. One of the few regional or global actors with the potential to affect significantly whether and how China moves to democracy is Taiwan itself. Should the island continue to be gripped by political deadlock, enmity, and rising nationalist pressure for Taiwan independence, this would likely dampen Chinese enthusiasm for democracy at the level of societal norms and aspirations as well as elite political intentions. Worse still, political polarization and continuing moves by a new government in Taiwan to legally separate from China and further press the boundaries of Taiwan's separate identity could feed an intense nationalist reaction in China, and in a context of political crisis, provide grounds for reactionary forces to mobilize popular sentiment and tilt a future moment of possible democratic transition toward a right-wing military or nationalist dictatorship. By contrast, should Taiwan's politics stabilize and its leaders reach out to Beijing, then the political balance in China could well be tilted toward a more positive view of democracy. Probably no external event would redound more favorably for democratization in China than a political accommodation between Beijing and Taipei. With the election of Ma Ying-jeou to the presidency of Taiwan (as this book was going to press), some progress toward that seemed more feasible.

There is one potential additional parallel, however, between Taiwan and China, and it is an extension of the one shared causal driver in their democratizations: economic development. One aspect of economic development that helped to generate pressure for democratic change in Taiwan, by accelerating normative change and the growth of civil society, was the large number of social scientists, businesspeople, economists, technocrats, lawyers, and ultimately politicians who were trained in the United States. This training abroad, particularly in law and the social sciences, heavily disposed them to "Western democratic ideals."[30] More generally, as deLisle notes in Chapter 9, the density of social and economic ties between Taiwan and the West, especially Taiwan and the United States, gradually helped to shape the view in Taiwan that Taiwan could not become a fully modern country and a member of the club of advanced industrial countries without becoming a democracy.

Will Chinese political and social elites begin to think in a similar way as their country becomes increasingly rich, educated, and powerful? There is no guarantee; Singapore continues to defy the odds (though I do not believe it will do so indefinitely), and the one element that was missing from the path of Taiwan and Korea was the geopolitical weight for either system to become a global model in its own right. Increasingly, China will have that power. But it will also have, even if it is alongside booming growth, a vexing tangle of social, environmental, and governance problems that cannot be addressed unless the country allows much more individual and media freedom, social and political pluralism, and transparency and judicial independence as well as more competition for power than it has so far done. In other words, as development creates a more and more educated and resourceful society, but with deeper and deeper contradictions, China's leaders will have to accommodate democratic evolution in order to keep the system stable. The natural instinct will be to institute more economic and social freedom, judicial professionalism, and effective, accountable governance, but in the absence of real political competition: in other words, Singapore. But much as they might wish to make a soft landing to the Singaporean system as a long-term (if not permanent) way of governing, China is too large and diverse, its political rulers are too corrupt, and its problems are too deep for those very limited reforms to suffice. For one thing, as China moves in that direction, toward what the Chinese political scientist Pan Wei has termed (and advocated) as a "consultative rule of law regime," people will not rest content with the limited political freedom and space granted to them.[31] They will demand more freedom and more pluralism—partly because their political values and aspirations will have changed so much and partly because they will see that the only way to contain corruption in China at this point is to enable the people to replace their leaders in free, fair, and competitive elections.

In China, there will be no natural resting place, no enduring equilibrium for this process of governance reform short of democracy itself. This is why the Chinese Communist leaders sit on the horns of a dilemma. If they do not open up the political system and move toward democracy, they risk popular discontent exploding at some point as a more politically restless, resourceful, and assertive populace demands more freedom and more accountable governance while governance problems mount. If they do gradually introduce political competition at successively higher levels of authority while also expanding the scope for dissent and criticism, then they risk seeing the Chinese Communist Party's grip on power erode and eventually slip away—and possibly faster than happened in Taiwan. For as Bruce Gilley has written elsewhere, "the CCP [of the current era] is not the KMT [of Taiwan's democratizing era]. The power of the CCP . . . has weakened considerably in the post-Mao era. While it remains a dominant force when compared to society as a whole, it is probably not dominant enough to successfully carry out a phased political transition."[32]

At some point, then, China's rulers may be forced to pick their poison. They may be confronted with three options. One would be to begin democratization and try to negotiate guarantees of their political and financial interests before it is too late, while knowing that this process of opening could well bring their downfall from power. The second would be to sit tight and hope for the best (namely that they can kick the political problems down the road to the next generation of leaders), while knowing that "regimes that waited too long saw their rulers dragged from their offices and shot in the head."[33] The third would be to divert attention by using or manufacturing a crisis with the West, perhaps over Taiwan, to recover some temporary legitimacy for the regime and mobilize people behind it with nationalist fervor.

The third option is of course the most dangerous—for Taiwan, for the United States, for the world, and, not least, for China. Whether that becomes a serious option will depend in large measure on the environment China faces regionally and internationally—whether Taiwan seeks accommodation or independence; whether the world can avoid a global recession and cooperate to address the mounting shortages of energy, water, and other resources; and whether the United States can draw China into a new era of global partnership, as what Deputy Secretary of State Robert Zoellick termed in 2005 "a stakeholder that shares responsibility."[34] Doing so means that the United States must walk a fine line between respect for China's dignity and sovereignty as a rising great power and resistance to its efforts to defend or entrench authoritarian regimes in Asia and around the world. It means standing up rhetorically for principles of human rights and the rule of law in China and working patiently in private with Chinese leaders to keep human rights on the agenda, while recognizing that US leverage over China is extremely limited. Probably the most important thing that the United States can do is to create a benign environment for the tremendous developmental changes that China is undergoing to work their own autonomous effects in generating democratic change.

China today is dramatically different from Taiwan, then and now. Its path and pace of regime transformation will not follow Taiwan's. But many of the political and normative consequences of economic development will be the same. If new generations of Chinese political leaders, technocrats, entrepreneurs, intellectuals, and artists can be vigorously and yet respectfully engaged, the political outcome will, sooner or later, likely be the same as in Taiwan: some form of genuine democracy.

Notes

1. All of the figures are drawn, as noted in Figure 1.1, from Alan Heston, Robert Summers, and Bettina Aten, "Penn World Table Version 6.2," Center for International Comparisons of Production, Income, and Prices at the University of Pennsylvania, September 2006. Available at http://pwt.econ.upenn.edu/php_site/pwt_index.php.

2. Huntington 1991, 62, table 2.1, calculated the most likely zone of transition as those countries with a 1976 per capita gross national product (GNP) of $1,000 to $3,000—which would be roughly $2,500 to $7,400 in nominal year-2000 dollars. Between 1974 and 1990, 16 of the 21 nondemocratic countries in that income group democratized or liberalized politically, and five other states in that group were already democracies. It is difficult to transform that category from nominal into international prices because the latter figures must be computed for every country individually. The gap between China's nominal GDP per capita in 2004, $1,323, and the same figure in PPP dollars, $5,493, is much greater (about four to one) than the disparity for Brazil ($3,337 vs. $6,515) or Korea ($5,291 vs. $7,420) during their transition years (1985 and 1987 respectively). So although China in its nominal dollar per capita income is not yet in the prime of Huntington's zone of transition, when the figure is computed

more realistically in international prices, it is roughly equivalent to Brazil's per capita income and so has clearly entered the "zone of transition."

3. Rowen 2007, 28–29.
4. Ibid., 41.
5. Pei 2006, 2.
6. Gilley 2004a, 60–94.
7. Ibid., 73.
8. Ma 2007, 6.
9. Pei 2006, 209.
10. Ibid., 161–165. As in the United States and Europe, favored sectors for the mafia include real estate, transportation, and construction.
11. Ibid., 189, 191–196.
12. The figure rose to 90 percent in some cities. Saich 2007, 38.
13. Ibid., 39.
14. Pei 2006, 208.
15. Gilley 2004a, 38.
16. Ma 2007, 5.
17. Harding 2007.
18. Pei 2006, 175–176. The data on dams are from Gilley 2004a, 103. In 1975, he reports, twin dams burst in Henan Province, killing an estimated 300,000 people. No catastrophe on anything approaching such a scale could be covered up today in China, even with the level of state control of the Internet and other media.
19. Pei 2006, 170.
20. Gilley 2004a, 103.
21. Pei 2006, 210–212.
22. Chen An 2003.
23. That is no longer true since Hainan Island became a province in April 1988, but the Taiwan government at the time did not recognize that move. Republic of China 1997, 3.
24. If China broke apart into separate countries based on its provinces, nine of its provinces would be among the 30 most populous countries in the world.
25. Rustow 1970.
26. Dahl 1971, 16.
27. Chu Hai-yan 1994, 91–92. The Gini coefficient varies from 0 to 1, with 0 being most equal (indicating everyone having the same income) to 1 being most unequal (indicating control of all income by one individual).
28. Saich 2007, 40. But Gilley 2004a, 38, cites some sources indicating that it may be as high as 0.60, making it one of the most unequal in the world. Saich cites official sources as reporting the urban-rural income gap at 3.22 to 1 in 2005.
29. Diamond 2008, chap. 2 and appendix table 1.
30. Cheng 1989, 483.
31. For Pan Wei's influential essay and responses to it, including mine, see Zhao 2006.
32. Gilley 2004a, 100.
33. Ibid., 99.
34. Robert Zoellick, "Whither China: From Membership to Responsibility?" Remarks to the National Committee on US-China Relations, September 21, 2005. Available at http://usinfo.state.gov/eap/Archive/2005/Sep/22-290478.html.

References

Acemoglu, Daron, and James A. Robinson. 2006. *Economic Origins of Dictatorship and Democracy*. New York: Cambridge University Press.

Agence France Presse. 2001. "Despite Softening Tone, China Sticks to Hard Taiwan Line." January 10.

———. 2006. "China Warns Taiwan over 'Very Risky' Council Move." March 4.

Aikman, David. 2003. *Jesus in Beijing: How Christianity Is Changing China and Transforming the Global Balance of Power*. Washington, DC: Regnery.

Alford, William P., Robert P. Weller, Leslyn Hall, Karen R. Polenske, Yuanyuan Shen, and David Zweig. 2002. "The Human Dimensions of Pollution Policy Implementation: Air Quality in Rural China." *Journal of Contemporary China* 11, no. 32 (August): 495–513.

Almond, Gabriel A. 1983. "Corporatism, Pluralism, and Professional Memory." *World Politics* 35, no. 2: 245–260.

———. 1990. "The Study of Political Culture." In *A Discipline Divided: Schools and Sects in Political Science*, edited by Gabriel A. Almond, 138–169. London: Sage.

Almond, Gabriel A., and Sidney Verba. 1963. *The Civic Culture: Political Attitudes and Democracy in Five Nations*. Princeton, NJ: Princeton University Press.

Alpermann, Bjorn. 2006. "Wrapped Up in Cotton Wool: Political Integration of Private Entrepreneurs in Rural China." *China Journal* 56: 33–61.

American Law Institute. 1987. *Restatement of the Law (Third). Foreign Relations Law of the United States*. St. Paul, MN: American Law Institute.

Angle, Stephen C. 2005. "Decent Democratic Centralism." *Political Theory* 33, no. 4: 518–546.

Arendt, Hannah. 1958. *The Origins of Totalitarianism*. 2nd ed. New York: Meridian Books.

Ba, Alice D. 2006. "Who's Socializing Whom? Complex Engagement and Sino-ASEAN Relations." *Pacific Review* 19, no. 2: 16–35.

Bakken, Borge. 2004. "Norms, Values, and Cynical Games with Party Ideology." In *Bringing the Party Back In: How China Is Governed*, edited by Kjeld Erik Brodsgaard and Yongnian Zheng, 22–56. Singapore: East Asian Institute Eastern Universities Press.

Barme, Geremie R., and Gloria Davies. 2004. "Have We Been Noticed Yet? Intellectual Contestation and the Chinese Web." In *Chinese Intellectuals Between State and*

Market, edited by Edward Gu and Merle Goldman, 123–145 New York: Routledge Curzon.

Barr, Michael D. 2000. *Lee Kuan Yew: The Beliefs Behind the Man.* Washington, DC: Georgetown University Press.

Bauer, Joanne R., and Daniel A. Bell, eds. 1999. *The East Asian Challenge for Human Rights.* Cambridge: Cambridge University Press.

Baum, Richard. 1996. *Burying Mao.* Princeton, NJ: Princeton University Press.

Beja, Jean-Philippe. 2006. "The Changing Aspects of Civil Society in China." *Social Research* 73, no. 1: 53–74.

Bell, Daniel A. 1995. "Democracy in Confucian Societies: The Challenge of Justification." In *Towards Illiberal Democracy in Pacific Asia,* edited by Daniel A. Bell, David Brown, Kanishka Jayasuriya, and David Martin Jones, 17–40. New York: St. Martin's.

———. 2000. *East Meets West: Human Rights and Democracy in Asia.* Princeton, NJ: Princeton University Press.

———. 2006. *Beyond Liberal Democracy: Political Thinking for an East Asian Context.* Princeton, NJ: Princeton University Press.

Bellin, Eva. 2002. *Stalled Democracy: Capital, Labor, and the Paradox of State-Sponsored Development.* Ithaca, NY: Cornell University Press.

Bellows, Thomas J. 2000. *Taiwan and Inland China: Democratization, Political Participation, and Economic Development in the 1990s.* New York: Center of Asian Studies, St. John's University.

Benoit, Kenneth, and John W. Schiemann. 2001. "Institutional Choice in New Democracies." *Journal of Theoretical Politics* 13, no. 2: 153–183.

Berger, Peter L., and Michael H.H. Hsiao, eds. 1998. *In Search of an East Asian Development Model.* New Brunswick, NJ: Transaction.

Bermeo, Nancy. 1999. "Myths of Moderation: Confrontation and Conflict During Democratic Transitions." In *Transitions to Democracy,* edited by Lisa Anderson, 120–140. New York: Columbia University Press.

Bernstein, Thomas. 2006. "Village Democracy and Its Limits." *Asien* 99 (April): 29–41.

Boix, Charles, and Susan Stokes. 2003. "Endogenous Democratization." *World Politics* 55, no. 4: 517–549.

Booth, John. 1998. "The Somoza Regime in Nicaragua." In *Sultanistic Regimes,* edited by H. E. Chehabi and Juan J. Linz, 132–152. Baltimore: Johns Hopkins University Press.

Boretz, Avron. 2003. "Righteous Brothers and Demon Slayers: Subjectivities and Collective Identities in Taiwanese Temple Processions." In *Religion and the Formation of Taiwanese Identities,* edited by Paul R. Katz and Murray A. Rubenstein, 219–251. New York: Palgrave Macmillan.

Bradisher, Keith. 2006. "Defiant Leader Scraps Unification Panel with China." *New York Times,* February 27.

Brady, Henry, Sidney Verba, and Kay Schlozman. 1995. "Beyond SES: A Resource Model of Political Participation." *American Political Science Review* 89, no. 2: 271–294.

Branstetter, Lee, and Nicholas Lardy. 2005. "China's Embrace of Globalization." *Asia Program Special Report.* Washington, DC: Woodrow Wilson International Center for Scholars.

Bratton, Michael, and Robert Mattes. 2001. "Support for Democracy in Africa: Intrinsic or Instrumental." *British Journal of Political Science* 31, no. 4: 447.

Bratton, Michael, and Nicolas Van de Walle. 1997. *Democratic Experiments in Africa:*

Regime Transitions in Comparative Perspective. Cambridge Studies in Comparative Politics. Cambridge: Cambridge University Press.

Brinkley, Douglas. 1997. "Democratic Enlargement: The Clinton Doctrine." *Foreign Policy,* no. 106 (Spring): 110–127.

Brown, Harold, Joseph Prueher, and Adam Segal. 2003. *Chinese Military Power.* New York: Council on Foreign Relations.

Brown, Michael E., Sean M. Lynn-Jones, and Stephen E. Miller, eds. 1996. *Debating the Democratic Peace.* Cambridge, MA: MIT Press.

Buchanan, Allen. 2004. *Justice, Legitimacy, and Self-Determination.* Oxford: Oxford University Press.

Buckley, Chris. 2004. "U.S. Official, in Beijing, Questions Taiwan Referendum Plans." *New York Times,* January 31.

Bueno de Mesquita, Bruce, and George Downs. 2005. "Development and Democracy." *Foreign Affairs* 84, no. 5 (September–October): 77–86.

Bunce, Valerie. 2000. "Comparative Democratization: Big and Bounded Generalizations." *Comparative Political Studies* 33, no. 6: 703–734.

———. 2003. "Rethinking Recent Democratization: Lessons from the Postcommunist Experience." *World Politics* 55, no. 2 (January): 167–192.

Bunce, Valerie, and Sharon Wolchik. 2005. "Bringing Down Dictators: American Democracy Promotion and Electoral Revolutions in Postcommunist Eurasia." Working Paper Series, Cornell University Mario Einaudi Center for International Studies.

Buruma, Ian. 1996. "Taiwan's New Nationalists: Democracy with Taiwanese Characteristics." *Foreign Affairs* (July–August): 12–19.

Bush, George W. 2005. "There Is No Justice Without Freedom." Inaugural Address, January 20.

Bush, Richard C. 2004. *At Cross Purposes: U.S.-Taiwan Relations Since 1942.* Armonk, NY: M. E. Sharpe.

———. 2005. *Untying the Knot.* Washington, DC: Brookings Institution.

Cabestan, Jean-Pierre. 2006. "More Power to the People's Congresses?" *Asien* 99 (April): 42–69.

Cai Dingjian. 2005. "The Development of Constitutionalism in the Transition of Chinese Society." *Columbia Journal of Asian Law* 19, no. 1 (Spring–Fall): 1–29.

Campero, Guillermo. 1995. "Entrepreneurs Under the Military Regime." In *The Struggle for Democracy in Chile,* edited by Paul W. Drake and Ivan Jaksic, 128–161. Lincoln: University of Nebraska Press.

Cao Siyuan. 2003. Xiugai Xianfa: Baohu Meige Rende Hefa Quanli [*Revise the Constitution: Protect Individual Rights*]. Hong Kong: Shidai Chaoliu Press.

Carothers, Thomas. 2002. "The End of the Transition Paradigm." *Journal of Democracy* 13, no. 1: 5–21.

———. 2003. *Promoting the Rule of Law Abroad—The Problem of Knowledge.* Washington, DC: Carnegie Endowment for International Peace.

Carter Center. 1998. "Carter Center Delegation Report: Village Elections in China and Agreement on Cooperation with the Ministry of Civil Affairs, People's Republic of China." March 2. Available at www.cartercenter.org/documents/1156.pdf. Accessed July 21, 2007.

Central Committee, Chinese Communist Party. 2004. "Zhonggong zhongyang guanyu jiaqiang dang de zhizheng nengli jianshe de jueding" ["Decision on Enhancing the Party's Governing Capabilities"]. September 19.

Central News Agency. 2006. "Net Penetration Nears 68 Percent." *Taipei Times,* August 7, p. 12.

Central News Agency (Taiwan). 2004. "President Says Taiwan Sovereign State, No Need to Declare Independence." February 19.

———. 2005. "Opposition Taiwan Solidarity Union Unveils Draft of 'Anti-Annexation Law.'" March 11.

Chambers, Simone, and Will Kymlicka, eds. 2002. *Alternative Conceptions of Civil Society.* Princeton: NJ: Princeton University Press.

Chan, Joseph. 1999. "A Confucian Perspective on Human Rights for Contemporary China." In *The East Asian Challenge for Human Rights,* edited by Daniel A. Bell and Joanne Bauer, 212–240. Cambridge: Cambridge University Press.

Chan, Sylvia. 2002. *Liberalism, Democracy, and Development.* New York: Cambridge University Press.

Chandler, Stuart. 2004. *Establishing a Pure Land on Earth.* Honolulu: University of Hawaii Press.

Chang, S. C. 2005. "Taiwan President Outlines Proposed 'Second Phase' of Constitutional Reform." Central News Agency (Taiwan). May 22.

Chang Wen-Chen. 2001. "Transition to Democracy, Constitutionalism, and Judicial Activism: Taiwan in Comparative Constitutional Perspective." JSD diss., Yale Law School.

Chang Yu-tzung, Yun-han Chu, and Frank Tsai. 2005. "Confucianism and Democratic Values in Three Chinese Societies." *Issues and Studies* 41, no. 4 (December): 1–33.

Chang Yu-tzung, Yun-han Chu, and Cong-min Pak. 2007. "Authoritarian Nostalgia in Asia," *Journal of Democracy* 18, no. 3 (July): 66–80.

Chang Yu-tzung, Yun-han Chu, Fu Hu, and Huo-yan Shyu. 2004. *How Citizens Evaluate Taiwan's New Democracy.* Taipei: Asian Barometer Project Office.

Chao, Chien-min, and Chih-chia Hsu. 2006. "China Isolates Taiwan." In *China's Rise, Taiwan's Dilemmas, and International Peace,* edited by Edward Freidman, 67–95. New York: Routledge.

Chao, Chien-min, and Yeau-tarn Lee. 2006. "Transition in a Party-State System: Taiwan as a Model for China's Future Democratization." In *The Chinese Communist Party in Reform,* edited by Yongnian Zheng and Kjeld Erik Brodsgaard, 210–230. New York: Routledge.

Chao, Linda, and Ramon Meyers. 1998. *The First Chinese Democracy: Political Life in the Republic of China on Taiwan.* Baltimore: Johns Hopkins University Press.

Chase, Michael, and James Mulvenon. 2002. *You've Got Dissent! Chinese Dissident Use of the Internet and Beijing's Counter Strategies.* Santa Monica, CA: Rand.

Chen, Albert. 2004. *An Introduction to the Legal System of the People's Republic of China.* 3rd ed. Hong Kong: Butterworth's.

Chen An. 2003. "China's Changing of the Guard: The New Inequality." *Journal of Democracy* 14, no. 1: 51–59.

Chen Jie. 2004. *Popular Political Support in Urban China.* Stanford, CA: Stanford University Press.

———. 2006. "Civil Society, Grassroots Aspirations, and Diplomatic Isolation." In *China's Rise, Taiwan's Dilemmas, and International Peace,* edited by Edward Friedman, 110–129. London: Routledge.

Chen Lung-chu. 1991. "Self-Determination and World Public Order." *Notre Dame Law Review* 66: 1287–1310.

Chen Min-tong. 2007. "A Pragmatic Constitutional Solution." *Taipei Times,* April 5.

Chen, Nancy N. 2003. "Healing Sects and Anti-cult Campaigns." In *Religion in China Today,* edited by Daniel L. Overmeyer, 199–214. London: Cambridge University Press.

Chen Shui-bian. 2000. "Taiwan Stands Up: Toward the Dawn of a Rising Era." Inaugural Address, Taipei, May 20.

———. 2004a. "Paving the Way for a Sustainable Taiwan." Inaugural Address, Taipei, May 20.

———. 2004b. "President Chen's National Day Message." October 10.

Chen Tsung-fu. 2000. "The Rule of Law in Taiwan." In *The Rule of Law: Perspectives from the Pacific Rim,* edited by Jerome Cohen, 134–156. Washington, DC: The Manfield Center for Pacific Affairs.

———. 2001. "Interpretations of Grand Justice Council and the Establishment of Formally Rational Laws. Application of Max Weber's Theory." In *Committee for Publishing Essays in Honor of Professor Wen-shyong Lin,* edited by Contemporary Fundamental Legal Theory, 24–56. Taipei: Sharing Culture Publishing.

———. 2002. "Democracy and Rule of Law in Taiwan: The Judiciary's Authority and Credibility." Paper prepared for the Twentieth Annual Meeting of the Association of Third Word Studies, Taipei, December.

———. 2003. "The Rule of Law in Taiwan." In *Understanding China's Legal System,* edited by Stephen Hsu, 220–267. New York: NYU Press.

Chen Weitseng. 2000. *Law and Economic Miracle: The Interaction Between Economy and Legal System in Taiwan After World War II.* Taiwan: Angle Publishing.

———. 2002. "State, Market, and the Law: Law and Development in Taiwan." *Journal of the Humanities and Social Sciences* 40, no. 1 (March): 23–46.

Cheng Tun-jen. 1989. "Democratizing the Quasi-Leninist Regime in Taiwan." *World Politics* 41, no. 4: 471–499.

———. 1990. "Is the Dog Barking? The New Middle Class and Democratic Transition in East Asia." *International Studies Notes* 15, no. 1: 10–16.

———. 2001. "Transforming Taiwan's Economic Structure in the 20th Century." In *Taiwan in the Twentieth Century,* edited by Richard Louis Edmonds and Steven M. Goldstein, 101–134. New York: Cambridge University Press.

Cheng Tun-jen, and Stephan Haggard. 1992. "Regime Transformation in Taiwan: Theoretical and Comparative Perspectives." In *Political Change in Taiwan,* edited by Tun-jen Cheng and Stephan Haggard, 87–110. Boulder: Lynne Rienner.

Cheong Ching. 2003. "U.S. Taiwan Policy Set 31 Years Ago." *Straits Times,* December 20.

Chi, Wennie, and Y. F. Low. 2006. "Taiwan Pledges to Retain Cross-Strait Status-Quo." Central News Agency (Taiwan), March 25.

Chi Yingying. 2000. "China's Rural Challenge." *Harvard International Review* 22, no. 2 (Summer): 34–37.

Chin Ko-lin. 2003. *Heijin: Organized Crime, Business, and Politics in Taiwan.* Armonk, NY: M. E. Sharpe.

China Daily. 2001. "Safeguard Our Culture." June 19.

———. 2006. "Recall Vote in Taiwan Set for November 24." November 11.

China Post. 2002. "President Chen Explains His 'One Country on Each Side' Remarks." August 31.

———. 2006. "Chen Mulls Axing Reunification Council." January 30.

———. 2008. "Campaign Enters Final Week." January 7.

Chinese Academy of Social Sciences. 2002. *Bluebook on Chinese Society, 2002.* Beijing: Chinese Academy of Social Sciences Press.

Ching, Leo T.S. 2001. *Becoming "Japanese": Colonial Taiwan and the Politics of Identity Formation.* Los Angeles: University of California Press.

Ch'iu Chui-liang. 1995. *Democratizing Oriental Despotism: China from 4 May 1919 to 4 June 1989 and Taiwan from 28 February 1947 to 28 June 1990.* New York: St. Martin's Press.

Chiu Hei-yuan, and Li-hsiang Yao. 1986. "Taiwan Diqu Zongjiao Bianqian Zhi Tantao" ["Discussion of Religious Changes in the Taiwan Area"]. *Special Publication of the Institute of Ethnology, Academia Sinica* 16: 655–685.

Cho Hui-wan. 2007. "China-Taiwan Tug of War in the WTO." *Asian Survey* 45, no. 5: 736–755.

Chong, Alberto, and César Calderón. 2000. "Causality and Feedback Between Institutional Measures and Economic Growth." *Economics and Politics* 12, no. 1: 69–81.

Christensen, Thomas J. 2000. "Clarity on Taiwan." *Washington Post,* March 20.

———. 2002. "The Contemporary Security Dilemma: Deterring a Taiwan Conflict." *The Washington Quarterly* 25, no. 4: 7–21.

———. 2007. "Roundtable Briefing with Taiwan Media" (December 6). Available at http://www.state.gov/p/eap/rls/rm/2007/96691.htm.

Chu, Alice R. 2004. "Taiwan's Mass-Mediated Crisis Discourse." In *The Minor Arts of Daily Life: Popular Culture in Taiwan,* edited by David K. Jordan, Andrew D. Morris, and Marc L. Moskowitz, 89–110. Honolulu: University of Hawaii Press.

Chu Hai-yan. 1994. "Taiwanese Society in Transition: Reconciling Confucianism and Pluralism." In *The Other Taiwan: 1945 to the Present,* edited by Murray Rubenstein, 85–100. Armonk, NY: M. E. Sharpe.

Chu Yun-han. 1992. *Crafting Democracy in Taiwan.* National Policy Research Series no. 2. Taipei: Institute for National Policy Research.

———. 1994. "The Realignment of Business-Government Relations and Regime Transition in Taiwan." In *Business and Government in Industrialising Asia,* edited by Andrew MacIntrye, 113–141. Ithaca, NY: Cornell University Press.

———. 2006. "Third-Wave Democratization in East Asia: Challenges and Prospect." *Asien* 100 (July): 11–17.

Chu Yun-han, and Hu Fu. 1996. "Neo-authoritarianism, Polarized Conflict, and Populism in a Newly Democratizing Regime: Taiwan's Emerging Mass Politics." *Journal of Contemporary China* 5, no. 11 (Spring): 23–41.

Chu, Yun-han, Hu Fu, and Chung-in Moon. 1997. "South Korea and Taiwan: The International Context." In *Consolidating the Third Wave Democracies,* edited by Larry Diamond, Marc F. Plattner, Yun-han Chu, and Hung-mao Tien, 267–294. Baltimore: Johns Hopkins University Press.

Chu Yun-han, and Chang Yutzung. 2001. "Culture Shift and Regime Legitimacy: Comparing Inland China, Taiwan and Hong Kong." In *Chinese Political Culture,* edited by Shiping Hua, 320–347. New York: M. E. Sharpe.

Chung-yang Jih-pao. 1996. "Seeking Peaceful Reunification Is the Final Goal of Our Diplomatic Affairs." August 20.

———. 1999. "Text of President Lee Teng-hui's Interview with Deutsche Welle Radio." July 10.

Clarke, Donald. 2003. "Economic Development and the Rights Hypothesis: The China Problem." *American Journal of Comparative Law* 51, no. 89: 89–111.

Clarke, Donald C., Peter Murrell, and Susan H. Whiting. 2006. "The Role of Law in China's Economic Development." GWU Law School Public Law Research Papers 187 (January). Available at http://ssrn.com/abstract=878672.

Clinton, William J. 2000. "Remarks on Signing PNTR with China." October 10.

Cody, Edward, and Anthony Faiola. 2006. "Taiwan's President Set to Open Debate on New Constitution." *Washington Post,* March 14.

Cohen, Warren I. 1990. *America's Response to China.* New York: Columbia University Press.

Collier, David, and Fernando Henrique Cardoso. 1979. *The New Authoritarianism in Latin America.* Princeton, NJ: Princeton University Press.

Collier, Ruth Berins. 1999. *Paths Toward Democracy: The Working Class and Elites in Western Europe and South America.* Cambridge: Cambridge University Press.

Collier, Ruth Berins, and James Mahoney. 1997. "Adding Collective Actors to Collective Outcomes: Labor and Recent Democratization in South America and Southern Europe." *Comparative Politics* 29, no. 3: 285–303.

Comaroff, Jean. 1985. *Body of Power, Spirit of Resistance: The Culture and History of a South African People.* Chicago: University of Chicago Press.

Cong Yaping. 2004. "Listening to the Footstep of Democratic Elections." New China News Agency (August 12). Available at http://news.xinhuanet.com/comments/2004-08/12/.

Congressional-Executive Commission on China [CECC]. 2005. *Annual Report.* Washington, DC: US Government Printing Office.

Control Yuan, Republic of China, Taiwan. 2006. *1948–2005. Statistics on Cases of Impeachment.* Taipei: Government Information Office.

Cooney, Sean. 2004. "The Effects of Rule of Law Principles in Taiwan." In *Asian Discourses of Rule of Law: Theories and Implementation of Rule of Law in Twelve Asian Countries,* edited by Randall Peerenboom, 417–445. New York: Routledge Curzon.

Council on Foreign Relations (Independent Task Force). 2007. *U.S.-China Relations: An Affirmative Agenda, A Responsible Course.* New York: Council on Foreign Relations.

Crafts, Nicholas. 1997. "The Human Development Index and Changes in Standards of Living: Some Historical Comparisons." *European Review of Economic History* 1, no. 3: 299–322.

Curtis, Gerald L. 1998. "A 'Recipe' for Democratic Development." In *Democracy in East Asia,* edited by Larry Diamond and Marc F. Plattner, 217–223. Baltimore: Johns Hopkins University Press.

Dahl, Robert. 1971. *Polyarchy: Participation and Opposition.* New Haven, CT: Yale University Press.

Dalton, Russell J., and Nhu-Ngoc T. Ong. 2005. "Authority Orientation and Democratic Attitude: A Test of the 'Asian Values' Hypothesis." *Japanese Journal of Political Science* 6, no. 3: 1–21.

Daniels, Ronald J., and Michael J. Trebilcock. 2004. "The Political Economy of Rule of Law Reform in Developing Countries." Available at http://www.wdi.bus.umich.edu/global_conf/papers/revised/Trebilcock_Michael.pdf

de Bary, William Theodore. 1996. *The Trouble with Confucianism.* Cambridge, MA: Harvard University Press.

———. 1998. *Asian Values and Human Rights: A Confucian Communitarian Perspective.* Cambridge, MA: Harvard University Press.

Dean, Kenneth. 1997. "Ritual and Space: Civil Society or Popular Religion." In *Civil Society in China,* edited by Timothy Brook and B. Michael Frolic, 172–192. Armonk, NY: M. E. Sharpe.

deLisle, Jacques. 1998. "Sovereignty Resumed: China's Conception of Law for Hong Kong, and Its Implications for the SAR and US-PRC Relations." *Harvard Asia Quarterly* 3 (Summer): 21–27.

———. 1999. "Lex Americana?" *University of Pennsylvania Journal of International Economic Law* 20 (Summer): 179–308.

———. 2000a. "China's Approach to International Law: A Historical Perspective." *American Society of International Law Proceedings* 94: 267–275.

———. 2000b. "The Chinese Puzzle of Taiwan's Status." *Orbis* 44, no. 2 (Winter): 55–63.

———. 2002. "Law's Spectral Answers to the Cross-Strait Sovereignty Question." *Orbis* 46, no. 4 (Fall): 733–752.

———. 2003a. "Chasing the God of Wealth While Evading the Goddess of Democracy: Development, Democracy, and Law in Reform-Era China." In *Development and Democracy,* edited by Sunder Ramaswamy and Jeffrey W. Cason, 23–56. Hanover, NH: University Press of New England.

———. 2003b. "SARS and the Pathologies of Globalization and Transition in Greater China." *Orbis* 47, no. 4: 587–604.

———. 2004a. "The Aftermath of Taiwan's Presidential Election: A Symposium Report." *FPRI E-Note* (June 18).

———. 2004b. *Reforming/Replacing the ROC Constitution: Implications for Taiwan's State(like) Status.* Woodrow Wilson Center Asia Program Special Report. Washington, DC: Woodrow Wilson Center.

———. 2005. "Taiwan's Democracy and Lessons from Yet Another Election." *FPRI E-Note* (December 16). Available at http://www.fpri.org/enotes/20051216.asia.delisle.taiwanelectionlessons.html.

———. 2006a. "China and the WTO." In *China Under Hu Jintao,* edited by Tun-jen Cheng, Jacques deLisle, and Deborah Brown, 10–45. Singapore: World Scientific Press.

———. 2006b. "Free Trade Areas: Legal Aspects and the Politics of U.S., PRC, and Taiwan Participation." *FPRI E-Note* (November). Available at http://www.fpri.org/pubs/20061110.asia.delisle.freetradeareasusprctaiwan.html.

———. 2007a. "Into Africa: China's Quest for Resources and Influence." *FPRI E-Note* (February). Available at http://www.fpri.org/enotes/200702.delisle.intoafrica chinasquest.html.

———. 2007b. "Legislating the Cross-Strait Status Quo?" In *Economic Integration, Democratization, and National Security in East Asia,* edited by Peter C.Y. Chow. Northampton, MA: Edward Elgar.

———. 2008. "Legalization Without Democratization Under Hu Jintao." In *China's Changing Political Landscape,* edited by Cheng Li. Washington, DC: Brookings Institution.

Deutsche Presse-Agentur. 2006. "Interview: Chinese Premier on Reforms, Foreign Policy." September 9.

Dezalay, Yves, and Bryant G. Garth. 2002. *The Internationalization of Palace Wars: Lawyers, Economists, and the Contest to Transform Latin American States.* Chicago: University of Chicago.

Diamond, Larry. 1992. "Economic Development and Democracy Reconsidered." In *Reexamining Democracy: Essays in Honor of Seymour Martin Lipset,* edited by Gary Marks and Larry Jay Diamond, 93–139. Newbury Park, CA: Sage Publications.

———. 1993. "Political Culture and Democracy." In *Political Culture and Democracy in Developing Countries,* edited by Larry Diamond, 1–33. Boulder, CO: Lynne Rienner.

———. 1996. "Is the Third Wave Over?" *Journal of Democracy* 7, no. 3: 20–37.

———. 1999. *Developing Democracy: Towards Consolidation.* Baltimore: Johns Hopkins University Press.

———. 2002. "Thinking About Hybrid Regimes." *Journal of Democracy* 13, no. 2: 21–35.

———. 2008. *The Spirit of Democracy: The Struggle to Build Free Societies Throughout the World.* New York: Henry Holt.

Diamond, Larry, Marc F. Plattner, Tun-han Chu, and Hung-mao Tien, eds. 1997. *Consolidating Third-Wave Democracies: Regional Challenges.* Baltimore: Johns Hopkins University Press.

Dick, Howard. 2006. "Why Law Reforms Fail: Indonesia's Anti-corruption Reforms." In *Law Reform in Developing and Transitional States,* edited by Tim Lindsey. New York: Routledge.

Dickson, Bruce J. 1996. "The Kuomintang Before Democratization: Organizational Change and the Role of Elections." In *Taiwan's Electoral Politics and Democratic Transition: Riding the Third Wave,* edited by Charles Chi-hsiang Chang and Hung-mao Tien, 42–78. Armonk, NY: M. E. Sharpe.

———. 1997. *Democratization in China and Taiwan: The Adaptability of Leninist Parties.* Oxford: Clarendon Press.

———. 1998. "China's Democratization and the Taiwan Experience." *Asian Survey* 38, no. 4 (April): 349–364.

———. 2003. *Red Capitalists in China: The Party, Private Entrepreneurs, and Prospects for Political Change.* New York: Cambridge University Press.

———. 2004. "Dilemmas of Party Adaptation." In *State and Society in 21st-Century China,* edited by Peter Hays Gries and Stanley Rosen, 141–158. New York: Routledge Curzon.

———. 2006. "The Future of the Chinese Communist Party: Strategies of Survival and Prospects for Change." In *Charting China's Future,* edited by Jae Ho Chung, 21–49. Lanham, MD: Rowman and Littlefield.

Dittmer, Lowell. 2006. "Taiwan as a Factor in China's Quest for National Identity." *Journal of Contemporary China* 15, no. 49: 671–686.

Dogan, Mattei, and John Higley. 1998. *Elites, Crises, and the Origins of Regimes.* Lanham, MD: Rowman and Littlefield.

Dowdle, Michael. 2002. "Of Parliaments, Pragmatism, and the Dynamics of Constitutional Development: The Curious Case of China." *New York University Journal of International Law and Politics* 35, no. 1: 1–200.

Dupont, Alan. 1996. "Is There an 'Asian Way'?" *Survival* 38, no. 2: 13–33.

Easter, Gerald M. 1997. "Preference for Presidentialism." *World Politics* 49, no. 2: 184–212.

Eckstein, Harry. 1988. "A Culturalist Theory of Political Change." *American Political Science Review* 82, no. 3 (September): 789–804.

Economy, Elizabeth C. 2004. *The River Runs Black: The Environmental Challenge to China's Future.* Ithaca, NY: Cornell University Press.

———. 2007. "The Great Leap Backward?" *Foreign Affairs* 86, no. 5 (September–October): 38–60.

Economy, Elizabeth, and Michel Oksenberg, eds. 1999. *China Joins the World.* New York: Council on Foreign Relations Press.

Edwards, Bob, Michael W. Foley, and Mario Diani. 2001. *Beyond Tocqueville: Civil Society and the Social Capital Debate in Comparative Perspective.* Hanover, NH: University Press of New England.

Emmerson, Donald. 1995. "Singapore and the 'Asian Values' Debate." *Journal of Democracy* 6, no. 4: 95–105.

Epstein, David L., Robert Bates, Jack Goldstone, Ida Kristensen, and Sharyn O'Halloran. 2006. "Democratic Transitions." *American Journal of Political Science* 50, no. 3: 551–569.

Esarey, Ashley, and Xiao Qiang. 2008 (forthcoming). "Under the Radar: Political Expression in the Chinese Blogosphere." *Asian Survey.*

European Community. 1991. "Guidelines on the Recognition of New States in Eastern

Europe and in the Soviet Union." *International Legal Materials* 31 (December 16): 1486.

Fan Lizhu, ed. 2003. Quanqiuhuaxiade Shehui Bianqian yu Feizhengfu Zhuzhi [*Social Change and NGOs in a Globalized Society*]. Shanghai: Shanghai People's Press.

Fan Shuo. 1990. Ye Jianying Zai 1976 [*Ye Jianying in 1976*]. 2nd ed. Beijing: Central Party School Press.

Fan Yun. 2004. "Taiwan: No Civil Society, No Democracy." In *Civil Society and Political Change in Asia,* edited by Muthiah Alagappa, 164–190. Stanford, CA: Stanford University Press.

Farnsworth, Clyde H. 1980. "Assailing Beijing, House Votes a Rise in China's Tariffs." *New York Times,* October 19.

Fearon, John. 1994. "Domestic Political Audiences and the Escalation of International Disputes." *American Political Science Review* 88, no. 3: 577–592.

Feldman, Harvey. 2007. "President Reagan's Six Assurances to Taiwan and Their Meaning Today" (October 2). Available at http://www.heritage.org/Research/AsiaandthePacific/wm1653.cfm.

Fell, Daffyd. 2007. "Prospects for Taiwan's Upcoming Presidential Election." *Brookings Northeast Asia Commentary* (June). Available at http://www.brookings.ed/opinions/2007/06taiwan_fell.aspx?p=1.

Feng Yi. 2003. *Democracy, Governance, and Economic Performance: Theory and Evidence.* Cambridge: MIT Press.

Feuchtwang, Stephan. 2003. "Peasants, Democracy, and Anthropology: Questions of Local Loyalty." *Critique of Anthropology* 23, no. 3: 93–120.

Fewsmith, Joseph. 2001. *China Since Tiananmen: The Politics of Transition.* New York: Cambridge University Press.

———. 2004. "China's New Leadership: A One-Year Assessment." *Orbis* 48, no. 2 (Spring): 205–216.

Finkel, Steve. 1985. "The Effects of Participation on Political Efficacy: A Panel Analysis." *American Journal of Political Science* 29, no. 4: 891–913.

Finkel, Steve, Christopher Sabatini, and Gwendolyn Bevis. 2000. "Civic Education, Civil Society, and Political Mistrust in a Developing Democracy: The Case of the Dominican Republic." *World Development* 28, no. 11 (November): 1851–1874.

Flanagan, Scott, and Aie-Rie Lee. 2000. "Value Change and Democratic Reform in Japan and Korea." *Comparative Political Studies* 33, no. 5: 626–659.

Franck, Thomas. 1991. "The Emerging Right to Democratic Governance." *American Journal of International Law* 13, no. 4 (January): 46–91.

Friedman, Edward. 2006. "Jiang Zemin's Successors and China's Growing Rich-Poor Gap." In *China Under Hu Jintao,* edited by Tun-jen Cheng, Jacques deLisle, and Deborah Brown, 34–56. Singapore: World Scientific Press.

Fu Hualing. 2007. "The Myth of Prosecuted Lawyers: China's Relationship with Criminal Defense Attorneys." Working Papers, Yale University China Law Center.

Fu Hualing, and Richard Cullen. Forthcoming. *Weiquan (Rights Protection) Lawyering in an Authoritarian State: Toward Critical Lawyering.*

Fukuyama, Francis. 1992. *The End of History and the Last Man.* New York: Free Press.

———. 1995a. "Confucianism and Democracy." *Journal of Democracy* 6, no. 2: 20–33.

———. 1995b. "The Price of Culture." *Journal of Democracy* 6, no. 1: 7–14.

———. 1998. "The Illusion of Asian Exceptionalism." In *Democracy in East Asia,* edited by Larry Diamond and Marc F. Plattner, 224–227. Baltimore: Johns Hopkins University Press.

Fuller, Lon. 1964. *The Morality of Law.* New Haven. CT: Yale University Press.

Gaddis, John Lewis. 1997. *We Now Know: Rethinking Cold War History.* New York: Oxford University Press.

Gao Bingzhong. 2005. "Ethnography of a Building Both as Museum and Temple: On the Double-Naming Method as an Art of Politics." Paper presented at the Annual Meeting of the American Anthropological Association, Washington, DC, December.

Garver, John W. 1997. *Face Off: China, the United States, and Taiwan's Democratization.* Seattle: University of Washington Press.

Gates, Hill. 1981. "Ethnicity and Social Class." In *The Anthropology of Taiwanese Society,* edited by Hill Gates and Emily Martin Ahern, 241–281. Stanford, CA: Stanford University Press.

Geddes, Barbara. 1999. "What Do We Know About Democratization After Twenty Years?" *Annual Review of Political Science* 2: 115–144.

Gellner, Ernest. 1994. *Conditions of Liberty: Civil Society and its Rivals.* New York: Penguin Books.

Gerring, John, Philip Bond, William Brandt, and Carola Moreno. 2005. "Democracy and Economic Growth: A Historical Perspective." *World Politics* 57, no. 3: 323–364.

Gill, Graeme. 2000. *The Dynamics of Democratization: Elites, Civil Society, and the Transition Process.* New York: St. Martin's Press.

Gilley, Bruce. 2004a. *China's Democratic Future: How It Will Happen and Where It Will Lead.* New York: Columbia University Press.

———. 2004b. "The 'End of Politics' in Beijing." *China Journal* 51: 115–135.

———. 2006a. "Elite-Led Democratization in China: Prospects, Perils, and Policy Implications." *International Journal* 61, no. 2: 341–358.

———. 2006b. "The Meaning and Measure of State Legitimacy: Results for 72 Countries." *European Journal of Political Research* 45, no. 3: 499–525.

———. 2008. "Legitimacy and Institutional Change: The Case of China." *Comparative Political Studies* 41, no. 3: 1–20.

Ginsburg, Thomas. 2003. *Judicial Review in New Democracies: Constitutional Courts in Asian Cases.* New York: Cambridge University Press.

Girvin, Brian. 1989. "Change and Continuity in Liberal Democratic Political Culture." In *Contemporary Political Culture,* edited by John R. Gibbins, 31–51. London: Sage.

Glaser, Bonnie S., and Evan S. Medeiros. 2007. "The Changing Ecology of Foreign Policy-Making in China: The Ascension and Demise of the Theory of 'Peaceful Rise.'" *China Quarterly,* no. 190: 291–310.

Gold, Thomas B. 1987. *State and Society in the Taiwan Miracle.* Armonk, NY: M. E. Sharpe.

———. 1988. "Entrepreneurs, Multinationals, and the State." In *Contending Approaches to the Political Economy of Taiwan,* edited by Edwin A. Winckler and Susan Greenhalgh, 175–205. Armonk, NY: M. E. Sharpe.

———. 1994. "Civil Society and Taiwan's Quest for Identity." In *Cultural Change in Postwar Taiwan,* edited by Stevan Harrell and Huang Chun-chieh, 47–68. Taipei: SMC Publishing.

———. 1997. "Taiwan: Still Defying the Odds." In *Consolidating the Third Wave Democracies,* edited by Larry Diamond, Marc F. Plattner, Yun-han Chu, and Hung-mao Tien, 162–191. Baltimore: Johns Hopkins University Press.

Goldman, Merle. 1994. *Sowing the Seeds of Democracy in China: Political Reform in the Deng Xiaoping Era.* Cambridge, MA: Harvard University Press.

Goldman, Merle, and Elizabeth Perry, eds. 2002. *Changing Meanings of Citizenship in Modern China.* Cambridge, MA: Harvard University Press.

Goldstein, Avery. 2005. *Rising to the Challenge: China's Grand Strategy and International Security.* Stanford, CA: Stanford University Press.

Goodman, David. 1999. "The New Middle Class." In *The Paradox of China's Post-Mao Reforms,* edited by Merle Goldman and Roderick MacFarquhar, 241–282. Cambridge, MA: Harvard University Press.

———. 2001. "The Interdependence of State and Society: The Political Sociology of Local Leadership." In *Remaking the Chinese State: Strategies, Society, and Security,* edited by Chien-min Chao and Bruce J. Dickson, 132–155. London: Routledge.

Goodwin, Jeff. 2001. *No Other Way Out: States and Revolutionary Movements, 1945–1991.* Cambridge: Cambridge University Press.

Government Information Office, ROC. 1994. *Republic of China on Taiwan and the United Nations: Questions and Answers.* Taipei.

———. 2005. *The Significance of Taiwan's Constitutional Reforms.* Taipei.

Greenhalgh, Susan. 1984. "Networks and Their Nodes: Urban Society on Taiwan." *The China Quarterly*, no. 99: 529–552.

———. 1988. "Families and Networks in Taiwan's Economic Development." In *Contending Approaches to the Political Economy of Taiwan,* edited by Edwin A. Winckler and Susan Greenhalgh, 224–245. Armonk, NY: M. E. Sharpe.

Gries, Peter Hays. 2004. *China's New Nationalism.* Berkeley: University of California Press.

Grindle, Merilee Serrill. 2000. *Audacious Reforms: Institutional Invention and Democracy in Latin America.* Baltimore: Johns Hopkins University Press.

Guo Xiaoqin. 2003. *State and Society in China's Democratic Transition: Confucianism, Leninism, and Economic Development.* New York: Routledge.

Haggard, Stephan. 1990. *Pathways from the Periphery.* Ithaca, NY: Cornell University Press.

Haggard, Stephan, and Robert R. Kaufman. 1995. T*he Political Economy of Democratic Transitions.* Princeton, NJ: Princeton University Press.

Haggard, Stephan, and A. MacIntyre. 2000. "The Politics of Moral Hazard: The Origins of Financial Crisis in Korea, Thailand, and Indonesia." In *Tigers in Distress,* edited by Francisco L. Rivera-Batiz and Arvid Lukauskus, 85–109. London: Edward Elgar.

Hahm, Chaibong. 1997. "The Confucian Political Discourse and the Politics of Reform in Korea." *The Korea Journal* 37, no. 4 (Winter): 65–77.

Hahm, Chaihark. 2004. "Rule of Law in South Korea: Rhetoric and Implementation." In *Asian Discourses of Rule of Law: Theories and Implementation of Rule of Law in Twelve Asian Countries,* edited by Randall Peerenboom, 385–416. New York: Routledge Curzon.

Hall, Peter A., and Rosemary C.R. Taylor. 1996. "Political Science and the Three New Institutionalisms." *Political Studies* 44, no. 5: 936–957.

Halperin, Morton H., Joseph T. Siegle, and Michael M. Weinstein. 2005. *The Democracy Advantage: How Democracies Promote Prosperity and Peace.* New York: Routledge.

Hamilton, Gary G. 1998. "Culture and Organization in Taiwan's Market Economy." In *Market Cultures: Society and Values in the New Asian Capitalisms,* edited by Robert W. Hefner, 41–77. Singapore: Institute of Southeast Asian Studies.

Hamrin, Carol Lee, and Timothy Cheek, eds. 1986. *China's Establishment Intellectuals.* Armonk, NY: M. E. Sharpe.

Han, San-Jin. 2001. "Modernization and the Rise of Civil Society: The Role of the 'Middling Grassroots' for Democratization in Korea." *Human Studies* 24, no. 1–2: 113–132.

Hand, Keith. 2007. "Using a Law for a Righteous Purpose: The Sun Zhigang Incident and Evolving Forms of Citizen's Action in China." *Columbia Journal of Transnational Law* 45, no. 3: 114–195.

Hannum, Hurst. 1990. *Autonomy, Sovereignty, and Self-Determination.* Rev. ed. Philadelphia: University of Pennsylvania Press.

Harding, Harry. 2005. "Change and Continuity in the Bush Administration's Asia Policy." In *George W. Bush and East Asia,* edited by Robert M. Hathaway and Wilson Lee, 45–86. Washington, DC: Woodrow Wilson International Center for Scholars.

———. 2007. "China: Think Again!" *Foreign Policy* 159, no. 2: 26–32.

He Baogang, and Youxing Lang. 2002. *Xunzhao Minzhu yu Guanwei de Pingheng— Zhejiang* S*heng Cunmin Xuanju Jingyan Yanjiu* [*In Search of a Balance Between Democracy and Authority—The Experience of Zhejiang Province in Village Elections*]. Wuhan: Huazhong Normal University Press.

Hellman, Joel S., Geraint Jones, and Daniel Kaufmann. 2003. "Seize the State, Seize the Day: State Capture, Corruption, and Influence in Transition." *Journal of Comparative Economics* 31, no. 4: 751–773.

Herschensohn, Bruce. 2002. *Across the Taiwan Strait: Democracy: The Bridge Between Inland China and Taiwan.* Lanham, MD: Lexington Books.

Ho Ming-sho. 2007. "The Rise and Fall of Leninist Control in Taiwan's Industry." *The China Quarterly,* no. 189: 162–179.

Hoare, Quitin, and Geoffrey Nowell Smith, eds. 1971. *Selections from the Prison Notebooks of Antonio Gramsci.* New York: International Publishers.

Hoffmann, Stanley. 1978. *Primacy or World Order.* New York: McGraw Hill.

Holbig, Heike. 2006. "Ideological Reform and Political Legitimacy in China: Challenges in the Post-Jiang Era." In *Legitimacy and Efficiency in Political Systems.* Hamburg: German Institute of Global and Area Studies. Available at http://www.giga-hamburg.de/english/index.php?file=rp1.html&folder=rp1.

Hollifield, J., and Calvin C. Jillson. 2000. *Pathways to Democracy: The Political Economy of Democratic Transitions.* New York: Routledge.

Hood, Steven. 1997. *The Kuomintang and the Democratization of Taiwan.* Boulder, CO: Westview.

Horowitz, Donald. 2002. "Constitutional Design: Proposals Versus Processes." In *The Architecture of Democracy: Constitutional Design, Conflict Management, and Democracy,* edited by Andrew Reynolds, 15–36. Oxford: Oxford University Press.

Hough, Jerry F. 1977. *The Soviet Union and Social Science Theory.* Russian Research Center Studies. Cambridge, MA: Harvard University Press.

Howe, Christopher. 1998. "The Taiwan Economy: The Transition to Maturity and the Political Economy of Its Changing International Status." In *Contemporary Taiwan,* edited by David L. Shambaugh, 167–187. Oxford: Oxford University Press.

Hsiao, Hsin-huang Michael. 1995a. "The Growing Asia-Pacific Concern Among Taiwan's NGOs." In *Emerging Civil Society in the Asia Pacific Community: Singapore and Tokyo,* edited by Tadashi Yamoto, 239–240. Singapore and Tokyo: Institute for Southeast Asian Studies and Japan Center for International Exchange.

———. 1995b. "The State and Business Relations in Taiwan." *Journal of Far Eastern Business* 1, no. 3: 76–97.

———. 2005. "Recapturing Taiwan's Democratization Experience." Speech presented at the First Biennial Conference of the World Forum on Asia, Taipei, September 15–17.

Hsiao, Hsin-huang Michael, ed. 1993. *Discovery of the Middle Classes in East Asia.* Taipei: Institute of Ethnology, Academia Sinica.

Hsiao, Hsin-huang Michael, and Hagen Koo. 1997. "The Middle Classes and Democratization." In *Consolidating the Third Wave Democracies,* edited by Larry Diamond, Marc F. Plattner, Yun-han Chu, and Hung-mao Tien, 312–333. Baltimore: Johns Hopkins University Press.

Hsiau A-chin. 2000. *Contemporary Taiwanese Nationalism.* New York: Routledge.

Hsu Chieh-ling. 1997. *Zhanhou Taiwan Shiji* [Taiwan's Postwar History]. Taipei: Weitang Press.

Hsu Leonard. 2005. *The Political Philosophy of Confucianism.* London: Rutledge.

Hsueh Hua-yuan. 1996. *Ziyou Zhongguo yu Minzhu Xianzheng: 1950 Niandai Taiwan Sixiangshi de Yige Kaocha* [Free China and the State of Democracy: A Study of Intellectual History in the 1950s Era]. Taipei: Daoxiang Press.

Hu Cheng-fen. 2005. "Taiwan's Geopolitics and Chiang Ching-kuo's Decision to Democratize Taiwan." *Greater China* 5, no. 1 (Winter): 26–44.

Hu Fu. 1998. *Zhengzhi Wenhua yu Zhengzhi Shenghuo* [Political Culture and Political Life]. Taipei: Sanmin Publishing House.

Hu Jintao. 2005. "Do Best to Seek Peaceful Reunification, but Never Tolerate 'Taiwan Independence.'" *Xinhua,* March 4.

———. 2007. "Political Report to the Seventeenth National Congress of the Chinese Communist Party," October 15.

Hu Shaohua. 1997. "Confucianism and Western Democracy." *Journal of Contemporary China* 6, no. 15: 347–363.

Hua Shiping, ed. 2001. *Chinese Political Culture, 1989–2000.* Armonk, NY: M. E. Sharpe.

Huang Chien-yu, Julia. 2001. "Recapturing Charisma: Emotion and Rationalization in a Globalizing Buddhist Movement from Taiwan." PhD diss., Boston University.

Huang Chien-yu, Julia, and Robert P. Weller. 1998. "Merit and Mothering: Women and Social Welfare in Taiwanese Buddhism." *Journal of Asian Studies* 57, no. 2 (May): 379–396.

Huang Teh-fu. 1996. "Elections and the Evolution of the Kuomintang." In *Taiwan's Electoral Politics and Democratic Transition,* edited by Hung-mao Tien, 105–136. Armonk, NY: M. E. Sharpe.

Huang Weiping. 1998. Zhongguo Zhengzhi Tizhi Gaige Zonghengtan [*General Thoughts on Political Reform in China*]. Beijing: Central Translation and Editing Press.

Huang Yanzhong. 2006. "Is the Chinese State Apparatus Being Revamped?" In *China Under Hu Jintao,* edited by Tun-jen Cheng, Jacques deLisle, and Deborah Brown, 86–103. Singapore: World Scientific Press.

Huang Yasheng. 2003. "One Country, Two Systems: Foreign-invested Enterprises and Domestic Firms in China." *China Economic Review* 14, no. 4: 404–416.

Huber, Evelyne, and John Stephens. 1999. "The Bourgeoisie and Democracy: Historical and Contemporary Perspectives." *Social Research* 66, no. 3: 759–788.

Hughes, Christopher. 1997. *Taiwan and Chinese Nationalism: National Identity and Status in International Society.* London: Routledge.

Huntington, Samuel P. 1968. *Political Order in Changing Societies.* London: Yale University Press.

———. 1991. *The Third Wave: Democratization in the Late Twentieth Century.* Norman: University of Oklahoma Press.

———. 1996. *The Clash of Civilizations.* New York: Simon and Schuster.

Inglehart, Ronald. 1990. *Culture Shift: In Advanced Industrial Society.* Princeton, NJ: Princeton University Press.

———. 1997. *Modernization and Postmodernization: Cultural, Economic, and Political Change in 43 Societies.* Princeton, NJ: Princeton University Press.

————. 2000. "Culture and Democracy." In *Culture Matters: How Values Shape Human Progress,* edited by Samuel P. Huntington and Lawrence E. Harrison, 80–97. New York: Basic Books.

Inglehart, Ronald, and Christian Welzel. 2005. *Modernization, Cultural Change, and Democracy: The Human Development Sequence.* Cambridge: Cambridge University Press.

Inkeles, Alex, and David Horton Smith. 1974. *Becoming Modern: Individual Change in Six Developing Countries.* Cambridge, MA: Harvard University Press.

International Committee for Human Rights in Taiwan. 1987. *Taiwan Communique* 29 (March).

Jacobs, Bruce. 2006. "One China, Diplomatic Isolation, and a Separate Taiwan." In *China's Rise, Taiwan's Dilemmas, and International Peace,* edited by Edward Freidman, 34–58. New York: Routledge.

Jacobs, J. Bruce. 1981. "Political Opposition and Taiwan's Political Future." *The Australian Journal of Chinese Affairs,* no. 6 (July): 21–44.

Jian Chen. 2001. *Mao's China and the Cold War.* Chapel Hill: University of North Carolina Press.

Jiang Zemin. 1995. "Eight Point Proposal" (January 30). Available at http://www.gwytb.gov.cn:8088/detail.asp?table=JiangEP&title=Jiang+Zemin's+Eight-point+Proposal&m_id=3.

————. 2001. "Speech at the 80th Anniversary of the Founding of the CCP." *People's Daily,* July 1.

————. 2002. "Speech at the Central Party School." *People's Daily,* May 31.

Jiang Zhuqing. 2005. "Hu Calls for Harmonious World at Summit." *China Daily,* September 16.

Jiefang Jun Bao. 1999. "Lee Teng-hui, Don't Play with Fire." July 15.

Jing Jun. 2000. "Environmental Protests in Rural China." In *Chinese Society: Change, Conflict, and Resistance,* edited by Mark Selden and Elizabeth J. Perry, 34–67. New York: Routledge.

Johnson, Chalmers. 1987. "Political Institutions and Economic Performance." In *The Political Economy of the New Asian Industrialism,* edited by Frederic C. Deyo, 136–164. Ithaca, NY: Cornell University Press.

"Joint Communiqué of the United States of America and the People's Republic of China." 1972. Shanghai, February 28.

"Joint Communiqué of the United States of America and the People's Republic of China." 1978/1979. Washington and Beijing, December 15–January 1.

"Joint Communiqué of the United States of America and the People's Republic of China." 1982. August 17.

Jones Luong, Pauline. 2002. *Institutional Change and Political Continuity in Post-Soviet Central Asia: Power, Perceptions, and Pacts.* Cambridge Studies in Comparative Politics. New York: Cambridge University Press.

Judicial Yuan. 2004. "Survey of the Quality of Judicial Service." Available at http://www.judicial.gov.tw/juds/index1.htm.

————. 2005a. "Oral History on Senior Legal Professionals in Taiwan." Vol. 1.

————. 2005b. "Survey of Civil, Criminal, and Juvenile Trial Cases." Available at http://www.judicial.gov.tw/juds/index1.htm.

————. 2005c. "Survey of the Quality of Judicial Service." Available at http://www.judicial.gov.tw/juds/index1.htm.

————. 2006. "Survey of Lawyers' Satisfaction of Judicial Reforms." Available at http://www.judicial.gov.tw/juds/index1.htm.

Judicial Yuan, Republic of China, Taiwan. 2006. *1950–2005, Judicial Statistics Yearbook.* Taipei: Government Information Office.

Karatnycky, Adrian, and Peter Ackerman. 2005. *How Freedom Is Won: From Civic Resistance to Durable Democracy.* Washington, DC: Freedom House.

Kaufmann, Daniel, Aart Kraay, and Massimo Mastruzzi. 2005. *Governance Matters III: Governance Indicators for 1996–2004.* Washington, DC: World Bank.

Kennedy, Ryan. 2004. "Re-Conceptualizing the Social Requisites of Democracy: A Conditional Probability Analysis of Modernization Theory." Paper presented at the Annual Meeting of the Midwest Political Science Association, Chicago, April 15. Available at http://www.allacademic.com/meta/p84080_index.html.

Kennedy, Scott. 2005. *The Business of Lobbying in China.* Cambridge, MA: Harvard University Press.

Kerr, George H. 1974. *Licensed Revolution and the Home Rule Movement 1895–1945.* Honolulu: University of Hawaii Press.

Kessler, Glenn. 2004. "U.S. Cautions Taiwan on Independence." *Washington Post,* April 22.

Keyser, Catherine H. 2003. *Professionalizing Research in Post-Mao China: The System Reform Institute and Policy Making.* Armonk, NY: M. E. Sharpe.

Kim Dae Jung. 1994. "Is Culture Destiny? The Myth of Asia's Anti-Democratic Values." *Foreign Affairs* 73, no. 6 (November/December): 189–194.

Kissinger, Henry. 1979. *White House Years.* Boston: Little, Brown.

Ko Shu-ling. 2006. "Chen Proposes Change of Constitution." *Taipei Times,* September 25.

Kristof, Nicholas D. 1998. "Clinton in China: Taiwan; Taipei Is on Alert for Sign of Betrayal." *New York Times,* June 29.

Kuhn, Anthony. 2004. "Political Business." *Far Eastern Economic Review* 167, no. 33 (August): 32–35.

Kuhn, Robert Lawrence. 2004. *The Man Who Changed China: The Life and Legacy of Jiang Zemin.* New York: Crown Publishers.

Kurlantzick, Joshua. 2007. *Charm Offensive: How China's Soft Power Is Transforming the World.* New Haven: Yale University Press.

Kyodo News Service. 2004a. "China Warns It Won't Be Indifferent If Chaos Erupts in Taiwan." March 26.

———. 2004b. "Chinese State Media Blast Taiwan Election, Referendum." March 22.

Lai I-chung. 2007. "17th Chinese Communist Party Congress: Policy Implications on Taiwan." *China Brief* (Jamestown Foundation) 7, no. 21 (November 14). Available at http://www.jamestown.org/publications_view.php?publication_id=4.

Lai Ming-yan. 2008. *Nativism and Modernity: Cultural Contestations in China and Taiwan Under Global Capitalism.* Albany: State University of New York Press.

Lai Tse-han, Ramon H. Myers, and Wei Wou. 1991. *A Tragic Beginning: The Taiwan Uprising of February 28, 1947.* Stanford, CA: Stanford University Press.

Lakshnan, Indira A.R. 2002. "China's Reforms Turn Costly." *Boston Globe,* July 22, 2002, sec. A.

Laliberté, Andre. 2004. *The Politics of Buddhist Organizations in Taiwan, 1989–2003.* London: Routledge Curzon.

Lam, Willy Wo-Lap. 1995. *China After Deng Xiaoping: The Power Struggle in Beijing Since Tiananmen.* Singapore: J. Wiley and Sons.

———. 1999. *The Era of Jiang Zemin.* Singapore: Prentice Hall.

———. 2004. "Cross-Strait Relations in Taiwan's Presidential Elections." *China Brief* (Jamestown Foundation) 4, no. 6 (March 19).

———. 2006. "Ebb and Glow of 'Color Revolutions.'" *Pingguo Ribao* (Hong Kong), April 11.

Langston, Joy. 2006. "Elite Ruptures: When Do Ruling Parties Split?" In *Electoral*

Authoritarianism: The Dynamics of Unfree Competition, edited by Andreas Schedler, 57–75. Boulder, CO: Lynne Rienner Publishers.

Lardy, Nicholas R. 2002. *Integrating China into the Global Economy.* Washington, DC: Brookings Institution

Laris, Michael, and John Pomfret. 1999. "Sssshhh! This Is a Secret Election: Chinese Quietly Test Democratic Waters." *Washington Post,* January 27, sec. A.

Lawrence, Susan V. 2000. "Three Cheers for the Party." *Far Eastern Economic Review* 163, no. 43 (October): 32–35.

League of Nations. 1933. *Montevideo Convention on the Rights and Duties of States.* League of Nations Treaty Series 19.

Lee Junshan. 2002. "Primary Causes of Asian Democratization: Dispelling Conventional Myths." *Asian Survey* 42, no. 6: 821–837.

Lee Teng-hui. 1995. "'Always in My Heart'—Speech at Cornell University." Available at http://www.news.cornell.edu/campus/Lee/Lee_Speech.html.

———. 1996. "'A New Phase of the Taiwan Experience Is Underway'—Full Text of Address by ROC President Lee Teng-hui." Taipei.

———. 1999. "Understanding Taiwan: Bridging the Perception Gap." *Foreign Affairs* 78, no. 6: 9–14.

Lei Fei-lung. 1992. "The Electoral System and Voting Behavior in Taiwan." In *Political Change in Taiwan,* edited by T. J. Cheng and Stephan Haggard, 149–176. Boulder, CO: Lynne Rienner.

Li Baojie, Cheng Yifeng, and Wang Mian. 2007. "Soft Power, a New Focus at China's 'Two Sessions.'" *Xinhua,* March 14.

Li Cheng. 2005. "The New Bipartisanship Within the Chinese Communist Party." *Orbis* 49, no. 3: 387–400.

Li Cheng, and Lynn White. 1990. "Elite Transformation and Modern Change in Inland China and Taiwan: Empirical Data and the Theory of Technocracy." *China Quarterly* 121, no. 1: 1–35.

Li Fangchao. 2007. "Referendum Bid Could Lead to 'High Risk Period.'" *China Daily,* December 18.

Li He. 2006. "Emergence of the Chinese Middle Class and Its Implications." *Asian Affairs: An American Review* 33, no. 2: 67–83.

Li Hongbin, Lingsheng Meng, and Junsen Zhang. 2006. "Why Do Entrepreneurs Enter Politics? Evidence from China." *Economic Inquiry* 44, no. 3: 559–578.

Li Hsiao-feng. 2001. "Types of Political Cases During the Martial Law Era in Taiwan." In *A Legal and Historical Analysis of Political Cases During Martial Law Era,* edited by Tsu-hsiu Nee, 234–257. Taipei: Compensation Foundation for Improper Verdicts.

Li Liaiang. 1999. "The Two-Ballot System in Shanxi Province: Subjecting Village Party Secretaries to a Public Vote." *China Quarterly,* no. 42 (July): 103–118.

Li Yongzhong. 2003. "Juece, zhixing, jiandu sanquan fenli xiang xietiao" ["Separation and Coordination Among Three Powers of Policymaking, Policy Implementation, and Supervision"]. *Mingjian,* no. 30: 3–11.

Lieberthal, Kenneth. 1995. "A New China Strategy: The Challenge." *Foreign Affairs* (November/December): 35–43.

Liebman, Benjamin. 2007. "China's Courts: Restricted Reforms." *China Quarterly* 191: 620–638.

Lilley, James, and David Shambaugh, eds. 1999. *China's Military Faces the Future.* Washington, DC: American Enterprise Institute.

Lin Chia-lung. 1998. "Path to Democracy: Taiwan in Comparative Perspective." PhD diss., Yale University.

Lin, Frederick Chao-Chun. 2006. "The Implementation of Human Rights Law in Taiwan." In *Human Rights in Asia: A Comparative Legal Study of Twelve Asian Jurisdictions,* edited by Randall Peerenboom, Carole J. Petersen, and Albert H.Y. Chen, 298–319. New York: Routledge Curzon.

Lin, Jih-wen. 2006. "The Politics of Reform in Japan and Taiwan." *Journal of Democracy* 17, no. 2 (April): 118–131.

Lin Man-houng. 2006. "Elite Survival in Regime Transition: Government-Merchant Cooperation in Taiwan's Trade with Japan, 1950–1961." In *The International Order of Asia in the 1930s and 1950s,* edited by Shigeru Akita and Nick White, 113–145. New York: Ashgate.

Lin Zhen. 2005. "Shilun Taiwan minzhuhuade dongyin" ["On the Reasons for Taiwan's Democratization"]. *Journal of Hehai University* 7, no. 2: 54–59.

Lindberg, Staffan I. 2006. *Democracy and Elections in Africa.* Baltimore: Johns Hopkins University Press.

Lindblom, Charles E. 1977. *Politics and Markets.* New York: Basic Books.

Ling, L.H.M., and Chih-yu Shih. 1998. "Confucianism with a Liberal Face: The Meaning of Democratic Politics in Postcolonial Taiwan." *Review of Politics* 60, no. 1: 55–82.

Link, Perry. 2002. "The Anaconda in the Chandelier: Censorship in China Today." *New York Review of Books* 49, no. 6 (April 2002): 12–16.

Linz, Juan J., and Alfred Stepan. 1996a. *Problems of Democratic Transition and Consolidation: Southern Europe, South America, and Post-Communist Europe.* Baltimore: John Hopkins University Press.

———. 1996b. "Toward Consolidated Democracies." *Journal of Democracy* 7, no. 2: 24–33.

Liu Heng-Wen. 2002. "A Study of the Judges and Prosecutors in Postwar Taiwan: An Observation Focused on Their Training Culture." *Journal of the Humanities and Social Sciences* 40, no. 1 (March): 2–14.

Liu I-chou. 1999. "The Development of the Opposition." In *Democratization in Taiwan: Implications for China,* edited by Steve Tsang and Hung-mao Tien, 67–84. Hong Kong: Hong Kong University Press.

Liu, Philip. 1997. "John Chang Explains ROC's Position to L.A. Audience," Central News Agency (Taiwan), June 17.

Liu v. Republic of China. 1989. 642 F. Supp. 297 (N.D. Cal. 1986), 892 F.2d 1419 (9th Cir. 1989).

Lo Chih-cheng. 2004. "Taiwan: The China Factor." *Taiwan Perspective* (e-paper), February 26.

Londregan, John B., and Keith T. Poole. 1996. "Does High Income Promote Democracy?" *World Politics* 49, no. 1: 1–30.

Low, Y. F. 2005. "Taiwan's Opposition TSU Urges 'Defensive Referendum Against Chinese Law.'" Central News Agency (Taiwan), March 8.

Lu, Alexander Ya-li. 1992. "Political Opposition in Taiwan: The Development of the Democratic Progressive Party." In *Political Change in Taiwan,* edited by Tun-jen Cheng and Stephan Haggard, 121–146. Boulder: Lynne Rienner Publishers.

Lu Hsiu-lien. 1992. *Chongshen Meilidao [Reconsidering the Formosa Magazine Incident].* Taipei: Independent Evening News Press.

———. 2006. "Prison to Power: Lu Hsiu-lien and the Democratization of Taiwan." Unpublished manuscript, October.

Lu Xueyi, ed. 2004. *Dangdai Zhongguo Shehui Liudong [Social Mobility in Contemporary China].* Beijing: Social Science Documents Press.

Lubman, Stanley B. 1999. *Bird in a Cage: Legal Reforms in China After Mao.* Stanford, CA: Stanford University Press.

Lynch, Daniel C. 2006. *Rising China and Asian Democratization: Socialization to "Global Culture" in Political Transformations of Thailand, China, and Taiwan.* Stanford, CA: Stanford University Press.

Ma Haijun. 2005. "Taiwan Zhengzhi Minzhuhuazhongde Mincui Zhuyi" ["Rich Peasants in the Process of Taiwan's Democratization"]. *Socialism Studies* 2, no. 1: 45–58.

Ma Ying. 2007. "China's Stubborn Anti-Democracy." *Policy Review* 141, no. 2: 3–8.

Ma Ying-jeou. 2008. "International Conference on Confidence-Building Measures: Successful Cases and Implications for the Taiwan Strait." January 16.

Madsen, Richard. 2007. *Democracy's Dharma: Religious Renaissance and Political Development in Taiwan.* Berkeley, CA: University of California Press.

Madsen, Richard, and Tracy B. Strong, eds. 2003. *The Many and the One: Religious and Secular Perspectives on Ethical Pluralism in the Modern World.* Princeton, NJ: Princeton University Press.

Mainland Affairs Council, Republic of China. 1993. *There Is No "Taiwan Question"; There Is Only a "China Question": Views on the Chinese Communists' White Paper, "The Taiwan Question and Reunification of China."* Taipei: Government Information Office.

———. 1994. *Explanation of Relations Across the Taiwan Strait.* Taipei: Government Information Office.

Mainwaring, Scott, and Anibal Perez-Linan. 2003. "Level of Development and Democracy." *Comparative Political Studies* 36, no. 9: 1031–1168.

Mann, James. 1998. *About Face.* New York: Knopf.

———. 2007. *The China Fantasy.* New York: Viking Press.

McCubbin, Mathew, and Thomas Schwartz. 1984. "Congressional Oversight Overlooked: Police Patrol Versus Fire Alarms." *American Journal of Political Science* 28, no. 1: 165–179.

McDonough, Peter, Samuel Barnes, and Antonio Lopez Pina. 1994. "The Nature of Political Support and Legitimacy in Spain." *Comparative Political Studies* 27, no. 3 (October): 349–380.

McFaul, Michael. 2001. "A Mixed Record, an Uncertain Future." *Journal of Democracy* 12, no. 4 (October): 87–94.

———. 2002. "The Fourth Wave of Democracy and Dictatorship: Noncooperative Transitions in the Post-Communist World." *World Politics* 54, no. 2: 212–244.

Meaney, Constance Squires. 1992. "Liberalization, Democratization, and the Role of the KMT." In *Political Change in Taiwan,* edited by Tun-jen Cheng and Stephan Haggard, 95–120. Boulder, CO: Lynne Rienner.

Mearsheimer, John J. 2003. *The Tragedy of Great Power Politics.* New York: W. W. Norton.

Mill, John Stuart. 1861/1958. *Considerations on Representative Government.* New York: Bobbs-Merrill.

Ming Pao (Hong Kong). 2000. "Beijing Continues to Exert Pressure on Chen Shui-bian." May 21.

Mo Ming. *90 Percent of China's Billionaires Are Children of Senior Officials.* Available at http://financenews.sina.com/ausdaily/000-000-107-105/202/2006-10-19/1509124173.shtml.

Moody, Peter. 1992. *Political Change on Taiwan: A Study of Ruling Party Adaptability.* New York: Praeger.

Moore, Barrington, Jr. 1966. *Social Origins of Dictatorship and Democracy.* Boston: Beacon Press.

Mote, Frederick W. 1989. *Intellectual Foundations of China.* New York: McGraw-Hill.

Muller, Edward, and Mitchell Seligson. 1994. "Civic Culture and Democracy: The

Question of Causal Relationships." *American Political Science Review* 88, no. 3 (September): 635–667.

Myers, Ramon H. 1984. "The Economic Transformation of the Republic of China on Taiwan." *China Quarterly* 99: 500–528.

———. 1991. *A Tragic Beginning: The Taiwan Uprising of February 28, 1947.* Stanford, CA: Stanford University Press.

Nathan, Andrew J. 1993. "The Legislative Yuan Elections in Taiwan: Consequences of the Electoral System." *Asian Survey* 33, no. 4 (April): 424–438.

———. 1996. "China's Constitutionalist Option." *Journal of Democracy* 7, no. 4: 43–57.

———. 2001. "The Tiananmen Papers: An Editor's Reflections." *China Quarterly* 167, no. 3: 724–737.

———. 2003. "Authoritarian Resilience: China's Changing of the Guard." *Journal of Democracy* 14, no. 1: 6–17.

———. 2006. "Is Communist Party Rule Sustainable in China?" Paper presented at the conference on "Reframing China Policy: The Carnegie Debates," Washington, DC, October 5.

———. 2007. "China's Political Trajectory: What Are Chinese Saying?" Paper presented at the conference on "Changes in China's Political Landscape: The 17th Party Congress and Beyond," John L. Thornton China Center, Brookings Institution, Washington, DC, April 12.

Nathan, Andrew J., and Bruce Gilley. 2002. *China's New Rulers: The Secret Files.* New York: New York Review of Books.

Nathan, Andrew J., and Helena V.S. Ho. 1997. "The Decision for Reform in Taiwan." In Andrew J. Nathan. *China's Transition.* New York: Columbia University Press.

Nathan, Andrew J., and Robert S. Ross. 1997. *The Great Wall and the Empty Fortress: China's Search for Security.* New York: W. W. Norton.

National Assembly, ROC. 2005. Revised Additional Articles of the ROC Constitution (June 10).

National Unification Council and Executive Yuan, ROC. 1991. "Guidelines for National Unification."

Negroponte, John D. 2007. "Interview by Naichian Mo of Phoenix TV" (August 27). Available at http://www.state.gov/s/d/2007/91479.htm.

NGO Affairs Committee, Ministry of Foreign Affairs, Republic of China (Taiwan). 2006. *Taiwan's NGOs Reaching Out to the World.* Taipei: Government Information Office.

Ng-Quinn, Michael. 2006. "The Normative Justification of Traditional Chinese Authoritarianism." *Critical Review of International Social and Political Philosophy* 9, no. 3: 379–397.

Nie, Norman, G. Bingham Powell, and Kenneth Prewitt. 1969. "Social Structure and Political Participation." *American Political Science Review* 63, no. 2 (June): 361–378.

Norris, Pippa. 1999. "Introduction: The Growth of Critical Citizens." In *Critical Citizens: Global Support for Democratic Governance,* edited by Pippa Norris, 1–30. Oxford: Oxford University Press.

O'Brien, Kevin J. 1990. "Is China's National People's Congress a 'Conservative' Legislature?" *Asian Survey* 30, no. 8 (August): 782–794.

———. 1994a ."Agents and Remonstrators: Role Accumulation by Chinese People's Congress Deputies." *China Quarterly* 138 (June): 359–380.

———. 1994b. "Chinese People's Congresses and Legislative Embeddedness: Understanding Early Organizational Development." *Comparative Political Studies* 27, no. 1 (April): 80–107.

————. 1994c. "Implementing Political Reform in China's Villages." *Australian Journal of Chinese Affairs* 32 (July): 33–59.

————. 2002. "Villagers, Elections, and Citizenship." In *Changing Meanings of Citizenship in Modern China,* edited by Merle Goldman and Elizabeth J. Perry, 212–231. Cambridge, MA: Harvard University Press.

O'Brien, Kevin J., and Liaiang Li. 2004. "Suing the Local State: Administrative Litigation in Rural China." *China Journal* 51 (January): 75–96.

O'Donnell, Guillermo A. 1973. *Modernization and Bureaucratic-Authoritarianism: Studies in South American Politics.* Berkeley, CA: Institute of International Studies.

O'Donnell, Guillermo A., and Philippe C. Schmitter. 1986. *Transitions from Authoritarian Rule: Tentative Conclusions About Uncertain Democracies.* Baltimore: Johns Hopkins University Press.

Office of Legislative Affairs, Republic of China, Taiwan. 2008. "Undertaking Administration According to Law: Review and Prognosis, Report Prepared for the Asian Development Bank."

Office of the President of the ROC. 2003. President Chen's Interview by *New York Times* (December 5). Available at http://www.roc-taiwan.org.sg/taiwan/4-oa/20031205/2003120501.html.

————. 2004. "President Chen's Televised Statement of the Peace Referendum on March 20," January 16.

Oi, Jean C. 1996. "Economic Development, Stability, and Democratic Village Self-governance." In *China Review,* edited by Maurice Brosseau, Suzanne Pepper, and Tsang Shu-ki, 136–141. Hong Kong: The Chinese University Press.

————. 2003. "State Responses to Rural Discontent in China: Tax-for-Fee Reform and Increased Party Control." In *Asia Program Special Report No. 108: Crisis in the Hinterland: Rural Discontent in China.* Washington, DC: Woodrow Wilson International Center for Scholars.

————. 2004. "Realms of Freedom in Post-Mao China." In *Realms of Freedom in Modern China,* edited by William C. Kirby, 264–284. Stanford, CA: Stanford University Press.

Olson, Mancur. 1971. *The Logic of Collective Action: Public Goods and the Theory of Groups.* 2nd ed. Cambridge, MA: Harvard University Press.

Ong Hwee Hwee. 2007. "New Leader Bound by Referendum, Says Chen." *Straits Times,* December 27.

Orentlicher, Diane F. 1998. "Separation Anxiety." *Yale Journal of International Law* 23 (Winter): 1–78.

Packenham, Robert A. 1973. *Liberal America and the Third World.* Princeton, NJ: Princeton University Press.

Page, Jeremy. 2002. "China Opens Up Political Debate to Strengthen Party." Reuters News Agency, July 20.

Pan Wei. 2003. "Toward a Consultative Rule of Law Regime in China." *Journal of Contemporary China* 12, no. 34: 3–43.

Pangalangan, Raul C. 2004. "The Philippine 'People Power' Constitution, Rule of Law, and the Limits of Liberal Constitutionalism." In *Asian Discourses of Rule of Law: Theories and Implementation of Rule of Law in Twelve Asian Countries,* edited by Randall Peerenboom, 371–384. London: Routledge Curzon.

Park Chong-Min and Doh Chull Shin. 2006. "Do Asian Values Deter Popular Support for Democracy in South Korea?" *Asian Survey* 46, no. 3 (May–June): 341–361.

Parris, Kristen. 1999. "The Rise of Private Business Interests." In *The Paradox of China's Post-Mao Reforms,* edited by Merle Goldman and Roderick MacFarquhar, 262–282. Cambridge, MA: Harvard University Press.

Pastor, Robert, and Tan Qingshan. 2000. "The Meaning of China's Village Elections." *China Quarterly* 162 (June): 490–512.

Pearson, Margaret. 1997. *China's New Business Elite: The Political Consequences of Economic Reform.* Berkeley: University of California Press.

Peerenboom, Randall. 2002. *China's Long March Toward Rule of Law.* Cambridge: Cambridge University Press.

———. 2003. "Networks, Rule of Law, and Economic Growth in China: The Elusive Pursuit of the Right Combination of Public and Private Ordering." *Global Economic Review* 31, no. 2: 1–31.

———. 2004. "Show Me the Money: The Dominance of Wealth in Determining Rights Performance in Asia." *Duke Journal of Comparative and International Law* 15: 75–152.

———. 2005. "Assessing Human Rights in China: Why the Double Standards?" *Cornell Journal of International Law* 38: 23–45.

———. 2007a. *China Modernizes: Threat to the West or Model for the Rest?* Oxford: Oxford University Press.

———. Forthcoming. *Judicial Independence in China.*

Peerenboom, Randall, et al., eds. 2006. *Human Rights in Asia.* London: Routledge.

Pei Minxin. 2003a. "China's Changing of the Guard: Contradictory Trends and Confusing Signals." *Journal of Democracy* 14, no. 1: 77–81.

———. 2003b. "Rights and Resistance: The Changing Contexts of the Dissident Movement." In *Chinese Society: Change, Conflict, and Resistance*, 2nd ed., edited by Elizabeth J. Perry and Mark Selden, 23–46. London: Routledge Curzon.

———. 2006. *China's Trapped Transition: The Limits of Developmental Autocracy.* Cambridge, MA: Harvard University Press.

Peng Ming-min. 1994. *A Taste of Freedom.* Irvine, CA: Taiwan Publishing.

Phillips, Stephen. 2007. "Between Assimilation and Independence: Taiwanese Political Aspirations Under Nationalist Chinese Rule, 1945–1948." In *Taiwan: A New History,* edited by Murray A. Rubinstein, 223–256. Armonk, NY: M. E. Sharpe.

Pils, Eva. 2007. "Asking the Tiger for His Skin: Rights Activism in China." *Fordham International Law Journal* 30: 340–356.

Pinkney, Robert. 2003. *Democracy in the Third World.* 2nd ed. Boulder, CO: Lynne Rienner.

Pistor, Katharina, and Phillip Wellons. 1999. *The Role of Law and Legal Institutions in Asian Economic Development 1960–1995.* New York: Oxford University Press.

Pollack, Jonathan D. 2005. "The Bush Administration and East Asia: Does the United States Need a New Regional Strategy?" In *George W. Bush and East Asia,* edited by Robert M. Hathaway and Wilson Lee, 45–89. Washington, DC: Woodrow Wilson International Center for Scholars.

PRC Supreme Court. 2005. *Work Report.* Available at http://www.court.gov.cn/work/200503180013.htm.

Przeworski, Adam, Michael E. Alvarez, Jose Antonio Cheibub, and Fernando Limongi. 2000. *Democracy and Development: Political Institutions and Well-being in the World, 1950–1990.* Cambridge: Cambridge University Press.

Przeworski, Adam, and Fernando Limongi. 1997. "Modernization: Theories and Facts." *World Politics* 49, no. 2: 155–183.

Putnam, Robert D. 2000. *Bowling Alone: The Collapse and Revival of American Community.* New York: Simon and Schuster.

Putnam, Robert D., Robert Leonardi, and Raffaella Naneeti. 1993. *Making Democracy Work: Civic Traditions in Italy.* Ithaca, NY: Cornell University Press.

Pye, Lucian W. 1985. *Asian Power and Politics.* Cambridge, MA: Harvard Belknap.

———. 2001. "Civility, Social Capital, and Civil Society in Asia." In *Patterns of Social Capital: Stability and Change in Historical Perspective,* edited by Robert I. Rothberg, 375–394. Cambridge: Cambridge University Press.

Qian Qichen. 2002. "Speech by Vice Premier Qian Qichen at the Forum to Commemorate the Seventh Anniversary of President Jiang Zemin's Important Speech Entitled 'Continuing to Endeavour for the Accomplishment of the Grand Cause of Reunification of the Motherland,'" Beijing, January 24.

Reagan, Ronald. 1982. "Speech to the House of Commons," June 8.

———. 1983. "Remarks at the Annual Convention of the National Association of Evangelicals," March 8.

Reardon-Anderson, James. 1992. *Pollution, Politics, and Foreign Investment in Taiwan: The Lukang Rebellion.* Armonk, NY: M. E. Sharpe.

Reed, Benjamin L. 2003. "Democratizing the Neighbourhood? New Private Housing and Home-Owner Self-Organization in Urban China." *China Journal* 49 (January): 31–60.

"Remarks by President Bush and Premier Wen Jiabao at Photo Opportunity." 2003 (December 9). Available at http://www.whitehouse.gov/news/releases/2003/12/20031209-2.html.

Renmin Ribao. 1991. "Build Up a Great Wall of Steel Against Peaceful Evolution." August 19.

———. 1999. "Undermining the One China Principle Is the Crucial Issue." July 14.

———. 2001. "Cross-Strait Relations Can Only Be Improved by Recognizing the 1992 Consensus." May 1.

Reporters Without Borders. 2006. "Annual Report." Available at http://www.rsf.org/rubrique.php3?id_rubrique=639. Accessed December 26, 2006.

Republic of China. 1990. Executive Order No. 12711. "Policy Implementation with Respect to Nationals of the People's Republic of China." April 11.

———. 1993. Executive Order No. 12850. "Conditions for Renewal of Most-Favored-Nation Status for the People's Republic of China in 1994." May 28.

———. 1997. *The Republic of China Yearbook 1997.* Tapei: Government Information Office.

Rice, Condoleezza. 2005. "Remarks at Princeton University's Celebration of the 75th Anniversary of the Woodrow Wilson School" (September 30). Available at http://www.state.gov/secretary/rm/2005/54176.htm.

Rigger, Shelley. 1999. *Politics in Taiwan: Voting for Democracy.* New York: Routledge.

———. 2001. *From Opposition to Power: Taiwan's Democratic Progressive Party.* Boulder: Lynne Rienner.

———. 2005. "Party Politics and Taiwan's External Relations." *Orbis* 49, no. 3 (Summer): 413–428.

Rigobon, Roberto, and Dani Rodrik. 2005. "Rule of Law, Democracy, Openness, and Income: Estimating the Interrelationships." *Economics of Transition* 13, no. 3: 533–364.

Robinson, James A., and Deborah A. Brown. 2000. "Taiwan's 2000 Presidential Election." *Orbis* 44, no. 4: 599–613.

Rose-Ackerman, Susan. 1999. *Corruption and Government: Causes, Consequences, and Reform.* Cambridge: Cambridge University Press.

Rosen, Stanley. 2004. "The Victory of Materialism: Aspirations to Join China's Urban Moneyed Classes and the Commercialization of Education." *The China Journal,* no. 51: 27–51.

Rosenblum, Nancy L., and Robert C. Post, eds. 2002. *Civil Society and Government.* Princeton, NJ: Princeton University Press.

Ross, Robert S. 2000. "The 1995–1996 Taiwan Strait Confrontation: Coercion, Credibility, and the Use of Force." *International Security* 25, no. 2: 87–123.

Ross, Robert S. 2006. "Taiwan's Fading Independence Movement." *Foreign Affairs* 85, no. 2 (March–April): 141–148.

Rowen, Henry. 2007. "When Will the Chinese People Be Free?" *Journal of Democracy* 18, no. 3: 38–52.

Roy, Denny. 2003. *Taiwan: A Political History.* Ithaca, NY: Cornell University Press.

Rueschemeyer, Dietrich, Evelyne Huber Stephens, and John D. Stephens. 1992. *Capitalist Development and Democracy.* Cambridge: Polity Press.

Rustow, Dankwart. 1970. "Transitions to Democracy: Toward a Dynamic Model." *Comparative Politics* 2, no. 2: 337–363.

Saich, Tony. 2000. "Negotiating the State: The Development of Social Organizations in China." *China Quarterly,* no. 161: 124–141.

———. 2007. "China in 2006: Focus on Social Development." *Asian Survey* 47, no. 1: 32–42.

Sartori, Giovanni. 1970. "Concept Misformation in Comparative Politics." *American Political Science Review* 64, no. 4 (December): 1033–1053.

Scalapino, Robert. 1996. "Foreword." In *Taiwan's Electoral Politics and Democratic Transition: Riding the Third Wave,* edited by Hung-mao Tien, ix–xiv. Armonk, NY: M. E. Sharpe.

———. 1998. "A Tale of Three Systems." In *Democracy in East Asia,* edited by Larry Diamond and Marc F. Plattner, 228–233. Baltimore: Johns Hopkins University Press.

Schwartz, Benjamin I. 1996. *China and Other Matters.* Cambridge, MA: Harvard University Press.

Sciolino, Elaine. 2002. "Records Dispute Kissinger on His '71 Visit to China." *New York Times,* February 28.

Shain, Yossi, Juan J. Linz, and Lynn Berat. 1995. *Between States: Interim Governments and Democratic Transitions.* Cambridge Studies in Comparative Politics. Cambridge: Cambridge University Press.

Shen Kui. 2003. "Is It the Beginning of the Era of the Rule of the Constitution? Reinterpreting China's 'First Constitutional Case.'" *Pacific Rim Law and Policy Journal* 12, no. 1: 199–232.

Shi Tianjian. 1997. *Political Participation in Beijing.* Cambridge, MA: Harvard University Press.

———. 2000. "Cultural Values and Democracy in the People's Republic of China." *China Quarterly,* no. 162 (June): 540–559.

———. 2001. "Cultural Values and Political Trust: A Comparison of the People's Republic of China and Taiwan." *Comparative Politics* 33, no. 4 (July): 401–419.

Shi, Weimin. 2006. "Ji guibu yizhi qianli—2000–2005 nian zhongguo minzhu zhengzhi jianshe huigu" ["Take a Long March Starting from Small Steps—Reflection of China's Democratic Development from 2000 to 2005"]. *Politics of China,* no. 1: 72–75.

Shiau Chyuan-jenq. 1996. "Elections and the Changing State-Business Relationship." In *Taiwan's Electoral Politics and Democratic Transition: Riding the Third Wave,* edited by Hung-mao Tien, 213–225. Armonk, NY: M. E. Sharpe.

———. 1999. "Civil Society and Democratization." In *Democratization in Taiwan: Implications for China,* edited by Steve Tsang and Hung-mao Tien, 101–115. Hong Kong: Hong Kong University Press.

Shih Ying-ying. 2006. "MAC Warns China Not to Dupe Taiwanese." *Taipei Times,* April 21.

Shin Doh Chull. 1999. *Mass Politics and Culture in Democratizing Korea.* New York: Cambridge University Press.

Shin Doh Chull, and Huo-yan Shyu. 1997. "Political Ambivalence in South Korea and Taiwan." *Journal of Democracy* 8, no. 3: 109–124.

Shue, Vivienne. 1994. "State Power and Social Organization in China." In *State Power and Social Forces,* edited by Joel Migdal, Atul Kohli, and Vivienne Shue, 65–88. Cambridge: Cambridge University Press.

———. 2004. "Legitimacy Crisis in China?" In *State and Society in 21st-Century China: Crisis, Contention, and Legitimation,* edited by Peter Hays Gries and Stanley Rosen. New York: Routledge Curzon.

Siew, Vincent C. 1997. *Cross-Strait Relations: Retrospect and Prospects.* Taipei: Mainland Affairs Council.

Silva, Eduardo. 2002. "State-Business Relations in Latin America." In *Emerging Market Democracies: East Asia and Latin America,* edited by Laurence Whitehead, 63–102. Baltimore: Johns Hopkins University Press.

"Six Assurances to Taiwan." 1982. (July). Available at http://www.taiwandocuments. org/assurances.htm.

Solinger, Dorothy J. 1984. *Chinese Business Under Socialism: The Politics of Domestic Commerce, 1949–1980.* Berkeley: University of California Press.

———. 1992. "Urban Entrepreneurs and the State: The Merger of State and Society." In *State and Society in China: The Consequences of Reform,* edited by Arthur Rosenbaum, 121–141. Boulder, CO: Westview Press.

———. 2003. "State and Society in Urban China in the Wake of the 16th Party Congress." *China Quarterly,* no. 176 (December): 943–959.

Song Qiang, et al. 1996. *Zhongguo Keyi Shuo Bu* [China Can Say No]. Beijing: China Industrial and Commercial Press.

State Council. 2005a. *Building of Political Democracy in China.* Beijing: Information Office of the State Council of the People's Republic of China.

———. 2005b. "China's Peaceful Development Road." White Paper, December 22.

Steinmo, Sven, Kathleen Thelen, and Frank Longstreth, eds. 1992. *Structuring Politics: Historical Institutionalism in Comparative Perspective.* New York: Cambridge University Press.

Stepan, Alfred. 1985. "State Power and the Strength of Civil Society in the Southern Cone of Latin America." In *Bringing the State Back In,* edited by Peter R. Evans, Dietrich Rueschemeyer, and Theda Skocpol, 317–343. Cambridge: Cambridge University Press.

Straits Times (Singapore). 2004. "How China Views DPM's Visit to Taiwan." July 14.

Sutter, Robert G. 2005. *China's Rise in Asia.* Lanham, MD: Rowland and Littlefield.

Sun, Yan. 2005. "Corruption, Growth, and Reform: The Chinese Enigma." *Current History* (September): 257–263.

Svensson, Marina. 1999. "A Hundred Year Long Debate." *China Rights Forum* (Spring): 20–25.

Swaine, Michael D. 2004. "Trouble in Taiwan." *Foreign Affairs* (March–April): 34–45.

Tai Hai. 2000. "One-China Principle Is Not Imposed on Taiwan." Xinhua News Agency, May 23.

Taiwan Affairs Office of the State Council of the PRC. 1993. "The One China Principle and the Taiwan Issue." White Paper.

———. 2000a. "The One-China Principle and the Taiwan Question." White Paper.

———. 2000b. "Statement on the Question of Current Cross-Strait Relations." May 20.

Taiwan News. 2003. "New Constitution Crucial for Democracy, Chen Says." October 1.
———. 2004. "AIT Official Says U.S. Support of New Constitution Has Its Limits." April 27.
Taiwan Relations Act. 1979. Public Law 96-8, 22 U.S.C., sections 3301–3316.
Tamney, Joseph B., and Linda Chiang. 2002. *Modernization, Globalization, and Confucianism in Chinese Societies.* Westport, CT: Praeger Press.
Tang Wenfang. 2001. "Political and Social Trends in the Post-Deng Urban China: Crisis or Stability?" *China Quarterly,* no. 168: 890–909.
———. 2005. *Public Opinion and Political Change in China.* Stanford, CA: Stanford University Press.
Tang Wenfang, and William L. Parish. 2000. *Chinese Urban Life Under Reform: The Changing Social Contract.* Cambridge Modern China Series. Cambridge: Cambridge University Press.
Tanner, Murray Scott. 2005. "Campaign-Style Policing in China and Its Critics." In *Crime, Punishment, and Policing in China,* edited by Borge Bakken, 171–188. Lanham, MD: Rowman and Littlefield.
Taylor, Jay. 2000. *The Generalissimo's Son: Chiang Ching-kuo and the Revolutions in China and Taiwan.* Cambridge, MA: Harvard University Press.
Thornton, Patricia M. 2003. "The New Cybersects." In *Chinese Society: Change, Conflict, and Resistance,* 2nd ed., edited by Elizabeth J. Perry and Mark Selden, 247–270. New York: Routledge Curzon.
Tien, Hung-mao. 1989. *The Great Transformation: Political and Social Change in the Republic of China.* Stanford, CA: Stanford University Press.
———. 1992a. "Taiwan's Evolution Toward Democracy: A Historical Perspective." In *Taiwan: Beyond the Economic Miracle,* edited by Denis Fred Simon and Michael Y.M. Kau, 45–68. Armonk, NY: M. E. Sharpe.
———. 1992b. "Transformation of an Authoritarian Party State: Taiwan's Development Experience." In *Political Change in Taiwan,* edited by Tun-jen Cheng and Stephan Haggard, 33–55. Boulder: Lynne Rienner Publishers.
Tien, Hung-mao, ed. 1996. *Taiwan's Electoral Politics and Democratic Transition: Riding the Third Wave.* Armonk, NY: M. E. Sharpe.
Tien, Hung-mao, and Tun-jen Cheng. 1997. "Crafting Democratic Institutions in Taiwan." *The China Journal,* no. 37 (January): 1–27.
Tien, Hung-mao, and Yun-han Chu. 1998. "Building Democracy in Taiwan." In *Contemporary Taiwan,* edited by David L. Shambaugh, 123–145. Oxford: Oxford University Press.
Tilly, Charles. 1982. "Routine Conflicts and Peasant Rebellions in Seventeenth-Century France." In *Power and Protest in the Countryside: Rural Unrest in Asia, Europe, and Latin America,* edited by Robert P. Weller and Scott E. Guggenheim, 13–41. Durham, NC: Duke University Press.
Tocqueville, Alexis de, and Stephen D. Grant. 2000. *Democracy in America.* Indianapolis: Hackett.
Tomba, Luigi. 2004. "Creating an Urban Middle Class: Social Engineering in Beijing." *The China Journal,* no. 51: 1–26.
Transparency International. 2005. "Global Corruption Report: Corruption in Judicial Systems." Available at http://www.transparency.org/publications/publications.
———. 2007. "Global Corruption Report: Corruption in Judicial Systems." Available at http://www.transparency.org/publications/publications.
Tremewan, Christopher. 1993. "Human Rights in Asia." *The Pacific Review* 6, no. 1: 17–30.
Tsai, Kellee S. 2002. *Back-Alley Banking: Private Entrepreneurs in China.* Ithaca, NY: Cornell University Press.

————. 2005. "Capitalists Without a Class: Political Diversity Among Private Entrepreneurs in China." *Comparative Political Studies* 38, no. 9: 1130–1158.

————. 2007. *Capitalism Without Democracy: The Politics of Private Sector Development in China.* Ithaca, NY: Cornell University Press.

Tsai, Lily Lee. 2004. "The Informal State: Governance and Public Goods Provision in Rural China" (PhD diss., Harvard University).

Tsang, Steve Yui-Sang. 1998. "Transforming a Party State into a Democracy." In *Democratization in Taiwan: Implications for China,* edited by Steve Yui-Sang Tsang and Hung-mao Tien, 1–22. New York: St. Martin's Press.

Tu Weiming. 1996. "Cultural Identity and the Politics of Recognition in Contemporary Taiwan." *China Quarterly,* no. 184: 1115–1140.

————. 1998. "Human Rights as a Confucian Moral Discourse." In *Confucianism and Human Rights,* edited by William Theodore de Bary and Weiming Tu, 297–308. New York: Columbia University Press.

Tu Weiming, ed. 1996. *Confucian Traditions in East Asian Modernity.* Cambridge, MA: Harvard University Press.

Tu Weiming, Milan Hejtmanek, and Alan Wachman, eds. 1992. *The Confucian World Observed: A Contemporary Discussion of Confucian Humanism in East Asia.* Honolulu: East-West Center Press.

Tucker, Nancy Bernkopf. 2005. "Taiwan Expendable? Nixon and Kissinger Go to China." *Journal of American History* 92, no. 1: 109–135.

Tucker, Nancy Bernkopf, ed. 2005. *Dangerous Strait.* New York: Columbia University Press.

Tyler, Patrick. 2000. *A Great Wall.* New York: Public Affairs Press.

Unger, Jonathan. 2006. "China's Conservative Middle Class." *Far Eastern Economic Review* 169, no. 3 (April): 27–31.

Unger, Jonathan, and Anita Chan. 1995. "China, Corporatism, and the East Asian Model." *The Australian Journal of China Affairs* 33: 29–53.

United Nations General Assembly. 1971. *Restoration of the Lawful Rights of the People's Republic of China in the United Nations.* Resolution 2758 (XXVI). October 25.

US Department of State. 2004. *Country Reports on Human Rights Practices 2003: China.* Available at http://www.state.gov/g/drl/rls/hrrpt/2003/27768.htm.

Van Rooij, Benjamin. 2006. *Regulating Land Reform and Pollution in China: Lawmaking, Compliance, and Enforcement; Theory and Cases.* Leiden, the Netherlands: Leiden University Press.

Vanhanen, Tatu. 2003. *Democratization: A Comparative Analysis of 170 Countries.* Routledge Research in Comparative Politics. London: Routledge.

Vassilev, Rossen. 1999. "Modernization Theory Revisited: The Case of Bulgaria." *East European Politics and Societies* 13, no. 3: 566–599.

Vogel, Ezra F. 1991. *The Four Little Dragons: The Spread of Industrialization in East Asia.* Cambridge, MA: Harvard University Press.

Wachman, Alan M. 1994. *Taiwan: National Identity and Democratization.* Armonk, NY: M. E. Sharpe.

Wade, Robert. 1990. *Governing the Market: Economic Theory and the Role of Government in East Asian Industrialization.* Princeton, NJ: Princeton University Press.

Walder, Andrew G. 1986. *Communist Neo-Traditionalism: Work and Authority in Chinese Industry.* Berkeley: University of California Press.

Waldron, Arthur. 2004. "How Would Democracy Change China?" *Orbis* 48, no. 2: 247–261.

Wang Chaohua, ed. 2003. *One China, Many Paths*. London: Verso.

Wang Hui. 2003. *China's New Order: Society, Politics, and Economy in Transition*. Cambridge, MA: Harvard University Press.

Wang, Peter Chen-mian. 2007. "A Bastion Created, a Regime Reformed, an Economy Reengineered, 1949–1970." In *Taiwan: A New History*, edited by Murray A. Rubinstein, 195–234. Armonk, NY: M. E. Sharpe.

Wang, Ruth. 2007. "U.N. Referendum Bid to Let People Refuse Unification." Central News Agency, December 5.

Wang Tay-sheng. 2002. "The Legal Development of Taiwan in the 20th Century: Toward a Liberal and Democratic Country." *Pacific Rim Law and Policy Journal* 11, no. 3: 531–559.

Wang Tay-sheng, Hua-yuan Hsue, and Shih-Jay Huang. 2006. *Trace the Track of Taiwan Law: One Hundred Important Legal Affairs and Legal History Analysis*. Taipei: Wunan Publishing.

Wang Tay-sheng, and Wen-Liang Tseng. 2005. *The History of Taipei Bar Association in the 20th Century*. Taipei: Yushan She Publishing.

Wang Te-chun. 2004. "Beijing Experts Explain the Anti-Secession Law." *Ta Kung Pao*, December 18.

Wang Yanlai. 2003. *China's Economic Development and Democratization*. Aldershot, UK: Ashgate.

Wang Yeyang. 2006. "Jiang Jingguo yu guomindangde minzhuhua zhuanxing" ["Chiang Ching-Kuo and the Kuomintang's Democratic Transition"]. *Yanhuang Chunqiu*, no. 5: 25–27.

Wang Zhengxu. 2005. "Before the Emergence of Critical Citizens: Economic Development and Political Trust in China." *International Review of Sociology* 15, no. 1: 155–171.

Wank, David L. 1999. *Commodifying Communism: Business, Trust, and Politics in a Chinese City*. Cambridge: Cambridge University Press.

Waterbury, John. 1999. "Fortuitous Byproducts." In *Transitions to Democracy*, edited by Lisa Anderson, 261–289. New York: Columbia University Press.

Way, Lucan. 2006. "Authoritarian Failure: How Does State Weakness Strengthen Electoral Competition?" In *Electoral Authoritarianism: The Dynamics of Unfree Competition*, edited by Andreas Schedler, 167–180. Boulder, CO: Lynne Rienner Publishers.

Weller, Robert P. 1999. *Alternate Civilities: Democracy and Culture in China and Taiwan*. Boulder, CO: Westview.

———. 2005. "Civil Associations and Autonomy Under Three Regimes." In *Civil Life, Globalization, and Political Change in Asia: Organizing Between Family and State,* edited by Robert P. Weller, 76–94. London: Routledge.

———. 2006. *Discovering Nature: Globalization and Environmental Culture in China and Taiwan*. Cambridge: Cambridge University Press.

Weller, Robert P., ed. 2005. *Civil Life, Globalization, and Political Change in Asia: Organizing Between Family and State*. London: Routledge.

Weller, Robert P., and Hsin-Huang Michael Hsiao. 2003. "The Transformation of Chinese Civil Associations in Taiwan, Hong Kong, and South China." In *Civil Society in Asia*, edited by David C. Schak and Wayne Hudson, 160–179. Hampshire, UK: Ashgate.

White, Gordon, Jude Howell, and Shang Xiaoyuan. 1996. *In Search of Civil Society: Market Reform and Social Change in Contemporary China*. Oxford: Clarendon Press.

Winckler, Edwin A. 1994. "Cultural Policy on Postwar Taiwan." In *Cultural Change in*

Postwar Taiwan, edited by Stevan Harrell and Chun-chieh Huang, 42–87. Boulder: Westview.

Winn, Jane Kaufman, and Tang-chi Yeh. 1995. "Advocating Democracy: The Role of Lawyers in Taiwan's Political Transformation." *Law and Social Inquiry* 20, no. 2: 580–581.

Wolf, Martin. 2005. "China's Rise Need Not Bring Conflict." *Financial Times,* September 14. Available at http://search.ft.com/ftArticle?queryText=China%E2% 80%99s+Rise+Need+Not+Bring+Conflict&y=10&aje=true&x=21&id=0509140 06814&ct=0&nclick_check=1.

World Bank. 1993. *The East Asian Miracle: Economic Growth and Public Policy.* New York: Oxford University Press, 1993.

Wright, Teresa. 2001. *The Perils of Protest: State Repression and Student Activism in China and Taiwan.* Honolulu: University of Hawaii Press.

———. 2004. "China Democracy Party: Intellectuals and the Politics of Protest in the 1980s–90s." In *Chinese Intellectuals Between State and Market,* edited by Edward Gu and Merle Goldman, 158–180. New York: Routledge Curzon.

———. 2006. "Review Article: Why Hasn't Economic Development Brought Democracy to China?" Unpublished paper.

Wu Guoguang. 1997. *Zhao Ziyang yu Zhengzhi gaige* [*Zhao Ziyang and Political Reform*]. Hong Kong: Pacific Press.

Wu, Joseph. 1995. *Taiwan's Democratization: Forces Behind the New Momentum.* New York: Oxford University Press.

Wu, Lilian, 1999. "U.S. Knows ROC Policy Toward Mainland Unchanged: MOFA." Central News Agency (Taiwan), July 16.

———. 2006. "President Accuses Opposition Leaders of 'Singing Duet with China.'" Central News Agency (Taiwan), February 15.

Wu, Sofia. 2007. "Name Change Aimed at Emerging from Martial Law Shadows: President." Central News Agency (Taiwan), May 19.

———. 2007. "Name Change Marks No Violation of Commitments to U.S.: President." Central News Agency (Taiwan), February 15.

Wu Yongping. 2005. *A Political Explanation of Economic Growth: State Survival, Bureaucratic Polices, and Private Enterprises in the Making of Taiwan's Economy, 1950–1985.* Cambridge, MA: Harvard University Press.

Wu Yu. 2007. "Holding a Referendum to Join the United Nations Incites Populism and Endangers Peace in the Taiwan Strait." *Xinhua,* September 16.

Xinhua. 1981. "Chairman Ye Jianying's Elaborations on Policy Concerning Return of Taiwan to the Motherland and Peaceful Reunification." September 30. Available at http://wcm.fmprc.gov.cn/eng/ljzg/3568/t17783.htm.

———. 2000. "President Jiang Urges US to Respect China's Sovereignty, Territorial Integrity." September 9.

———. 2004a. "Anti-Secession Law Reflects 'Common Will of All Chinese People.'" December 29.

———. 2004b. "U.S. Human Rights Draft Resolution Against China Doomed to Fail." April 16.

———. 2006a. "China 'Regrets' U.S. Assessment of Its WTO Compliance." December 17.

———. 2006b. "Taiwan Leader Chen Shui-bian Apologizes over Scandals." May 20.

Yahuda, Michael. 1996. "The International Standing of the Republic of China on Taiwan." *China Quarterly,* no. 148 (December): 1319–1356.

Yan Jiaqi. 1996. *Minzhu Zenyang Cai Neng Laidao Zhongguo?* [*How Can Democracy Finally Come to China?*]. Taipei: Yuan Liu Press.

Yang Dali. 2004. *Remaking the Chinese Leviathan: Market Transition and the Politics of Governance in China.* Stanford, CA: Stanford University Press.

Yang, David. 2007. "Classing Ethnicity: Class, Ethnicity, and the Mass Politics of Taiwan's Democratic Transition." Irvine: Center for the Study of Democracy, University of California at Irvine.

Yang, Deshan. 2002. "Developing Socialist Political Civilization." Available at http://xinhuanet.com. Accessed September 6, 2002.

Yang Jianli. 2004. *Feibaoli Kangzheng Yu Xianzheng Gaige: Lun Zhongguo Minzhuhua Zhi Lu* [*Non-Violent Struggle and Constitutional Reform: On China's Road to Democracy*]. Hong Kong: Kaifang Press.

Yang, Mayfair Mei-hui. 1994. *Gifts, Favors, and Banquets.* Ithaca, NY: Cornell University Press.

Ye Jianying. 1979. "Message to Compatriots in Taiwan." Reprinted in *Beijing Review,* January 1.

Ye Weishi. 2002. "Sange daibiao zhongyao sixiang xingcheng he fazhang mailuo" ["The Formation and Development of the Important Thought of 'Three Represents'"]. *Jiefang Ribao,* July 2.

Yeh Junn-ron. 2003. *Democratic Transition and Constitutional Change.* Taipei: Angle Publishing.

Young, Susan. 1995. *Private Business and Economic Reform in China.* Armonk, NY: M. E. Sharpe.

Yu Keping. 2002. "Toward an Incremental Democracy and Governance: Chinese Theories and Assessment Criteria." *New Political Science* 24, no. 2: 181–199.

Yu Zheng. 2007. "Communist Reform Broadens Democracy." Xianhua News Agency, October 17.

Zakaria, Fareed. 2003. *The Future of Freedom: Illiberal Democracy at Home and Abroad.* New York: W. W. Norton.

Zhang Boshu. 2007. *Taiwan Minzhu Zhuanxing Yu Xiandaihua Dui Dalu Xianzheng Gaigede Qishi* [*Lessons for China's Constitutional Reforms from Taiwan's Democratic Transition and Modernization*]. Beijing: Chinese Academy of Social Sciences.

Zhang Liang, Andrew J. Nathan, and Perry Link. 2001. *The Tiananmen Papers.* New York: Public Affairs.

Zhang Shu Guang. 1992. *Deterrence and Strategic Culture: Chinese-American Confrontations, 1949–1958.* Ithaca, NY: Cornell University Press.

Zhang Ye. 1995. "Chinese NGOs: A Survey Report." In *Emerging Civil Society in the Asia Pacific Community,* edited by Tadashi Yamamoto. Singapore: Institute for Southeast Asian Studies; Tokyo: Japan Center for International Exchange.

Zhao Jia. 1998. "Minzhu xuanju minzhu juece minzhu guanli minzhu jiandu: woguo liucheng nongcun queli cunmin zizhi zhidu" ["Democratic Election, Democratic Decision-making, Democratic Management and Democratic Supervision: 60 Percent of Chinese Villages Have Established Villagers' Self-Government Systems"]. *People's Daily,* November 6.

Zhao Suisheng. 2006. *Debating Political Reform in China: Rule of Law vs. Democratization.* Armonk, NY: M. E. Sharpe.

Zheng Bijian. 2005. "China's 'Peaceful Rise' to Great Power Status." *Foreign Affairs* (September/October): 18.

Zheng Shiping. 2003. "Leadership Change, Legitimacy, and Party Transition in China." *Journal of Chinese Political Science* 8, no. 1/2: 47–63.

Zhong Wen. 2004. "Complex, Changeable Taiwan Situation." *Xinhua,* January 25.

Zhong Yang. 2000. "Voter Apathy in China's Grassroots Election." Paper presented at the 15th Annual Conference of the Association of Chinese Political Studies on China's Reform from a Global Perspective, College of Charleston, November 11–12.

———. 2006. "Grassroots Democracy in the Chinese Countryside: A Democratic Breakthrough?" Unpublished manuscript.

Zhong Yang, and Jie Chen. 2002. "To Vote or Not to Vote: An Analysis of Peasants' Participation in Chinese Village Elections." *Comparative Political Studies* 35, no. 6 (August): 686–712.

Zhou Yezhong. 2006. *Xianzheng Zhongguo Yanjiu* [*Research on Constitutional Government in China*]. Wuhan: Wuhan University Press.

Zhu Jianling. 2006. "Chen Ruiren qisushu: xiang wuxing daodan shejin dalu sifa jie" ["Chen Ruiren's Lawsuit Has Entered Mainland Legal Circles Like an Invisible Guided Missile"]. *China Times*, November 21, sec. 1.

Zhuge Muqun. 1998. *Xianzheng Zhongguo* [*Constitutional China*]. Brampton, ON: Mirror Books.

Zong Fengming. 2005. *Lixiang, Xinnian, Zhuiqiu: Wode Rensheng Huigu Yu Fansi: He Zhao Ziyang Tanhuade Yixie Huiyi* [*Ideals, Trust, and Searching: Rethinking and Recalling My Life: Some Memories of Discussions with Zhao Ziyang*]. Hong Kong: Global Press.

———. 2007. *Zhao Ziyang Ruanjinzhongde Tanhua* [*Zhao Ziyang's House Arrest Memoirs*]. Hong Kong: Open Magazine Press.

Zweig, David. 2002. *Internationalizing China.* Ithaca, NY: Cornell University Press.

The Contributors

Weitseng Chen is the Hewlett Fellow at the Center on Democracy, Development, and the Rule of Law, Stanford University. He received his JSD from Yale Law School. His research interests include law and development, foreign direct investment and the transitional legal system, the legal behavior of foreign investors in China, and East Asian legal studies, particularly in the Greater China area.

Tun-jen Cheng is Class of 1935 professor of government at the College of William and Mary. He has published extensively on East Asian political economy and democratic change, including most recently *China Under Hu Jintao* (coedited with Jacques deLisle and Deborah Brown) and *Religious Organizations and Democracy in Contemporary Asia*. Professor Cheng was editor-in-chief of *American Asian Review* and is editor of the *Taiwan Journal of Democracy*.

Yun-han Chu is distinguished research fellow of the Institute of Political Science at Academia Sinica and professor of political science of National Taiwan University. He is the author of *Crafting Democracy in Taiwan*.

Jacques deLisle is Stephen A. Cozen Professor of Law at the University of Pennsylvania. DeLisle's research focuses on the law and politics of China, China's approach to international law, Taiwan's international status, legal change and economic reform in China, Hong Kong's transition to and political-legal development under Chinese rule, and public international law.

Larry Diamond is senior fellow at the Hoover Institution, Stanford University, and founding coeditor of the *Journal of Democracy*. At Stanford University, he is professor by courtesy of political science and sociology and coordinates the democracy program of the new Center on Democracy, Development, and the Rule of Law. His research and policy analyses are focused on the relationship among democracy, governance, and development in poor countries, particularly in Africa. Diamond is the author of *Squandered Victory: The American Occupation and the Bungled Effort to Bring Democracy to Iraq* and *Developing Democracy: Toward Consolidation.*

Ashley Esarey is An Wang Postdoctoral Fellow of the Fairbank Center for Chinese Studies at Harvard University. He researches the effect of mass media and the Internet on political discourse and democratization. Esarey has served as a consultant for Freedom House's Freedom in the World and Freedom of the Press surveys.

Bruce Gilley is assistant professor of political science at Portland State University. His research centers on democracy, legitimacy, and global politics. His recent books include *China's Democratic Future* and *The Right to Rule: How States Win and Lose Legitimacy.*

Merle Goldman is professor emerita of history at Boston University and Research Associate of the Fairbank Center for Chinese Studies at Harvard University. Her most recent book is *From Comrade to Citizen: The Struggle for Political Rights in China.*

Gang Lin is an adjunct professor at American University. He served as program associate in the Washington-based Woodrow Wilson Center's Asia Program (1999–2005) and as president of the Association of Chinese Political Studies (1998–1999). His research interests include China's political development, Taiwan's domestic politics and cross-Strait relations, US-China relations, and democracy and democratization.

Richard Madsen is distinguished professor and chair of the Sociology Department at the University of California, San Diego, and a coauthor (with Robert Bellah et al.) of the *The Good Society* and *Habits of the Heart,* which received the *Los Angeles Times* Book Award and was jury nominated for the Pulitzer Prize.

Randall Peerenboom is the director of the Oxford Foundation for Law, Justice, and Society Rule of Law in China Programme, an associate fellow of the Oxford University Center for Socio-Legal Studies, and a law professor at La Trobe University. Recent books include *China Modernizes: Threat to the West or Model for the Rest?* and *China's Long March Toward Rule of Law.*

Dorothy J. Solinger is professor of political science and adjunct senior research scholar at the Weatherhead East Asian Institute of Columbia University. She is also the author of *Terms of Attachment: Global Liaisons and Labor's Losses in China, France, and Mexico, 1980–2000* (forthcoming) and *Contesting Citizenship in Urban China.* She has written on Chinese internal migration, comparative political economy, and the domestic social effects of economic reform.

Robert P. Weller is professor and chair of anthropology at Boston University and research associate at the Institute on Culture, Religion, and World Affairs there. His most recent books include *Discovering Nature: Globalization and Environmental Culture in China and Taiwan* and *Alternate Civilities: Chinese Culture and the Prospects for Democracy.*

Index

295

Kennedy, Scott, 104
Kissinger, Henry, 55, 187
KMT (Kuomintang): authoritarian rule
by, 8, 186; civil society and, 83–89;
Commission of Economic Reform
established by, 156*n15*; commitment
to legality, 142; decrease in support
for, 215; defeat of, 2, 54; early
organizational development of, 161;
experiments with local democracy by,
16; founding of, 162; hegemonic
power of, 169; implementation of
investment policies by, 156*n16*;
international pressures on, 13,
171–172; legitimacy of, 142;
liberalization faction in, 54; local
elections and, 164–172; monopoly of
power by, 162; as opposition party,
161; plans to retake China by, 3, 54;
reconciliation with Communist party,
15; relinquished executive power,
161; retreat to Taiwan by, 3; role in
rule of law transition, 138–144;
"Taiwanization" of, 194;
transformation of, 164–172. *See also*
Taiwan
Koo Chen-fu, 190
Kuan Chung, 229

Laos: authoritarianism in, 21; legal
system in, 138
Latin America: bureaucratic
authoritarianism, 21; democratic
transition in, 218, 252; education
levels in, 245; regime support from
business class in, 10; reversal of
democracy in, 11; rule of law systems
in, 154; tariff rates in, 145; Third
Wave democratization in, 4
Lee Chen-yuan, 59
Lee Teng-hui, 50, 53, 58, 59, 60, 74,
76*n6*, 77*n19*, 142, 194, 196, 198, 199,
219, 220, 223, 228, 229, 236, 252
Lee Yuan-tseh, 61
Legalism, 66
Legal systems: autonomy in, 137;
autonomy of courts, 142, 143; checks
and balances mechanisms in, 140;
civil society and, 137; corruption in,
143; demands on, 150; development
of, 135–155; East Asia Model and,

136–138; infrastructure for
transactions through, 145; judicial
independence and, 137; in People's
Republic of China, 144–151;
strengthening of, 11; strengthening of
judiciary, 143; in Taiwan, 138–144
Legislative Yuan (Taiwan), 3, 53, 56, 58,
60, 61, 76*n6*, 78*n45*
Lei Chen, 54, 55
Liao Cheng-hao, 61
Liberalization: limits to in Chinese
societies, 8, 9; political, 2, 49, 166,
170, 188, 215
Liberty Times (publication), 62
Lien Chan, 59, 60, 197
Life and Environment (publication), 120
Li Huan, 180
Li Keqiang, 3, 227
Lin, Edgar, 120
Liang Congjie, 121
Lin Chun-i, 120
Lindblom, Charles, 98
Lin Hwai-min, 124
Link, Perry, 67
Lin Yang-kang, 229
Lin Yi-hsiung, 57
Linz, Juan, 51, 182*n3*
Lin Zhen, 239
Lu Hsiu-lien, 56, 58, 60, 77*n19*, 77*n33*,
77*n35*, 156*n20*
Luo Gan, 230
Lu Xueyi, 109

Madsen, Richard, 9, 10, 79–93
Malaysia: authoritarianism in, 21; legal
systems in, 137; nonliberal
democracy in, 137; rule of law in,
144
Mao Zedong, 2, 13, 49, 51, 52, 66, 69,
73, 78*n50*, 80, 90, 103, 228, 243
Martial law, 4
Ma Ying-jeou, 61, 144, 197
Media: control of, 53; free, 56, 58; mass,
50, 62–63; organizations, 53;
programming, 62; radio, 62;
restrictions on, 150; state control of,
50; television, 62
Mei-li Tao (publication), 188
Modernization, 100; Confucian values
and, 30, 31; democracy and, 29;
economic, 162, 189; impact on

About the Book

What is the nature of the political changes under way in China? Might China become a democracy? And what lessons, if any, might Taiwan's experiences of political change and democratization hold for China's future? The authors of this book consider these questions through a structured comparison of Taiwan's historical experience with the current period of economic and social change in the PRC. The authors also provide a more focused analysis of China's current, and possible future, politics.

Bruce Gilley is assistant professor of political science at Portland State University. His numerous publications include *China's Democratic Future, Model Rebels: The Rise and Fall of China's Richest Village,* and *Tiger on the Brink: Jiang Zemin and China's New Elite.* **Larry Diamond** is senior fellow at the Hoover Institution, Stanford University, and founding coeditor of the *Journal of Democracy.* Among his many works on democracy and democratization are *The Spirit of Democracy: The Struggle to Build Free Societies Throughout the World* and *Developing Democracy: Toward Consolidation.*